The Ecology of Violent Extremism

About the Peace and Security in the 21st Century Series

Until recently, security was defined mostly in geopolitical terms with the assumption that it could only be achieved through at least the threat of military force. Today, however, people from as different backgrounds as planners in the Pentagon and veteran peace activists think in terms of human or global security, where no one is secure unless everyone is secure in all areas of their lives. This means that it is impossible nowadays to separate issues of war and peace, the environment, sustainability, identity, global health, and the like.

The books in this series aim to make sense of this changing world of peace and security by investigating security issues and peace efforts that involve cooperation at several levels. By looking at how security and peace interrelate at various stages of conflict, the series explores new ideas for a fast-changing world and seeks to redefine and rethink what peace and security mean in the first decades of the new century.

Multidisciplinary in approach and authorship, the books cover a variety of topics, focusing on the overarching theme that students, scholars, practitioners, and policy makers have to find new models and theories to account for, diagnose, and respond to the difficulties of a more complex world. Authors are established scholars and practitioners in their fields of expertise.

In addition, it is hoped that the series will contribute to bringing together authors and readers in concrete, applied projects, and thus help create, under the sponsorship of Alliance for Peacebuilding (AfP), a community of practice.

The series is sponsored by the AfP (http://www.allianceforpeacebuilding.org) and edited by Charles Hauss, government liaison.

The Ecology of Violent Extremism

Perspectives on Peacebuilding and Human Security

Edited by Lisa Schirch

ROWMAN & LITTLEFIELD
INTERNATIONAL
London • New York

Permission credit lines available at the back of the book.
Published by Rowman & Littlefield
A wholly owned subsidiary of The Rowman & Littlefield Publishing Group, Inc.
4501 Forbes Boulevard, Suite 200, Lanham, Maryland 20706
www.rowman.com

Unit A, Whitacre Mews, 26–34 Stannary Street, London SE11 4AB

British Library Cataloguing in Publication Information Available

Library of Congress Cataloging-in-Publication Data

Names: Schirch, Lisa, editor.
Title: The ecology of violent extremism : perspectives on peacebuilding and human security / edited by Lisa Schirch.
Description: London ; New York : Rowman & Littlefield International, [2018] | Series: Peace and security in the 21st century | Includes bibliographical references and index.
Identifiers: LCCN 2018021147 (print) | LCCN 2018023048 (ebook) | ISBN 9781786608475 (electronic) | ISBN 9781786608468 (cloth : alk. paper) | ISBN 9781786608451 (pbk. : alk. paper)
Subjects: LCSH: Terrorism. | Political violence. | Radicalism. | Human security. | Peace-building.
Classification: LCC HV6431 (ebook) | LCC HV6431 .E366 2018 (print) | DDC 363.325--dc23
LC record available at https://lccn.loc.gov/2018021147

∞™ The paper used in this publication meets the minimum requirements of American National Standard for Information Sciences—Permanence of Paper for Printed Library Materials, ANSI/NISO Z39.48–1992.

Printed in the United States of America

Contents

Foreword ix
Kevin Clements, Toda Peace Institute

Preface xi
Lisa Schirch, Toda Peace Institute, Alliance for Peacebuilding

How to Use This Book xvii

Acronyms xix

SECTION I: THE ECOLOGY OF VIOLENT EXTREMISM 1

Section I Introduction 3

1 The Landscape of Terror 5
Lisa Schirch

2 Mapping the Ecology of Violent Extremism: Correlations and Theories of Change 21
Lisa Schirch

3 Unintended Impacts and Ecological Metaphors of Violent Extremism 53
Lisa Schirch

SECTION II: ECOLOGICAL ANALYSIS OF VIOLENT EXTREMISM 65

Section II Introduction 67

4 Alt-Right and Jihad 69
Scott Atran

5 Radical Islamist and Radical Christianist Nuclear Terrorism 81
Frances Flannery

6 The Private Sector and Violent Extremism 87
Stone Conroy

7 The Neurobiology of Violent Extremism 94
Mari Fitzduff

8 Youth and the Security Sector: VE as a Function of Y 103
Mark Hamilton

9 Advancing a Gender Perspective and Women's Participation in Preventing and Countering Violent Extremism 110
Rafia Bhulai

10 Climate Change and Violent Extremism 116
Lisa Schirch

SECTION III: THE ECOLOGY OF COUNTERTERRORISM 123

Section III Introduction 125

11 Principles of Effective Counterterrorism 127
Alistair Millar

12 Overcoming Violent Extremism in the Middle East: Lessons from the Arab Spring 139
Sverre Lodgaard

13 Civil Society Engagement to Prevent Violent Extremism 149
David Cortright

14 Six Principles for Enabling State Responses 157
Lena Slachmuijlder

15 Legal Restrictions and Counterterrorism 166
Kay Guinane

16 Proscribing Peace: The Impact of Terrorist Listing on Peacebuilding Organizations 174
Teresa Dumasy and Sophie Haspeslagh

SECTION IV: THE ECOLOGY OF PREVENTING/ COUNTERING VIOLENT EXTREMISM (P/CVE) 185

Section IV Introduction 187

17 The Evolution of Countering Violent Extremism Policy 189
Elizabeth Hume and Laura Strawmyer

18 Countering Violent Extremism Framework 197
Humera Khan and Adnan Ansari

19 Countering Violent Extremism in the United States: Unscientific and Stigmatizing National Security Theater 210
Arjun S. Sethi

20 Islamization, Securitization, and Peacebuilding Approaches to Preventing and Countering Violent Extremism 218
Mohammed Abu-Nimer

21 Countering Violent Extremism; Disarmament, Demobilization, and Reintegration; Social Capital; and the "Women, Peace and Security" Agenda 226
Dean Piedmont and Gabrielle Belli

SECTION V: THE ECOLOGY OF PEACEBUILDING **237**

Section V Introduction 239

22 Addressing Terrorism: A Theory of Change Approach 241
John Paul Lederach

23 Negotiation and Violent Extremism: Why Engage and Why Not? 255
I. William Zartman and Guy Olivier Faure

24 Peacebuilding Principles for Transforming Violent Extremism 268
Lena Slachmuijlder

25 Peacebuilding Approaches to Working with Young People 277
Lakshitha Saji Prelis, Michael Shipler, Rachel Walsh Taza, and Lena Slachmuijlder

26 Peacebuilding Narratives and Countering Violent Extremism 284
Lena Slachmuijlder

27 A Peacebuilding Approach to Media and Conflict-Sensitive Journalism 291
Myriam Aziz and Lisa Schirch

28 To Defeat Terrorism, Use "People Power" 297
Maria J. Stephan and Leanne Erdberg

29 Preventing Violence through a Trauma-Healing Approach 300
Veronica Laveta

SECTION VI: CASE STUDIES 311

Section VI Introduction 313

30 The Ecology of Violent Extremism in Kenya 315
Millicent Otieno

31 Preventing and Countering Violent Extremism through Empowering Women Economically and Socially in Pakistan 324
Mossarat Qadeem

32 The Radical Muslim and the Radical Mennonite: An Interfaith Encounter for Peace in Indonesia 333
Agnes Chen, Paulus Hartono, and Agus Suyanto

33 What Works to Prevent Violent Extremism: Lessons from Employment and Education Programs 340
Rebecca Wolfe and Keith Proctor

34 A Child-Focused Perspective on the Preventing and Countering Violent Extremism Paradigm 351
Matthew J. O. Scott

35 Putting Human Dignity at the Center: An Alternative Perspective on "Countering Violent Extremism" 358
Aaron Chassy and Nell Bolton

36 Toward a Synergy of Approaches to Human Security—Policy Recommendations 370
Lisa Schirch

Notes 377

Bibliography 385

Index 421

About the Contributors 429

Foreword

The Toda Peace Institute is delighted that we have been able to nurture this book as it has evolved over the past two years. The Toda Peace Institute is an independent, nonpartisan institute committed to advancing a more just and peaceful world through policy-oriented peace research and practice. We commission evidence-based research; convene multitrack and multidisciplinary problem-solving workshops and seminars; and promote dialogue across ethnic, cultural, religious, and political divides. Our aim is to catalyze practical, policy-oriented conversations among theoretical experts, practitioners, policy makers, and civil society leaders in order to discern innovative and creative solutions to the major problems confronting the world in the twenty-first century.

We believe that this book does exactly that. It provides an extensive analysis of the sources of violent extremism; considers and critiques orthodox responses to such behavior; and maps out systematic, creative, and nonviolent alternatives. It needs to be read by policy makers, academics, and the general public because it provides a much-needed counterweight to all those who seek military solutions to what are complex, interconnected "wicked problems."

This book developed out of a two-day conference organized by the Alliance for Peacebuilding, Eastern Mennonite University—The Center for Justice and Peacebuilding, and the Toda Peace Institute in Harrisonburg, Virginia, during November 5–6, 2016. This meeting brought together leading theorists and practitioners, with extensive experience in the field of peacebuilding, negotiation, governance, democratic processes, intergroup dialogue, and the use of media to address key drivers of violent conflict. In order to break out of violent responses to extremism (which often seem to generate more violence and death), the authors in this book were asked to discuss an ecological or systems approach to violent extremism (VE). This is because ecological approaches to violent extremism pay much more attention to broader contextual and systemic issues than is common in most mainstream media and political analyses. Most "orthodox" counterterrorism strategies offer simplistic examinations of violent extremism by focusing solely on the individuals and groups using terror, without examining the broader factors driving or mitigating such behavior. The chapter authors document human security and peacebuilding approaches to violent extremism with vivid examples of how to address, for example, political conflicts, economic and social tensions, and trauma linked with humiliation.

The meeting that initiated this book coincided with the election of Donald J. Trump to the presidency of the United States. The book's major messages and themes have become more rather than less relevant in the face of resurgent nationalist sentiment (fear of the other) and popular support for coercive and militarized solutions to problems rather than negotiated ones. Lisa and her authors present a systematic and critical alternative to those currently being pursued by the United States. It is our hope that key policy makers will read the book and be willing to change course so that those who currently choose violence will have other nonviolent means at their disposal, thereby pursuing justice and peace by peaceful, rather than violent, means.

As editor of this volume and North American research director for the Toda Peace Institute, as well as senior policy advisor for the Alliance for Peacebuilding, Lisa Schirch is an outstanding scholar and practitioner who has spent a lot of time understanding what it means to build peace. She is a "pracademic" who knows from experience that peace is built from the bottom up, not the top down, by locals rather than foreign actors and with wisdom that flows from locality rather than Western metropoles.

Kevin Clements
Toda Peace Institute

Preface

In 2007, I landed in Sri Lanka to an airport in chaos. The Tamil Tigers had just bombed the airport and the city of Colombo in one of their last efforts to press the government for their independence. Mine was the last plane in before the airport shut down for over a week. The local peacebuilding and development colleagues who had invited me to come drove me to the hotel along the coastline. There we found bombshells littered on the grass around the hotel. Hotel staff oriented us about where to go should there be another flyover attack. For the next two weeks, we offered trainings to local humanitarian and development groups on preventing violent conflict and building peace.

That wasn't my first or last brush with nonstate terrorism. In 2001, the attacks on 9/11 began a long journey to apply the research and practice of conflict transformation and peacebuilding to the security threats posed by terrorism. In 2002, I spent a year in Kenya and Ghana studying local responses to terrorism on a Fulbright fellowship with my husband and young daughter. The US Embassy in Kenya sent us regular warnings about impending terrorism while we lived in a village outside Nairobi. We went on lockdown with the giraffes and water buffalo that wandered through the national park outside our home.

Many of the world's finest researchers on terrorism spend their time interviewing people who subscribe to violent extremist beliefs. Jessica Stern's book *Terror in the Name of God* interviews anti-abortion activists in the Army of God, white nationalists, and others who advocate terrorism. Scott Atran's book *Talking to the Enemy* documents his interviews with a wide range of young men in Asia and the Middle East.

This book takes a different approach. It documents the stories and perspectives of those working mostly at the community level to stem the spread of the poison of violent extremism.

In 2005, I flew through Baghdad to Erbil, Kurdistan, to provide training for my local colleagues in Iraq about how to combine peacebuilding and development. Here I learned the most important lesson of my lifetime: local peacebuilders were far more sophisticated than any outsiders in thinking through the causes of terrorism and how to respond to it.

An Iraq nongovernmental organization (NGO) called REACH was implementing what seemed to me to be the best practices for development and peacebuilding, and, oddly enough, also for preventing violent extremism and terrorism already back in 2005. REACH's staff of Kurdish, Arab, Sunni, and Shia development practitioners sat with me at the University of Sulaimani in Kurdistan. There was more collective wisdom in that room about what to do to prevent terrorism and violent extremism than any military conference I have attended (and I attend regularly) over the past twenty years.

REACH's method was simple but elegant. First, they visit a community and ask whether the community would like to work on a collective process. While they are all Iraqis, they come from different regions, hold different ethnicities (Arab and Kurd), and belong to different sects of Islam. So, while they are "insiders" compared to the international forces or international NGOs, they are still "outsiders" to the local communities where they work. In addition to their expertise in the field of development and NGO management, they have a variety of other capacities. Unlike most foreigners, they understand the language, the regional political and economic history, the culture and religious tensions, and how to get things done. Their resources come from both local and international donors. But the most important resource they have that foreigners lack is trust and legitimacy based on their previous work and reputation.

If the community answers positively, REACH staff provide initial training in governance, decision making, and conflict transformation skills. The community chooses diverse representatives to take part in a community governing council that will help to set development priorities to determine a project. For example, some communities might prioritize early childhood education, digging a well and water management, or maternal health care. Once the community decides upon its priorities, this council guides the process to determine how diverse members in the community can benefit from the project. This requires building relationships of trust, open communication, and collective problem-solving skills.

Violent extremist groups attempted to recruit young men in the villages where REACH worked. They found it much more difficult to "divide and conquer" communities that had governing councils and interethnic, interreligious relationships across the lines of conflict. REACH's peacebuilding and development processes were like a vaccine, inoculating communities against the virus of violent extremism.

These women and men from REACH knew how to foster locally owned, sustainable education, health care, water management, and governance systems. They had been drawing on peacebuilding skills like dialogue and negotiation in their development work for years. I felt like I learned more than I taught. Westerners are not out in front of these questions. Local community leaders, innovating their own locally generated solutions, are my teachers.

Since 2005, I have continued to travel and work in regions plagued with terrorism. In Afghanistan, I researched local peacebuilding experts' insights on how to design a comprehensive peace process. In Pakistan, Israel, Palestine, Jordan, and elsewhere, I visited local peacebuilding programs to document how local people conceive not only of the problem of violent extremism and terrorism but also what they see as the solutions.

My Iraqi and Kurdish colleagues in Erbil said something life changing to me back in 2005. They said, "Security doesn't land in a helicopter. It grows from the ground up. It is great that you and others come here to talk to us about peacebuilding, but what we really need you to do is talk to your own government and military about how to respond to terrorism. They need to listen to local people. They need to understand peacebuilding alternatives. They are making the problem worse, not better."

While I had made a career out of listening and talking to local civil society leaders responding to violent conflict before 2005, they pointed me in a new direction: to my own government and the US military. In 2006, I embarked on a journey to follow their advice. I spent a sabbatical year attending military conferences and listening in to congressional security briefings. I made contact with nearly every peace and justice lobby group in Washington, DC. I received initial foundation grants to begin an initiative to bring civil society voices with an expertise in peacebuilding from places like Iraq and Afghanistan to Washington, DC.

The premise was this: the people impacted by US policies should have a voice in shaping them. We coined the term "democratic policy making." With my staff, we brought delegations of local peacebuilding experts from Pakistan, Iraq, Afghanistan, Somalia, and elsewhere to talk with congressional offices about how to prevent violent extremism and terrorism. Many of the congressional officers noted that it was their first time to meet a person from these countries, and some said it was their first time meeting a Muslim person. They noted that this seemed strange, since they spend so much of their work talking about US policy toward these countries.

While Congress remained wary of listening to local people, the US military was far more open. I came to understand that Congress primarily trusted military leaders to tell them about security. If I wanted to change the way Congress thought about terrorism, I would need to influence the US military. I imagined that might be difficult. Surprisingly, I could not keep up with the invitations I received from US military training centers across the country. Military leaders more than anyone understood that there was not a military solution in Iraq and Afghanistan. They knew how to take down a government supporting terrorism. They did not know how to rebuild a government or how to interact with local civil society to build peace from the ground up.

To my surprise, I found myself giving keynote speeches and sitting on panels at the Pentagon seated between ambassadors and military generals. Every week I gave trainings at different military bases on how security personnel could best listen to and understand local civil society while respecting the Geneva Convention's legal framework for civil-military relations.

Many in Washington, DC, and other Western capitals believe their own lazy meme that "there is no local capacity." They spend their days making decisions for people in other parts of the world with the naive belief that local people are either terrorists or victims. They lack any knowledge of local leadership or the thousands of initiatives that local people are taking in every country in the world.

Even at the US State Department, many had never heard the word "civil society"—a term widely used around the world to describe the positive contributions groups of people make outside government and business. When I informed the head of the new State Department "Conflict Stabilization Operations" (CSO), tasked with conflict prevention and peacebuilding, that their abbreviation might be confusing since thousands of local civil society organizations (CSOs) already used this abbreviation to talk about their own nongovernmental peacebuilding initiatives, I was told, "Well they are going to have to change their name."

While commissioned to write a peacebuilding strategy for the UN Development Program (UNDP), a high-level UN official edited the document. Where I had written a key priority for UNDP was to "map local capacity in peacebuilding," he scratched in an addition, changing the sentence to "mapping the lack of local capacity in peacebuilding." At the world's centers of power, there is a striking absence of understanding of local civil society's responses to violence. And there is a confounding arrogance that Westerners know better than locals about what to do.

Most books about violent extremism are written by daring researchers who venture out to the corners of the world to interview extremists themselves to discover their motivations and worldview. This book is a bit different. This book emerges out of decades of interviews and research not of violent extremists but of local people who are analyzing and responding to these threats within their own context.

The book also reflects countless seminars, forums, and conversations with US and NATO military personnel about the challenge of terrorism. They more than anyone else in government have the on-the-ground experience to know that current counterterrorism frameworks are not working. Many military personnel who have lost their friends and colleagues in this long and endless war on terror know they need new approaches and ways of understanding the problem.

I have lost three of my colleagues to terrorism. In Iraq, my former student and colleague Tom Fox was kidnapped by the Swords of Righteousness Brigade on his way home from a visit with Muslim clerics in 2005 with a group called Christian Peacemaker Teams. Tom had been documenting human rights violations in US counterterrorism efforts. After four months in captivity, Tom was killed, but the rest of his group was released (Brown 2008).

Glen Lapp worked for Mennonite Central Committee in Afghanistan. He was my local host, translator, and guide on my visits to Kabul. Glen was a nurse, working with an eye clinic. A terrorist group killed him along with a group of nine other medical staff and humanitarians in the northern mountains of Afghanistan in 2010. Like other humanitarians working in Afghanistan, this team was a target for armed opposition groups who viewed all foreigners as occupiers or spies (Nordland 2010).

Javaid Akhtar was the director of Just Peace Initiatives (JPI), a local Pakistani civil society group that uses mediation and other peacebuilding processes between tribal leaders and Pakistan government officials to find solutions to prevent violence. JPI was founded by Ali Gohar, another former student from Eastern Mennonite University. Javaid hosted me in Pakistan and set up many of the meetings I had with local peacebuilding organizations who were responding to violent extremism in April 2012. Javaid was assassinated by militant groups opposing his work with JPI as he stepped out of his car in a remote village where he had been called to mediate a dispute.

This book is dedicated to Tom, Glen, and Javaid and to the countless other local peacebuilders who lost their lives as they attempted to address the root causes of terrorism.

Lisa Schirch
Toda Peace Institute
Alliance for Peacebuilding

How to Use This Book

This book has four intended audiences and purposes:

First, it serves as *a textbook for students* to learn the landscape of research and theories related to violent extremism. It is a survey text that maps out more than twenty-five factors that correlate with violent extremism. As a textbook, the book also introduces readers to a range of different types of interventions or theories of change to prevent and stop violent extremism: counterterrorism, preventing and countering violent extremism (P/CVE), and peacebuilding.

Second, *as a reader on violent extremism*, the book includes a broad range of authors, including select writings from some of the world's finest researchers and practitioners. Each author takes an ecological approach, viewing violent extremism as emerging from a complex, dynamic system.

Third, the book serves as an *overview for policy makers and general public* who desire a basic understanding of the causes and potential solutions to violent extremism. This book is written for government staff, police and military personnel, development workers, and peacebuilders to help prepare for their work.

Fourth, the book offers *a new systems-based, human security framework* to understand violent extremism. A toxic cocktail of factors interact with each other to create the dynamics that give rise to violent extremism. Responses to violent extremism can also boomerang. Counterterrorism bombing can end up increasing recruitment, and CVE programs can inadvertently make it more difficult for local communities to respond and prevent violent extremism. Using ecological metaphors, the book offers insights into how violent extremism and the responses to it all interact with each other in an ecological system.

Finally, this book documents a unique set of "peacebuilding approaches to violent extremism" written by peacebuilding scholars and practitioners not found in any other book. In this new approach, peacebuilding is an important paradigm for preventing and responding to violent extremism and takes a distinct approach from counterterrorism and P/CVE.

No book can be comprehensive in reviewing the thousands of articles and books published on this topic. But unlike other books that focus on one or two main theories about violent extremism, this book covers a wide range of possible causes of and cures for violent extremism. Many of the popular assumptions about violent extremism have little evidence supporting them. In part, this book asks readers to bring a critical eye to the wide-ranging articles and news shows on violent extremism and terrorism.

Acronyms

CT	Counterterrorism
CVE	Countering Violent Extremism
ISIS/ISIL/DAESH	The group that calls itself the Islamic State
P/CVE	Preventing and Countering Violent Extremism
PVE	Preventing Violent Extremism
TVE	Transforming Violent Extremism

Section I

THE ECOLOGY OF VIOLENT EXTREMISM

Section I

Introduction

The first three chapters offer definitions and conceptual frameworks for this book. Chapter 1, "The Landscape of Terror," includes definitions; a discussion of debates on key terms; and the social, political, and economic importance of the topics of terrorism and violent extremism. Chapter 2, "Mapping the Ecology of Violent Extremism," offers a conceptual framework for this topic. This chapter also includes a survey and discussion of research on over two dozen factors or themes related to violent extremism. Chapter 3, "Unintended Impacts and Ecological Metaphors of Violent Extremism," defines three types of interventions, counterterrorism, preventing and countering violent extremism (P/CVE), and peacebuilding. This chapter lists the critiques and ways in which these interventions may undermine each other. Two ecological metaphors for understanding violent extremism create awareness of how interventions lacking an appreciation for ecological systems can cause harm. A human security framework concludes this section and offers a paradigm for imagining how counterterrorism, P/CVE, and peacebuilding might work together synergistically.

Chapter 1

The Landscape of Terror

Lisa Schirch

Terrorism is the use of violence against civilians to achieve an ideological goal. Violent extremism (VE) refers to the *beliefs* that encourage, condone, justify, or support terrorism (FBI 2016) . News media keeps us alarmed with the close-up images of terrorism's devastation. How do we attempt to prevent and respond to violent extremism and terrorism in ways that do not inadvertently fuel it?

Violent extremism and terrorism do not grow like a virus in a sterile research lab. Like the ecology of our planet, which is an interacting system of plants, animals, weather, and geological components, VE and terrorism are ecological phenomena. They emerge out of a complex environment of vulnerable individuals, community grievances, national ideological campaigns, and global factors. The word "ecology" refers to the study of something within an ecosystem. An "ecosystem" is a connected set of interrelated parts. An ecological or systems-based analysis of violent extremism looks at interrelationships among humans, the institutions they create, social patterns of relationships, and their environment.

Principles from the field of "systems theory" and environmental sciences are relevant to understanding violent extremism. Systems theory is an interdisciplinary study of how parts of a system interact with each other. When one part of a system malfunctions, it affects the entire system. Making an intervention in one part of the system can affect other areas. Systems theorists believe that a part of a system can be understood only by examining its relationship to other parts. A system is a complex environment where there is no simple "cause" and "effect" reaction chain where an action leads to predictable results. VE takes place in complex environments, where there are political conflicts, economic pressures, business interests, drug profits, climate change–induced droughts, easy access to weapons, and multiple divisions within society between religious and ethnic groups.

This book looks at the ecology of VE to understand the problem from a systemic point of view. While many books offer one or two hypotheses for preventing terrorism, this book gives readers the tools to look at VE and terrorism from many different angles. Readers will finish this book recognizing the debates within the definitions of terrorism and VE, identifying over twenty-five factors that correlate to VE, and understanding the ecology of interventions to address VE and terrorism, including counterterrorism, preventing/countering VE (P/CVE), and peacebuilding. This chapter begins by identifying the importance of studying terror, terrorism, and VE in terms of the array of costs on society, including civilian deaths, economic costs, and costs on civil liberties from both terrorism and counterterrorism. It then identifies the debates on and definitions of the terms "violent extremism" and "terrorism."

WHAT IS TERROR?

The word "terror" comes from the Latin word *terreo*, meaning to fill with panic, alarm, and great fear. Human beings die in many ways, but only some of those ways invoke terror. What gives terrorism its name? What about terrorism makes us panic and fills us with fear?

Terrorism is not scary because of the *number* of people it kills. Other threats kill far more people, as illustrated in Table 1.1. The Global Terrorism Index reports that over 25,000 people died from terrorism in 2016 (GTI 2017, 42). Most deaths from terrorism happen in just a few countries that are also experiencing civil war, such as Nigeria, Iraq, and Syria. In comparison, in 2016, 157,000 people died from violent conflicts, and there were 50 million displaced people and refugees (Institute for Security Studies 2017).

Deaths from terrorism and war combined are still far less than those resulted from other threats. Heart disease and stroke killed 15 million people, and injuries from road accidents killed 1.3 million, globally in 2015 (World Health Organization 2017). In 2016, over 42,000 people died from opioid overdose in the United States alone (CDC 2018).

Table 1.1. Comparison of Death Rates

Deaths from Terrorism in 2016	*Deaths from Violent Conflict in 2016*	*Deaths from Heart Disease in 2015*	*Deaths from Road Accidents in 2015*	*Deaths from Opioid Overdose in the United States in 2016*
25,000+	157,000+	15 million	1.3 million	42,000

Yet people globally continue to rate terrorism as one of the most important public issues in opinion surveys. Funding levels for preventing and responding to terrorism far outweigh prevention of other causes of death that affect far more people. Taxpayers around the world are spending billions on counterterrorism. Understanding violent extremism and terrorism is important for the sheer amount of funding and the trade-offs of this priority for public spending as opposed to other public health concerns.

Terrorism often takes its aim not at military personnel or government staff but at unarmed civilians. Terrorism does not pose a great threat to states. Terrorism is an attack on society and human security. It is the intentional spreading of fear. Just as some people would rather die from a bee sting than a shark or lion attack, it seems that the methods of death from terrorism aim to repulse and disgust.

Media images of beheadings, body parts from car bombs, and children wrapped in white sheets terrify people. Terrorism sets off powerful psychological processes that animate human flight-or-fight behavior (Nacos 2016).

Terrorism is scary for a number of reasons:

- Deaths from terrorism are often gruesome.
- Terrorism targets civilians who lack protection, making people feel unsafe in public.
- Terrorism is relatively random, and the public is unable to take precautions.
- News media heightens fear by sharing photos and gory details.
- Political leaders and arms dealers benefit from inflated threat perception.

People who want to postpone death can alter their lives in many ways. They exercise, resist addictive junk food and drugs, and sleep and relax to postpone death from heart disease (Leahy 2008). Terrorism is far less predictable. It happens in shopping centers in Nairobi, bookstores in Baghdad, a Christmas market in Berlin, coffee shops in Paris, and on public streets around the world. Terrorism terrifies people because it is so random. People cannot make predictions that enable them to postpone death from terrorism. Terrorism causes symptoms of anxiety and depression (Marshall et al. 2007). Incidences of posttraumatic stress disorder (PTSD) increase after an incidence of terror (Silver et al. 2002).

The attacks on September 11 created the possibility that individuals or groups could use a civilian plane to attack key parts of a society. If the fourth plane on 9/11 had hit the White House or the Capitol, the ability for the United States to respond might have been far more difficult. The threat of terrorism has a lot to do with "what ifs" rather than the threats seen year after year since 2001. The risk that state or nonstate groups could commit an act of terrorism with nuclear, chemical, or biological weapons is potentially catastrophic.

THE ECOLOGICAL COSTS OF TERRORISM

Terrorism destroys lives, property, and a sense of security. An ecological view of terrorism also requires looking at other costs, including the human, financial, and civil freedoms lost that correlate with counterterrorism approaches.

Increased Terrorism Correlates with Increased Counterterrorism

What is the relationship between the increase in both terrorism and counterterrorism? Is there an increase in counterterrorism programs because there is an increase in terrorism caused by other factors? Or do counterterrorism programs increase terrorism? If there is a correlation between terrorism and counterterrorism programs, what are the hypotheses to explain the correlation (Cordesman 2017)?

In the past fifteen years, most regions of the world have seen an increase in terrorism with deaths increasing by 247 percent in the past ten years (GTI 2017, 42, 30). At the same time, there has been a significant increase in funding and programs in counterterrorism. The US military is conducting counterterror activities in seventy-six countries (Costs of War 2018). *Washington Post* investigators documenting the security increase after 9/11 in their "Top Secret America" project concluded, "The top-secret world the government created in response to the terrorist attacks of Sept. 11, 2001, has become so large, so unwieldy and so secretive that no one knows how much money it costs, how many people it employs, how many programs exist within it or exactly how many agencies do the same work" (Priest and Arkin 2010).

The link between counterterrorism efforts and terrorism can be seen in a variety of research reports, particularly from security experts who insist that drone warfare creates more terrorists than it kills by serving as a recruiting tool (Abbas 2013). For example, a 2009 study of the drivers of radicalization in Afghanistan found that support for the Taliban and Hizb-i Islami terrorist groups grew primarily because of government corruption and violent or offensive behavior of foreign forces in counterterrorism operations (Ladbury 2009). In Kenya, 65 percent of al-Shabaab members stated they joined this terrorist group due to the Kenyan government's repressive counterterror strategy and 97 percent said they believed that Islam was under attack (ISS 2014).

The Death Toll from Terrorism Is Equal to, or Possibly a Third Less Than, the Death Toll from Counterterrorism

Deaths from terrorism have dramatically increased since 2000. At the same time, civilian deaths from counterterrorism are also increasing. Many of the

Table 1.2. Deaths from Terrorism and Counterterrorism

Annual Death Toll from Terrorism in 2000	*Average Annual Death Toll from Terrorism since 2013*	*Conservative Estimate of Average Annual Death Toll from War on Terror from 2001 to 2016*	*Approximate Death Toll from War on Terror from 2001 to 2016*
Less than 5,000	25,000–33,000	24,666	370,000 to 1 million

157,000 civilian deaths and millions of displaced people in violent conflicts in 2016 were a result of the war on terror and counterterrorism. Counterterrorism operations each year kill as many, or up to three times as many, civilians as those who have died from terrorism. US general Stanley A. McCrystal asserted, "I believe the perception caused by civilian casualties is one of the most dangerous enemies we face" in his inaugural speech as commander of the International Security Assistance Force in Afghanistan in June 2009 (Ackerman 2010). Table 1.2 identifies the human costs of terrorism and counterterrorism operations, including the war on terror.

In 2000, fewer than 5,000 people died from terrorism each year. Since 2013, between 25,000 and 33,000 people die from terrorism each year, mostly in a handful of countries experiencing civil war (GTI 2017, 15). From 2001 to 2016, researchers estimate somewhere between 370,000 people (Crawford 2017) and 1 million people (PSR 2015, 15) died in the counterterrorism wars in Iraq, Afghanistan, and Pakistan.[1] Based on the lower number of 370,000 deaths, that is approximately 24,666 per year. More than 10 million Afghan, Iraqi, and Pakistani people have become refugees or internally displaced persons, many living in grossly inadequate conditions, since the beginning of the war on terror (Costs of War 2018). This human suffering is also part of the calculation on the costs of terrorism.

The Economic Impact of Terrorism Is Less Than the Economic Impact of Counterterrorism

Estimates of the economic costs of terrorism and counterterrorism are complex to calculate. There is no single counterterrorism budget, and all budget numbers are imperfect estimates. But even given variations in methods of calculation, the global economic cost of counterterrorism is far more than the economic cost of terrorism. Yet few researchers compare and contrast costs from terrorism and counterterrorism. While hundreds of researchers look at the correlates of terrorism, there is a surprising lack of attention on what seems like a fairly obvious research question: Why is terrorism increasing at the same time that investments in counterterrorism programs are increasing?

Committing acts of terror is relatively inexpensive compared to the cost of war. Three-quarters of terror attacks in Europe cost less than $10,000 (Oftedal 2015, 3). The global economic impact of terrorism in 2000 was $9 billion. Since 2013, the economic impact varies between $71 billion and $104 billion. The total economic impact of terrorism between 2001 and 2016 was $724 billion (GTI 2017, 80).

In contrast, the United States has spent approximately somewhere between $1.7 trillion (GAO 2018) and $5.6 trillion on counterterrorism since 2001 (Costs of War 2018). In 2001, the United States spent approximately $30 billion a year on the war on terrorism, which consisted mostly of counterterrorism operations, to a high of $235 billion in 2008 at the height of the wars in Iraq and Afghanistan. In 2018, the projected war on terror budget is estimated at $126.8 billion (DoD 2017).

It is not possible to precisely calculate total European Union (EU) and member state spending on counterterrorism, but the approximate EU spending per year on counterterrorism is estimated to have increased from €5.7 million in 2002 to €93.5 million in 2009 (Sgueo 2016). In 2013, the US government reportedly budgeted over $16 billion for counterterrorism intelligence gathering alone (Pew 2013).

According to the calculations illustrated in Table 1.3, the economic cost of counterterrorism is far greater than the economic cost of terrorism. The cost of counterterrorism may even be up to 5 trillion dollars more costly. Furthermore, every dollar spent on counterterrorism is a dollar not spent on peacebuilding, education, health care, or other priorities. In the ecology of VE, there are trade-offs in costs related to preventing terrorism. In 2016, the total expenditure for all peacekeeping operations and peacebuilding efforts amounted to approximately $21.8 billion (Luengo-Cabrera and Butler 2017). According to the Global Peace Index, the international community would have saved $552.1 billion if they had allocated peacebuilding funding to the ten most at-risk countries to develop inclusive political processes, support governance, and protect human security and if these investments had prevented conflict (GPI 2017, 76).

Table 1.3. Comparison of Economic Costs of Terrorism and Counterterrorism

Cost to Plan and Carry Out a Terror Attack in Europe	*Global Impact of Terrorism between 2001 and 2016*	*U.S. Spending on Counterterrorism between 2000 and 2017*	*Amount That Would Have Been Saved If Peacebuilding Funded for Ten Most At-Risk Countries*
$10,000	$724 billion	Between $1.7 and $5.6 trillion	$552 billion

The Increase in Terrorism and Counterterrorism Correlates with a Decrease in Political Rights and Civic Freedoms

The Global Terrorism Index consistently finds a strong correlation between state political repression and terrorism. Where there is more state repression and political violence, there is more terrorism. The correlation between counterterrorism and political repression is also strong. In their annual quantitative evaluation of global political rights and civil liberties, Freedom House concludes there is a vicious cycle between government abuse and radicalization. "When more countries are autocratic and repressive, treaties and alliances crumble, nations and entire regions become unstable, and violent extremists have greater room to operate" (Freedom House 2018, 2).

Political and civil liberties have steadily decreased since 2005. In 2017, more countries declined in their levels of political rights and civil freedom than those that increased (Freedom House 2018, 1). From 2000 to 2017, 99 percent of all deaths due to terrorism took place in countries in conflict or with high levels of political terror, in which the state uses repressive violence against civilians. A wide variety of institutions and researchers conclude from these correlations that counterterrorism is increasing, not decreasing, terrorism. But this correlation is not easy to prove (Hafner-Burton and Shapiro 2010).

Most government-funded researchers do not count state terrorism that takes place under the umbrella of counterterrorism. In the United States, for example, one senior US researcher notes, "[E]xcessive repression in the name of counterterrorism, and state repression that amounts to de facto state terrorism, are not reported as terrorism even when they have such impacts. The grave limits in the counterterrorism activity of various states—many US partners and allies—are only officially reported on only in the State Department annual human rights report and by human rights NGOs" (Cordesman 2016).

Many civil society groups view counterterrorism "lawfare" as a convenient cover for authoritarian governments to wage war on democracy and civil society. For example, Kenya is using counterterrorism financing laws to freeze the assets of Kenyan human rights organizations that work primarily to support democracy and human rights in the country rife with government corruption.

While the impact of terrorism is relatively small, the combined impact of terrorism and counterterrorism is having a significant impact on the globe. A relatively small group of individuals and groups using terrorism have managed to change the policy priorities, redirect funding to counterterrorism priorities, begin wars with a significant toll on civilian lives, and provide cover for authoritarian governments to limit civil liberties.

WHAT IS TERRORISM, AND WHAT IS NOT TERRORISM?

Terrorism is distinct from other forms of violence in a number of ways, even though there is no agreed-upon definition. For this book, *terrorism* is (1) the intention to spread fear by dramatic violent acts, (2) against unarmed civilians and civilian property, and (3) to achieve an ideological goal.

There are two important debates on the definition of terrorism. First, there is a debate over whether terrorism is violence primarily against civilians or whether terrorism is violence against either governments or civilians. Second, there is a debate over whether terrorism is carried out only by nonstate actors or whether both state and nonstate actors can commit terrorism. These debates center on definitions of *the target* of violence (civilians or government) and on *who* is carrying out violence (state or nonstate armed actors).

THE DEBATE ON TERRORISM, CIVILIANS, AND HUMAN SECURITY

Terrorism is unique from other forms of violence in that it targets civilians and civilian property, such as hospitals, schools, business centers, and homes. In international and noninternational war, the target of violence is usually another armed group, not civilians. International law uses the term "noncombatants" to refer to civilians. Noncombatants can include military or government personnel who are unarmed and not serving as active combatants. International law defines who and what is or is not a legitimate target. Terrorism can be a tactic in a war or insurgency, but it is an illegal tactic.

The Global Terrorism Database (GDT) classifies terrorist acts according to whether an intentional attack includes "some level of violence or immediate threat of violence including property violence, as well as violence against people." GDT further qualifies that "there must be evidence of an intention to coerce, intimidate, or convey some other message to a larger audience (or audiences) than the immediate victims." The GDT determines this by identifying whether the perpetrators make pre- or postattack statements, their past statements or attacks on civilians, or the target/victim, weapon, or attack type (GTD 2017, 9–10). This definition includes, for example, the 9/11 attacks on the Pentagon; even though this is a military installation, it was full of unarmed, noncombatant civilian government personnel. The GDT diagnoses terrorism as attempts to, in the words of US government policy, "intimidate or coerce a civilian population to influence the policy of a government by intimidation or coercion, or to affect the conduct of a government by mass destruction, assassination, or kidnapping" (18 U.S. Code § 2331 2010). In contrast to the definition of terrorism, hate crimes, which include similar forms of violence against civilians based on their race, ethnicity, religion, gender, or sexual orientation, do not aim to change government policy.

The debate here is whether terrorism intends to challenge a government or whether its challenge is primarily to civilians and the broader society. Some scholars argue that terrorism is, by definition, a challenge to the state (Rubenstein 1987). While terrorist groups may threaten civilians as leverage to coerce or pressure a government, the goal may be simply to kill civilians because they want the civilians to die, migrate, change their beliefs, or take some action. The motivations and beliefs that underlie an intention to kill civilians set terrorism apart from other forms of violence.

THE DEBATE ON STATE AND NONSTATE TERRORISM

The debate about whether the term "terrorism" covers both state and nonstate violence against civilians is complex. In public discourse, many news sources use the term "terrorist" to refer to a nonstate individual or group that uses the tactic of terrorism to pursue political goals. There are two reasons why many researchers and governments focus only on nonstate actors committing terrorism: states have legal authority to use violence, and states lack intention to kill civilians. But other scholars insist that state terrorism and state-sponsored terrorism should be part of the discussion on terrorism.

Legal Authority

The Geneva Conventions and other forms of international law identify what is deemed lawful and legitimate military action even if it may result in civilian deaths. Some states define "terrorism" as the "unlawful" use of violence and use the term to identify nonstate groups that do not have legal authority to use violence. For example, the GDT explicitly states that the term "terrorism" does not apply to states. Terrorism is a violent act "outside the context of legitimate warfare activities" and "outside the parameters permitted by international humanitarian law (particularly the prohibition against deliberately targeting civilians or non-combatants)" (GTD 2017, 10). For example, a terrorist group such as ISIS uses both insurgent violence against state military forces in Syria, Iraq, and Egypt and terrorism against civilians, such as its attacks on Egyptian Sufi Muslims and Christians. These attacks on civilians are illegal according to international humanitarian law.

State Intention, "Collateral Damage," and Civilian Deaths

Some scholars argue that states rarely intentionally target civilians even though they may kill civilians in the course of pursuing their political goals. "Collateral damage" is the term governments use to refer to unintended civilian deaths that result from military strikes on legitimate targets such as military personnel or objects. Unlike terrorist groups, some argue that states do not intend to spread fear and terror on civilians (Schmid 2011, 48). While nonstate terrorist groups want the media to cover their grisly attacks on civilians, states do not want media coverage, and many go to great lengths to deny responsibility (Nacos 2016, 13).

State Terrorism

Other researchers argue state terrorism is the state's violence directly targeting civilians (Nairn and James 2005). States do sometimes target civilians, and sometimes they terrorize civilians in ways that are deemed legal. During World War II, the German state set up human killing factories whose sole purpose was to kill Jews, homosexuals, Gypsies, the disabled, and other people. The United States used a nuclear bomb in World War II knowing that thousands of Japanese civilians would die. State warfare strategies such as the use of nuclear or biological weapons and shock and awe military tactics do not distinguish between combatants and noncombatants. The Geneva Conventions mandate that the military benefit must justify the number of civilians killed. Because the idea of "military benefit" is not precisely defined, it is difficult to prove that a state has acted illegally when it kills thousands of civilians as its collateral damage in a war.

When state security forces carry out genocide or even just use violent repression against parts of the civilian population, this also is brutal violence targeting civilians. States use repressive violence to terrorize civilians for a variety of reasons, such as forcing them off land, suppressing their opposition, or preventing civilians from reporting on government corruption. State violence against civilians meets the definition of terrorism, as it is used as a means of provoking fear and intimidation so that a government can achieve its goals. State violence such as disappearances, assassinations, torture, and massacres of certain populations are violations of the Universal Declaration of Human Rights and other international frameworks.

State-Sponsored Terrorism

State-sponsored terrorism refers to a state's providing weapons, funding, and cover for terrorist groups in order to achieve goals shared by the state and its

Table 1.4. Coding Terrorism

	Ideological Goal	*Violence Targeting Civilians*
International war	Yes	Sometimes
Nuclear war	Yes	Yes
Civil war or insurgency	Yes	Sometimes
State repression	Yes	Yes
Genocide	Yes	Yes
Sexual and gender-based violence (SGBV)	No	Yes
Mafia violence	No	Yes
Gun violence	No	Yes

nonstate partner organizations (James and Friedman 2006). In many countries, authoritarian governments sponsor nonstate groups to carry out violence against certain parts of the population to achieve shared goals.

This book accepts that states and nonstate groups both use terrorism, the deliberate targeting of civilians to achieve a goal. However, this is not a book that focuses on state-sponsored terror, state violence, and war or acts of terror committed by states. This book has a narrower focus simply because there are many other books on state-based violence like international and civil war as well as state-based genocide or human rights violations against civilians. This book does explore how state-based responses to terrorism become part of the ecology of causes driving VE.

However, there are limitations on the term "terrorism" that are important to mention here. Some use the term "terrorism" to refer to any group that uses violence targeting civilians, including, for example, sexual and gender-based violence (SGBV) such as rape, mafia violence, or gun violence such as school shootings. But these forms of violence lack a coherent ideological goal. Table 1.4 illustrates how the term "terrorism" applies to certain types of violence.

WHAT IS VIOLENT EXTREMISM, AND WHAT IS NOT?

Surveys of people in the Muslim world found that most thought the "Global War on Terror" (GWOT) was code for a "Global War on Islam." Polls found that most Muslims surveyed perceived the policies of the United States and other Western governments as part of the upsurge in support for terrorism (Pew 2007). To respond to this critique of the focus on Islam in the "war on terror," governments began using the term "violent extremism" as a way of identifying the specific types of "extreme" beliefs that lead to terrorism (Schmitt and Shanker 2005).

What looks extreme to some looks moral to others. Some governments categorize any type of protest against it as VE. Is a nonviolent movement to oust a brutal dictator extreme? Is a community group protesting government corruption extreme? Is extremism defined by governments or by standards such as human rights and international law?

Martin Luther King Jr. commented on this dilemma as some white leaders referred to him and the nonviolent civil rights movement as extremists. "The question is not whether we will be extremists, but what kind of extremists we will be. Will we be extremists for hate or for love? Will we be extremists for the preservation of injustice or for the extension of justice? . . . The nation and the world are in dire need of creative extremists" (King 1963). Robert F. Kennedy added to the understanding of extremism in his writing "Extremism: Left and Right." "What is objectionable, what is dangerous about extremists is not that they are extreme, but that they are intolerant" (Kennedy 1964: 3). VE is intolerant toward some groups and justifies killing as a form of revenge, purification, or removal of some groups of people.

Violent extremism is a belief system that justifies killing civilians. White nationalists kill people of color because they strive to create a pure white nation. ISIS kills Christians, Shia Muslims, and others because they aim to create a pure Sunni Muslim state or "caliphate." Jewish "hilltop youth" advocate using violence to push Palestinians out of the West Bank to create a pure Jewish community in Judea and Samaria. In India, the Shiv Sena party advocates attacking Muslims and Christians to create a pure Hindu state. In Burma, the Ma Ba Tha Buddhist movement advocated for the removal of the Rohingya Muslims that resulted in a massacre of thousands of civilians. In each of these cases, violent extremists argued that their political or religious goals could be achieved by only killing or removing a certain kind of civilian.

CHARACTERISTICS OF VIOLENT EXTREMIST BELIEFS

There are four characteristics of violent extremist beliefs.

Violence

Violent extremism is a belief that violence is necessary because it is tactically superior and/or redemptive.

- *Tactical superiority:* Belief that violence is a superior method of pursuing their goals and more likely to be effective than other methods
- *Redemptive:* Belief that violence is a necessary process to bring about change by transforming those willing to carry out violence

Civilian Targets

Violent extremism justifies the use of brutal violence against unarmed civilians to achieve purification of society and/or because civilians are responsible for their government.

- *Purification:* Belief in purifying society by killing, removing, controlling, or converting those civilians deemed inferior or outsiders or are guilty and deserving of death because of their skin color, ethnicity, or beliefs
- *Responsibility:* Belief that civilians are responsible for the actions of government and military who act on their behalf

Authoritarian Narrative

Violent extremists usually believe in an authoritarian narrative that is intolerant and patriarchal and opposes participatory democracy.

- *Intolerant:* Belief that people who are different racially, ethnically, religiously, or ideologically are inferior and/or should live separately in "pure" communities
- *Patriarchal:* Belief in exclusively male leadership and/or that women are property to control and should not hold public roles
- *Authoritarian:* Belief in authoritarian decision making and opposition to democratic practices of participatory decision making or cultural diversity

Ideological Goals

Violent extremism includes ideological goals related to their identity and/or grievances.

- *Ideological identity:* Belief that ideology is more important than nationality
- *Response to grievance:* Belief in the need to challenge, change, disrupt, and destroy the current government or respond to a grievance by supporting a different ideology

EXAMPLES OF WHAT IS AND IS NOT VIOLENT EXTREMISM

These characteristics of VE narrow the scope of analysis for this book. Violent extremist groups believe that brutal violence to civilians is necessary, hold a superiority narrative supporting authoritarianism, and have an ideological goal. Here are three examples of the relationship between violent extremist ideologies and acts of terror.

In August 2017, white nationalists joined a march in Charlottesville, Virginia, to protest the plan to remove a statue of Confederate general Robert E. Lee from the city park. The "Unite the Right" rally asserted white superiority, threatened local Jewish synagogues and African Americans, and asserted white nationalism as an ideology. One of the white nationalists rammed his car into a street of counter protestors, killing one young woman. White nationalism fits each characteristic of a violent extremist belief system. White nationalists killed or injured over one hundred people, often targeting women, Jews, Muslims, and people of color in the United States between 2014 and 2017. White nationalists are mostly young white men, bonded together with a political goal to assert that their white identity is under attack by multiculturalism and political correctness. White nationalists' online propaganda provides an ideology that explains to young men why they are unemployed or do not have sexual partners. Immigrants, Jews, African Americans, Latinos, and empowered women are deemed inferior and responsible for their woes. White nationalist media includes explicit directions on how to carry out brutal violence against civilians to fulfill political goals using a superiority narrative (Hawkes and Amend 2018).

In Orlando, Florida, in June 2016, a lone man planned and carried out an attack on a gay nightclub killing fifty people. The gunman Omar Mateen was an Afghan refugee with a history of mental illness. A debate in the media began about whether to call the attack terrorism or gun violence. On the right, Republicans argued "radical Islam" was to blame, citing the religion of the attackers. On the left, Democrats asserted loose gun laws had failed to prevent the ill man from buying weapons and ammunition to carry out the attack. Investigators eventually found a tape on which the gunman had pledged allegiance to ISIS and explained his political goal was to stop US violence in Iraq and Syria against Muslims. The victims were civilians. Mateen's homophobic beliefs had led him to attack the gay nightclub, where he himself had frequented. The people in the nightclub had nothing to do with US policy in the Middle East. Omar Mateen acted on his own. But he had subscribed to a violent extremist ideology and with clear political goals, superiority narratives, and a belief that brute violence to civilians was necessary.

In the Palestinian-controlled West Bank city of Hebron, a Jewish settler Baruch Goldstein armed with a gun and an ideology of superiority and natural rights of Jews to the land of Israel walked into a crowded mosque and opened fire killing twenty-nine Muslim worshippers in 1994. As part of the Jewish minority in the city, Goldstein belonged to Kahanist Kach movement that Israel designated as a terrorist organization. Kahanists believe acts of terror against

Palestinian civilians are a necessary tactic to achieve the political goals of Jewish settlements to clear the region of what Kahanists call "terrorist" Arabs.

These are three examples of violent extremist's beliefs that led to terrorism. It is also important to identify what is not VE. In many countries, governments label civil society groups and nonviolent social movements protesting government corruption, police brutality, and discrimination as posing a terrorist threat. Civil society groups that hold one of these political goals but reject violence against civilians and embrace diversity and democracy are not violent extremists.

After al-Shabaab massacred 148 students at Garissa University in Kenya in 2015, the Kenyan government froze the bank accounts of two human rights organizations, Haki Africa and Muslims for Human Rights, under the accusation that they had supported the attack. Civil society groups wrote an open letter to the government denouncing the freeze (Kenya Human Rights Organizations Are Not Terrorist Organizations 2015). In following years, the Kenyan government has gone on to freeze bank accounts and deregister hundreds of other civil society organizations with no proven link to violent extremist beliefs or organizations. It appears as if the government uses counterterrorism laws in its effort to disempower civil society at large. Al-Shabaab is a terrorist group. The human rights groups monitoring government corruption and counterterrorism efforts are not terrorist groups.

The Black Lives Matter (BLM) movement in the United States is another such example. The Federal Bureau of Investigation (FBI) and US Department of Homeland Security monitor the BLM movement for what they refer to as "black supremacist extremists" or "black identity extremists." The FBI asserts that these groups aim to use aggressive, retaliatory violence in response to perceived police brutality against African Americans. The BLM movement leaders have repeatedly denounced these accusations, reaffirming their commitment to human rights for all people and their rejection of the use of violence. Analysts of violent extremism note that the FBI surveillance of African American nonviolent activists as potential violent extremists is a flagrant attempt to undermine a legitimate protest movement (Cohen 2017). BLM movement leaders do not justify killing, nor do they articulate a superiority narrative.

Finally, a number of researchers note the similarity between school shootings and terrorism in the United States. Most school shootings are carried out by white young men with mental illness; loneliness; a desire to prove their masculinity; and hatred or intolerance for girls, women, sports jocks, and other groups in their schools. Like terrorism, school shooters intend to inflict mass casualties and create brutal violent spectacles. But unlike terrorism, there is no coherent ideology or goal. While the solutions to prevent school shootings may look very similar to the strategies for preventing terrorism, these are related, but not identical, problems.

In sum, a simple chart as illustrated in Table 1.5 with a definition helps to define what is and is not VE. A political goal is necessary but not sufficient characteristic of VE.

Table 1.5. Coding Violent Extremism

	Ideological Goals	*Superiority Narrative Intolerant of Diversity*	*Belief in Brutal Violence against Civilians*	*Violent Extremists?*
White nationalists	X	X	X	Yes
Orlando shooter/ ISIS	X	X	X	Yes
Kahanists	X	X	X	Yes
Kenyan human rights organizations	X			No
Black Lives Matter	X			No
U.S. school shooters		X	X	No

CONCLUSION

This chapter explored definitions of terror, terrorism, and VE. It listed reasons why the study of VE and terrorism is important. In sum, terrorism is terrifying not so much for how many people it kills. VE and terrorism are important because of the high costs of counterterrorism and the war on terror, the large numbers of civilian deaths in these operations, and the correlation in decreased civil liberties that has come with counterterrorism. The next chapters identify the elements that contribute to these problems and the range of interventions to prevent, reduce, and stop VE and terrorism.

Chapter 2

Mapping the Ecology of Violent Extremism

Correlations and Theories of Change

Lisa Schirch

Researchers share anecdotes and hold grand theories on the causes of violent extremism (VE) and terrorism. Most researchers focus on one factor that correlates or may contribute to VE. There is not one main factor that drives individuals and groups to adopt violent extremist beliefs and to commit terrorism. In the ecology of VE, a combination of factors correlates with a person adopting VE beliefs. This chapter offers a survey of the correlations or hypotheses about what contributes to VE.

Quantitative researchers offer specific data sets on lone actors, the size and numbers of members of terrorist groups, and the number and geographic location of attacks and numbers of civilians killed. Qualitative researchers offer anecdotes and psychological insight on the identities, grievances, and ideology of interview subjects who are themselves violent extremists supporting terrorism or know those who are. Some offer grand theories and highlight key patterns in the growth and dynamics of VE.

While there are a plethora of research projects and reports analyzing data about VE, the quality of this research is still lacking. Many of the purported factors driving VE and the so-called warning signs in use by police and intelligence officers today are based on little supporting research. For example, the Federal Bureau of Investigation's (FBI) online program "Don't Be a Puppet" identifies that a lack of excitement, a sense of purpose, importance, morality, or a sense of alienation, anxiety, and painful experiences correlate with VE. Yet polls indicate that large numbers of people feel lonely, experience anxiety, and have an unfulfilled desire for meaning in life. These indicators offer little assistance for determining who will and who will not adopt violent extremist beliefs or commit an act of terror.

Most VE research projects are inductive; they examine data on individuals or groups that have already carried out terrorism and determine correlations such as these individuals seemed lonely, were depressed, wanted adventure, experienced an identity crisis, were unemployed, expressed political grievances, or embraced apocalyptic religious ideas. In contrast, solid research would develop hypotheses with the establishment of a control group to determine which of the factors correlates to VE and whether the correlation is strong or weak. To do this, researchers would need to follow many people who all had the same types of life exposure. A control group of people, for example, who experience social isolation, lack of meaning, identity crisis, unemployment, political grievances, and a strong commitment to religion but do not join violent extremist groups could disprove or weaken the sense that these are indicators of VE in any context. And since every context is distinct, there will never be a one-sizefits-all explanation. Research cannot predict who or how many people will or will not adopt VE beliefs or commit acts of terror.

This chapter begins with a "map" of the ecology of VE. Every intervention has an implicit or explicit theory of change, a strategic narrative about how to address VE and terrorism. The map starts with the idea of a "context." Researchers identify over 25 factors that correlate with VE that emerge from the context. There are distinct theories of change for each of these 25 factors.

A LINEAR METAPHOR

Figure 2.1 illustrates how the concepts of context, recruitment, VE, planning, and terrorism relate to each other in theory. The diagram makes this process look deceptively linear. Contrary to widespread belief, there is

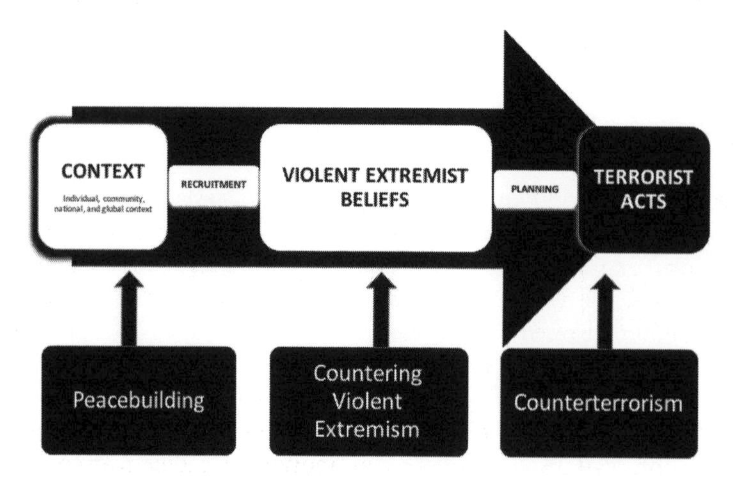

Figure 2.1. Arrow Model of Violent Extremism

nothing sequential about this process. There is no direct line between context and action. An arrow is simply a metaphor, a symbol that can help describe the relationship between parts of the ecology of VE. Chapter 3 gives other, nonlinear metaphors. The linear "arrow diagram" in Figure 2.1 is helpful simply to delineate different terms. Terrorist acts emerge from planning, which emerges from violent extremist beliefs, which emerge from recruitment. And context affects all these elements. Chapter 3 will explain further how three paradigms of interventions—counterterrorism, CVE, and peacebuilding—relate to this model.

PLANNING

Counterterrorism interventions focus mostly on the "planning" element in Figure 2.1. When individuals or groups are making plans, receiving funding, buying weapons, and training recruits, the chance of violent action is high. In theory, counterterrorism measures aim to respond to these immediate threats. At the most basic level, analysis centers on finding the specific people who belong to a violent extremist or terrorist group or who are planning to recruit others to join. Who is buying weapons and planning an attack? Who is joining a group and undergoing rituals of membership? Is a terrorist group accessing outside funding? What plans are they making? These questions require a brief description of the types of VE actors.

Types of Violent Extremist Actors

There are a variety of types of violent extremist organizations that support and/or carry out terrorism. These include the following:

Lone Actors and Lost Dogs

While the media often calls individuals who commit acts of terror "a lone wolf," some argue this is "way too appealing of a brand" and that these individuals more closely resemble "lost dogs"—a less appealing term (Dana Eyre, sociologist, in discussion with the author. January 20, 2018). Individuals who plan and carry out terrorist acts rarely are truly acting on their own. In most cases, the writings, videos, or communication of a wider violent extremist group inspired them to act.

The Profiles of Individual Radicalization in the United States (PIRUS) database contains information on approximately 1,500 individuals who "radicalized" to the point of engaging in violent and/or nonviolent criminal behavior. PIRUS has found that individual radicalization happens slowly, often over a period of five or more years between the adoption of violent extremist beliefs and taking criminal or violent action against others. This means there is often adequate time for family, friends, and community members to identify VE beliefs and take preventive action. According to PIRUS, the Internet is almost always involved in recruitment. Those individuals with past records of criminal behavior are more likely to move from belief to violent action. Those who are married, have children, or are older are less likely to move from belief to violent acts than those who are both young and unmarried (Jensen, James, and Tinsley 2016).

Leaderless Resistance, Impromptu Hives, and Unstructured Networks

Some violent extremist networks are unstructured and take place mostly via online networks. Someone can put out a call on these networks and mobilize people to take collective violent action. In Germany, for example, fluid groups of people form a crowd to commit violent hate crimes against Muslim refugees (Koehler 2016). In the United States, the Army of God is a Christian terrorist organization that is an example of "leaderless resistance." It publishes the names online of medical doctors who provide abortion as a call for anyone reading the list to kill them (Stern 2003).

Structured Local and Global Networks

Highly structured violent extremist groups such as the Ku Klux Klan (KKK) or ISIS also exist. These groups are unique from the others in that they may offer training, regular meetings, and have official leadership. Most structured terrorist groups and networks do not last. Like business start-ups, they have a high rate of failure. Approximately 50 percent of groups do not last longer than one year (Phillips 2017).

Funding and Weapons Access

Each type of violent extremist actor must find funding and access weapons so that they have the means to carry out an attack. While war is an expensive effort, terrorism can be done relatively cheaply. The rapid spread and availability of cheap guns and other weapons have created a "democratization of violence." Homemade bombs can be strapped on individuals' bodies, to cars or trucks, or put on train tracks. More sophisticated terrorist networks with regular funding and the ability to do long-term planning can learn how to fly planes as bombs like Al-Qaeda did on 9/11. Terrorist groups can also plant long-term employees in nuclear power plants to gain access to use nuclear power as a weapon. Larger and more complex plans requiring greater funding are also easier to detect and foil.

RECRUITMENT

Researchers also identify patterns of how individuals become motivated to join a VE group. *Radicalization* refers to the process by which individuals develop violent extremist beliefs and/or behaviors. Early ideas about radicalization imagined a "conveyor belt" in which a person became more religious, adopted violent extremist beliefs, and then committed acts of terror. But multiple researchers have found no profile, personality type, hallmarks, or common pathways toward VE and debunk the idea that a certain type of person adopts an ideology and becomes a terrorist. There is no "radicalization pathway," and there is no checklist that can predict VE. For one young man who adopts violent extremist beliefs, it is a combination of his older brother's influence, a religious uncle articulating a violent theology, a lack of job opportunities, anger at economic and political injustice by corrupt governments, and a desire to be admired by his friends. For another young person, a sense of being lost in modern society, feeling that his or her group is suffering humiliation, and a desire for adventure and meaning combine to attract him or her to the violent extremist narrative.

Scholars contest the concept of radicalization (Patel and Koushik 2017). Figure 2.1 uses the term "recruitment" instead of "radicalization." At some point, individuals cross from a situation where they may be susceptible to violent extremist narratives to a point in which they believe them and commit to them. For many violent extremists, the belief system does not ever take the form of violent action. Recruitment to a group or a cause can happen almost anywhere. But researchers point to four main locations or contexts where individuals make a commitment to join a violent extremist group.

Family and Community Recruitment

Social networks seem to play a significant role for people who develop violent extremist beliefs. Family and community ties create a sense of tribal loyalty. Researchers find that these social bonds are more important than ideology (Atran 2010; Sageman 2008). Friends and family make decisions together to join a group or to carry out an attack (Burke 2015). Individuals joining ISIS in Syria are recruited mostly by family and peers (Barrett 2014). Of US citizens who joined ISIS, three-fifths had a relative who had already joined (Bergen et al. 2016). In the majority of cases of lone-actor terrorism in the United States, 83 percent had a family member or friend who knew their grievances, 79 percent had shared their violent extremist beliefs, and in 64 percent of the cases, the family and friends were aware the individual was planning to commit a terrorist act (Gill, Horgan, and Deckert 2014). This does not mean that every family member or friend is aware or supportive of

VE. Social networks of VE among friends and family are difficult to discover. Every soccer field, coffee shop, diner, and street hangout spot on the planet is a potential recruitment arena.

Theories of Change

Counterterrorism interventions seek to find these individuals and groups to arrest and detain them, deter them from carrying out an attack, or destroy them through violent force.

Counterterrorism intelligence gathering attempts to identify family and friendship networks involved in spreading ideas of VE. Some programs focus on the children of those involved in terrorism. For example, a school in Indonesia works with the children of those family members convicted of terrorism to help them understand and develop immunity to the appeal of VE (VICE 2018). In other cases, countries use counterterrorism force to threaten, intimidate, and extract information from family and friends of those involved in terrorism. In both Israel (Schwartz 2014) and Russia (Kramer 2016), government forces routinely destroy the homes of individuals accused of terrorism. In both cases, researchers assert that such tactics result in further spreading violent extremist beliefs to entire communities that seek revenge.

Online Recruitment

The role of the Internet and social media in motivating and organizing people to embrace VE is unclear. Terrorist groups attempt to entice people to join their movement on Facebook, Twitter, websites, and online newsletters. Extremist groups are investing in compelling online video propaganda (Rieger, Frischlich, and Bente 2013). In the United States, the anti-abortion Army of God publishes the names and home addresses of doctors who perform abortions through their website to recruit individuals to kill them. A 2016 study found that each day ISIS produces an average of three videos, fifteen photographic reports, 90,000 social media reports, and 46,000–70,000 pro-ISIS Twitter posts (Radsch 2016). Likewise, white nationalists use online recruitment to find recruits through boosting young white men's self-esteem by telling them that they are part of a superior race, that they belong to the white nation, and that they can take out their revenge on women and minority groups. These sites target angry, lonely, insecure young men and promise them belonging to an elite group (Lapowsky 2017).

In popular media and government policy groups, there is an assumption that all these social media efforts by violent extremist groups result in actual online recruitment. However, there are no large-scale, empirical studies that confirm a correlation between Internet messages and recruitment to engage in

VE (McCants 2011). Some scholars remain skeptical of a significant role for the Internet in processes of violent radicalization (Conway 2016).

For example, news stories initially reported three teenage girls in London responded to a call for "Jihadi girl power" from ISIS on Twitter to go to Syria (Saleh 2014). But later research played down the role of the Internet, finding that it was a female friend who enticed them to Syria. The Internet facilitated their travel to Syria and perhaps added to the appeal through photos and memes showing other Western girls living with ISIS. But without a personal contact or the friendship they found with each other, the girls would likely not have joined ISIS (Shackle 2016). Some assert that only one in five ISIS foreign fighters is recruited online (Perliger and Milton 2016).

Theories of Change

Government counterterrorism programs are shutting down websites preaching violent extremist beliefs and limiting civil liberties, including access and freedom of expression in response to the perceived threat of online recruiting. Donors and security agencies are also investing in online counternarrative programs to compete with the recruiters. Slachmuijlder's chapter 26 in this book explores how peacebuilding alternative narratives can address online recruiting.

Recruitment at Religious Sites

There is no data to suggest that religious sites are primary locations for recruitment. Government agencies tend to target mosques or Islamic community centers as potential recruitment sites. In their view, young Muslim men attending frequent prayers on their own look vulnerable to violent extremist groups who might seek to use these sites to recruit individuals. Researchers dispute this correlation noting that the soccer field and coffee shop are much more likely places for recruitment (Atran 2010).

Theories of Change

Counterterrorism's focus on monitoring religious sites as a way of preventing VE lacks research to affirm its effectiveness. It has also been an unpopular feature, for it views Muslim communities with suspicion and asks Muslim leaders to identify potential recruits. Seeking intelligence information from untrained religious leaders is perceived as part of a so-called war on Islam. It also puts untrained religious leaders in the position of attempting to understand and act on unproven correlations and assumptions. Some argue that this approach actually reinforces community grievances and that this can increase the appeal of VE groups (Patel and Koushik 2017).

Prison Recruitment

In some countries, prisons have been central to the spread of violent extremist beliefs. Some view the prison setting as a potential enabling environment where prisoners can exchange information, spread violent extremist beliefs, and recruit and even plan for future terrorism outside of the prison. Researchers focus on risk factors to identify how to prevent or stop the spread of VE in prison settings. In some cases, a charismatic advocate for VE, gang violence, or overcrowding can have some psychological impact on prisoners (Silke and Veldhuis 2017).

Theories of Change

Rehabilitation and reintegration are theories of change to address the potential for recruitment and radicalization in prison settings. Researchers in Indonesia found four factors that related to successful rehabilitation and reintegration of those arrested for terrorism. First, deradicalization programs isolate prisoners away from others convicted of terrorism. Second, prisoners receive incentives such as better living conditions and economic aid for engaging in deradicalization programs. Third, former militants debate with prisoners on violent extremist ideology. Fourth, workshops on anger management, employment, and other practical skills help the inmates develop new goals and relationships in the outside world (Sukabdi 2015). Researchers find that in most cases, religion is a positive force for prisoners, helping them acknowledge past wrongs and develop a more positive identity and sense of purpose. It can even help to "deradicalize" people by giving other religious pathways for acting. In rare cases, prison inmates do embrace radical religious theologies and violent extremist beliefs (Silke and Veldhuis 2017).

Reintegration of armed groups engaged in terrorist acts happens within a process of disarmament, demobilization, and reintegration (DDR). It includes social cohesion programs, economic aid to help former combatants and extremists reintegrate into society, and education to prepare them to find alternative livelihoods. The Rome Memorandum on Good Practices for Rehabilitation and Reintegration of Violent Extremist Offenders outlines best practices for DDR for violent extremist groups. The chapter by Piedmont and Belli (chapter 21) in this volume explores DDR and VE.

CONTEXT

The arrow diagram in Figure 2.1 takes place in a broader context. The context is not just at the beginning of this arrow. It surrounds the entire arrow, as illustrated in Figure 2.2. Contexts are constantly shifting. What motivated first-generation jihadi fighters from Muslim countries is different from third- and fourth-generation fighters (Roy 2017). What motivates white extremist groups is different from what motivates Jewish or Buddhist extremists. The local context matters to every aspect of recruitment, VE beliefs, planning, and terrorist acts.

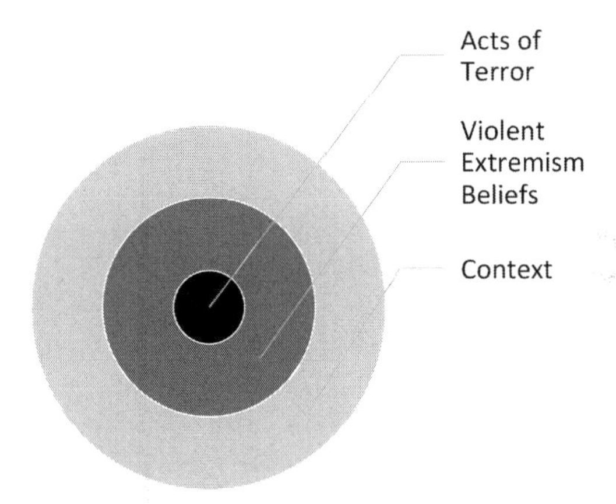

Figure 2.2. Nested Model of Violent Extremism

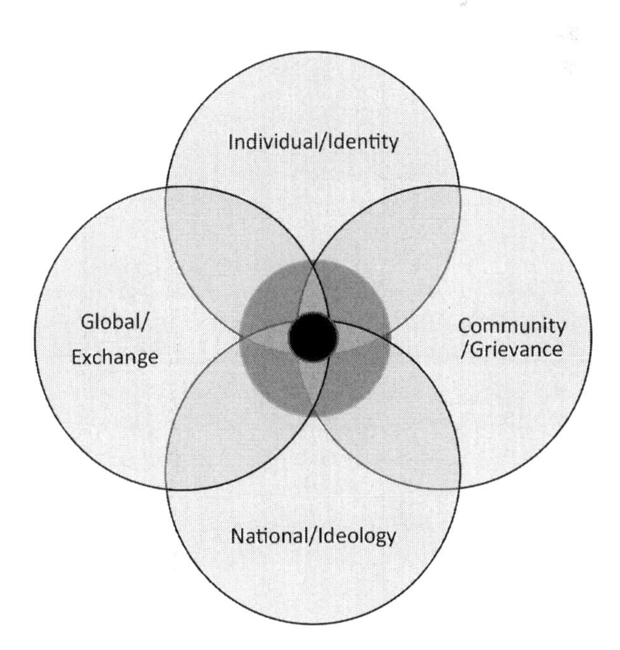

Figure 2.3. Four Categories of Context

The concentric circles in Figure 2.2 help to illustrate how beliefs and actions are nested within a wider context. Figure 2.3 then illustrates that there are four interrelated categories or dimensions of the wider context within which violent extremist beliefs and acts of terror take place.

- *Individual/Identity context* includes the factors that relate to an individual's identity.
- *Community/Grievance context* relates to sense of perceived grievances, often expressed at the community level.
- *National/Ideology context* relates to religious, political, economic, and social ideologies, often expressed at the national level.
- *Global/Exchange context* relates to the global exchange of military forces, guns, ideas, and weather patterns.

The metaphor of a plant with deep roots illustrates the underlying factors in the context that correlate with the growth of VE. Some plants have roots that can reproduce themselves if cut off at ground level. Superficial efforts to eradicate VE may temporarily halt the growth of the plant above ground. But without addressing the roots, the plant can regenerate growth (Schirch 2014). Superficial interventions that simply kill or arrest people without addressing root causes are unlikely to offer sustainable change. And, in fact, research confirms that killing individuals may worsen grievances, because perceptions of injustice and military/security force abuse strongly correlate with terrorism (GTI 2017). VE and terrorism correlate with roots in each of these areas: identity, grievance, ideology, and global exchange.

IDENTITY CONTEXT

A person's identity is his or her sense of his or her place in the world and where he or she belongs. Everyone has a need for a sense of identity and belonging. Every individual belongs to a variety of diverse cultural identity groups, including their ethnicity, religion, class, sex, educational level, geographic location, languages, and so on (Schirch 2014). These groups share values, beliefs, and behaviors that define them and set them apart from other groups.

Conflict between groups is common. An "in group" criticizes an "out group" for believing or behaving in a way that they find unacceptable. Group identity dynamics make it difficult for people to feel a sense of belonging to a group while not engaging in conflict with other groups. Some men view feminism as "anti-male" because it focuses on women's rights as human beings. Some white people view the Black Lives Matter movement as a threat because it focuses on the value of black lives.

Psychologist Erik Erikson defined an "identity crisis" as a failure of young people to develop a positive self-image and sense of social belonging (Erikson 1970). Historically, people traveled less, encountered fewer people from other cultures, and had stronger ties to community. Some scholars blame globalization, the process of increased economic, political, and social exchange around the world, for shifting the way people relate to each other and instigating identity crises (Babran 2008). Others blame increasing individualism as fragmenting strong cultural ties and communities. And still others see transition and migration resulting from climate change, economic pressure, and violent conflict as creating an identity crisis in individuals who have become untied to their cultural communities. Atran's chapter in this book (chapter 4) describes the attraction of VE as part of "civilizations unraveling," and people, especially young people, become "unmoored from their traditions" and "flail about" in search of a meaningful identity. "The new world disorder puts us all at risk in this global age, where non-state forces volcanically erupt through the nation-state system, spreading noxious, violent memes."

There are a wide range of issues related to identity. These include the following:

Adventure, Heroism, Glory, and Significance

Anecdotal evidence suggests some young people join violent extremist groups so that they can travel and experience the world and gain social significance and glorification. Most of these stories include young men who while living in the West travel to Afghanistan or Syria and do so because they want to transform from being a "nobody in a run-down suburb to a heroic warrior battling dark forces" (Bartlett 2011). Researchers argue young men and women join violent extremist causes because they seek glory, heroism, meaning, and significance in the world. They view Al-Qaeda and other violent extremist groups as networks pitching a narrative where individuals can become "stars" and achieve glory through dramatic terrorist theatre (Roy 2017). Anti-abortion "soldiers" in the Army of God kill abortion doctors, and in return peers reward them with praise. Palestinian martyrs who attack Israeli civilians in suicide bombings are rewarded with posters celebrating their attacks.

Social Isolation, Loneliness, and Need for Belonging

Some researchers find a correlation between VE and a sense of social marginalization and disenfranchisement. This is seemingly at odds with the finding that friends and family vulnerable to VE are the most likely to recruit others. Isolation is cited as a correlation with lone actors because they are often unconnected to social networks and act relatively independently, want a sense of belonging, and thrive off the tight social relationships in some of these groups. Analyses of individuals who committed mass acts of terror against civilians indicate that social isolation and loneliness do correlate, at least in some cases, with their development of VE beliefs (Hug 2013).

Transition and Migration

The argument that transition and migration correlate with VE relates to social isolation and identity crises. The hypothesis is that people who have left their home communities have fewer social ties, are more likely to be unemployed, and are more vulnerable to VE. Anti-immigration policies thrive on this hypothesis. Some researchers argue that immigration correlates with 88 percent of terrorist attacks in the United States between 1975 and 2015. But anti-immigration policies often have nothing to do with evidence-based research. No migrants from the six countries included in the recent U.S. immigration ban committed any terrorism (Nowrasteh 2016).

Trauma and Fear

Trauma refers to an emotional wound that results from experiencing or witnessing a traumatic event, especially deliberate violence. Trauma produces fear and anxiety, a sense of lack of control, an insult to identity, or a threat of physical injury. Fear is another potential factor for those who join VE organizations. Al-Qaeda propaganda repeatedly asserts that Christians and Jews want to destroy Islam. Many recruits are afraid of attacks on Islam and want to defend their religion and the identity their religion provides to them. Likewise, among white extremists, fear of the destruction of white culture and identity motivates some to join these groups. Identity groups based on fear of another group often hold a narrative where the survival of their own in-group depends on the death and destruction of some other group. Christian white extremists carry out the majority of terrorist acts in the United States, usually targeting African Americans, Jews, and Muslims whom they see as threatening their white identity (START 2017).

Humiliation

Numerous researchers identify humiliation as a primary emotion related to VE (Moisi 2007). However, some research with individuals who espouse VE ideas concludes that it is not direct humiliation but rather indirect observation of people of their own group experiencing humiliation that motivates the desire for revenge through terrorism (Atran 2010). Similarly, interviews with individuals who committed brutal violence revealed that they all carried out this violence in an effort to replace shame, humiliation, disrespect, and ridicule with self-esteem and respect (Gilligan 2001).

Mental Health, Neuroscience, and Hormones

Mental health is another individual factor related to identity. Some researchers identify a pattern of depression and mental illness in those who join violent extremist groups (Bhui et al. 2012). Other researchers assert that neurological processes impact vulnerability to violent extremist propaganda such as online videos. MRI scans can show whether these images engage emotional and cognitive elements of the brain (Basick 2015). Still other researchers assert that less than 10 percent of the VE cases involved individuals with either a diagnosed or a reported suspected presence of a mental health condition (PIRUS n.d.). Fitzduff's chapter in this book (chapter 7) explores this research on the brain, hormones, and biology.

Sex

There is a variety of evidence that some people join violent extremist groups because of the desire to have sex. ISIS entices young women to fly to Syria to be "jihadi brides" (Saltman and Smith 2015). In Iraq, ISIS systematically raped thousands of Yezidi women and girls. Young men join Hamas and other groups with the promise of seventy-two virgins. Boko Haram kidnaps and rapes women and girls, forcing some into marriage and sexual servitude (Zenn and Pearson 2014). Rape is seen as a weapon and recruiting tool for VE groups in countries like Nigeria, where gender-based violence is rampant (Searcey 2017). White nationalists express anger at not having access to women and sex. While traditionally antigay, white nationalists have recently begun recruiting white gay men by playing on their fears of immigrants and Muslims and offering promises of sex (Minkowitz 2017).

Gender Roles

Men carry out most acts of terror. But women also join VE groups and carry out attacks. And at least in some countries, women support terrorism more than men do (Fair and Shepherd 2006). Gender roles, the social norms and expectations of masculinity and femininity, push boys and girls as well as men and women toward VE beliefs in different ways. Gender refers to the cultural and social characteristics that society expects of males and females.

Violence-based rites of passage for boys to become men exist in many cultures. Cultures and societies want men to be tough and strong. Media images of masculinity portray a "hypermasculine" expectation that males will kill without regret and will show no remorse (Kratz 1999). Research on "toxic masculinity" suggests young men find an appeal in VE beliefs and acts of terror as rites of passage for their own unsure gender conformity. Afraid of being seen as homosexual or feminine, some suspect young men commit acts of terror in an attempt to prove their manhood (Haider 2016; Kimmel 2018). In the United States, a number of researchers view school shootings, almost all of which are carried out by young men, and terrorism as motivated by similar violent notions of masculinity. The principal feature of gun violence in American schools, theaters, night clubs, and shopping centers involves young male efforts to garner respect and attention related to their threatened sense of manhood (Kellner 2008). Psychologists analyzing the violence of young white extremists in Charlottesville, Virginia, in 2017 also point to the central role of toxic masculinity (Williams 2017).

Female gender roles are also linked to VE. Some scholars suggest women carry out up to a quarter of all terrorist attacks (Bloom 2011). This may be in part because they may not be searched or suspected as much as their male counterparts. Research on women who join ISIS describes the range of factors pushing and pulling women into ISIS, including anger at oppression of Muslims, desire to aid the ISIS goal of state-building, and desire to belong and have a group identity (Fink, Zeiger, and Bhulai 2016). ISIS uses female-specific messages to recruit girls and women. "Jihadi girl power" messages, for example, stress the empowerment and capability of women to support ISIS in its mission while promising women agency, voice, and access to their rights, even while these promises are usually not truthful (Havlicek 2015). Recruitment of girls and women to join VE groups can mirror the tactics and stages that sexual predators use to groom victims. Once they join, women play a variety of roles, including brides to male fighters and online recruiters attempting to lure other women to join the movement (Saltman and Smith 2015). In addition, a survey of 6,000 Muslims in fourteen countries found females were more likely to support terrorism than were males (Fair and Shepherd 2006).

Theories of Change

There are a variety of theories of change to address these individual, identity-based factors. Anti-immigration policies are one response to the correlation between VE and the identity crises linked to transition and migration. Some researchers assert that improving humanitarian responses to support refugees and migrants would put the emphasis on finding sustainable solutions and human rights–based support and development options for migrants (Koser 2015b). Antidiscrimination and antiracism efforts aim to reduce racism and prejudice between social groups and can help to affirm identity groups while also asserting the equality of all human beings and their rights to equal opportunities and treatment. Young people seeking opportunities to become heroes and achieve empowerment and social significance can find other pathways through opportunities to travel, participate in sports or arts groups, or civic engagement work to address social justice issues.

Some theories of change to address individual-level correlations to VE are similar to remedies to other social problems like gangs, delinquency, and youth criminal activity. A central principle of identity-based solutions is that people engaging in conflict with another group need ways of feeling positive about their identity. People will be willing to kill and die if they think they are protecting their identity and dignity (Gilligan 2001). Psychologists argue that emotional literacy is an antidote to VE, teaching people how to cognitively challenge irrational convictions; understand emotions such as sadness, envy, and hate; and manage anger and boredom. Emotional literacy teaches people how to understand and be mindful of connections between thinking, feeling, and acting. It can also empower people to challenge manipulation and psychological control mechanisms (Liechtenstein 2015).

Resilience refers to the capacity to respond to, adapt to, absorb or survive a crisis or severe change. Psycho-social trauma healing addresses the psychological wounds of those who have been affected by conflict and foster resilience. Intergroup dialogue bringing groups together to jointly work on shared interests can help a positive sense of identity. Psychosocial support through trauma healing and community affirmation of different identity groups can address fear, humiliation, and mental health aspects of VE. This public health approach to VE includes community-led preventative programming to build resilience against recruitment to VE through education, dialogue, and counseling. This can include school-based and faith-based mental health interventions as well as screening for mental health and trauma (Weine et al. 2015). Education about sex and sexual integrity can combat the ignorance stemming from extremely restrictive religious messages and/or vulgar pornography.

Community-led CVE programs attempt to track individuals who may be suffering an identity crisis of some sort. Chapters in this book by Ansari and Khan and Qadeem (chapters 18 and 31) give examples of programs to address these individual identity factors. This book's chapters by Hamilton and Prelis, Shipler, Walsh, and Slachmuijlder (chapters 8 and 25) illustrate how some peacebuilding groups are working with youth to address these factors.

Other interventions include theories of change based on changing gender norms and increasing the participation of women and youth in shaping VE interventions. Some programs advocate affirming a wider range of expressions of masculinity that might include new rites of passage to manhood that involve public service rather than violence (Ezekilov 2017). There is extensive research on the positive roles women can play in preventing VE (Fink, Zeiger, and Bhulai 2016). Chapters by Bhulai, Fitzduff, and Piedmont and Belli (chapters 7, 9, and 21) in this book explore the role of gender in VE and women's roles in preventing VE.

COMMUNITY/GRIEVANCE CONTEXT

Many violent extremist groups view national and even global economic, political, and social systems as oppressive to their group, whether they be white nationalists, Jewish settlers, or Buddhist monks. Some researchers insist grievances play little role in driving VE and are simply justifications to mobilize supporters (Roy 2017). But major research studies with big data sets prove that political, economic, and social grievances correlate strongly with VE.

Political Grievances

The Global Terrorism Index finds a strong correlation between conflict, political violence, and terrorism; most terrorism takes place in countries that are also experiencing an armed conflict or high levels of political or state terror where there are state-sanctioned killings, torture, disappearances, and political imprisonment. In 2016, 99 percent of deaths due to terrorist attacks occurred in countries in these two categories (GTI 2017, 62). In developing countries, internal conflict and political terror result in a decrease in civil liberties and an increase in political tension. These experiences correlate with the individual and group grievances by violent extremist groups (GTI 2017, 64). The countries most affected by the nonviolent protests in the Arab Spring, for example, are now the countries that suffer most from terrorism (GTI 2017). The Arab Spring expressed public grievances about economic conditions, political freedoms, and government corruption, among other issues. Before the Arab Spring began, Libya and Syria had no deaths from terrorism. A civil war emerged in both countries after the Arab Spring. Deaths from terrorism dramatically increased.

Likewise, a UNDP study of 500 former members of violent extremist groups finds a strong correlation between political grievances and VE, and that abuses by state security forces were often the "tipping point" that propelled an individual to join a VE group.

> [D]isaffection with government is highest by significant margins among the *Journey to Extremism* respondents who were recruited by violent extremist

> groups across several key indicators. These include: belief that government only looks after the interests of a few; low level of trust in government authorities; and experience, or willingness to report experience, of bribe-paying. Grievances against security actors, as well as politicians, are particularly marked, with an average of 78 percent rating low levels of trust in the police, politicians and military. Those most susceptible to recruitment express a significantly lower degree of confidence in the potential for democratic institutions to deliver progress or meaningful change. . . . A striking 71 percent pointed to "government action", including "killing of a family member or friend" or "arrest of a family member or friend", as the incident that prompted them to join. (UNDP 2017, 5)

The UNDP study also surveyed individuals who had positive views of government programs. This group had less likelihood of joining a VE group, confirming government provision of services as a source of resilience that prevents vulnerability to VE. UNDP comments that this strong correlation calls into question counterterrorism programs that are known for human rights abuses and simultaneously drain government funds that could provide public services that might better prevent VE.

In Afghanistan, researchers found that the two main reasons men join the Taliban are a frustration with a predatory and corrupt government that cannot deliver justice or security and the perceived predatory behavior of foreign forces (Ladbury 2009). Corruption in Afghanistan is vast, and a number of scholars note the significant role corruption plays in driving VE (Chayes 2016). Osama bin Laden wrote in *The Encyclopedia of the Afghan Jihad* about his frustration with Muslims' political marginalization by Western Judeo-Christian powers (Gerecht 2002). Bin Laden perceived that Western Christians held most political power and could press for their political interests, whereas Muslims were persecuted and excluded from international political decision making.

The US Agency for International Development (USAID) identifies seven political characteristics that correlate with VE. These include (1) denial of basic political rights and civil liberties; (2) gross violations of human rights; (3) corruption and impunity for elites; (4) safe havens, poorly governed or ungoverned areas; (5) violent local conflicts that can be exploited (6) state sponsorship of violent extremist groups; and (7) weak or nonexistent oppositions (USAID 2009).

Economic Grievances

There is a long history of research correlating economic status and political violence (Gurr 1970; Krueger 2007). Poverty itself does not correlate with terrorism. However, there is more terrorism in poor countries than in rich countries. The correlation between economic status and VE relates to perceptions of injustice rather than economic levels on their own. Relative deprivation is the frustration experienced when expectations for economic prosperity are higher than what is possible. Researchers also refer to a hypothesis that VE also correlates with the so-called youth bulge, a shift in the age of the general population toward a concentration of large numbers of youth and young adults looking for work while relatively few older adults are retiring from work. Countries with a youth bulge are thought to have higher unemployment and youth who may feel frustrated at their lack of opportunities and may provide a cheap source of labor for violent extremist groups (Urdal 2007).

In some regions, Africa in particular, there is some research to suggest that payments and economic incentives entice poor young men (and some women) to join violent extremist groups. In the UNDP study of VE in Africa, economic incentives were the tipping point for just 13 percent who joined a VE group (UNDP 2017, 58). However, research found that ordinary Nigerians perceived that money and economic marginalization were primary factors (Ewi and Salifu 2017). Other researchers find that, at least in some regions, those belonging to a violent extremist group may feel insulted at payment and view their motivation as solely in response to a religious call or sacred duty (Atran and Axelrod 2008).

In Pakistan, researchers found less support for major violent extremist groups among poorer Pakistanis than among middle-class Pakistanis. Those who were given information emphasizing economic inequalities perceived greater injustice and also felt less support for violent extremist groups (Fair et al. 2016). However, in the European Union, immigrant youth experience much higher levels of unemployment than do native-born citizens. In Belgium, young immigrants are 64 percent more likely to be unemployed than those born in Belgium. Young immigrants from Belgium left their homes in Europe to join ISIS in Iraq and Syria (GTI 2017, 65). In this context, relative deprivation seems to have the opposite effect as it does in Pakistan, spurring greater support for VE.

Few violent extremist organizations articulate economic grievances such as poverty or lack of public services in their recruiting materials or publications justifying their terror. Political grievances of identity and political exclusion and repression are far more prevalent. Those who carry out terrorist attacks come from a variety of economic backgrounds. Often the leadership of terrorist groups is highly educated and wealthy or middle class. In some countries, the so-called foot soldiers of terrorist groups are less educated or illiterate and poor.

However, Osama bin Laden articulated economic grievances against global economic trade policies that disenfranchised and discriminated against the

Muslim world. Bin Laden viewed American policy of supporting corrupt Arab leaders as a result of its desire for economic dominance and exploitation or "globalization." Bin Laden denounced US policy that would put American greed above the dignity of Muslim civilians (Lewis 2001). Al-Qaeda claims it is using an economic warfare strategy aimed to use terrorist attacks, such as the one against the capitalist symbol of the World Trade Center, which would invite Western capitalist countries to invest in a large military response that would "bleed until bankrupt" the West (Gartenstein-Ross 2011).

Social Grievances

Social grievances relate to a lack of society-wide social cohesion, social capital, as well as social exclusion, and discrimination. Sociologists measure social cohesion based on a variety of factors, including the number and strength of relationships between people in the same group, the incentives they receive for loyalty with others in their group, and the strength of their social norms or the values and behaviors that they share with each other. Social cohesion can also refer to relationships between groups. Groups with strong internal cohesion, for example, tend to have strong in-group loyalty but often they conflict with the out-group. A society has strong social cohesion when there are many cross-cutting relationships between social groups. Social capital refers to the number and quality of relationships an individual or group has available to them. Social capital allows people to address their interests and pursue their goals. An individual who has a relatively small social network and that is exposed to violent extremist beliefs has a relatively weaker social capital. They may believe they have no way of addressing their social, economic, or political grievances.

The Global Terrorism Index separates the correlations with terrorism in Organisation for Economic Cooperation and Development (OECD) and non-OECD countries. The OECD includes thirty-five economically advanced countries primarily in Europe and North America. Those OECD countries that are involved in external conflict, lack economic opportunity, and have low social cohesion and social alienation are more likely to have incidents of terrorism (GTI 2017, 64).

In Europe, for example, some locally born white citizens discriminate against young migrants from other religions and parts of the world. While white citizens may have relatively strong social cohesion and social capital with other white members of society, they may perceive migrants as a threat. They may hold racist social attitudes and discriminate against migrants. Young Muslims living in Europe have relatively fewer social networks to achieve their social, political, and economic goals. They may have strong in-group social capital but lack a sense of cohesion in the broader society.

They may experience a sense of social exclusion and discrimination by white Europeans in terms of finding housing, jobs, or how local businesses, educators, police, and government agents treat them. Several researchers indicate a clear correlation between grievances related to lack of social cohesion and VE (Schmid 2016).

Theories of Change

Grievances such as political and economic disenfranchisement do not have an easy fix. Few counterterrorism and CVE programs try to address the root causes of grievances that correlate with VE. But given the strength of the correlation between grievances and VE, policies and programs to address grievances are necessary for preventing VE. The UN Secretary General stated that research convinced him that "the creation of open, equitable, inclusive and pluralist societies, based on the full respect of human rights and with economic opportunities for all, represents the most tangible and meaningful alternative to violent extremism" (UNDP 2017, iii).

Nonviolent civil resistance movements have a history of bringing about social, political, and economic change that far exceeds the success rate of violent movements (Chenoweth and Stephan 2011). Civil resistance movements are already working on many of the same grievances expressed by those who join violent extremist groups. And nonviolent movements "absorb" and rechannel youth alienation, providing a positive mission for change. Stephan and Erdberg's chapter in this book (chapter 28) discusses the importance of nonviolent civil resistance as a way to address the political and structural root causes of VE.

The literature on good governance, security-sector reform, and improving the quality of state–society relations is vast. But most of these peacebuilding strategies (Serwer and Thomson 2007) are not employed directly to address VE. And, as noted earlier, counterterrorism policies in many countries exacerbate the problems of political grievances and worsen state–society relations.

Peacebuilding programs that address the following sectors could help to prevent VE and also address many other economic, political, and social problems. The effectiveness of programs can be measured by public perceptions of performance in each of these areas. In the 2017 UNDP study of VE in Africa, researchers found that people who did not join VE groups felt more positive about state performance in these areas of governance (UNDP 2017).

Politically Stable Democracy

States that uphold human rights, civil freedoms, and democratic decision making enjoy greater peace and security (GPI 2017). Preventing VE and terrorism requires reforming governance to address corruption and supporting democratic reforms by improving the state–society relationship. Since terrorism correlates with political conflict, a robust and comprehensive peace process involving all sectors of society can address political conflicts that may be root causes of terrorism. Chapters in this book by Lederach (chapter 22), Zartman (chapter 23), and Slachmuijlder (chapter 14) illustrate this approach.

Sustainable Economy

Improving basic economic security, rewarding entrepreneurship, managing sustainable use of resources, reducing the gap between rich and poor, and fostering economic stability for all people can improve security (Ghanem 2015; Keefer and Loayza 2008; Kessels and Nemr 2016). Chapters in this book by Conroy and Wolfe and Proctor (chapters 6 and 33) identify how government support programs and private-sector growth and job creation can be part of the solution to VE.

Safe and Secure Environment

Community security, freedom of movement, and freedom from fear are necessary for human security and prevention of VE. Security forces should protect all civilians, regardless of their identity. For security forces that have been abusive to the population, a transparent process of security sector reform should enable increased accountability and strategies, including community policing that improves state–society relationships. In addition, disarmament, demobilization, and reintegration (DDR) processes to address former non-state armed groups can improve human security and prevent VE. Chapters by Millar, Lodgaard, and Piedmont and Belli (chapters 11, 12, and 21) in this book illustrate the role and behavior of security forces in counterterrorism operations and DDR processes related to VE.

Justice and Rule of Law

When people believe the justice system is unfair or illegitimate, they may not use it to pursue their grievances. Preventing VE requires people to perceive that they have predictable social relations and a justice system that is coherent and legitimate and that uses just legal frameworks to monitor and protect human rights. Effective counterterrorism requires good criminal justice practices, including constitutional reform and rule-of-law-based criminal justice systems, anti-money laundering cooperation, cooperative intelligence sharing and investigations, evidence and investigation standards, and rehabilitation and reintegration programs (GCCS 2015). Civil society has an important role in monitoring government corruption and promoting the rule of law in regions such as South Asia (GCCS et al. 2015).

Social and Cultural Well-Being

When people perceive that they have a sense of meaning and social order in their lives along with respect, dignity, identity, and a sense of belonging, VE may be less likely. Chapters by Hamilton, Laveta, Chassy and Bolton, Scott, Slachmuijlder (chapter 24), and Abu-Nimer in this book address how a range of peacebuilding efforts, including psychosocial recovery and trauma healing, may also be helpful.

Preventing and countering violent extremism and peacebuilding interventions aim to improve social integration, social cohesion, and resilience in communities. Some of these programs aim to help migrants and other groups integrate into society. Others build social capital so that communities can respond to crises with built-in redundancy and horizontal leadership so that local leaders do not have to depend on top-down decision making.

IDEOLOGY CONTEXT

An ideology is a system of ideas, beliefs, and values that shape how an individual or group understands and interacts in the world. Ideology defines what is right or wrong and prescribes how to change or fix the world. An ideology responds to a grievance and creates an alternative vision of what the world should look like.

Political Ideologies

Violent extremist groups support authoritarian political structures and oppose democracy and political systems that represent diverse political interests and ideas.

Social Ideologies

Race is a historical and social construct without biological basis. There are more genetic differences within groups of people than between them. Nazi racial ideology was responsible for the deaths of 6 million Jews as well as millions more Roma people, LGBTQ people, and disabled people. Yet racial ideologies still have strong membership in many countries. In Europe and North America, white supremacy combats multiculturalism and "race mixing." White nationalism calls on white people to fight in a "holy racial war" to create pure white states (Klassen 1986). To the white nationalist, white supremacy is the opposite of multiculturalism and diversity. Purity narratives urge members of a group to kill or exterminate people of other races so that the society can reach its potential. VE groups espousing racial ideology often see governments tolerating or supporting diversity as part of the problem. The Kahanist movement in Israel, for example, opposes Palestinians on what they see as Jewish land, and they oppose the Israeli government for not pushing Palestinians off the land.

Economic Ideologies

Violent extremist groups rarely outline an economic ideology to address economic grievances. Some credit the anarchist-communist movement, which held an economic and political ideology, for creating modern terrorism (Jasanoff 2016). In their attempt to collapse the state and create a communal society, anarchist terrorists took aim at civilians. But today, few VE groups espouse an economic ideology.

Religious Ideologies

Pew polling found that 84 percent of the world's population identifies with religious beliefs (Pew 2012). Most religious people do not engage in VE. Yet many commentators on terrorism continue to blame religion, and specifically Islam, for terrorism. There are correlations between religion and VE. But contrary to popular opinion, most terrorists do not have extensive religious training, nor are they more religiously knowledgeable or devout than other people who reject VE. A survey of five hundred members of violent extremist groups in Africa found that over half felt their religion (Islam in most cases) was under attack, and yet over half acknowledged that they only held limited understanding of their religion (UNDP 2017). There are four aspects of the role of religion in VE.

Religion as Theological Justification for Terrorism

Most religions have teachings that limit violence, particularly against innocent civilians. VE groups use theological justifications for attacks on civilians. Some religious groups dehumanize other groups through a religious lens, posing their own group as "good" and the civilian enemy as "evil." Religious purity narratives then argue that a pure religion requires violence against an "other." Religious groups offer a theology of "redemptive violence," whereby violent action toward an enemy is a necessary religious requirement (Wink 1986). Religious apocalypticism is the extreme manifestation of theological justification for killing civilians. Terror groups use a religious framework that divides the world into good and evil and see themselves as the midwives birthing the purification of evil through dramatic violent destruction. Flannery's chapter in this book (chapter 5) explores religious apocalypticism in more depth.

Religion as a Pathway for Political and Economic Grievances

Public opinion polls in 2005 found that while most Muslims opposed Al-Qaeda and other terrorist groups and supported democracy, most Muslims disagreed with the US-led war in Iraq and Afghanistan (Kohut 2005). Research suggests most Muslims in the United States believe there is discrimination against Muslims (Lipka 2017). Grievances can also drive people to adopt fundamentalist religious ideologies. ISIS's narrative can be summed up as this: "Islam is under attack. ISIS will defend Islam and create an Islamic Caliphate."

ISIS supporters hold a religious and political ideology. ISIS believes in the superiority of Salafi religious ideas, belongs to the social group of Sunni Islam, and believes in authoritarian rule. Scholars point to the Shia-Sunni divide as driven more by political calculations than religious differences (Hunter 2013). Political and economic marginalization of Sunni Muslims in Iraq and Syria correlated with the rise of ISIS and its fundamentalist Salafi version of Islam.

Political grievances also translate into religious frameworks in the United States. White poor communities in the American South, frustrated with their stagnant economy and relative lack of political voice, compared with other parts of the United States, adopted fundamentalist and evangelical forms of Christianity at higher rates. Some of these began to embrace elements of white nationalism. Some evolved into the Christian Identity movement, the ideology of white nationalism, as a reaction to the political challenge they perceived (Berry 2017).

Religion as Source of Identity

Fundamentalist versions of Christianity, Islam, Buddhism, Hinduism, Judaism, and other religions operate as ideologies. Religious fundamentalism is a set of ideas that view the world as a struggle between good and evil. Scholars view fundamentalism as a reaction to an increasingly complex and ambiguous world (Schultz 2005). Fundamentalism offers a simplistic understanding of how the world works and provides a narrative that explains the world in terms of good versus evil. Fundamentalism rejects diversity of opinion and requires loyalty to authoritarian leaders. Fundamentalist religious ideologies are appealing to individuals experiencing an identity crisis or overwhelmed with a world of complex ideas and ambiguity. Some researchers suggest that fundamentalist religious groups may particularly attract individuals struggling with a sense of humiliation, loneliness, a desire to belong, sexual frustration, confusion over gender roles, and in transition (Schultz 2005). For example, violent extremist groups in Europe may recruit Muslims who feel marginalized by their country of citizenship. Religious groups provide an alternative identity for belonging, finding meaningful work, and taking collective action in these contexts (Mandaville and Nozell 2017).

Religion as a "Spiritual High" of Belonging to VE Groups

Researchers find that some join VE groups because killing on behalf of a religious calling gives an intense spiritual high that makes an individual feel part of a group (Atran 2010). Some describe a spiritual calling or addiction to carrying out religiously motivated terrorism (Stern 2003). The Latin root of the word "religion" is "ligar"—the same root of the word "ligament," the connective tissue between muscle and bone. Sacred experiences often relate to feeling strong bonds with others. "Religion" is about connecting or reconnecting. Religion includes a set of laws, rituals, and experiences that bind people together. From the earliest expressions of religion, this "wholeness" or "holiness" was felt as a sacred, religious experience (Ehrenreich 1997). Emile Durkheim refers to this as the "inherent social nature of religion" in his sociological analysis of *The Elementary Forms of the Religious Life* where everyday life is "profane" and people have religious or "sacred" experiences in collective social gatherings (Durkheim 1915).

Theories of Change

There are a variety of methods to address VE ideologies. Counterterrorism experts created elaborate diagrams and checklists to identify the religious or political ideologies of people they thought might commit a terrorist act. They identified individuals who were, for example, attending religious services, growing a beard, wearing religious clothing, critical of the US bombing in Iraq, or resentful of FBI monitoring of Muslims. Researchers have debunked this theory (Wilton Park 2016). Many argue religion plays a more complex role in VE that requires an ecological, contextual approach to "right size" the role of religious analyses and interventions (Park 2016).

Counterterrorism and P/CVE use "counternarratives" to combat violent extremist ideology. In the so-called war of ideas, responding to ideological drivers of VE through "counternarratives" attempts to dissuade, challenge, or falsify ideological beliefs. This is a tempting theory of change, as spreading countering narratives via the media is far easier than making fundamental change in global politics or economics. However, most of these ideologies relate to grievances. And grievances do require more substantial political and economic changes.

Some governments are pushing religious leaders to deliver moderate religious messages to counter the narratives of violent extremists. This can backfire in a variety of ways. If governments view criticism of military policy, for example, as "radical" then being "moderate" means these religious leaders must stop their fair critique and democratic discussion. Religious leaders who push back against the expression of political grievance or criticism of Western policy, or who are viewed by their communities as agents of intelligence and government spying, are likely to lose all authority and possibly their lives. Religious actors may have an important role in affirming and redirecting these grievances. Any encouragement for moderation requires much further discussion on the specific definition of what is extreme. As noted earlier, killing civilians is a radical idea, departing from most religious and social norms. Religious leaders have an authority to speak on the norms protecting human life in every context. But religious leaders should not be asked to counter expression of political grievances or economic injustices (Mandaville and Nozell 2017, 10). Chapters by Abu-Nimer, Sethi, and Hume (chapters 17, 19, and 20) address these challenges and opportunities in this book.

Furthermore, challenging and "deprogramming" people who hold VE ideologies often require a more robust program of daily personal contact. British programs for Nazi prisoners after World War II offer theories of change that explain how to deradicalize people who hold racial ideologies. The goal was to ensure "long-term ideological victory" over the Nazi belief system by changing the group attitudes through a variety of activities that aimed to demoralize Nazi prisoners and reorient them toward democratic values (Cooper 2013). The German Institute on Radicalization and De-Radicalization Studies continues doing this type of work today in a program called Exit that helps young people leave neo-Nazi groups.

In the United States, an organization called Life after Hate carries out these types of programs for white nationalists (Life after Hate n.d.). Run by individuals who were previously members of VE groups, Life after Hate counters messages of hate online and runs programs to help others counter VE in their schools and community groups. Life after Hate emphasizes the role of compassion for self and others, noting that people must overcome the shame they may feel having belonged to a VE group.

Human rights and peace education is another theory of change for addressing ideologies related to VE. Many young people have exposure to violent ideologies that press for change but do not have information or knowledge about nonviolent methods of change, or human rights. Education in these areas can provide options and skills for channeling individual and group frustrations toward productive change.

Engaging religious actors is a relatively new focus in government P/CVE efforts. Governments are recognizing the necessity of religious literacy in achieving their foreign policy goals (Appleby and Cizik 2010). Diplomats often take a secular approach to their work. The failure of US foreign policy planners in Iraq to understand the division between Shia and Sunni Muslims and the debate on whether it is primarily about religion or politics is one of the most flagrant examples. Religious literacy training for diplomats is preparation for a strategy to engage religious actors "early and often" rather than consulting with them after decisions have already been made. Religious actors also seek training to learn skills in interreligious dialogue and how to improve their access to media to broadcast messages of religious tolerance and understanding. Dialogue and relationship building is a theory of change that asserts the possibility that members of violent extremist groups can break stereotypes and rehumanize people they have demonized. This type of engagement can feel abusive to those belonging to groups who receive violence from violent extremists, so engagement should always be fully informed of the risks of further harm and pain.

GLOBAL CONTEXT

At the global level, there are four factors that correlate with VE: international military intervention, the global weapons trade, climate change, and media. Globalization is the process of global exchange and interdependence that is facilitated by increased communication and transportation of people, objects, and ideas.

International Military Intervention

In his 2004 video to American citizens, Osama bin Laden said, "We want to restore freedom to our nation. Just as you lay waste to our nation, so shall we lay waste to yours. No one except a dumb thief plays with the security of others and then makes himself believe he will be secure" (bin Laden 2004). Perceived injustice at the presence of foreign troops is widely seen as correlating with an increase in terrorism. As illustrated in chapter 1, data on the increase in military funding for the war on terror correlates with an increase in terrorism. Researchers note the United States is targeted more frequently than other countries because of the extent of US military involvement abroad (Choi 2011). There is a US counterterrorism military presence in seventy-six countries (Costs of War 2018). There are signs that intelligence agencies and the public recognize that foreign military intervention can increase rather than decrease terrorism (Robbins 2017). In response to the increased threat from terrorism caused by foreign military intervention, the logical next step would be withdrawal of international forces and a shift of attention to diplomatic solutions and addressing corruption. The chapter by Lodgaard (chapter 12) on the Arab Spring addresses some of these themes and issues.

Global Weapons Trade

The easy access to and spread of cheap weapons correlates with the increase in terrorism in the past twenty years (Stohl n.d.). The UN Security Council has adopted several resolutions urging governments to stop the abundance of weapons, military equipment, drones, and improvised explosive devices that fall into the hands of ISIS, Al-Qaeda, and other terrorist groups (UNSC 2016, 2017b, 2001). Efforts to stop the cheap and easy access to weapons include the International Small Arms Control Standards, which is a UN-led effort to provide guidance on how to reduce the flow of small arms as part of the UN Coordinating Action on Small Arms (CASA) mechanism. The International Action Network on Small Arms (IANSA) is a global movement against gun violence that links organizations working to stop the proliferation and misuse of small arms and light weapons. These organizations contend with weapons-producing corporations that battle all legislation and efforts to stem trade in weapons, even those efforts that attempt to keep weapons from being sold to terrorist groups (Walsh and Abdelaziz 2018).

Climate Change

Climate change does not directly cause violent conflict. Environmental impacts from climate change such as varied rainfall, changes in temperatures, and stronger storms create economic impacts such as failure of family farms. This in turn creates social and political changes such as migration to cities and increased pressure on governments. Military leaders view climate change as a "threat multiplier" potentially escalating the war on terror. In response, communities are mitigating the effects of climate change and managing a transformation to sustainability and using peacebuilding and environmental mediation to help manage conflicts related to the environment. Chapter 10 in this book gives a wider view on climate change and VE.

Media Coverage

The global news media also plays a role in VE. Some see the media's role as fanning the flames of terrorism by giving terrorist groups the "oxygen" of media attention, which they need in order to terrorize people. The media also spreads awareness of injustice, grievances, and ideologies to both highlight and garner a response to public grievances. While national public news stations provide high journalistic value and present relatively objective presentation of facts, these news sources are under threat from news programs that heighten emotional responses and sensationalize the news in order to improve their ratings. The chapters by Slachmuijlder (chapter 26) and Aziz and Schirch (chapter 27) address the role of the media and narratives that can improve understanding of the root causes of VE as well as possible solutions to address political, social, and economic grievances.

CONCLUSION

The factors that correlate with VE are immense and diverse. Preventing VE and terrorism requires a comprehensive approach involving concerted work on many of the areas in this chapter. Table 2.1 provides a reference for the correlations and theories of change explored in this chapter. Chapter 3 explores how interventions into VE and terrorism may undermine or counteract each other. In an ecological system, even well-intended efforts can end up backfiring.

Table 2.1. Correlations and Theories of Change Chart

Planning		
VE Factor	**Description**	**Theories of Change**
Planning	Planning to carry out an attack	Use of police and military force to deter, disrupt, detain, destroy VE groups' planning and training for attacks
Training	Training to prepare for an attack	
Funding	Obtaining funding to buy weapons and carry out an attack	Laws restricting funding to VE groups, selling weapons to VE groups
Recruitment		
VE Factor	**Description**	**Theories of Change**
Family and community	Social bonds and loyalty to friends and family	Psychosocial support services and trauma-recovery programs for families
Online	Messages, photos, songs, and videos on Twitter, Facebook, websites, and chat rooms	Online messages to support nonviolent belief and action to address grievances
Religious setting	Locations owned by religious groups	Community-led programs to support nonviolent action to address grievances
Prison	Criminal justice locations for incarceration	Prison-based programs to rehabilitate and deradicalize

(Continued)

Table 2.1. (Continued)

Individual Identity Context		
VE Factor	**Description**	**Theories of Change**
Adventure, significance	Desire for exotic travel or new experiences and sense of glory	Opportunities for travel; creation of new "hero" groups
Social isolation	Sense of isolation and desire for group membership	Civic engagement, sports, arts, and other groups to provide belonging
Transition and migration	Uprooted community with unsettled or unpredictable future	Psychosocial support services; community organizing
Trauma and Fear	Perception of insults, powerless, attacks or threats to identity or life	Trauma healing and resilience, affirmation for identity groups; human rights education; dialogue
Humiliation	Perception of disrespect and desire for power for revenge and to gain respect	Symbolic gestures of respect; principle of dignity and human rights in all interventions
Mental health, hormones	Biological and physical aspects that contribute to VE beliefs	Community support to channel biophysical aspects; psychosocial support services and trauma-recovery programs
Sex	Interest in sexual rewards for participating in terrorism	Gender awareness training; organized sports activities
Gender roles	Social norms for men and women encourage participation in VE	Gender awareness training; inclusion of women in VE interventions
Community Grievance Context		
VE Factor	**Description**	**Theories of Change**
General VE grievances	Grievances against the state and/or society	Counterterrorism/CVE counternarratives to alter perceptions of grievances
		Nonviolent civil resistance to push for changes to address grievances
		Improve state–society relationship with peacebuilding efforts

Political grievances	Civil war or insurgency with armed groups challenging state governance	Political peace process with disarmament, demobilization, and reintegration
	Perception that state power is elite-captured	Democratic reforms and participatory governance
	Perception that Western countries dominate global politics	Reform global political institutions to increase representation and empowerment of non-Western states
	Graft, bribery, and corruption to favor elites	Reform of national governance to increase transparency and reduce corruption; support justice, rule of law
	State military or police repression of population and/or inability to protect people from nonstate group threats	Security-sector reform to increase adherence to human rights and international humanitarian law, and civilian oversight and human security
Economic grievances	Relative deprivation between groups, perceived inequality with structural privileges	State grants to community for community-led sustainable economic development
	Interest in money or other financial incentives	Promotion of private-sector growth and job creation
	Perception that trade system favors wealthy nations	Economic and trade reforms to support fair trade
Social grievances	Weak relational ties between social groups and strong relational ties within	Intergroup dialogue, programs, and projects to enhance social well-being
		Social capital and networking opportunities
	Perception of social exclusion	Social cohesion programs

(Continued)

Table 2.1. (Continued)

National Ideology Context		
VE Factor	**Description**	**Theories of Change**
VE ideology	Violence to civilians perceived as necessary	Counternarratives to challenge ideology and positive peacebuilding narratives
Political ideology	Authoritarian leadership and opposition to democracy	Peace education, collaborative decision making, and dialogue forums
Social ideology	Hierarchical social relationships between groups	Human rights education and social justice programs
Economic ideology	Critique of economic systems	Economic reforms, economic justice, fair trade
Religious ideology	Religious doctrine, values, or goals	Intra- and interreligious dialogue
		Engage religious actors
Global Context		
International military intervention	Perceived injustice at the presence of foreign troops	Withdrawal of international forces and shift of attention to diplomatic solutions and addressing corruption
Weapons trade	Easy access to weapons	Slow and stop the flow of weapons
Media coverage of VE	Disproportionate sense of threat and sensational coverage that magnifies fear to increase profit	Conflict sensitive journalism that addresses complexity, root causes, and information to manage fear
Climate change	Rapid environmental changes destabilize societies	Prevent, mitigate, and adapt to climate change

Chapter 3

Unintended Impacts and Ecological Metaphors of Violent Extremism

Lisa Schirch

There is no "silver bullet" that can isolate and solve the problem of violent extremism (VE). There are no smart bombs or programs in government reform, employment generation, religious moderation, or youth empowerment that can untangle the knot of terrorism. Finding a way to prevent, manage, and stop VE and terrorism requires a systems-based approach. Any intervention will have consequences on the rest of the ecology. There is no such thing as a "surgical strike" that affects only terrorist groups. Interventions into VE make changes throughout the system. Improving human security requires careful attempts to take actions recognizing the interdependence of the stakeholders and the issues.

INTERVENTIONS TO ADDRESS VIOLENT EXTREMISM AND TERRORISM

Figure 2.1 maps how interventions such as counterterrorism, preventing and countering violent extremism (P/CVE), and peacebuilding respond to terrorist acts, violent extremist beliefs, and the context that gives rise to these problems. Each paradigm is an umbrella term used to describe a variety of strategies or interventions.

Counterterrorism

Counterterrorism aims to stop terrorist acts by disrupting, deterring, dismantling, isolating, detaining, or destroying terrorist organizations and networks to prevent attacks and plans, as illustrated in Figure 2.1. Counterterrorism includes intelligence gathering to identify individuals and groups that hold violent extremist beliefs. Counterterrorism includes the use of force (warfare and policing) against individuals and groups that use terrorism. The United Nations and many countries have complex measures in place to criminalize terrorism financing, to enhance domestic and international cooperation to identify groups planning terrorist acts. They produce lists of designated terrorist organizations and cooperate on identifying terrorism financing indicators. Counterterrorism's lawfare takes a criminal justice approach to make the support and funding of terrorist groups illegal. Counterterrorism also includes the use of legal restrictions (also known as "lawfare") that prevent individuals and groups, including civil society, from relating in any way to groups listed as terrorist organizations. Section 3 in this book explores the best practices of counterterrorism as well as the negative impacts on civil society.

Preventing and Countering Violent Extremism

The focus of *P/CVE* is addressing beliefs that precede terrorist actions, as illustrated in Figure 2.1. The US government developed the concept of P/CVE in 2010 in response to the growing understanding of the role of families, communities, and institutions in responding to violent extremist beliefs. The 2011 White House CVE plan states that the goal of CVE is to "prevent violent extremists and their supporters from inspiring, radicalizing, financing, or recruiting individuals or groups in the United States to commit acts of violence" (The White House 2011). The United Nations and some countries favor the term "preventing violent extremism" (PVE) rather than CVE. In practice, PVE and CVE interventions are similar, and thus, this book just uses the term "P/CVE." P/CVE is primarily a nonmilitary but government-led paradigm for responding to VE. Governments fund and direct civil society organizations to run P/CVE programs that engage communities to improve trust and communication and prevent at-risk individuals from joining violent extremist groups. P/CVE aims to help people move away from violent extremist beliefs through rehabilitation and reintegration efforts. Some civil society groups criticize CVE as an intervention aimed at supporting and mirroring the "counter" frame of "counterterrorism" as it is also involved in intelligence gathering and law enforcement–led interdiction or disruption through arrest, prosecution, and incarceration. *CVE-specific programs* have explicit CVE goals as their primary objective. *CVE-relevant programs* reduce vulnerability toward violence and establish stronger and more resilient communities. Section 4 in this book explores the pros and cons of P/CVE programming.

Peacebuilding

Peacebuilding attempts to address the broad context where VE and terrorism take place, as illustrated in Figure 2.1. Peacebuilding includes a wide range of efforts by diverse actors in government and civil society at the community, national, and international levels to address the immediate impacts and root causes by managing political conflict and reforming governance processes. Peacebuilding includes activities designed to prevent conflict through addressing both structural and proximate causes of violence, delegitimizing violence as a dispute resolution strategy, building capacity within society to peacefully manage disputes, and reducing vulnerability to triggers that may spark violence. "Peacebuilding" began as a civil society term and set of efforts, but now many governments, international organizations, and the United Nations have peacebuilding programs. Local-level peacebuilding emerges from the community. Top-down peacebuilding is directed by governments or international organizations. These different forms of peacebuilding share similar principles of building relationships across the lines of conflict, looking for common ground while identifying differences and focusing on creative problem solving. Like P/CVE, peacebuilding emphasizes building resilient communities. Resilience is the ability to respond to challenging circumstances through adaptation and the strength that comes from information, networking, and innovation. Section 5 in this book identifies a range of peacebuilding approaches to VE.

Counterterrorism, P/CVE, and peacebuilding interventions operate on different analyses of the problem of VE and different theories of change or strategic narratives about how to address a particular challenge. Counterterrorism is based on a theory of change that the use of force and legal restrictions can isolate, destroy, detain, or deter terrorism. P/CVE is based on a theory of change that communities can interrupt the recruitment process and build their resilience to prevent people from a VE belief system. Peacebuilding is based on a theory of change related to building and transforming relationships and structures to address the root causes of the grievances and violence within the broader context where VE and terrorism take place.

ACTORS AND AGENTS OF CHANGE IN COMPLEX ENVIRONMENTS

Violent extremism takes place in a *complex environment*, a dynamic system where there are many different groups with diverse interests. No one group can control or dominate the space. Attempts by any one group to solve an issue without involving other groups are likely to cause new, unexpected issues. Solutions to VE require coordination between different groups of stakeholders. Many different stakeholders play roles and hold responsibilities for achieving sustainable peace and human security. No one stakeholder can achieve their goals without coordinating with others.

Counterterrorism efforts are exclusively led by the military and specific government agencies. P/CVE is government-led, but many civil society groups and even media agencies actively take government funding and participate in P/CVE programs. Peacebuilding emphasizes the need for "local ownership," an empowered civil society, and community-led efforts. Both P/CVE and peacebuilding advocate "whole of society" efforts including not only security forces but also government, civil society, business, academic, religious, media, and other stakeholders. Most books on VE and terrorism focus on two groups: nonstate terrorist groups and states responding to terrorism. This book recognizes that there are more stakeholders affected by VE and intervening in ways that seek to prevent VE.

Civil society refers to nongovernmental, voluntary groups of people that organize themselves on behalf of interest groups or local communities. Civil society takes collective action for shared interests. Civil society is nonprofit and independent from government and the business sector. Civil society includes traditional forms of collective action such as tribal groups, local religious institutions, and community-based traditional associations. Civil society also includes "modern" forms of collective action such as educational institutions, labor unions, industry associations, sports and arts associations, and clubs. Independent news and entertainment media are considered part of civil society. Nongovernmental organizations (NGOs) are also considered a type of civil society organization. This book includes examples of *local* civil society organizations (CSOs) such as the Kenya Human Rights Commission, Indonesian religious leaders, and the PAIMAN Alumni Trust in Pakistan. It also includes examples from *international* NGOs such as Catholic Relief Services, World Vision International, Mercy Corps, and Search for Common Ground.

Terrorism attacks civilians and civil society groups and property such as universities and schools, religious centers, NGO offices, and women's centers. The debate over the beliefs of VE takes place in civil society, on the news media, on social media, in religious centers, and at kitchen tables. Civil society is also the target of many counterterrorism and P/CVE programs.

Civil society is neither all good nor all bad. Like governments and security forces, civil society has the potential to contribute to or detract from human security. A handful of the thousands of civil society organizations in the world do fund and support terrorist groups. Yet some governments clamp down on all forms of civil society, failing to recognize that preventing VE and terrorism requires civil society participation and leadership. Government counterterrorism tactics freeze NGOs' bank accounts and raid offices in response. But P/CVE and peacebuilding interventions also recognize that civil society plays key roles in partnership with government to address factors that correlate with VE. And civil society holds the state to account for good governance, and this too can help address a major factor driving VE: abusive security forces and corrupt governance (Bassuener and Kinsman 2013). Civil society organizations are not contractors or "implementing partners" simply doing work that the government tells them to do. Civil society requires political independence and trust with local communities.

The challenge is to create a synergy between the interventions of different stakeholders to prevent and stop VE and terrorism. This is difficult for the following reasons:

- Stakeholders' views on what the problem is at hand may be irreconcilable, and the solutions they propose will therefore be incompatible.
- Stakeholders may not, on their own, have enough knowledge or complete information about a given problem and may propose inadequate solutions.
- The problem of VE is connected to many other problems, and every effort to solve it may create new, unintended problems.

The range of stakeholders affected by and intervening to prevent VE is part of the complexity of addressing the ecology of VE.

WICKED PROBLEMS AND UNINTENDED IMPACTS OF INTERVENTIONS

Violent extremism is a wicked problem. Wicked problems are difficult to define or complex issues that resist easy solutions. Wicked problems affect every level of society, often lasting for generations. Efforts to solve wicked problems may have the unintended effect of making the problem worse. Interventions to prevent or stop VE and terrorism can have unintended impacts that worsen VE. Just as the factors correlating with VE interact with each other, so too do VE interventions affect each other. Recognizing this complex web of relationships between correlations and interventions into VE is the purpose of this book.

Currently, interventions to prevent and respond to VE and terrorism conflict with and undermine each other. On their own, each of these approaches is insufficient. Each approach also has considerable drawbacks, unintended consequences, and critiques as illustrated in Table 3.1 and discussed in greater length in Cortright, Guinane, Dumasy and Haspeslagh, Abu-Nimer, and Sethi's chapters in this book (chapters 13, 15, 16, 19, and 20).

Yet each of these paradigms also makes a strong case for how they prevent and stop VE and terrorism. Counterterrorism also correlates with prevention of attacks. In Organisation for Economic Cooperation and Development (OECD) countries, counterterrorism intelligence gathering has helped to thwart nearly half of all terrorist attacks (GTI 2017, 56). This is evidence that

Table 3.1. Critiques and Unintended Impacts of Counterterrorism, CVE, and Peacebuilding

	Critiques and Unintended Impacts of VE Interventions
Counterterrorism	Researchers, civil society, United Nations, and government staff articulate a range of problems with the current practice of counterterrorism (CT) around the world. • CT does not address root causes of VE or terrorism and diverts funds away from solutions with greater promise of effectiveness. • CT's use of force can escalate grievances and contribute to increasing recruitment to violent extremist groups. • States use CT as an excuse to use repression against nonviolent forms of dissent against state corruption or abuses. • CT reduces civil liberties and violates democratic principles by targeting Muslims or other minority groups. • CT places legal restrictions on humanitarian assistance, development, governance, and peacebuilding—which all help to prevent violent extremism.
P/CVE	Community and civil society leaders articulate a range of problems with the current practice of P/CVE around the world. • P/CVE usually focuses on targeting "at-risk" individuals and addressing their individual grievances and has not focused enough on addressing broader community political, social, and economic grievances. • P/CVE can further exacerbate political and social grievances if P/CVE efforts target minority communities. • P/CVE risks further isolating and marginalizing people by calling them "at-risk" rather than empowering them to take action to address their own grievances through other channels. • P/CVE is too closely identified with counterterrorism and its goal of intelligence gathering and reducing community trust in peacebuilding. • P/CVE asks community leaders to spy on their communities. • P/CVE unfairly targets Muslim communities even in places like Europe and North America where white nationalists commit more acts of terror.
Peacebuilding	The U.S. Supreme Court identified four types of risks of peacebuilding engagement with listed armed groups to justify the absolute prohibition on engagement. These are: • Peacebuilding negotiations may help terrorist groups gain legitimacy and skills, which may help them recruit, finance, and carry out terrorism. • Peacebuilding processes may help terrorist groups gain resources allowing them to use other resources for terrorism. • Peacebuilding negotiations may help terrorist groups buy time and serve as a way of recovering from attacks against them or pretending to be cooperative while preparing for renewed attacks. • Peacebuilding efforts are outside of government control and may affect government foreign policy and relationships with allies.

counterterrorism intelligence investigations and policing contribute to stopping terror attacks. P/CVE programs such as the ones described by Qadeem and Khan and Ansari in this book (chapters 18 and 31) illustrate how these programs prevent people from joining VE groups and build community resilience. Peacebuilding makes important contributions to preventing VE by addressing underlying political grievances, promoting ideologies of tolerance and democratic decision making, and creating resilient governance structures. Ecological thinking can help address the problems and critiques of unintended impacts that make these interventions less effective.

ECOLOGICAL METAPHORS FOR VIOLENT EXTREMISM

Metaphors are powerful forms of communication because they hold a great deal of information in a short or concise format. Skillful use of metaphors can change public conversations by creating a new "frame" that creates a new shared understanding of the problem and a set of solutions that cannot be seen in other frames (Lakoff 2014). Metaphors help us understand complex ideas. They make it easier to understand or imagine connections.

The idea of an "ecology" of VE is a metaphor in itself. It communicates that VE is not something separate from the rest of society. Those who commit acts of terror emerge out of society. An ecological understanding of terror requires that we imagine solutions that reduce VE while strengthening and not weakening the social, political, and economic context.

Two ecological metaphors provide insight into how to intervene without causing greater harm. Metaphors of the natural world are more apt descriptors of the complex system influencing who will and who will not commit an act of terror. In each metaphor, the interconnectedness between parts of the system increases the challenge of finding a solution that does not destroy other parts of the system. These metaphors help to identify the importance of taking a systems-based approach to understanding and intervening to prevent VE.

But metaphors are not perfect. And sometimes metaphors can also serve to trap people into simplistic solutions. Popular discourse often compares fighting terrorism to "draining swamps" and "curing cancer." The simplistic usage of these metaphors has been inadequate and even harmful. And yet, with a deeper look, both of these metaphors can also help us imagine a more effective response by synergizing counterterrorism, P/CVE, and peacebuilding.

The Swamp Metaphor

Swamps are an interesting metaphor when it comes to terrorism. After 9/11, military generals and news media relied heavily on the swamp metaphor.

Iraq was compared to a "quagmire," which is another word for a swamp. There was talk of "draining the swamp," which conjured images of alligators stranded in a dry lakebed that could then be killed (Lakoff 2001). The swamp metaphor suggested that something in the very nature of swamps themselves was evil. Destroying swamps became a metaphor for bombing villages and cities where terror groups lived (Katzman 2015; Steuter and Wills 2009).

But destroying villages and cities has not slowed the growth of terror groups. Instead of getting rid of the problem of swamps (presumably alligators and snakes), bombing created a landscape with less resilience and more vulnerability to VE. This usage of the swamp metaphor was quite ineffective at describing how to prevent terrorism. But the swamp metaphor itself, as an ecological system, does have promise.

Imagine a swamp as a metaphor for society. A healthy swamp manages droughts and floods, and even toxic chemicals dumped into it. There is a balance and interdependence among the creatures in the swamp. Alligators and snakes are not the terrorists in this swamp society. They are simply part of the healthy ecosystem.

Rather, poisons such as toxic chemicals dumped into this swamp are the metaphor for violent extremist beliefs. The chemicals will affect that swamp. Some of the plants and animals will get sick, and some will die. Some of those that fall ill will recover and adapt. Mushrooms and some plants will filter out the toxins and help to purify the swamp. Cause and effect will be obscure. Correlations between elements in the swamp and its recovery or death will be complex. The researchers' job in the swamp is to observe the interconnectedness. What elements of the swamp are working together to build resilience to the toxins? What parts of the swamp are most vulnerable to the toxins? And who is dumping the toxins into the swamp?

When oil spilled into the Gulf of Mexico, oil companies dumped a chemical called Corexit to break down the oil. But researchers found this intervention actually caused even more deaths of organisms (Katzman 2015). Pouring chemicals into the ocean to break down other toxins is a bit like using bombs to kill terrorist groups. These solutions may have the intended effect of targeting the toxins and terrorists. But these solutions also create more of the same problem.

If VE is like a poison in the swamp of our society, draining the swamp or pouring in more toxins to try to neutralize the existing toxins is not a solution. To quote another metaphor, draining the swamp literally lets the baby out with the bathwater. It does not make sense to kill society in order to save it. In the real world, toxic chemicals in swamps correlate with a marked increase in cancer in animals and humans near the swamp (Marcus 1983). And that leads us to the second metaphor.

The Cancer Metaphor

The cancer metaphor may seem like an alternative to the "drain the swamp" metaphor. Central Intelligence Agency (CIA) director John Brennan used the cancer metaphor as a way of expressing a desire not to destroy the society (or the swamp) when he called the United States to "eliminate the cancerous tumor called an Al-Qaeda terrorist while limiting damage to the tissues around it" (Knefel 2016). Military strategists use the cancer metaphor to talk about "surgical strikes" and "parent tumors" in Syria and Iraq that breed cancer cells that can float through the rest of the body and grow elsewhere. Terrorists are like cancer cells in this metaphor. They must be cut out and bombed with radiation before they kill the rest of the body (Curt 2001; Ganor 2010; Yilmaz 2013). But the military usage of the cancer metaphor actually is not keeping up with the science of cancer.

Unlike a virus or bacterial disease, cancer cells begin as normal cells native to our bodies. This also reflects the origin of violent extremists; they are people who start out as nonviolent humans in society. Like radicalized individuals who are not violent, cells can undergo mutations without being considered cancerous. Cells only gain the cancerous label when they invade neighboring locations in the same organ. A cancer cell never can transform back into a healthy cell. But unlike cancer cells, individuals who embrace violent extremist beliefs or commit acts of terror can and do transform back into healthy individuals (Price 2017). So, the cancer metaphor can give us the sense that VE is incurable. But that is not exactly accurate.

The most basic intervention to stop the spread of cancer is surgery, which removes the cancerous tissue from the body with the least amount of trauma to the surrounding tissue. This is comparable to police action for VE, to remove the violent extremist cells from the surrounding community. But surgery can backfire. It weakens the body's immune response and damages other healthy tissues.

Other treatments for cancer include high doses of chemotherapy and radiation. Early versions of chemotherapy and radiation ended up killing many people. Doctors did not keep track of which patients died from cancer and which died from radiation or chemotherapy poisoning because it was often difficult to tell. Like dumping chemicals into a swamp to clean up the toxins, chemotherapy had unintended negative consequences in the ecology of the body. For example, chemotherapy for women with breast cancer did prove that it could kill breast cancer cells. But many forms of chemotherapy give women endometrial cancer and blood clots, causing more women to die. Radiation and chemotherapy kill cancerous cells, but they also can poison other healthy cells and weaken the immune system. The typical usage of the cancer metaphor does not offer a positive or realistic understanding of human body and health via radiation-targeted strikes or chemotherapy.

However, new treatments for cancer have far more to do with building the resilience of the body's immune system rather than "killing" the cancer cells. Immunotherapy stimulates the immune system to recognize and respond to specific forms of cancer cells. This would be comparable to P/CVE and peacebuilding resilience programs that foster a healthier state–society relationship and strong communities that are immune to the threat of VE. Other newer generations of cancer treatments include chemicals found naturally in foods that reduce and regulate blood-vessel growth, since cancerous cells require high blood flows. This is comparable to violent extremist interventions that attempt to interrupt financial support for violent extremist groups.

HUMAN SECURITY

Human security is distinct from national security, as illustrated in Table 3.2. *Human security* refers to the security of individuals and communities. Human security can include living with a freedom from fear, freedom from want, and freedom to live in dignity. Individuals and communities measure their human security in different ways, depending on their context. Threats to human security include violence caused by both state and nonstate armed groups, poverty, economic inequality, discrimination, environmental degradation, health, and other factors that undermine individual and community well-being. From a human security perspective, terrorism is an intentional attack against civilians.

In contrast, *national security* or state-centric security refers to the national interests of the state. In most states, national interests include protection of

Table 3.2. Comparing National Security and Human Security

	National Security	*Human Security*
Goal	Focus on state interests	Focus on safety of individuals and communities
Actors	Primarily military and police	Many different stakeholders, including civilian government agencies, military, police, and civil society, including religious, education, community, and other societal groups
Analysis	Focus on specific individuals and groups as threats	Focus on wider political, economic, social structures that give rise to violence

territory, a legal order, economic interests, geopolitical interests, ideological values, and citizens. The less the gap between government and civil society's identification of national interests, the more likely the state and civil society can coordinate with each other to pursue human security.

While national security and human security approaches sometimes overlap, they are often not the same. In some countries, there is very little attention to human security and an exclusive commitment to national security with an emphasis on elite economic or geopolitical interests. In these cases, there is a tension between civil society's interest in human security and state's national security interests. A dialogue between security policy makers, security forces, and civil society can help identify common ground in national security and human security perspectives and also appreciate the areas where their approaches are different (Schirch and Mancini-Griffoli 2016).

If an armed group is using terrorism to attack civilians and overthrow a government, this impacts human security. But if the government also violates human rights and uses military repression, this too impacts human security. In this case, a national security strategy may understand the underlying security challenge as the state lacking a monopoly of force. As a consequence, the national security actor may ask the international community for more weapons and to provide training in counterterrorism. In contrast, a human security strategy will understand the challenge as the state lacking public legitimacy. A human security strategy might therefore focus on empowering civil society to hold their government to account for the grievances that drive support for insurgents.

Human security requires a careful combination of rights-based, people-centered approaches to counterterrorism, P/CVE-specific programs, and peacebuilding (Schirch 2016). But instead of working synergistically, there is currently conflict and tension between these approaches.

HOW AN ECOLOGICAL APPROACH CONTRIBUTES TO HUMAN SECURITY

Counterterrorism, P/CVE, and peacebuilding can all work together to support human security. But this requires an ecological analysis to understand how current manifestations of these three paradigms undermine each other in the ecology of VE. An ecological approach to violent extremism seeks a synergy between counterterrorism, P/CVE, and peacebuilding. A synergy brings the energy of different elements together to create an impact greater than the sum of their parts. This book emphasizes the need to "de-conflict" or reduce the negative impact these interventions have on each other and the broader context.

This "ecological approach" to VE requires the following:

- Using peacebuilding processes to address the underlying political and governance factors and to build the resilience of the whole system to prevent and respond to VE
- Using a rights-based, community-led approach to P/CVE to address specific problems that appear to be driving VE and rehabilitate and reintegrate former members of VE groups
- Using human rights–based counterterrorism intelligence and policing to stop individuals and groups preparing for terrorist attacks

Counterterrorism that protects civilians, minimizes the use of force, relies on nonlethal weapons, and abides by human rights laws could better reinforce human security while addressing urgent and impending attacks. P/CVE could be more effective if clear strategies existed to separate P/CVE from counterterrorism. Counterterrorism surveillance programs should not be hidden as P/CVE programs or target and collect intelligence from local communities. Peacebuilding could be more effective if it emphasized a more robust effort to facilitate communication and build relationships between the state, especially the security sector, and local populations. A focus on facilitating the state–society relationship is one of the most promising approaches to preventing VE.

Section II

ECOLOGICAL ANALYSIS OF VIOLENT EXTREMISM

Section II

Introduction

This section gives a view of diverse lenses or ways of understanding violent extremism (VE).

In chapter 4, "Alt-Right and Jihad," Scott Atran compares the elements of VE in radical Muslim and Christian groups, noting the similar identity crises, community grievances, and nationalist ideologies in both movements. Frances Flannery similarly draws parallels in the violent religious theologies of these groups in her chapter, chapter 5, "Radical Islamist and Radical Christianist Nuclear Terrorism."

Next, Stone Conroy analyzes the role of the private sector and VE in chapter 6, "The Private Sector and Violent Extremism." In chapter 7, "The Neurobiology of Violent Extremism," Mari Fitzduff describes the genetic, neurobiological, and hormonal factors that may influence young men and some women to joining violent extremist groups. Mark Hamilton looks at youth and the security sector in chapter 8, "Youth and the Security Sector," and proposes a constructive dialogue between the two groups. Rafia Bhulai identifies a range of issues related to gender and the role of women in VE in chapter 9, "Gender and the Role of Women in Violent Extremism." The last chapter in this section, chapter 10, "Climate Change and Violent Extremism," explores climate change and VE, reinforcing again that VE takes place in an "ecology" where environmental impacts translate to economic, political, and security impacts.

Chapter 4

Alt-Right and Jihad

Scott Atran

The last of the shell-shocked were being evacuated as I headed from home toward Las Ramblas, Barcelona's famed tourist-filled walkway in August 2017. Another disgruntled "soldier of ISIS" had just ploughed his van into the crowd there, killing fourteen and wounding more than one hundred people from nearly three dozen nations. I had just dropped off my wife's niece to meet friends by the Plaça Catalunya, near where the rampage began. It was déjà vu and dread again, evoking the Paris massacre at the Bataclan theater and the café La Belle Équipe in 2015, next door to where my daughter lived. At a seafront promenade south of the city, a car of five knife-wielding ISIS kamikazes mowed down a woman before police killed them all. One teenage attacker had posted on the web two years ago that on his "first day as King of the World" he would "kill infidels and leave only Muslims [who] followed religion."

As I approached the police security line in Barcelona, someone thought they heard a noise, a rumor of another attack; someone else saw a sudden movement by a darker-skinned man, an unanticipated fall by an onlooker—or perhaps nothing at all. People surged, screamed, cried, and then it all stopped as suddenly as it had started. The strategy in hitting any of the unlimited soft targets in our societies is to undermine people's faith that government can provide security while increasing suspicion and hatred against those who are different so they will see that trying to live in peace only brings pain.

The next day, along the wide shopping boulevard that ends in the Plaça Catalunya, there was a minute of silence and then tears and applause. For a few hours, Spain's people had come together to show, as the Spanish prime minister Mariano Rajoy bellowed, "our values and way of life will triumph," but without a hint of how—just as the British prime minister Theresa May had proclaimed "our values will prevail" last March when yet another petty criminal, "born again" into the salvational grace of radical Islam, killed and wounded pedestrians after driving across Westminster Bridge.

Over the course of these events, pundits and politicians repeated platitudes and then tore into one another for not having a clue about how to stop what everyone knew was coming next. One of the problems may be looking at radical Islam instead of larger, more global forces worldwide. These attacks are unleashed from the dark side of globalization, where desire for liberal democracy is lost.

The week before the Barcelona attack, the terrorist in Charlottesville, Virginia, was a white supremacist who maimed and killed people nearly at random with his vehicle in a fashion painfully familiar to the ISIS-inspired killings in London, Nice, Berlin, and Stockholm. It was an act recently repeated in Manhattan by a man pledged to ISIS, who killed eight pedestrians and wounded twelve with a rental truck. An acquaintance and activist from the attacker's immigrant community described him in the *New York Times* as someone initially unremarkable who had developed "monsters inside." So, too, according to the Charlottesville attacker's former history teacher: "This was something that was growing in him. . . . He had this fascination with Nazism [and] white supremacist views."

Whether alt-right or radical Islam, the values of liberal and open democracy increasingly appear to be losing ground around the world to those of narrow, xenophobic ethno-nationalisms and radical ideologies. Our research team at Artis International and the Centre for the Resolution of Intractable Conflict at Oxford University has found that these forces are clobbering free societies today much like Fascists and Communists did back in the 1920s and 1930s. In Hungary, we find that youth strongly support the government's call for restoring "national cohesion" (Daily News 2017), lost with the fall of Miklós Horthy's Fascist and pro-Nazi regime; the call to root out "cosmopolitan" and "globalist" values is strong. In Iraq, we find that nearly all of the young people we have interviewed who are coming out from under Islamic State rule in Mosul initially welcomed it for stability and security amid the chaos following the US invasion—until they were alienated by the ever-increasing brutality.

According to the World Values Survey, the majority of Europeans do not believe that living in a democratic country is "absolutely important" for them. This includes most young Germans under age thirty and especially their elders in former communist East Germany who, in September, voted into Parliament the right-wing populist party Alternative for Germany. In April 2017, Marine Le Pen's hard-right National Front and Jean-Luc Mélenchon's hard-left Unbowed France together captured nearly half of the French vote of people age eighteen to thirty-four in first-round national elections. And in the United States, political scientists Roberto Foa and Yascha Mounk find that nearly half of American citizens lack faith in democracy; more than one-third of young high-income earners actually favor army rule, presumably to halt rising social unrest linked to income inequality, job insecurity, and persistent failures in racial integration and cultural assimilation in an age of identity politics (Foa and Mounk 2017).

In our own research in France and Spain, we find little willingness to make costly sacrifice for democracy, especially compared to the willingness to fight and die for jihad in Europe, North Africa, and the Middle East (Sheikh, Gómez, and Atran 2016). Our wide-ranging interviews and psychological experiments have uncovered not a "clash of civilizations," as Poland's interior minister declared in reaction to events in Barcelona, but civilization's unraveling, as young people unmoored from traditions flail about in search of a social identity that gives personal significance and glory (Poland 2017). Individuals radicalize to find firm identity in a flattened world. In this new reality, vertical lines of communication between generations are replaced by horizontal peer-to-peer attachments that can span the globe, albeit in vanishingly narrow channels of ideas and information. Our research has shown that, despite its vitriol against "globalists," today's alt-right movement involves the same narrow-minded global weave of tweets, blogs, and chat rooms linking physical groups across the world as the jihadi movement.

The new world disorder puts us all at greater risk in this global age, where nonstate forces volcanically erupt through the nation-state system, spreading noxious, violent memes. The Western creations of the nation-state and the relatively open markets that today dominate the global political and economic order (and to which non-Western powers like China and Russia also subscribe) have largely supplanted age-old forms of governance, social formations, and economic activity that involved whole communities of people that once intimately knew one another. Instead, rising populations and urbanization, extensive and rapid communications and transportation, and science and technology have transformed people in the farthest reaches of the planet into competitive players seeking progress and personal fulfillment through material accumulation and its symbols. But market-driven competition often comes at steep personal and social cost. When communities lack enough time to adapt to all the innovation and change, its members may fall short of their aspirations; anxiety and alienation bubble up, and violence can erupt along prevailing political and religious fault lines.

It was religious philosopher Søren Kierkegaard who first discussed "the dizziness of freedom" and the social disruption that it creates. Seizing on the idea in *Escape from Freedom*, humanist philosopher Erich Fromm argued that too much freedom caused many to seek elimination of uncertainty in authoritarian systems (Fromm 1941). This has combined with what social psychologist Arie Kruglanski calls "the search for significance," propelling both violent jihadists and militant supporters of populist ethno-nationalist movements worldwide. In the wake of these forces, we see what psychologist Michele Gelfand describes as a "tightening" of political cultures, featuring intolerance of behaviors that differ from the norm (Gelfand 2011). Thus, in our recent fieldwork with youth emerging from under ISIS rule in Mosul, we find that although ISIS may have lost its state, the caliphate, it hasn't necessarily lost allegiance among the people to its core values of strict religious rule and rejection of democracy. As one young man put it, "Sharia is God telling you what to do. . . . Democracy is humans causing wars and distrust. To be free to do whatever you want leads to many problems and divisions and corruption in society."

World history from the nineteenth century onward illustrates the impact of globalizing trends. After the massive bloodletting of the French Revolution and Napoleonic Wars from 1789 to 1815, governing elites tried to find consensus on how Europe, and the expanding colonial world it dominated, would be run. For a hundred years, from the Congress of Vienna in 1815 to the outbreak of World War I in 1914, this informal international collaboration basically maintained the integrity of existing empires and nation-states. The order endured despite popular uprisings like the French Revolution of 1830 and the continent-wide 1848 revolution, both erupting over lack of rights and social protection for peasants and workers in industrializing societies. And it held fast in the face of conflicts like the Crimean War (1853–1856), a Russian quest to extend its reach. Britain, especially, repeatedly intervened to maintain Europe's balance of power at home and abroad. But the gap separating elite values and popular needs—along with the willingness of one, then the other, of Europe's powers to break the consensus—ultimately unwound the world order.

By the end of the nineteenth century, this order had attained heightened levels of globalization, liberating human beings from near-exclusive reliance on wind, water, and muscle power. Advancements in transportation included worldwide construction of roads and railroads, steamships across the waterways, and later automobiles. Communication technology included the telegraph and later telephone, film, and radio. Scientific prowess multiplied, and capital flowed. People moved freely around the world; Russia and Turkey alone required passports.

But just as today, the rapid, radical changes produced countercultural pressures, with social revolutionaries and anarchists propelling a wave of transnational terror that began shortly before the assassination of Russia's tsar Alexander II in 1881. This terrorist wave extended through to the assassinations of the prime ministers of France in 1894 and Spain in 1897; the empress of Austria in 1898 and the king of Italy in 1900; and finally, the killing of US president William McKinley in 1901. It involved bombings of "bourgeois" civilians in cafes and theatres across Europe and North America before abating with the onset of World War I.

The ineffective response of those in power, likewise, resembled what we see today. Affected states initially lashed out in stunned bafflement, often missing their illusive targets but hitting upon those unrelated to terrorist acts. This included, for example, violent repression of the trade union and labor movements that arose in late nineteenth-century Europe and the United States. Nations reacted by adding or reinforcing state security organizations: Russia's Okhrana, created in 1881, was a precursor of the NKVD and KGB; Britain founded New Scotland Yard in 1890; and France's Direction Centrale de Renseignements Généraux came in 1907, followed by the US Bureau of Investigation in 1908, a precursor of the Federal Bureau of Investigation (FBI).

In his first annual message to Congress after McKinley's death, US president Theodore Roosevelt declared that "when compared with the suppression of anarchy, every other question sinks into insignificance" (Roosevelt 1901). He offered a corollary to the Monroe Doctrine: anarchy's "general loosening of the ties of civilised society, may in America as elsewhere, ultimately require intervention by some civilised nation, and may lead the United States, however reluctantly . . . to the exercise of an international police power." The war against anarchy and terror even helped to justify the brutal repression of a native insurgency against the US "civilizing mission" and rule in Muslim areas of the Philippines.

Ultimately, the anarchist's diffuse movement lost steam, but globalism and the reactions to it propelled other forces to the fore. In the Soviet Union, peasants and workers embraced Communism and acceded to the suppression of all dissent that came with Stalinism. The Nazis preached the revival of the nation and a race war against the forces of cosmopolitanism and cultural diversity, and tens of millions of people in Germany's advanced industrial society groveled at Hitler's feet.

And in the United States, from the late nineteenth century on, we saw the rise of the Ku Klux Klan (KKK). The Klan had three iterations in the United States, starting with its founding in 1866 by southern whites to fight reconstruction, including policies to give African Americans equal rights. It was temporarily crushed but rose again in 1915 in the wake of burgeoning immigration to stand against not just black Americans but also Roman Catholics, Jews, and foreigners of any ilk. By the 1920s, at its height, the KKK's membership of some 4 million came from all layers of majority culture in the U.S. heartland. By 1927, members of the KKK had found fellow travellers—those embracing Charles Lindbergh and his America First Committee, with its Fascist and anti-Semitic rhetoric endorsing an isolationist United States that would not oppose Hitler or the Nazis in the lead-up to World War II.

Today, the parallels between the alt-Right and radical jihadism are clear, illustrated by the late William Luther Pierce III. I met the tall, soft-spoken physicist in 1980, when I sought to learn how he had hosted the French Holocaust denier Robert Faurisson. By then one of the most persuasive voices of the white supremacist movement, he told me that "evil is the failure to recognise the necessity of race war," and indeed, he had strategized mass revolt and white nationalist revolution through his group, the National Alliance.

These were the ideas that inspired Timothy McVeigh, who was executed for bombing a federal office building in Oklahoma City in April 1995, killing 168 and injuring over 600. The dream of a race war also inspired Dylann Roof to murder nine people at the Emanuel African Methodist Church in Charleston in June 2015. With his act, he believed, the war would come a few years hence, and he'd be revered. These kinds of acts aim to incite retaliatory measures of repression and violence against whites, including a tightening of gun laws, much as ISIS aims to accomplish repression of Muslims through acts of terror in the West.

White supremacist and jihadi groups parallel one another not only in strategy and tactics but also in messaging. Klansman and Aryan Nations member Louis Beam published his 1983 manifesto, "Leaderless Resistance," in *The Seditionist*, as a social resistance strategy for white nationalists (Beam 1992). Like the jihadi movement, it rejects commanding antigovernment acts from the leaders of a top-down hierarchy in favor of letting independent groups and individuals act on their own. And it rejects direct messaging in favor of inferred messaging—all to prevent authorities from decapitating the movement or assigning legal responsibility for cause and effect.

When Mustafa Setmariam (a.k.a. Abu Musab as-Suri) published Al-Qaeda's strategy for jihad as "The Call for Global Islamic Resistance" in 2004, one could just as well have been reading an exegesis on *The Seditionist* and Louis Beam (as-Suri 2004). Like Beam, Setmariam adopted the theme of leaderless resistance: "[S]pontaneous operations performed by individuals and cells here and there over the whole world, without connection between them, have put local and international intelligence apparatuses in a state of confusion."

There *are* leaders, of course—founders of groups or those who analyze conditions and formulate plans. Whether jihadist or alt-Right, these figures are often educated and well-off. Osama bin Laden was famously a multimillionaire who studied economics and civil engineering. His successor as head of Al-Qaeda, Ayman al-Zawahiri, is a surgeon from a distinguished and prosperous family of doctors and scholars. ISIS leader Abu Bakr al-Baghdadi received a PhD from the University of Baghdad. Charles Lindbergh was not just an aviator but also the son of a lawyer and a US Congressman. William Pierce was a physicist descended from southern aristocracy. Richard Spencer, the president of the alt-Right's preeminent think tank, the National Policy

Institute, is the son of an ophthalmologist and an heir to a cotton-field fortune, who received his MA in humanities from the University of Chicago. Across the wide swath of revolutionary and insurgent groups, founders are usually members of the middle or upper class, who then reach out to the more marginalized, less educated, and poorer masses to increase potency.

Leaders may be highborn, but whether jihadist or alt-Right, mass recruitment is not primarily top-down but peer-to-peer. The Soufan Group, which provides strategic security intelligence services to governments and multinational organizations, explains that individuals are "motivated to travel to Iraq and Syria by friends, family, or influential members of their communities" (Barret 2014). Data assembled by the International Centre for the Study of Radicalisation at King's College London indicate that approximately 75 percent of those who join the Islamic State at home or abroad do so in preexisting groups (Bond 2014). According to West Point's Combating Terrorism Center, only one in five ISIS foreign fighters were recruited directly through social media, although social media greatly facilitates the jihadi movement's global communication and integration (Perliger and Milton 2016).

But even more than today's jihadists (where personal networks rooted in immigrant neighborhoods and clustered in particular towns and foreign territories remain key to recruitment), the alt-Right grassroots movement has coalesced online, on the dark side of social media. Before the predominance of the Internet, there were fringe newsletters, radio programs, and rallies, like the attempted Nazi march in Skokie, Illinois, in 1977 whose case went before the US Supreme Court, and the short-lived KKK demonstration in Warren, Ohio, in 1998. But the rise of social media has allowed people who might want to be part of the white supremacist movement to adhere without incurring the stigma previously associated with physically joining.

As political scientist Richard Hasen describes it, social media lowers "the collective action problem" of an individual going it alone because you can see that there are people out there like you to share risks (Hasen 2017). Neuropsychologist Molly Crockett notes that outrage-inducing messages appear to be more prevalent and potent online, with social media magnifying its triggers and reducing its personal costs (Crockett 2017).

Moreover, research by sociologist Mark Granovetter shows that once an expected threshold of there being people like you is appreciably surpassed, then the number and pace of people who join the fold can rapidly ratchet up (Granovetter 1978). Thus, the *Daily Stormer* can boast in a recent online Sunday edition of being "the biggest pro-white publication in the history of the world. With 6 million monthly unique visitors, we trounced the circulation of the Third Reich's most popular tabloid *Der Sturmer*, which had 250,000."

From jihadis in Europe to white supremacists in the United States, people most susceptible to joining radical groups are youth in their teens and twenties seeking community and purpose. The attraction of community is especially keen where there are sentiments of social exclusion or community collapse, whether or not accompanied by economic deprivation. It is a sense of purpose that most readily propels action and sacrifice, including a willingness to fight and die—especially when that purpose is perceived to be in defense of transcendent values dissociated from material costs or consequences.

In our studies across Europe, North Africa, and the Middle East, we find that when membership in a tight community combines with a commitment to transcendent values, the willingness to make costly sacrifices will rise. The idea is to encourage devoted action for the sake of absolute values that fuse community and purpose (Sheikh, Gómez, and Atran 2016).

This applies to the alt-Right as well. Just look at Patrik Hermansson's undercover investigation of the extreme Right for the anti-racist group Hope Not Hate (Hermansson 2017). Like recruiters who seek to bring in people from the larger Muslim community through cultural mixers and gatherings and then nudge them toward jihadi values, the alt-Right aims "to bring the [white] mainstream towards us," as far-Right Scottish YouTube vlogger Colin Robertson put it, by avoiding the stereotypical "race hate" line and by relentlessly focusing on what Aryan Nations portrays as "a spiritual-based, numinous way of living."

A core value shared by alt-Right proponents and jihadists is hatred of Jews. Beam called for linking up the far-Right in the United States with the "liberation movements" of Libya, Syria, Iran, and Palestine. In 2002, in a speech that he gave shortly before he died, William Pierce declared that "when Osama bin Laden attacked the United States on September 11 the year before, he did much more than send us a message that Muslims are not happy about what the Jews . . . are doing to the Palestinians. . . . He forced the whole subject of US policy in the Middle East into the open: the subject of American interests versus Jewish interests, of Jewish media control and its influence on governmental policy. He broke the taboo. He exposed the treason. In the long run that may more than compensate for the 3,000 American lives that were lost" (Pierce 2002).

In 2007, Aryan Nations argued for an "Aryan Jihad" to destroy the "Judaic-tyrannical" system of "so-called Western democratic states." Dylann Roof also saw the link: when questioned by a court examiner, he said he was "like a Palestinian in an Israeli jail after killing nine people . . . the Palestinian would not be upset or have any regret" (RX 2007).

Of course, white supremacists and jihadis have different worldviews, even if the slippery Jew or rootless Zionist is a sacrificial scapegoat in both. Our team asked white supremacists and jihadis whether a child born to Jewish parents but adopted by them since birth would grow up to be like other Jews or like their adoptive parents. White supremacists invariably say that a born

Jew is always a Jew who must be eliminated. Jihadis mostly say that a person born to Jews (or any other group) can grow up to be a Muslim holy warrior, or *mujahedin*, if raised in the House of Islam.

Different, but not different enough. That's because the reaction to outside threat is a deep human tendency—when an in-group feels threatened by an out-group, violence and hatred are not the anomalies but the rule for nearly all cultures throughout human history.

In *The Descent of Man*, Charles Darwin cast this devotion to the group as moral and fit, required for better-endowed winning groups in history's competition for survival and dominance. Across cultures, the strongest group identities are bounded by sacred values like unwillingness to sell out one's religion or country for material trade-offs (Atran and Ginges 2012). "Is this not because God and society are one and the same?", French sociologist Émile Durkheim famously conjectured. Revolutionaries and insurgents willing to sacrifice for cause and group have long tended to prevail with considerably less firepower and manpower than the state armies and police forces they oppose.

Fearful of the chauvinism and xenophobia that fed two world wars, many Western leaders and press simply denounce national identity or cultural preference as "bigoted" or "racist" and show an ostrich-like blindness to panhuman preferences for one's own. This leaves the field wide open for the offensive of white nationalist groups of the alt-Right or the far-Right's less overtly racist alt-Light defenders of "Western culture" against the onslaught of Islam, globalism, migration, feminism, and homosexuality.

So how might we intervene? At the 2017 World Economic Forum in Davos, Switzerland, where I presented some of our research findings, I had the impression that most people in attendance thought that the recent surge of jihadism and xenophobic ethno-national populism were just atavistic blips in the ineluctable progress of globalization that were destined to soon go away. That to me was the most worrisome feature of Davos, whose denizens basically run the world (or try to). Few there seemed willing to change their policies or behavior. They seemed to view the left-behinds of the dark side of globalization as simply losers who might be given a handout when artificial intelligence and robots deny them any chance for a decent living.

To end these worries, there was earnest talk among the spectacularly wealthy of a universal guaranteed income for the economically disadvantaged. Yet poor people rarely instigate violent overthrows of established order. Indeed, a guaranteed income for people without purpose or significance in life would more likely radicalize them than create quiet sheep. The doyens of Davos thereby could be subsidizing their own extinction.

Providing jobs that deny people dignity or the dream of a worthy life would likely fare no better. Instead, the first part of a more considered solution lies in understanding how human these violent responses are. In our preferred world of liberal democracy and human rights, violence—especially extreme forms of mass bloodshed—are deemed pathological. But across most of human history and culture, violence against outsider groups has been considered an act of moral virtue, for without a claim to virtue it is difficult, if not inconceivable, to want to eliminate large numbers of people innocent of direct harm to others.

But what messages could compete? For some, reinforcing our own values of representative government, with equal opportunity and justice before the law and unfettered debate, may provide a way forward in life. Preserving what is left of the planet's fauna and flora and avoiding environmental catastrophes may offer a new course for others. Others still might be inspired by antinuclear activities to fight what is probably humanity's greatest threat.

News media can help. Rapid diffusion of fake news, conspiracy theories, and other forms of propaganda is rife. With the decline of public-service national and local news to provide a consensus about reality, false information encourages people to form mistaken beliefs that are skewed to their prejudices. We need to revive local news as a public service for citizens, without imposing censorship, and convince national media and Internet giants like Google and Facebook that the First Amendment right of individuals to information may not apply equally to any source without caveat, such as the Russian government seeking to sway US elections or hate groups hell-bent on ethnic cleansing.

But even if news coverage improves, no message will spread and endure in a social vacuum. Instead, to thwart the recruitment process, we need intimate engagement with communities at risk. When I was conducting research in Jordan, an imam who formerly recruited for ISIS told me that "the young who came to us were not to be lectured at like witless children. We have to provide a better message, but a positive one." He went on to say that the message needs to be in a cultural frame that inspires them "from within their hearts."

The hurdle is high. The mixed neighborhoods I've studied in Paris, Brussels, and Ripoll, Spain (where the Barcelona killers plotted) contain parallel universes in which North African immigrants and natives fail to greet or even look at one another and where neighbors only know that the other is "an Arab" or not. Yet without intimate engagement between the groups, violent passions will continue their viral spread through social networks in distressed places across the world.

Hands-on social engagement, on the other hand, has already helped turn youth away from local gangs. Criminologist David Kennedy has demonstrated significant homicide reduction among gangs and drug crews through community work. Based on his observations that offenders within communities operate in groups, he spearheaded a program in cities across the United

States to bring youth into contact with respected community members, social services, and law enforcement officials, avoiding arrests and preventing death (Kennedy 2011).

One important strategy is learning from radical Islamist groups, ranging from the largely nonviolent Muslim Brotherhood to Al-Qaeda, whose outreach approach to social services and charity work (*dawah*) appears to offer greater success than calls to extremism. For example, in the al-Mahra governorate in Yemen, Al-Qaeda is the dominant jihadi group. Middle East scholar Elisabeth Kendall found that 56 percent of Al-Qaeda tweets were directed toward community development projects, often focusing on youth (only 3 percent concerned punishments). She sought to counteract Al-Qaeda's appeal with a parallel campaign run through a local nonprofit organization, Mahra Youth Unity Association, to enlist youth in community service and development work, initially relying mostly on print media and direct community engagement to promote school initiatives for peacebuilding, environmental cleanup, and so on. These efforts generated wide involvement of local youth and leaders in vulnerable, hard-to-reach desert communities. Now, her intervention work increasingly also uses social media.

Community engagement can also help counteract the alt-Right's appeal. In Germany, the Violence Prevention Network and Exit Germany have used outreach initiatives to turn around hundreds of far-right supporters. These initiatives focus on intimate "counter-engagement" involving quality time with youth to develop a sense of worth and purpose; they build social relationships within the community and avoid mass "counternarrative" messages, which have not worked. Exit Motala in Sweden, started by a school welfare worker and a local police officer to beat gangs at their own game of offering belonging, now also focus on young women susceptible to racist recruitment, providing a variety of social activities, ranging from theater, sports, cooking, and car repairs to outings at the Swedish Parliament and Jewish museum in Stockholm.

At the very least, we must embed ourselves within actual communities to understand which approach may work best. A necessary focus of this effort must be youth, who form the bulk of today's extremist recruits and tomorrow's most vulnerable populations. Volunteers for Al-Qaeda, the Islamic State, and many extreme nationalist groups are often youth in transitional stages in their lives—immigrants, students, and people between jobs and before finding their mates. Having left their homes, they seek new families of friends and fellow travellers to find purpose and significance. The ability to understand the realities facing young people will determine whether the transnational scourge of VE continues and surges or abates.

We need to alter the approach to youth. Right now, young people, especially young men (although increasingly young women), are viewed mostly as part of a "youth bulge," a problem to be pummeled, rather than as a "youth boom"—the world's most creative force, holding the promise for a better future, without violence in the mix. Let us help these young people realize their hopes and dreams and take agency over their own lives (Atran 2015). The best strategy could be showing them how they might successfully navigate their ideas in the labyrinths of power and prevailing institutions to change the world without violence. This is a goal of the United Network of Young Peacebuilders, which was instrumental in promoting UN Security Council Resolution 2250 that urges member states to give youth a greater voice in decision making to confront VE. But for now, that goal is only a hope.

Few of us will ever be free from the anxiety of never-ending change and choice. Some may never escape the hopeless delusion that life must never shift, a sense that can only lead to dread of difference in others. But we still share common grounds of shared passions and ideas in a world where all but the too-far-gone can live with more than a minimum of liberty and happiness, if given half a chance. It is for this chance that some of our forebears fought a revolution, civil war, and world wars.

Chapter 5

Radical Islamist and Radical Christianist Nuclear Terrorism

Frances Flannery

Terrorist groups such as Al-Qaeda, ISIS/Daesh, and some white nationalist groups (intersecting with the so-called alt-right) have sufficient motivation to inflict mass casualties under the right circumstances. Such actions fit the radical apocalyptic ideology that informs their overlapping worldviews—similar ideological structures that simply swap the face of the enemy and the righteous.[1] Both reinterpret their parent religions of Islam and Christianity through a violent apocalyptic ideology, which they fold into aspirations of radical new political systems that are either Islamist or Christianist in nature. Representatives from these groups have already attempted to procure nuclear weapons, made plans to do so, threatened nuclear power plants, or aspired to start a nuclear war as part of a divine, unfolding plan.

Grasping the radical apocalyptic religious framework that makes terrorism, including nuclear terrorism, "rational" from the perspectives of some of the leaders of these groups is essential for forming coherent policies that effectively counter the threat. By "apocalyptic," I do not simply mean "eschatological," that is, focused on end-time scenarios. For specialists in apocalypticism such as myself, the term "apocalyptic" has a broader meaning. I define apocalypticism as an orientation to reality that maintains that the transcendent realm has sent a revelation to a select few persons, the righteous. They believe that this revelation discloses the ultimate reality: that evil forces rule the mundane realm—our world as it now is. The world is thus divided simply into good versus evil, and the apocalyptic believers believe themselves to be on the side of the good. Here and now, the righteous feel oppressed, while evil flourishes. However, they believe that someday there will be a transcendent intervention that will dramatically change the operation of history by overcoming evil. The righteous will finally be vindicated: it is their destiny (Flannery 2016, 2–3). Al-Qaeda and Daesh are both apocalyptic by this definition, with different timetables and specific scenarios for the end-time events. Some white nationalist groups are also apocalyptic by this definition; they just imagine different players in the roles of the wicked (people of color/Israel/Jews/the Middle East/China) versus the transcendent (e.g., white God-given America/Germany/the Netherlands/Greece). The January 2017 election of President Donald Trump to the White House has empowered some constituencies that have felt ignored and impotent, as the world has become increasingly interconnected, diverse, and global. Unfortunately, among the president's supporters are white nationalist groups in the United States and Europe, which have seized on nativist and anti-immigrant remarks by Trump and former White House chief strategist Steve Bannon, an alt-right ideologue. Some supporters have high hopes for radical change that will rid their nation of its cultural and religious diversity, as well as its "political correctness," all of which they see as problems.

Recently, several factors have conflated to lend greater inspiration to radical apocalyptic terrorist groups. The Syrian conflict constitutes perhaps the greatest generator of grievances, radicalization, and terrorist actions in the world of radical Islamists, as the death toll of those killed climbs to almost *half a million*. The Trump administration's sharply contested executive order banning all refugees for four months and travel from seven nations (with exceptions made for non-Muslims) feeds the ideology of a clash of civilizations and enhances radical Islamist propaganda. Even the loss of territory in the so-called caliphate may have an unintended effect in propelling a few toward escalation and flashy, violent, and theatrical actions in the United States as well as in Europe, in order to secure Daesh's eschatological role. Competition between Daesh and Al-Qaeda also increases the probability of escalation from Al-Qaeda, since Daesh's loss of territory will be their moment to reassert themselves as the "alpha-endtime players" in the room.[2] Characterizations of the clash of civilizations embolden not only radical Islamists but radical Christianists in the United States and Europe as well. The rise of nativism, hate speech and demonization of others, vesting hope in a single authority, and belief in a God-given national destiny do as well.

If such persons subscribe to an apocalyptic worldview, they may view this change as the awaited vindication of the righteous. However, if they then suffer reversals—whether personally, societally, or politically—to this temporary empowerment, there is an increased chance of a violent backlash or even terrorism, whether from lone actors or small, radicalized groups.

Certainly, not every member of radical Islamist and radical Christianist groups is apocalyptic or even motivated by religion—people have different reasons for joining radical groups. However, this apocalyptic framework is the ideological worldview that the leadership uses to impart coherence to their message, actions, and goals. While apocalypticism is *not* violent in and of itself, and may even be a peaceful theology, a tiny minority of people in apocalyptic religions also subscribe to four additional reality propositions or indicators of radical or violent apocalypticism (Flannery 2016, 59–83).

The first indicator of radical apocalypticism is *authoritarian interpretation.* While all apocalyptic believers believe in some original revelation, such as the Bible or the Quran, radical apocalyptic believers maintain that *they* are the only ones who know how to interpret it. They are the *only ones* who know the truth; there is no room for reasonable dissent, discussion, or other interpretations. Leaders in these groups, such as Al-Qaeda's bin Laden or Daesh's al-Baghdadi, can amass power through acting as an interpreter of divine revelation or by claiming a role as the sole person/group who understands what *is destined* to happen. No such single leader has yet emerged clearly as the hero of the white nationalist movement. Instead, the trend is a social media or fringe media campaign spouting authoritative propaganda from a variety of sources that often take the form of conspiracy theories revealing the "real" workings of world and national power and the cycles of history (Barkun 1997).

The second indicator of radical apocalypticism is *active eschatology*, a belief that not only is some kind of transformation coming to history but also that the "righteous" must act to *actively trigger those end-time events.* Bin Laden acted in anticipation of the Hour or Last Day yet showed relative patience in waiting to form a caliphate *after* broad strategic interests were well secured (Flannery 2016, 53). Daesh, on the other hand, was formed under an urgent eschatology. Al-Baghdadi appears to preach that the establishment of the so-called caliphate now will trigger a series of end-time events: a final battle in Dabiq, Syria, between Daesh and Turkey/the United States, the coming of Christ who will defeat the Antichrist, and the Mahdi figure who will unite all remaining true believers (McCants 2015).

White nationalism in the United States, while not a unified movement, has been strongly influenced by the *Turner Diaries*, a virtual Bible of the white racist right, which leads some to believe that whites must prepare for an impending American race war that is akin to Armageddon. In fact, triggering this race war was part of the impetus for the actions of (domestic terrorists) Timothy McVeigh, Dylann Roof, and the leaders of the now-defunct Christian Identity group, the Covenant, Sword, and Arm of the Lord (Flannery 2016, 143–185). Some support a "Fourth Turning" theory of American history in which the United States is destined to engage soon in a cataclysmic and bloody war, after which it will emerge victorious in a new triumphant phase (Lopez 2017).

The third reality proposition that radical apocalyptic groups share is identifying evil not just as cosmic evil but as *concrete evil* that takes the form of *groups of people*, a thought process known as "othering." For Al-Qaeda,

Daesh, and many white nationalists, the world is a clash of civilizations that represent Good versus Evil. For radical Islamist and Christianist groups alike, the imaginary cosmic divide is manifested as "Islam" versus "the West"; they simply differ on which side is evil and which side is good. All such radical apocalyptists view the moderates whom they think *should* be on their side as hypocrites at the very least, or as the incarnation of evil at the worst. Hence, Daesh considers the worst of Satan's followers to be Shi'ite Muslims and moderate Sunnis, and Al-Qaeda targeted eight times as many Muslims as non-Muslims from 2001 to 2009 (Al-Obaidi, Abdullah, and Helfstein 2009). In fact, 82–97 percent of the victims of terrorism worldwide are Muslims[3] (Alexander and Moore 2015). Similarly, white nationalists are just as inclined to distrust white liberal journalists, judges, or professors as they are certain refugees, immigrants, or foreigners whom they see as a threat. This type of "othering" results in extremely intense "in-group" bonds of communal identity that may indeed be the strongest motivation for radicalization (Flannery 2016, 72–73, 227–230).

The final indicator of radical apocalypticism involves some legitimizing theology of *redemptive violence*. Most religious terrorists come from a parent religion that forbids the kind of violence that terrorism embraces. Yet radical Islamist and Christianist ideologues reinterpret and contradict their parent traditions while still claiming their allegiance to Islam and Christianity. Going against the core interpretations of peace in Islam and Christianity, they believe that they are divinely appointed to exact vengeance or that their violence is divinely approved because the end goal—the cleansing of the world of evil—is worth any suffering. Such violence may seem not only divinely legitimized but also macho and cool, playing into social constructions of an empowering masculinity that facilitates religiously sanctioned violence. And there is no greater symbol of redemptive violence than inflicting mass annihilation on the enemy through nuclear war or terrorism.

THE THREAT OF NUCLEAR TERRORISM

The 9/11 Commission reports that Al-Qaeda has long sought to procure nuclear weapons (9/11 Commission 2004). Daesh appears to have similar ambitions. In the May 2015 issue of *Dabiq*, the group's magazine, a writer outlined how a nuclear weapon could be smuggled from Pakistan to West Africa, South and Central America, and then up to and across the Mexico-US border (Cantlie 2016). The United Nations has warned that Daesh could also target nuclear power plants. A different scenario is envisioned in the *Turner Diaries*, in which the Organization, the white anti-federalist resistance movement, seizes Southern California and nuclear weapons from a military base, subsequently using them to trigger a larger nuclear war between the United States and the Soviet Union (Pierce 2002; Torres 2016). Trump's assertion before the 2016 election that he might use a nuclear weapon against ISIS fuels this scenario further and elevates nuclear war to the level of a national theology of redemptive violence (Post Opinions Staff 2016).

Overall, the worldview of radical apocalypticists means that they are governed by a different mental calculus than the rest of us. Since they find current institutions to be evil and oppressive, they wish to upend everything, to dissolve the current political systems or moral culture of our world. Policy makers must grasp that aggressive measures against them will never deter the ambition of apocalypticists, since feeling oppressed only feeds them. *Particularly in this age of the Internet, when ideology has such a far reach*, targeting their leaders with ridicule, removing their leaders through jailing, or eliminating leadership through targeted killing can actually worsen radicalization by energizing the ideology of oppression.

Nuclear terrorism remains a serious threat. While it is fairly difficult to steal nuclear materials, penetrate nuclear power plants, or radicalize (or compel) nuclear scientists, these things are not impossible. Moreover, evaluations of risk should be based on "agential risk," a concept coined by Phil Torres that argues that even given very low access to advanced technologies that can cause great harm, a few deeply committed agents still pose a greater threat than do many more noncommitted agents with greater access (Flannery 2016, 186–213; Torres 2016).

Nonstate terrorists are not the only possible sources of nuclear threat, and perhaps not even the most concerning. The danger of nuclear war between nuclear states, such as Pakistan and India, or the United States and North Korea or China, must be considered an even more ominous existential threat, given the geopolitical fallout. Candidate Trump's election speeches were peppered with all four indicators of radical apocalyptic ideology. President Trump's views on the use of nuclear weapons are unclear and, at the time of writing, tensions between the United States and North Korea remain high.

Radical apocalypticism is a cross-cultural ideology that has at its core the perception of vast oppression that will be cataclysmically upended. With their vast potential for destruction and cultural associations with doom, nuclear materials may be especially attractive for state and nonstate actors who are radical apocalypticists. The redress to this philosophy must not only come from policy makers in a top-down fashion, but change must also come from the grassroots level up. We have to *counter authoritarian interpretations* by creating societies that value civil debate and that protect the freedoms, welfare, and rights of the minority who dissent or are different. We have to *counter the climate that fosters belief in active eschatology* by supporting those organizations, including faith-based organizations and NGOs, that are working for social justice and the slow betterment of the world. Religious leaders in apocalyptic faiths have to remind their congregations that only God is in control of the timing of the end time or otherwise reinterpret or contest apocalyptic narratives. We have to counter "othering" by refusing to engage in hate speech, stereotyping, or discrimination against minorities and by fostering inclusion in our societies. We also have to refuse simple, binary divisions into *Good versus Evil persons*, even when we are speaking about terrorist groups. Why do people join Boko Haram? Sometimes, because they are kids who cannot afford an education. Finally, we have to *counter belief in redemptive violence*, including rethinking our national values and strategies in combating terrorism.

It will not be easy, but in order to successfully prevent nuclear catastrophes, we need to work in a myriad of ways, at multiple levels of society, toward long-term, systemic peace. This involves fostering the physical, psychological, material, cultural, religious, and ecological well-being of peoples across the globe and here at home.

Chapter 6

The Private Sector and Violent Extremism

Stone Conroy

An ecology of violent extremism (VE) would not be complete without mentioning the private sector and its integral role in the existing systems that create and counter violence. Despite this, most discussions about VE and preventing/countering violent extremism (P/CVE) ignore the private sector completely or only mention social media companies and the role they play.

While technology has certainly played a critical role in the spread of VE since the advent of the social media age, technology companies are not the only businesses in the VE ecosystem. Nor are they the only ones affected by the rise of VE, and the technology world is not the only private-sector industry that can help counter or prevent VE.

This chapter will examine every facet of the relationship between VE and the private sector: how violent extremists use technology platforms to propagate their rhetoric; which companies are working with governments and NGOs to disrupt or destroy information-sharing networks; and how the private sector is affected by VE, can help P/CVE, and how it can break down the current paradigm and create a more viable and virtuous alternative.

THE PRIVATE SECTOR AND VIOLENT EXTREMISM

When it comes to private-sector engagement, the focus on social media companies makes sense given that their platforms are used to facilitate the spread of information about VE. Governments have been eager to work with these organizations to curtail these communication flows, map networks of actors, and propagate counter-extremism narratives.

Organizations of all sizes are involved in P/CVE, and they are starting to work together and in junction with government entities to increase their efficacy. A Department of Homeland Security (DHS) report from the Countering Violent Extremism Subcommittee recommended the creation of a network that connects "non-profits and small businesses whose missions or interests overlap with CVE" with other organizations that have more resources to scale their impact (DHS 2016). A good example of this is Google, which is currently working with a small start-up called Moonshot CVE to develop a counter-messaging platform that runs on artificial intelligence (Greenberg 2016).

Entrepreneurs are as critical to CVE as well-established organizations. At the 2016 White House Global Entrepreneur Summit, former secretary of state John Kerry stated that "entrepreneurship is a rebuttal to extremism" because it provides a framework for jobs, hope, and prosperity (Dremann 2016). The DHS report also called for more engagement with "entrepreneurs and businesses leaders" and lamented the fact that "American donors and civic investors have not yet taken on the issue of the spread and impact of extremist ideology" despite many high-level attempts to convince them of the necessity of such investment. Engagement with investors and entrepreneurs has been a central mission of the Global Community Engagement and Resilience Fund, a public–private partnership designed to support local, community-level initiatives aimed at strengthening resilience against violent extremist agendas (GCERF n.d.).

VIOLENT EXTREMISM'S EFFECT ON THE PRIVATE SECTOR

Violent extremism negatively affects private-sector organizations from a financial standpoint as well. The Institute of Economics and Peace estimated that global terrorism cost $89.6 billion in 2015, and terrorism insurance sales have steadily risen in recent years with more than 60 percent of companies in the United States now insured (Rosand and Miller 2017).

As one expert notes, "Companies know that violence and terrorism are bad for business . . . it lowers productivity, stifles human potential, reduces consumer confidence, increases the price of risk and destroys infrastructure" (Eide 2015). The author of this article also notes that there is "greater awareness of these costs than ever before, and also greater willingness to partner in security-related dialogue and solutions" (Eide 2015). At a GCERF and the Institute for Security Studies (ISS) convening in June 2015 to discuss innovative approaches to countering VE, private-sector representatives shared examples of how "violent extremism threatens not only the safety of employees, but also negatively impacts the stability and development of business operations" (GCERF 2015).

In addition to the general effects of VE on the economy, businesses are affected in specific ways that lead to increased security costs or decreased profit from curtailed operations in high-threat areas. One article on the role of private companies in P/CVE stressed that companies across all sectors are "affected by threats against soft targets" and that businesses "must do more to help and to protect their own bottom line" (Rosand and Miller 2017). A study from 2008 noted that 90 percent of the critical infrastructure that might be targeted by violent extremists is owned by private sector (Nasser-Eddine et al. 2011). After the November 2015 attack in Paris, Air France lost an estimated $73.5 million, and the tourism industry (including hotels, airlines, and travel agents) suffered stock loses after the Brussels airport bombing.

As an alternative to divesting, scaling down operations, or increasing security expenditures, GCERF has started to develop joint "shared-value" initiatives with the private sector as a way for companies to "preserve and expand their investment and market share" in countries where VE is an issue (Koser 2016). If these initiatives are successful, companies may be able to invest in prevention measures that can help mitigate their losses.

PRIVATE INVESTMENTS IN COUNTERING VIOLENT EXTREMISM

The Overseas Private Investment Corporation (OPIC) has been working with American businesses to increase private investment in Jordan, including several enterprise lending programs that expand access to financial services to Jordanians. The CEO of OPIC noted that the institution was committed to ensuring Jordan's economic success—a major factor in preserving its status as a "bulwark against extremism" in the region (OPIC 2016).

GCERF is taking this idea one step further; at the Seventieth UN General Assembly in 2015, they featured a special address from the Swiss government entitled "Investing in Fragile Environments: The Role of the Private Sector in Countering Violent Extremism." The address included an appeal that was directed to private-sector representatives in the room: "You can offer more than jobs and salary; you can offer perspectives and opportunities for young people. You can keep them away from engaging in violent extremism." The address mentioned that private-sector engagement is not merely corporate social responsibility; it is actually "an investment in unleashing economic potential, in future growth and higher returns in new markets. It is thus a real business case" (The Federal Council of the Swiss Government 2015).

An article featured by the Council on Foreign Relations highlighted five ways the private sector can be engaged on this issue: making the business case, focusing on outcomes, starting local, seeking core competencies rather than capital, and widening the focus of interventions around the world. It mentioned that "an investment in countering violent extremism is an investment in future growth" of affected regions (Koser 2015a).

At another GCERF event in Washington, DC, in the summer of 2016, participants suggested that governments should create incentive structures to encourage the private sector to invest in P/CVE. As an example, GCERF launched PVE initiatives in Nigeria with matching funding to leverage private-sector investment (GCERF 2016). There have been significant hurdles in convincing private entities to invest in these programs, however; a CSIS report noted that private investment has been "very disappointing, largely because of concerns about working on issues linked to counterterrorism and being perceived as agents of the U.S. government" (Green and Proctor 2016).

PUBLIC–PRIVATE PARTNERSHIPS

Given that economic factors such as employment are sometimes a factor in extremist recruitment, the private sector can play an important role in reducing these risks. As one expert notes, "Companies are in a unique position to partner with governments and civil society in a long-term effort to address the conditions that underlie the spread of extremist ideologies and recruitment" (Eide 2015). Another author notes that the private sector can interact with individuals whom governments cannot, especially people with criminal records or "formers"—those who used to belong to extremist groups (Jamal 2014).

A good example of partnerships is the Strong Cities Network (SCN), which was launched by the United Nations in 2015 and is the "first ever global network of mayors, municipal-level policy makers and practitioners united in building social cohesion and community resilience to counter violent extremism" (SCN n.d.). The SCN has a working group dedicated to public–private partnerships, and their flagship project was the creation of Public-Private Community Initiatives (PPCIs), which use "private sector experience in harnessing public aspiration to market social change" (SCN 2016). A statement of purpose about the PPCIs noted the following:

- There are many great examples of public–private partnerships but very few on the sharp end of CVE policy.
- CVE is a difficult sell to private companies, which can feel that it is too politically sensitive and associated with a political agenda.
- Public–private partnerships on CVE activities need to be community-led rather than local government-led.
- Community organizations—which are best placed to appeal to private companies and foundations for CVE public–private partnerships—may not

have the private-sector experiences to formulate and design pitches that are compelling (particularly financially) to private companies and foundations (SCN 2016).

The private sector also has a wealth of information about risk management and security that could be of assistance. As one author notes, "Companies today often need to operate in risky locations, or in places where there is no or very limited government. Their wealth of experience in building resilience is invaluable, yet they are not normally involved in the formulation of security strategies" (Eide 2015).

A project manager at the Institute for Strategic Dialogue, a think tank that is attempting to engage more with businesses and convince them of the necessity of working to prevent or counter VE, said, "The only group in society with the expertise to counter extremism online is the private sector; their engagement is no longer optional, it's crucial" (Jamal 2014). The executive director of the Counter Extremism Project echoed this statement, saying, "The private sector absolutely has a role to play in the counterterrorism space because of how extremists are using essentially private sector tools to communicate and radicalize" (Weinger 2016).

Technology companies remain a large segment of the private sector's engagement with P/CVE, although some technology initiatives have links to other business sectors. The Institute for Strategic Dialogue, for example, runs a social network platform called Against Violent Extremism (AVE), which brings together former members from a wide variety of extremist groups (from former white supremacists in the United States to former Al-Qaeda members in the Middle East) and survivors of VE to help them exchange ideas and build initiatives dedicated to P/CVE (Against Violent Extremism n.d.). Some of the projects include the *Abdullah-X Show*, an Internet cartoon that espouses anti-extremist messages, and "Own Your Brain," a series of workshops designed to teach participants how extremist groups manipulate people into joining them (Bharath 2016).

FROM VIOLENT EXTREMISM TO VIRTUOUS ENTERPRISES

The true power of the private sector in P/CVE lies in its ability to provide purpose and empowerment to those seeking—and finding—meaning in the ideologies of extremist groups. A good example of how the private sector could provide an alternative path can be found in Northern Nigeria, home to the terrorist group Boko Haram. A study released in the fall of 2016 by the nonprofit organization Mercy Corps describes how Boko Haram provides financial services to businesses and individuals as a means of recruitment. While some people are forced or deceived into receiving these financial services (which include loans, gifts, and in-kind contributions), others willingly accepted them due to a lack of alternatives and an understanding that these services would act as a "catalyst for starting or growing their enterprises and achieving a better economic situation for themselves and their families" (Mercy Corp 2016).

Another study that examined CVE programs in Northern Nigeria had similar findings—interviews with youth revealed that Boko Haram's promises of financial support were attractive, given the lack of alternatives and a strong desire for economic empowerment and opportunity. Young people who participated in CVE programs noted that although they appreciated the lessons taught during the program about tolerance and civic engagement, they were concerned about the sustainability of these teachings in the face of poverty and lack of meaningful economic opportunities (Odafen 2016).

If a viable strategy to preventing or countering Boko Haram's recruitment is increasing economic opportunities for young people, engagement with the private sector is critical. As one expert points out, "Companies have a natural, and essential, role to play in reducing the drivers of extremism, and this is to create jobs" (Eide 2015). Simply creating jobs is not enough, however—the work must be empowering, providing people with a sense of pride and purpose.

Engagement with private sector on P/CVE can be more effective if the framing shifts from combatting a negative to promoting a positive. By tapping into the desires expressed by those young Nigerians seeking purpose and prosperity—rather than treating them as potential Boko Haram recruits—the companies can provide a positive alternative to VE in the form of "virtuous enterprise." This new paradigm has an additional benefit in that it aligns with the incentives of private-sector entities to increase profits and—as is increasingly the case around the world—to provide some social benefit at the same time.

Affinis Labs is a great example of this. Affinis is an award-winning social enterprise that leverages innovation and entrepreneurship to tackle pressing global challenges (Amanullah 2015). As an incubator and accelerator, Affinis provides support for start-up companies with a positive social mission, with a specific focus on young Muslims with innovative business ideas. Examples of their work include a "hackathon" in Dhaka, Bangladesh, to promote storytelling and social harmony (in partnership with Facebook, Google, and the UN Development Program), the launch of a Youth Entrepreneurship Hub in the Middle East and North Africa, and the incubation of a business called "Little Big Kids," which produces children's books with Muslim characters and Islamic themes (Little Big Kids n.d.).

While the Lab is primarily focused on promoting the development of virtuous enterprises of any kind, it does explicitly work on projects in the P/CVE realm. Affinis cohosted a three-day hackathon with Google and Facebook called "No2H8," where participants worked collaboratively on developing online tools to counter hate speech (No H28 n.d.). In fact, the company was founded with the goal of providing "innovative goods & services that enhance identity and help counter violent extremism" and has since expanded its vision to empowering all Muslim social ventures regardless of their mission (PRWeb 2015).

"We realized that the more empowered young people are, the less they gravitate to extremist movements," said one of the cofounders of Affinis Labs, Shahed Amanullah (Field 2016). In another interview, he highlighted how Affinis fits within the virtuous enterprise paradigm when he said, "We see enormous market needs as well as opportunities to use market forces to generate significant social good" (PRWeb 2015).

CONCLUSION

As Espen Eide notes, there will be no clear path to "victory" over VE, but success can be achieved "when we partner to build more inclusive, more just, tolerant and open societies" (Eide 2015). After Global Partnerships Week in 2016, the event's organizing body, Concordia, released a statement on partnerships for countering VE that noted "success lies in a partnership's ability to leverage private sector expertise, efficiency, and scale alongside government scope, reach, and influence" (Silva 2016).

Partnering with private-sector entities is important to P/CVE and essential to creating the virtuous enterprises that represent a positive goal rather than the countering of a negative one. The private sector has the chance to follow in the footsteps of Affinis Labs and use market forces to generate social good in the pursuit of prosperity and purpose.

Chapter 7

The Neurobiology of Violent Extremism

Mari Fitzduff

Recent advances in neuroscience and biopsychology are increasing our understanding of the ways in which our biological predispositions can affect our behavior. Such insights can help us understand why people are attracted to fundamentalist ideological causes, for which they are prepared to kill and be killed. Recently developed techniques such as genetic and hormonal testing, functional magnetic resonance imaging (fMRI), and electroencephalograms show just how strongly we can be influenced by our genetic, neurological, and hormonal tendencies, which in turn affect our individual and group responses to situations of conflict. Understanding our neural and biological legacies may help us to develop more effective strategies for preventing and managing violent extremism (VE).

IMPORTANT CAVEATS

There is no single biopsychological reason why people become violent extremists. Studies across ideologies and time describe the multifaceted nature of radicalization and its relationship to its environmental context. The Tamil Tigers/Sri Lanka, IRA/Ireland, ETTA/Basque country, Naxalites/India, Maoists/Nepal, and the many past and present Middle Eastern and African Jihadist groups will offer varying motives to explain their membership of their groups, and even within apparent identity groups motivations will vary widely, for example, Jihadist group members have varying motivations depending upon whether such recruits are from the Western world or from Asia, Africa, or the Middle East. There are, however, generic human biopsychological processes that predispose people to become members of such groups, and these are useful to remember when studying ways and means to prevent or halt such memberships.

It is also important to note that in studies of militant members of groups such as the Revolutionary Armed Forces of Colombia (FARC) in Colombia, or ISIS in the Middle East, or the Irish Republican Army (IRA) in Ireland, most show no signs of psychopathology (Dando 2016; Purtill 2015). And, although researchers found two genes, *monoamine oxidase* (*MAOA*) and *cadherin-13*, which when mutated appeared to correlate with violent, even homicidal, behavior, no connection between these naturally occurring regulators and the behavior of VE has been made (Knapton 2014). Nor can members of violent extremist groups be distinguished by the obscene violent tactics that some groups use. Such violence can and has been part and parcel of almost all militia groups, both legal and illegal throughout time. The Shankill Butchers in Ireland, cannibalism as part of war, wholesale bombings of innocent civilians, and the use of torture and biological weapons by many governments demonstrate that almost any belief system can justify and mandate horrifyingly violent behavior.[1]

Violent extremism is also not primarily about political, theological, or other beliefs. Researchers assert that ideology is usually not the primary motivating factor (Sageman 2008). Testosterone-driven young men looking to be heroic are not, by and large, involved in political or theological discussions. The adoption of a group ideology often occurs after an individual has joined an organization. Would-be recruits jihadists Yusuf Sarwar and Mohammed Ahmed ordered *Islam for Dummies* and *The Koran for Dummies* on Amazon just before they set out from Birmingham to join ISIL in Syria (Hassan 2014). In 2008, a classified briefing note on radicalization, prepared by MI5's behavioral science unit, suggested that, far from being religious zealots, a large number of those involved in terrorism do not practice their faith regularly (Travis 2008). It appears that the fascination that the Islamic State holds for thousands of French youths is not about the radicalization of Islam but the "Islamisation of radicality" (Oliver, 2017). Any ideology, including domestic ideologies, can provide a focus for VE.

Importantly, while this chapter will address the biological, genetic, hormonal, and neurological reasons that *predispose* many to the use of violence for ideological means, it should be remembered that such reasons *are not determinist*. A predisposition is a built-in tendency, which can be quite powerful but will only be harmful—or helpful—when such tendencies are stimulated within particular environments.

Given such caveats, what biopsychological processes facilitate membership of VE groups?

Feelings, not logic, are the main drivers in human decisions. People are more often ruled by their emotions than by logic, and this is particularly true at the age in which most young men join legal or illegal militias. There are two regions of the brain that are struggling for attention in young minds, that is, the amygdala, the part of the brain that processes our automatic/intuitive emotional impulses, and our prefrontal cortex that deals with our conscious/reasoned / logical responses to a situation. These "emotional" and "reasoning" minds coexist uneasily, and the amygdala is particularly inclined to dominate when we are under stress. For example, electroencephalogram (EECG) and hormonal and genetic testing reveal that we are more at the mercy of such biological tendencies when responding to conflict stimuli and to take our cues from what we feel, rather than what we think, and the emotional parts of our brain are particularly potent in those who are younger (Allard and Kensinger 2014).

MALE AND YOUNG

Recruits for VE groups are generally male and young, and their gender and attendant biological processes often facilitate their engagement in such groups. The neural circuitry of young adult brains lights up different neural pathways than older adults. These pathways rely heavily on emotions, favoring sensory reward and immediacy, and the excitement of action and social bonding with peers over potential future consequences. These pathways also diminish their tolerance for the complexities and ambiguities of differing moralities (Casey, Jones, and Somerville 2011).

Young men are flooded with testosterone, which makes them more likely to be risk takers, and eager to prove their masculinity (Steinberg 2013). Depending on the environment such characteristics can be positive or negative. There is a male-related age-crime curve, which transcends all cultures, which is flat until about age ten and peaks at about eighteen, which Baird attributes to a variety of neurochemical phenomena, which can be used for socially acceptable heroism—such as becoming firefighters and police or legal soldiers. Many young men will try to prove their status as tough and popular, and, in some cases, depending upon the environment and the opportunities available, aggressive and violent. While adolescent women also take greater risks, act impulsively, and can be more aggressive during young adulthood, they are more likely to heed social cues and to be reined in by social expectations (Baird 2011).

Hormones also play a role in the linking of sex and VE. Abu Bakr al-Baghdadi, the self-declared Muslim caliph of the Islamic State in Iraq and Syria chief, ordered that a marriage grant be given to all members of ISIL who wanted to enter matrimony, which included housing and a sum of $1,200. So many were the ISIL fighters who were unmarried and wanted a wife that they opened a "marriage bureau" for women who wanted to wed the group's fighters in Syria and Iraq (Al Arabiya 2014). Such offerings are very attractive to testosterone-filled young men, many of whom have lived in societies where premarital sex is forbidden and who had no obvious way of earning enough to enter into a normal marriage.

TO BE A HERO

The search for significance is a fundamental human motivation (Kruglanski et al. 2013) and is particularly important during adolescence. Radicalism—that is, the pursuit of fundamental political, economic, or social reforms—often provides a convenient track to significance. It can enable young men to shape their individual identity and to find their place in a group (Dugas and Kruglanski 2014). Such a quest for the heroic has always motivated young men to join violent groups such as the Christian Crusades, the Spanish civil war, the Irish Republican movement, International Maoist struggles, and Jihadist extremist movements. By fighting, young men can quickly gain the status of heroes, or where such are valued, as martyrs, particularly in contexts in which a young man's desire to gain individual significance is given little opportunity to develop in a socially positive manner.

Both the bodies and brains of young adults are also changing. Abstract concepts such as justice and politics begin to have appeal, and youth build a new sense of identity. A match of perceived injustice and grievances allied with their identity search is a potent mix for recruiters to extreme groups. Interestingly, the response to perceived injustice may be biologically disposed. It appears that it has shown that fairness is much more than a moral value or ideological construct but appears to have biological roots. When offered a fair deal, certain reward centers of the target's brain light up, specifically the ventral striatum, amygdala, orbitofrontal cortex (OFC), and ventromedial prefrontal cortex (VLPFC). On the other hand, unfair offers result in activity in the anterior insula—an area associated with contempt or disgust such as reactions to bad tastes or smells. These emotional firings are fast and automatic, so it appears that the emotional brain is overruling the more deliberate, rational mind. Faced with a conflict, the brain's default position is to demand a fair deal (Tabibnia and Lieberman 2007).

Studies conducted with members of the Sri Lankan terrorist organization the Liberation Tigers of Tamil Eelam found that the degree to which they felt anger or shame or feeling insignificant in the previous few weeks correlated with engaging in violent actions and supporting violent struggle against the Singhalese majority. Martin McGuinness, a Catholic in a Protestant-dominated Northern Ireland, and a major leader of the IRA, explained the reason for his IRA allegiance during the years of oppression he and his friends in Derry had endured at the hands of the British and the Ulster police: "I would have been ashamed not to join the IRA" (Elmhirst 2011).

For young men, joining a militia group can also be about a sense of responsibility to address historical injustices or to provide for their families. In Nigeria, it was broad frustration with the government that created initial community acceptance of Boko Haram, which took advantage of the deep grievances around government inadequacies and security abuses to gain a foothold in communities. Thus, many see violence as the only viable option left for them and their communities to regain any control over their lives. "Such young men convince themselves that they are righting epic wrongs, and many believe that their sacrifice (their 'martyrdom') is not only heroic but even chivalric" (Dickey 2009).

Yet many of those who are attracted to VE tend to be relatively well educated, come from affluent backgrounds, but are "frustrated achievers" in which their talents are not sufficiently utilized within their societal context. ISIS is able to recruit fighters from places like the United States and Western Europe who may be facing some sort of identity crisis, a desire for a personal sense of recognition that they cannot find at home. "For those who find themselves at odds with the culture of their parents, and yet are met with hostility from the culture of the society they live in, exiting the acculturation paradigm to embrace a third culture that provides them with a sense of belonging may be an appealing option" (Taylor 2015).

For some young men, the idea of adventure itself is enough to entice them to join militias. Evidence given in an Irish court in 2002 by John McDonaugh revealed that he had hung around a McDonalds in Dublin and collected five young men whom he had recruited for membership of an IRA extremist group Oglaigh na hEireann (Young Men of Ireland) training camp. According to one fourteen-year-old, he had been told he would learn about Irish history, be shown guns, and be allowed to fire blanks. There was no evidence of any motivation for his joining other than a possible adventure on the part of the young man (Wilson 2000).

A BAND OF BROTHERS

Adolescence and early adulthood are psychologically and hormonally confusing times. Lacking a group to belong to can create a sense of insecurity and identity confusion, which is why adolescents are so keen to "fit in" and belong. A sense of isolation and vulnerability seems to be especially strong in young men, and this may be the great majority of gang members are young males, since gangs can provide them with a strong sense of belonging and identity. According to Taylor, "Females don't seem to experience 'ego-separateness' to the same degree. It is unclear whether this is due to environmental factors, or innate psychological and biological ones, but females seem to be generally more relational than males, finding it easier to make connections and find emotional support" (Taylor 2015).

In seeking such group belonging, potential recruits are also unconsciously responding to the lure of another hormone—oxytocin. Oxytocin has various social and physiological functions in the brain and the body but is primarily known for its effect within groups where it increases a sense of belonging and of connectedness to the group and positively rewards cooperation. Spraying oxytocin into people's noses makes people more likely to cooperate in any group task (Stallen, De Dreu, and Shalvi 2012). It is heavily involved in rewarding the processes of group loyalty and belonging, and its rise can be measured in blood changes after social interactions. It reduces the fear of social betrayal in humans and is important for the inhibition of the brain regions such as the amygdala, which are associated with stress, fear, and anxiety. There is a genetic basis for oxytocin production and receptivity and may have had an evolutionary function. High levels of oxytocin may enable groups to thrive better than others by cooperating with each other and rewarding processes of group loyalty and belonging. The change in oxytocin after a social interaction can be measured in a person's blood. It has been shown that successful hunting increases testosterone, oxytocin, and cortisol in a subsistence population (Jaeggi et al. 2015). Surges of testosterone reinforce muscle regeneration after the hunt and are perhaps similar to the high we may experience after doing sports or other exercise, when we release a protein called BDNF (brain-derived neurotrophic factor), which has a protective and also reparative element to our memory neurons and can act as a physical reset switch.

Given such biophysical rewards, it is no wonder that adolescents join gangs. Once they are members of any peer group, new ideas and ways of acting become normal. While belonging to a group helps to alleviate their sense of separateness and strengthens their identity, it also makes them vulnerable to any form of extremism and their willingness to join up with groups such as the Islamic State as part of a sort of "super-gang." The rewards for bonding are particularly desirable in countries who are more collectivist in nature. Based on surveys of thousands of people in fifteen Arab and other countries, researchers found that Muslims who have a more collectivistic mentality are more likely to support terrorist attacks against Americans or Europeans than those with more individualistic leanings (Dugas and Kruglanski 2014).

US AND THEM

Unfortunately, while hormones such as oxytocin can increase levels of bonding within a group, it can also increase the member's suspicion and rejection of "others" outside the group or the tribe, and it makes people *less* likely to cooperate with members of an out-group. This has led to the suggestion that humans have evolved biologically for cooperation—but only with some people. There are also findings that suggest that out-group biases such as race bias may be a fear "prepared" by evolution and not purely contextual, as elements of the amygdala appear to be responsible for, and associated with, implicit, as opposed to explicit, attitudes toward racial out-groups (Brosch, Bar-David, and Phelps 2013).

Our attitude toward out-groups is also affected by what scientists call "mirror neurons." Brain imaging experiments using fMRI have shown that the human inferior frontal cortex and superior parietal lobe are active when a person is contemplating another person and using mirror neurons to connect or otherwise with another person or group. Such neurons appear to be linked to our capacity for empathy, the emotion that enables us to better understand other people's intentions, feelings, and emotions and allow us to see the world from another person's point of view. What seems to make terrorists essentially different from others is their ability to "switch off" their sense of empathy in relation to their chosen beliefs and goals and to those who do not share them. This may enable them to kill them without remorse.

THE NEED FOR CLOSURE

Not only do fundamentalist ideologies provide a strong sense of belonging assisted by the intoxication of oxytocin, but they also provide certainty—the conviction that they contain the truth, a conviction that is needed by some people more than others in order to stabilize their lives. People genetically differ in their dislike of ambiguity and their need for certainty. fMRI scans have shown that differences in genetics/biology influence differences in attitudes and beliefs. At one end of the spectrum, some people appear to have genetically greater sensitivity and dislike of uncertainty, and a greater need for order, structure, and clear beliefs in their lives—differences that can be observed from birth. On the other end of a continuum, there appear to be people who are genetically more open to new things and to new experiences that require cognitive complexity. They tend to show greater activity in the left insula of their brain and can better tolerate nuances of belief and certainty (Haidt 2003).

Extremist ideology is often more appealing to individuals who have a high need for closure (NFC) because such ideologies paint an unambiguous picture of the world they desire and what they want to eliminate. They answer the need for cognitive closure by eliminating ambiguity and confusion, often at the expense of what others would perceive as rationality. NFC is a mindset that sees the world in sharp definition, no shades of gray. Such views are highly attractive to young people who are seeking a clear-cut vision of life with which to identify and for coherence in their outlook and beliefs. ISIL calls address this need by calling for young people to join in building the caliphate and create a new, pure state uncorrupted by Western influences, in which all the norms are clear. Such clarity is welcome to those who have NFC.

The current world situation may constitute just such a confusing and threatening context for many as unprecedented waves of immigration dislocate millions of people, in a world of postdepression high unemployment levels, and many crumbling political orders. "All these engender unsettling, anxiety-inducing uncertainties, which prompt cravings for coherence and closure. Fundamentalist ideologies are quintessentially fit to satisfy just such cravings." A fundamentalist ideology offers a future that is predictable and controllable. "Such a perspective holds particular fascination for confused youths in transitional stages of their lives, who drift like rudderless ships and find themselves torn by conflicting cultural demands" (Kruglanski 2014). Many researchers have found significant statistical relations between NFC and extremism. This relationship was found regardless of where the researchers looked, for example, Morocco, Spain, the Philippines, Palestine, Northern Ireland, or Sri Lanka, although expressed differently by religious/cultural/political extremism (Dugas and Kruglanski 2014).

Interestingly, one study has shown empirically that among jihadist militia who live in Muslim majority countries, a high proportion are engineers (Gambetta and Hertog 2016).[2] The authors of the study propose two possible explanations for why engineers are recruited in such high numbers, that is, unmet professional expectations and personality types. The latter includes a desire to draw rigid boundaries between insiders and outsiders and a need for cognitive closure, which traits they argue, based on survey data, are stronger among engineers and weaker among humanities and social science graduates. Responding to the NFC phenomenon, the Sabaoon rehabilitation program for violent extremists in Pakistan uses an innovative model rooted in sociology and psychology that seeks to increase the integrative complexity (IC) of the students in order to decrease "black and white" thinking and improve critical thinking (Peraçha, Khan, and Savage 2012).

CONCLUSION

The involvement of young men in VE is often aided by a perfect storm of their hormonal tendencies, allied with a particular genetic makeup and an environment that favors simple worldviews over those that are more complex. Governments and communities need to provide a way for young men in particular to positively use their biopsychological energies and tendencies for the betterment of themselves and their communities. Curbing the attraction of violent extremist groups requires creating communities where people can bond with others as part of groups that are respected by one's neighbors, to be esteemed and not derided for what one's difference brings to a society, to be heroic in serving a positive and inclusive dream for all in one's society, to have an education that fosters an appreciation of more complex and nuanced thinking, and to harness hormonal and genetic energies that are evolutionarily developed to be used for the best and not the worst of our societies. A greater appreciation for our genetic and physical predispositions can strengthen our consideration of what we can learn from the emerging field of biopsychology to assist us in stemming the tide of VE.

Chapter 8

Youth and the Security Sector

VE as a Function of Y

Mark Hamilton

Most discussions of violent extremism in academic and policy circles highlight threats from exclusive religious ideologies and an anarchic global vision. We tend to focus on the discourses and messages of movement leaders to interpret the actions of young foot soldiers, with relatively little attention to the broader ecology of violent extremism (VE) discussed in this edited volume.

This chapter explores the predominant role of youth within an ecological vision of VE: *VE as function of Y* (highlighting the role of forgotten youth). It identifies three underlying mechanisms of armed mobilization. The chapter addresses the challenges of youth engaging with the security sector in fragile environments, with attention to a recent UN Security Council Resolution (UNSCR) 2250 on "Youth, Peace and Security." To close, recommendations are offered to improve engagement between marginalized youth communities and actors in the security sector.

WHY YOUTH MATTER

Why do youth matter for VE? In short, youth have been at the forefront of most social and political revolutions (and counterrevolutions) throughout the modern era. In the words of a European analyst, "The young generation is traditionally seen as one of the most dynamic mediums of social change." Youth are caught within a web of political, social, and cultural transitions and often are the demographic sector most open to new possibilities and social upheaval. Youth proved critical in fomenting the Protestant reformation in the 1500s and then solidifying Nazi institutional control centuries later. They led the US civil rights movement, Sandinista *revolución*, and

Palestinian *Intifada*.[1] Young actors filled the streets for the democratic "Color Revolutions" in Europe, served as "child soldiers" in Sierra Leone, and more recently flooded Syria and Iraq to fight with ISIL/Daesh.[2] Youth mobilization is not static or normatively positive or negative. It simply is, and, more often than not, it tends to challenge status quo relations, nationally and globally. As I have written elsewhere:

> Young people are engines of sociopolitical change, if not the main engineers. Power brokers in governments, civil society, and militant networks compete for their support (often in inverse order of priority), and youth have shown the mass power to get wheels turning for diverse vehicles of sociopolitical change.[3]

Viewed as an equation, I propose we start to think of *VE as a function of Y*, or violent extremism (VE) influenced by youth mobilization (Y). In spite of much political rhetoric and policy funding to the contrary, I wonder if understanding the VE message is actually secondary to better understanding young adherents and their motivations. A long history of social movements and armed mobilization betrays a consistent dependence on youth sectors. Perhaps VE "messaging" questions should be reframed: To what extent do young people buy in to a given message? Are they attracted to take up arms for the cause? How does the message tap into their hopes, dreams, beliefs, and fears? What are alternatives available to youth most vulnerable to VE messages?

MECHANISMS OF ARMED MOBILIZATION

As a scholar-practitioner, I have studied and presented in a number of global environments on the mobilization dynamics of armed conflict, particularly the question of how and why young people decide to join (or not join) groups dedicated to organized violence, including the category of "violent extremism" that has dominated headlines.

I have identified and empirically tested three major mechanisms that explain why youth join diverse armed groups. Mobilization tends to be driven by factors of (1) groups and identity, (2) grievance and perceived injustice, and (3) greed and incentives.

The *Groups and Identity* mechanism focuses on community proximity of a given armed group ("network contagion" effect) as well as cultural ripeness for rebellion: the extent to which an armed group's messaging and legitimacy have surpassed that of the governing regime and status quo politics, at least for a targeted cohort of recruits. Focus here is on the group that one belongs to and how community boundaries are drawn.

The *Grievances and Perceived Injustices* mechanism, meanwhile, highlights how communal frustrations and failed expectations are critical drivers

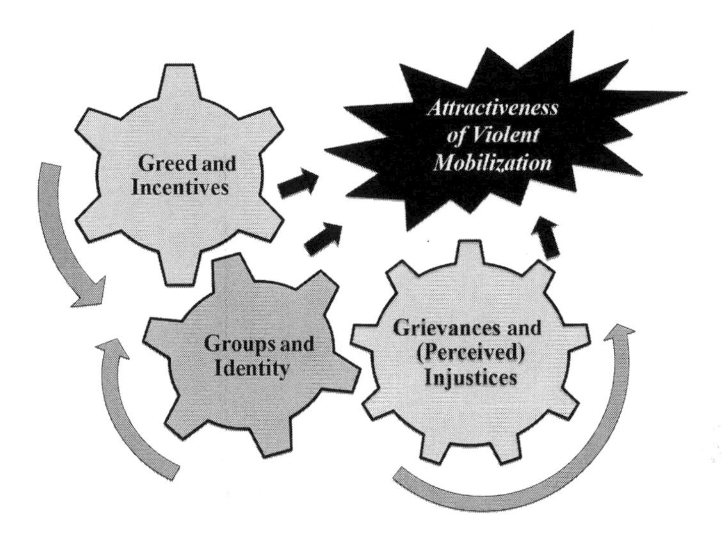

Figure 8.1. Mechanisms of Violent Mobilization

of mobilization. Armed groups leverage shortfalls in political and economic opportunities vis-à-vis community expectations. Gaps of "relative deprivation" may be measured against memories of past experience, the gains of a rival peer/communal group, or even idealized media images of worldly "success." In the realm of grievances, perceptions tend to trump empirical realities. Focus here is on the opportunities one is missing and who receives blame.

Finally, the *Greed and Incentives* mechanism draws from the economics discipline and stresses how incentive structures explain the dynamics of violent mobilization. Armed group recruitment depends on their ability to create favorable incentives for participation (and disincentives for desertion). Rewards, coercion, and capacity building are intertwined as strategies for successful mobilization, with a focus on organizations' competitive advantage and "political capital" to gain new recruits and retain supporters.

In my multimethod research, tracing South Asian and Central American conflicts over an extended time horizon, these three mechanisms have proven interlocking and interdependent (see Figure 8.1).[4] Their relative influence tends to shift across time and space and often varies considerably across conflict cases. These three mechanisms are best considered as part of a broader conflict system rather than as isolated theories.

During situations of crisis, policy responses often target mechanisms in isolation, importing "best practices" from other conflict zones (without appreciating local context nuances or the broader conflict system). These types of responses catalyze unforeseen consequences, including unleashing other "hidden" mechanisms of violent mobilization. A scenario initially driven by economic grievances may, through policy mismanagement, morph into protracted identity-based conflict or perhaps even a greed-driven proxy war.

A key lesson, then, is to move beyond surface-level appearances of mobilization, particularly related to VE: youth in any given community should not be assumed to be inherently violent, aggrieved, or greedy. It is important to conduct conflict analysis to better understand context, the primary and latent drivers of mobilization, and potential responses to mitigate these challenges (including analysis of attendant risks).[5]

YOUTH AND THE SECURITY SECTOR: A CHALLENGE FOR PRODUCTIVE ENGAGEMENT[6]

At the international level, UNSCR 2250—shepherded by Jordan through the most important UN security body in December 2015—offers a new reference point for those advocating for youth development and peacebuilding in zones of civil unrest. As framed in the resolution, youth should be considered as agents of change rather than simply passive recipients. Like UNSCR 1325 on women's peacebuilding roles, though, there is a challenge in moving from paper to practice, from elite global discourse to local realities.

My contribution on this issue is informed by years of work and research with youth communities, juxtaposed by more recent academic engagement with international security actors. I now teach peacebuilding and alternative, multidimensional approaches to security with senior-level police and military officers from throughout the Americas.[7]

The idea of "Youth, Peace and Security" envisioned in UNSCR 2250 is still far from reality. In many countries around the world, especially those ravaged by armed conflict, there is a major disconnect and a palpable distrust between the security sector on the one hand and marginalized youth communities on the other.

Young people are often afraid of encountering police and military actors in their communities. Even in a "peaceful" country like the United States, consider the rise of Black Lives Matter as an activist response to perceived injustice and abuse by police officers and broader security sector. Related groups have organized elsewhere around the globe, some in direct confrontation with authorities and others in the shadows.

Meanwhile, military and police forces do not need to be convinced that youth are critical players in security questions. These security actors are often laser-focused on youth sectors as they confront VE, insurgencies, and transnational crime.

In both cases, among youth communities and actors in the security sector, the tendency is to paint "the other" with a broad brush: all security officials are perceived as a threat or all youth are a threat. Reality, though, is usually more complex.

Youth care deeply about security issues in their communities; after all, they live there! Often young people are at the forefront of efforts to improve social conditions, facilitate dialogue, build their local economy, limit opportunities for crime, and so forth.

Meanwhile, I have found many security actors open to innovations in policies and responses. Based on failures in the field and awareness of an increasingly complex political-strategic environment, military and police leaders now see a bigger picture on inequality, institutional weakness, and the limitations of hard-line/coercive approaches.[8]

Moving forward, I recommend five key focus areas to engage the security gap in implementing UNSCR 2250, with attention to government and civil society–driven initiatives:

1. *Continued advocacy work on youth concerns:* Youth and related civil society organizations should continue to decry abuses, unjust targeting, corruption by security officers, and so on. Even amid other forms of engagement, it is important to maintain advocacy pressure on themes of youth interest.
2. *Community organizing to enhance security:* It is important to recognize that youth contribute to peaceful communities, especially when they receive support from elder partners in public, private, and nonprofit sectors. Consider the interventions of Barrios de Paz in Ecuador (addressing roots of gang mobilization) and Todos Somos Juarez in Mexico (organizing in civil society against a culture of fear and *narco* threats). In the former case, youth involved in the gang life of Guayaquil are now seeing alternative opportunities for social engagement, greater access to jobs/vocational training, and broadened networks of community support. In Mexico, meanwhile, the Todos Somos Juarez campaign leveraged a new type of community action in local civil society (connecting NGO actors, churches, business sector, etc.) to challenge criminal networks and limit societal violence. The focus of both programs—and others like them—is reversing the social exclusion and hopelessness for marginalized and conflict-affected community actors.[9] Around the world, young people have proven adept at catalyzing community change, especially with the benefit of multisector and multigenerational support.
3. *Opening up dialogue between youth and security sectors:* There is promise in seeking "common ground" across sectors via active listening sessions, thematic roundtables, and joint working groups. Nevertheless, it may be difficult to attract participants when there is significant distrust

or preconception of "the other." There is also an implicit power dynamic at play that undervalues youth perspectives in relation to the experience/authority of police and military actors. For this reason, it may be important for dialogue sessions to be convened by bridging organizations with legitimacy to "level the playing field" and let everyone be heard.[10]

4. *Interagency collaboration/whole-of-government focus:* This recommendation involves leveraging the contributions of multiple state offices and authorities, although it requires significant political will from government leaders and commitment to interagency coordination and trust building. Not unlike the community dialogue sessions discussed previously, interagency collaboration requires serious engagement of civil-military tensions and even cross-cultural relations. State agencies often operate from alternative paradigms and compete for budget dollars.
5. *Increased peacebuilding education and training:* Innovation is particularly important in the security sector, with attention to evidence-based models.[11] These include studies of community policing—learning from the work of Brazil's UPP (*Unidade de Polícia Pacificadora*, or Police Pacification Unit), which tried to follow up coercive, militarized interventions in favela communities of Rio de Janeiro to emphasize community presence, build relationships, and facilitate entry of other needed services and state institutions.[12] Security experts should consult other pilot initiatives and work on building practical peace literacy. Helpful resources are available from Saferworld, the Center for the Prevention of Violence (CEPREV) in Nicaragua, and Igarapé institute in Brazil.

I appreciate the joint civil-military curriculum on human security and peacebuilding developed by the Alliance for Peacebuilding, Global Partnership for the Prevention of Armed Conflict, and University of Notre Dame (Schirch 2016). Innovative programs by NGOs like Search for Common Ground in Lebanon and Indonesia on police and counterterrorism engagement are critical steps in the right direction. They create a conceptual frame for dialogue and greater understanding

I also hope the work we do at the Inter-American Defense College (IADC) helps to support regional efforts at security-sector reform, conflict analysis, and peacebuilding engagement. In master's-accredited and multilingual courses, we introduce military and police actors from more than fifteen countries to peacebuilding theories of change, Lederach's 3Ps (people, problem, process), and broad-based stakeholder analysis.[13] As part of the academic program, we challenge officials to design and assess holistic conflict interventions and offer an inclusive vision for positive youth engagement. The goal is to offer a wider aperture for analysis as they return home as senior security officials and security advisors.

CONCLUSION

This chapter has utilized the equation *VE as function of Y* to engage the role of youth in VE, and, more broadly, to explore critical mechanisms that tend to drive armed mobilization in fragile communities. It addresses challenges in young people's relationships with the security sector, with attention to UNSCR 2250 on "Youth, Peace and Security." To close, recommendations are offered to improve the quality of engagement of marginalized young people with military and police actors operating in their communities. Recommendations include improving youth engagement and advocacy, recognizing existing youth organizing on security, opening up brokered dialogue (between youth and security sectors), enhancing interagency and whole-of-government collaboration, and strengthening the role of peacebuilding education and training, particularly in the security sector. Youth matter in questions of VE, and we need to see them as part of a long-term solution and not just lemmings for ideologues.

Chapter 9

Advancing a Gender Perspective and Women's Participation in Preventing and Countering Violent Extremism

Rafia Bhulai

As the field of preventing and countering violent extremism (P/CVE) continues to develop, policy makers and practitioners increasingly recognize the importance of integrating a gender perspective and promoting women's participation in all aspects of P/CVE policy and practice. Critically, a more nuanced understanding of gender dynamics and awareness about the multiple roles of women has evolved—from regarding women and girls primarily as victims to recognizing their agency not only as preventers and peacebuilders but also as sympathizers, supporters, and perpetrators of violent extremist activities. This chapter explores the current discourse on gender and the roles of women in violent extremism and P/CVE and discusses the importance of meaningfully engaging women in prevention efforts.

WHY A GENDER PERSPECTIVE?

Integrating a gender perspective into P/CVE ensures that policy makers and practitioners consider the different experiences, effects, impacts, and needs of women, girls, men, and boys regarding their security, thus allowing for better tailored and hence more impactful interventions. A gender perspective "requires asking more detailed questions about both men and women's access to and control of resources, men and women's legal rights, and sociocultural beliefs and practices about the way women and men are expected to behave—and examining how all of these dynamics may change over time" (Fink, Zeiger, and Bhulai 2016, 37) Applying a gendered lens or analysis should therefore be part and parcel of a tailored approach to P/CVE that considers individual characteristics, such as age, socioeconomic background, motivations, and needs.

In P/CVE, incorporating a gender perspective involves examining how violent extremism affects or impacts women and men differently and accounting for this in P/CVE responses. There is overwhelming evidence of the adverse impact of violence and conflict on women and girls and the harmful practices they endure as a result, especially with regard to politics, health care, and education (Strachan and Haider 2015). Violent extremist groups like the Islamic State of Iraq and the Levant (ISIL), Al-Qaeda and affiliates, Boko Haram, and others exploit existing conflicts and crises around the world to gain new recruits and operational space (ICG 2016). Within these conflict dynamics, widespread acts of sexual and gender-based violence are being committed by violent extremist groups, including as a tactic of war (UNSC 2017a). Safeguarding women from violence and ensuring their rights and freedoms are protected not only help to improve their lives and those of their children but can also enhance societal security more widely (Hudson 2009).

Furthermore, a gender perspective involves considering if and how men and women follow different pathways to joining and supporting violent extremist groups and understanding how gendered narratives and dynamics inform recruitment and mobilization efforts. There is a tendency to view women as "passive or coerced actors or supporters rather than active participants or perpetrators of terrorism and violent extremism" (Fink, Zeiger, and Bhulai 2016, 9). However, history shows many examples of women planning, supporting, and executing terrorist attacks, from Northern Ireland to Sri Lanka.[1] Increasing numbers of women, particularly from Western countries, have journeyed to ISIL-controlled territory, with some reports suggesting that 10–20 percent of the foreign contingent are women (Bergen et al. 2016; van Ginkel and Entenmann 2016). A closer examination of women's motivations for supporting ISIL found that, not unlike their male counterparts, they do so due to, among other things, social or cultural isolation related to their identity, feelings of persecution of the international Muslim community, and anger or sadness over perceived international inaction to this persecution (Hoyle, Bradford, and Frenett 2015; Saltman and Smith 2015).

While the number of female combatants remains low, women can play and have played key roles in designing, attempting or executing attacks, garnering material support, disseminating propaganda, and, in the case of ISIL, migrating to Iraq and Syria to help build the caliphate (Alexander 2016). Critically, violent extremist groups like ISIL also utilize a gender perspective in their recruitment strategies to appeal to women and girls, often underscoring the crucial role of women to their mission or as an alternative means of female empowerment (Tarras-Wahlberg 2016). Indonesia, for instance, is witnessing a "new activism" of women in violent extremist movements, in which they have moved beyond "reproductive and nurturing roles" to recruitment (both online and offline), providing or facilitating material support to families of imprisoned and "martyred" fighters, or planning or perpetrating suicide attacks (IPAC 2017).

The spectrum of women's involvement in violent extremism and P/CVE is also exemplified in the Boko Haram insurgency and responses to it in Nigeria and the Lake Chad area:

> Boko Haram and the subsequent insurgency and counter-insurgency have dramatically changed the lives of thousands of women and girls, casting them voluntarily, by force or for lack of other options into new, evolving roles outside the domestic sphere. Some joined the movement, first as members of a religious community, later as insurgents, while many are targets of its violence. Some fight against it within local vigilante units; others play critical roles in relief and reconciliation, while many displaced by fighting find themselves with new responsibilities. (ICG 2016)

At the same time, a gendered approach to P/CVE also involves the role of men and masculinity and understanding how "gender identity, gender status, and gender rewards intertwine with the choices of men to become engaged in politically motivated violence" (Aoláin 2016). For example, ISIL uses hyper-masculine messages and draws on gendered expectations of men in their traditionally perceived roles as breadwinners and protectors of women and advocate for men's dominance over women, sometimes in the form of systemic rape (Van Leuven, Mazurana, and Gordon 2016). Relatedly, the history of abuse against women by perpetrators of the Boston, Orlando, Nice, and Westminster attacks, for example, raises additional questions about possible linkages between domestic violence and terrorism, a topic that undoubtedly warrants further empirical research.

WOMEN'S PARTICIPATION IN PREVENTING AND COUNTERING VIOLENT EXTREMISM

To ensure a nuanced and gendered perspective in P/CVE, it is important that women's contribution to the sustainability of international peace and security is better understood and aligned with P/CVE policy and practice (UN Women 2015). The need for women's participation and protection as a core component of peace and security efforts was formally institutionalized with the landmark adoption of UN Resolution 1325 (2000) and the seven follow-on resolutions on women, peace, and security (WPS).[2] Through their long-standing work in the field, WPS experts and practitioners offer critical insights, good practices, and lessons learned for strengthening P/CVE policy and programs. Moreover, women and women-led organizations have "unique credibility and authenticity . . . [and] understand the complexity of the challenges and the need for systems-wide, multi-sectoral approaches" to addressing the underlying drivers of violent extremism (WASL 2018).

Over the past five years, significant policy development on gender integration and women in counterterrorism and P/CVE emerged at the international level, particularly at the United Nations and the Global Counter-Terrorism Forum (GCTF). Notably, UN Security Council Resolution 2242 (2015), cosponsored by more than seventy member states, called for greater gender-sensitive research on the drivers of radicalization for women and the impact of counterterrorism activities on women and women's organizations. It also urged member states and the UN system to "ensure the participation and leadership of women and women's organizations in developing strategies" to counter terrorism and violent extremism and called for increased financing for projects related to P/CVE and counterterrorism that address a gender dimension, including women's empowerment. This recognition and accompanying policy frameworks are significant as they provide critical entry points for increased funding and operating space for women and women-led organizations that are often negatively impacted by violent extremism but remain at the front lines in safeguarding their families and communities.

Examples abound of women involved across the board in P/CVE—recognizing early signs of radicalization, intervening to dissuade individuals from supporting or joining violent extremist groups, and rehabilitating and reintegrating violent extremist offenders back into society (Bagenal 2017). Women and women-led organizations work to promote social harmony and community resilience through inter- and intrafaith and cross-cultural dialogues. They facilitate and provide rehabilitative services, such as psychosocial support, counseling, and trauma healing for both victims and violent extremist offenders and ensure their adequate reintegration into society. The role of mothers is also widely explored in P/CVE as one avenue to recognize early behavioral changes in children and provide powerful alternatives to violence due to mothers' unique position within their homes and communities (Schlaffer and Kropiunigg 2016). Nevertheless, caution should be taken in making assumptions or overemphasizing mother's roles as they are not always empowered to spot or respond to early warning signs or alert relevant authorities of their child's behavior, typically due to mistrust or fear among communities and for law enforcement.

OVERCOMING CHALLENGES

Despite significant progress within the past five years, a number of hurdles remain for civil society organizations, experts, and practitioners as they continue to advocate for women's participation in, and a gendered approach to, P/CVE policy and practice.

Gender and women's participation are still typically not a core component within P/CVE strategies and action plans and in their implementation processes. In some cases where gender is included, implementation is limited due to lack of political will, failure to localize the plan with communities or involve civil society, and/or little or no dedicated funding. While some governments claim that gender is mainstreamed throughout their strategies, history has shown that it is necessary to explicitly acknowledge the differential impacts of violence among men, boys, women, and girls to ensure that effective and context-specific solutions are developed and implemented. For instance, an assessment of the impact of the United Kingdom's counterterrorism policy on women and women's organizations found that the first iteration of the *Prevent* strategy contained an explicit focus on women, while the new strategy did not reference women, which led to a narrowing of funding for women's groups and put ethnic minority women at risk as the policy further empowered religious leaders and interfaith networks (Huckerby 2016).

Furthermore, a number of women's organizations working in the areas of peacebuilding, conflict resolution, development, and human rights report being "squeezed" between terrorism and counterterrorism and P/CVE (Huckerby 2011). These groups face constant threats from terrorist and violent extremist groups yet simultaneously face adverse effects of counterterrorism and P/CVE policies on their operations or feel that their work is being instrumentalized or securitized by actors in the security sector. In other instances, due to the very nature of their work (e.g., on gender equality and women's rights), they may be subjected to greater scrutiny and labeled as anti-government, which may lead to certain governments shutting down their operations (Duke Law 2017). Stakeholders interested in engaging women and women's organizations should allow these groups to determine if and how they participate in P/CVE efforts to alleviate unintended consequences.

At the same time, there are many women and women-led organizations already working on P/CVE and related initiatives. Many of these actors have indicated their desire to undertake P/CVE programming but lack the knowledge and organizational and technical capacity to address violent extremism. Nevertheless, some efforts are already underway to support community-led P/CVE efforts (Rosand 2016). Specifically, platforms have been created for information exchange among women-led organizations working in the areas of conflict prevention and peacebuilding, such as the Women's Alliance for Security Leadership (WASL), a network that brings together existing women rights and peace practitioners, organizations, and networks to collaborate in efforts to prevent extremism and promote peace (WASL 2018). Furthermore, the Global Solutions Exchange (GSX) was established as a mechanism to facilitate interactions between governments and independent civil society organizations around the world, such as members of WASL, to advocate for and help sustain a "communities-first, whole-of-society, and gender sensitive approach" to P/CVE (GSX 2017).

A number of structural, cultural, and societal challenges and often a lack of political will have hindered women's meaningful participation and equal representation in the security sector. For example, surveys show that Afghan communities are increasingly supportive of policewomen, but families and communities are still reluctant to encourage or allow female members to serve (Hancock 2013). This can be attributed to a multitude of issues including conservative cultural norms, pervasive sexual harassment and assault within the forces, and lack of adequate facilities, equipment, and child care for female personnel. Yet, research suggests that having more women in the security sector can improve effectiveness of these forces and help to address grievances held by local communities, such as human rights abuses, access marginalized communities, limit the use of excessive force, and more efficiently deescalate tension (Dhamapuri 2013; Lonsaway 2003; Peters 2014). Greater investments are therefore needed in training and technical assistance to support the recruitment, training, and professionalization of women in the security sector.

CONCLUSION

Despite notable efforts to promote gender integration and women's participation in P/CVE, references to gender and women are still often made in connection to sexual violence and as victims of terrorism and violent extremism, with little attention to topics such as women's leadership and autonomy, as well as their voluntary involvement in violence and terrorism. Integrating a gendered perspective in P/CVE requires in-depth analysis of the different experiences, motivations, effects, impacts, and needs of women, girls, men, and boys in both violent extremism and P/CVE policy and programming. This approach helps us better understand why, where, and how the inclusion of women in prevention efforts can be significant, critical, or counterproductive. Failure to recognize gender dynamics and complexities could lead to superficial and ineffective P/CVE policy and interventions.

The impact of conflict on women, the participation of women in terrorism, and roles of women in peacebuilding and security is nothing new. It is critical for P/CVE actors to leverage the vast knowledge, experiences, and lessons from existing practice, such as WPS, development, and human rights, to ensure the meaningful inclusion of women in the design, development, and implementation of P/CVE strategies and programs. Many existing efforts undertaken by women and women-led organizations in these areas offer illustrative examples of how to challenge violent extremists and their narratives. While these efforts may not be explicitly labeled "P/CVE," they demonstrate the valuable roles women can play in these efforts.

Chapter 10

Climate Change and Violent Extremism

Lisa Schirch

An ecological approach to violent extremism requires both a micro and a macro look at the trends that correlate with the increase in violent extremism. The 2014 report on *National Security and the Accelerating Risks of Climate Change*, written by eleven retired US military admirals and generals, concluded that climate change poses a serious threat to America's national security. The report also described how climate change weakens political systems. States unable to provide basic services correlate with social turmoil, the spread of violent extremist beliefs, and acts of terrorism when governments do not have the capacity to cope with large-scale disasters. The report stated that climate change acts as a "threat multiplier" for instability in some of the most volatile regions of the world. Today, the United Nations, European Union, and states around the world include climate change in their security analyses. And many researchers now assert there is a correlation between violent extremism and climate change.

Climate change does not directly cause conflict or terrorism. Climate change is neither necessary nor sufficient for violent extremist beliefs or terrorist acts. This chapter describes how some researchers are correlating climate change with ISIS violent extremism in Syria, the Arab Spring, and Boko Haram. However, climate change in Syria's neighboring states also experienced climate change impacts, but they did not have a correlation with a rise in terrorism. Other countries with significant levels of violent extremism and terrorism do not seem to have a correlation with climate change. To date, there is not enough evidence to conclude that climate change is a main factor or even a contributory factor to war or terrorism. Yet because there is no single factor that causes violent extremism and terrorism, it is important to understand the potential role of climate change and how it may trigger a series of economic, social, and political impacts that affect violent extremism.

Climate change alters complex, dynamic systems in ways that can contribute to conflict and may increase the likelihood of violence (Gleditsch, Nordas, and Salehyan 2007; Smith and Vivekananda 2007). The link between climate change and terrorism requires an ecological understanding. This chapter explores the correlation between climate change and regions that also are experiencing violent extremism and terrorism.

SYSTEMIC IMPACTS OF CLIMATE CHANGE

There is wide scientific consensus that climate change is happening, and it is a result of human activity like burning fossil fuels that release carbon into the atmosphere and meat consumption of animals like cows that produce huge quantities of methane gas. Scientists are uncertain of the pace of projected climate changes, but yearly reports indicate that climate change is occurring far more rapidly than scientists anticipated.

Climate change is causing changes in temperature, making areas colder and hotter than normal. Changing weather patterns alter global rainfall, causing droughts and desertification in some regions and floods and soil erosion in others. In some regions, the desert is spreading two or more miles per year, swallowing large swathes of agricultural land. Melting polar ice caps and glaciers increase river and sea levels. Warming trends increase the range and number of disease-carrying insects, spreading malaria and other deadly infections. Climate change also is increasing the frequency and severity of storms. Climate change impacts on the environment can also affect the economy, social and political systems, and peace and security.

Floods, droughts, severe storms, and insect infestations, for example, cause disruptions in food production. Shortages of water for irrigation and farm animals make agricultural work more difficult. Decrease in food production leads to increase in food prices. Droughts can make farming impossible, causing migration toward urban areas. Melting ice caps increase access to new oil reserves. This leads to decrease in the price of oil, increase in demand for oil, and in turn more carbon released into the atmosphere.

Climate change–induced drought in Central America is increasing the failure rate of family farms and the number of migrants seeking employment in other countries (Leutert 2017). In the Sahel, the spreading desert and droughts are creating new environmental migrants seeking refuge in Europe (Thomas 2013). In Bangladesh, shortages of arable land due to rising sea levels and stronger storms are increasing tensions between ethnic groups (Harris 2014).

As societies attempt to adapt to and mitigate the effects of climate change, social tensions can increase. Environmental migrants move because their former homes are under water, threatened too often by stronger storms, or are no longer livable because of drought. New mega-projects like dams, mass plantings, and irrigation channels designed to help mitigate climate change also alter the environment as well as economic, social, and political systems. In India, for example, entire villages are wiped out by mega dams developed to mitigate against the impacts of climate change–induced droughts and flooding (Doshi 2016).

It is unclear if and how environmental, economic, and social changes impact peace and security. Researchers hypothesize that climate shocks such as heat waves, stronger storms, and more frequent flooding and droughts put demands on governments to respond to public need. When governments are not able to adequately respond, social order begins to break down. While some argue this is especially true in so-called fragile states with governments that have fewer human and financial resources, it is also true of so-called strong states. Hurricane Katrina brought civil chaos despite the fact that the United States is a strong state.

Migration brings opportunities for economic growth with new workforces. But some populations view migrants as a cultural, religious, or economic threat (Gleditsch, Nordas, and Salehyan 2007). Even without significant migration, climate change–induced scarcities can exacerbate local competitions over water and land between ethnic and religious groups. In 2016, a

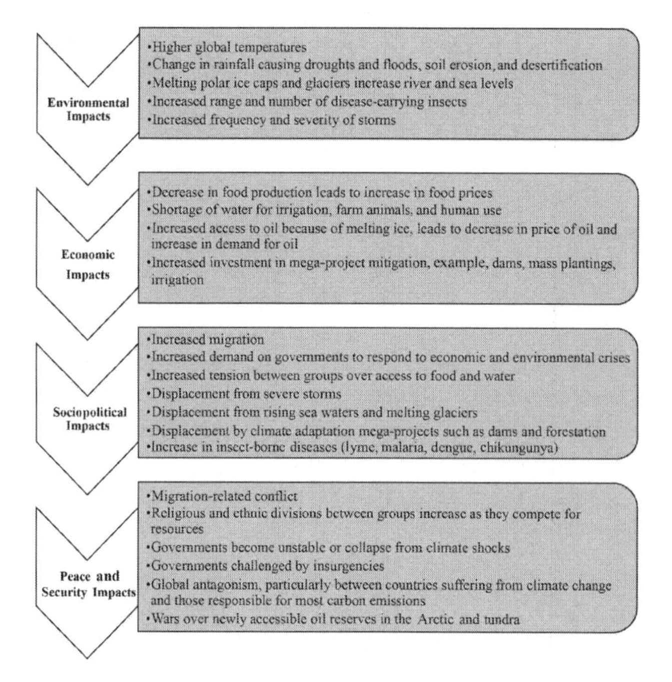

Figure 10.1. Correlations between Climate Change Impacts and Violent Extremism

report commissioned by the German government concluded that climate change is creating increased motivations for nonstate armed groups to control access to natural resources like water as a weapon of war (Nett and Rüttinger 2016). With the scarcity of food and water, violent extremist ideologies spread more quickly, and groups can recruit others by offering alternative livelihoods and access to scarce resources.

There is also a potential for global antagonism, particularly between countries suffering from climate change and those responsible for most carbon emissions. Some argue "climate migrants" should have the right to move to the countries that are producing greenhouse gases. "Millions should be able to go to the United States" (Harris 2014). There is also potential for war at the Arctic poles where melting ice creates a competition for access to oil reserves.

Figure 10.1 illustrates the cascade of changes that occur related to climate change. Environmental impacts lead to economic impacts. Economic impacts lead to social and political impacts. And in combination with all of these changes in the human and environmental ecology, conflict, violent extremism, and terrorism may erupt.

CORRELATIONS BETWEEN CLIMATE CHANGE AND VIOLENT EXTREMISM

Researchers bring a climate change lens to a range of contexts impacted by violent extremism and terrorism. In each of these cases, a complex and interdependent set of environmental, economic, political, and social factors interact and reinforce each other.

Syria

Syria is an oft-cited example of the correlation between climate change and civil war in which nonstate groups use terrorism. The story starts with climate change impacts. Climate change is responsible for weaker winds bringing less moisture from the Mediterranean Sea to agricultural regions in Syria. Weaker winds mean hotter temperatures. More heat increases evaporation in the already drought-affected area. These environmental changes created economic impacts: there were water shortages, so livestock died, and food prices increased. Economic impacts led to social changes; children grew sick and families left their farms and migrated to urban centers. Refugees from the Iraq War, where climate change–induced drought contributed to violent conflict, were already overcrowding cities in Syria. These social migration patterns translated to increased political pressure in Syria's cities where grievances against the state already existed (Kelly et al. 2015).

Arab Spring

Researchers studying the Arab Spring argue that climate change may have impacted the timing of the Arab Spring. There were a variety of interacting factors driving public frustration. Climate change–induced drought in China decreased wheat production. This had the effect of increasing wheat prices globally, including in the Middle East. Public frustration over the rising prices of food paired with political grievances over corruption led to frustration with government and a desire for greater democratic participation. Public protests ousted governments in Egypt and Tunisia (Werrell and Femia 2013).

Nigeria

Climate change–induced drought and desertification in Nigeria as well as the neighboring countries Niger and Chad have displaced over 200,000 farmers. Around Lake Chad, over seventy different ethnic groups compete for the increasingly scarce water. As the population increases, social, economic, and political pressure increases as well. A mix of desperation, unemployment, corrupt governance, abusive security forces, and frustration with international control over oil resources combine to give the Boko Haram insurgency fertile ground to recruit new members (Nett and Rüttinger 2016).

CLIMATE-SENSITIVE AND VIOLENT EXTREMISM–SENSITIVE DEVELOPMENT AND PEACEBUILDING

Climate-sensitive development includes mitigation, management, and adaptation programs to help people adapt locally to shifting climate impacts so that communities are more resilient to climate shocks. This includes creating new ways of reusing and conserving water, new drought-resistant plants, and efforts to reduce greenhouse gases. Sustainable development prevents instability, migration, humanitarian crises, the spread of violent extremist ideologies, and other security threats. Field-driven development solutions to environmental degradation are needed, with a particular emphasis on alternative livelihoods. For example, communities will be far more likely to return to cultivating drought-resistant crops, such as cassava, if there is market demand for them.

"Violent extremism–sensitive" development programs are sensitive to the potential threat of violent extremism. Integrated programming can address the threats of both climate change and violent extremism. This includes natural resource management and environmental governance programs in broader peacebuilding and peace and security operations.

Multitrack diplomatic efforts and mechanisms are needed for addressing environment-related tensions. Climate change presents an opportunity for increased multilateral cooperation on common threats. The Madrid Peace Process for the Middle East used water, migration, and other environmental issues to foster multilateral engagement between Israel and regional states. India, Pakistan, and China have cooperated on seismic disaster preparedness. NATO promoted dialogue and cooperation among former East Bloc countries on environmental issues.

Diplomatic efforts for multilateral engagement, cooperation, and tension reduction on common threats related to climate change. Dialogue and confidence-building platforms between diverse stakeholders can develop mechanisms for sharing natural resources and responding jointly to environmental threats. Working together, states and civil society can create a cost-effective infrastructure for prevention of climate-related conflict and violent extremism at the regional, national, and district levels, particularly in states susceptible to climate-related instability.

Section III

THE ECOLOGY OF COUNTERTERRORISM

Section III

Introduction

This section explores the opportunities and challenges of counterterrorism to prevent terrorism and foster human security.

In chapter 11, "Principles of Effective Counterterrorism," Alistair Millar offers best practices for counterterrorism that supports, rather than undermines, human rights. In chapter 12, "Military Interventions and Violent Extremism," Sverre Lodgaard identifies some of the problems with the war on terror as it has been implemented in the Middle East.

Next David Cortright defines the scope of the challenges of counterterrorism in the broader, long-term efforts in chapter 13, "The Role of Civil Society in Preventing Violent Extremism." Lena Slachmuijlder then offers a positive set of principles for how civil society organizations can engage in principled and constructive ways with state counterterrorism efforts in chapter 14, "Six Principles for Enabling State Responses."

The next three chapters look at the harmful impact counterterrorism legal frameworks have on the field of peacebuilding. In chapter 15, "Legal Restrictions and Violent Extremism," Kay Guinane offers an analysis of the specific legal restrictions imposed by counterterrorism laws on US civil society and the impacts on humanitarian, development, and peacebuilding NGOs. Next, the UK-based researchers Teresa Dumasy and Sophie Haspeslagh go into further detail on the impact of counterterrorism restrictions on peacebuilding organizations in their chapter 16, "The Impact of Terrorist Listing on Peacebuilding Organizations."

Chapter 11

Principles of Effective Counterterrorism

Alistair Millar

In aftermath of the 9/11 attacks in 2001, the United States actively pursued a costly Global War on Terrorism (GWOT), which placed too much emphasis on the military and was ill suited to address complex social and political problems that are at the core of violent extremism and terrorism. Indeed, in less than three years, the GWOT had become so untenable that even its most ardent proponents within the US government began to openly question its utility. It was clear that a more principled approach—to not only counter but also *prevent* terrorism—was needed. The changing nature of attacks and the recruitment methods used by terrorist organizations have forced counterterrorism experts and officials to reconsider their approach to a threat that is decentralized and becoming increasingly difficult to monitor and interdict. There is a growing realization that although kinetic military action and enhanced border security measures are still necessary, they are insufficient for addressing a threat that is often homegrown and does not require direct contact or training from members of a terrorist organization.

What had previously been a government and security-dominated conversation now includes a broader range of nongovernmental partners, such as those with expertise in relevant issues including education, development, media and strategic communications, youth engagement, and peacebuilding.

From 2004 until July 2017, I served as the executive director of the Global Center on Cooperative Security, a nonprofit organization that does research, makes policy recommendations, and builds the capacity of practitioners from governments and nongovernmental entities to improve and sustain security from terrorism and other transnational threats. When I founded the organization, we were named the Center on Global Counterterrorism Cooperation.

In 2014, we decided to rebrand and change our name to the Global Center on Cooperative Security to better reflect our organization's ability to go beyond the limited scope of counterterrorism toward a more inclusive, comprehensive goal of promoting cooperative security.

For the first decade having the term "counterterrorism" in our name was accurate and appropriate. It enabled us to participate in policy debates and play an integral role in reshaping tactical responses to terrorism into a more considered, strategic approach drawing from well-established social and economic development practice and policy. However, the term "counterterrorism" is no longer reflective of the diverse, cross-cutting, and multidimensional nature of our work. As our research, analysis, and programs tend toward approaches to security that are more integrative horizontally and vertically, the "counterterrorism" label is increasingly outdated. If we conceived of our initial mission in negative terms—to prevent and suppress terrorism—we believed it timely in 2014 to reframe our goal for the future in positive terms—to achieve collective security.

Former UN secretary-general Kofi Annan, in the executive summary of his report *In Larger Freedom: Towards Security, Development and Human Rights for All*, presented in advance of the Millennium Summit, asserted that

> [i]n a world of inter-connected threats and opportunities, it is in each country's self-interest that all of these challenges are addressed effectively. Hence, the cause of larger freedom can only be advanced by broad, deep and sustained global cooperation among States. The world needs strong and capable States, effective partnerships with civil society and the private sector, and agile and effective regional and global intergovernmental institutions to mobilize and coordinate collective action. (Annan 2005)

The phrase "cooperative security" was widely used during the Cold War in the development of a pan-European security architecture that introduced innovative confidence-building measures in the aftermath of two devastating world wars. The concept of cooperative security endures in today's world, which has become increasingly interconnected in all aspects—economic, social, and political. In this new global context, transnational terrorist and other violent or criminal groups have an expanded reach, which can only be halted, or at least significantly reduced, with coordinated and inclusive global efforts across multiple levels of engagement. This chapter briefly assesses how the principles of counterterrorism that we have advocated over the years have actually taken root in practice, with some examples from the United Nations' efforts at the multilateral level.

The Global Center was established to promote a more sustainable approach to countering terrorism by working with governments, international and regional organizations, and nongovernmental actors, such as civil society groups and survivors of terrorist violence. Our field research has taken place in Africa, the Americas, Asia, Europe, and Oceana.[1] We looked at what drives support for terrorism, and, counter to earlier conventional wisdom and contrary to what is often said by governments and repeated in the media, the literature on the subject shows that it is generally not religion, ideology, or the Internet that attracts would-be violent extremists. Rather, military or police abuses of one's own population are among the single-largest drivers of terrorist recruitment. Corruption and the biased delivery of public services that erodes the trust between the government and its citizens are also among the key sources of grievance within communities that terrorist propaganda exploits. The US Department of State's research from 2016 confirms this (Robinson 2016). In study after study, youth alienation and marginalization and a lack of trust between local authorities and communities have been found to fuel terrorist violence (Mercy Corps 2016).

CORE PRINCIPLES

Counterterrorism policy also requires a holistic effort to assess, prevent, deter, protect, and counter the problem. Based on the literature on this subject and interactions with our local partners, it is clear that there is a need for a more principled approach to countering terrorism. For the purpose of this chapter, I offer the following four principles, which are essential for guiding policy makers and practitioners:

1. *Holistic:* Bring together a wide array of essential component parts so that they are coherent and guided by a clear strategic vision outlining efforts to prevent as well as counter violent extremism over the near, medium, and long term with sufficient resources to sustain those efforts. As Paul Pillar noted in his seminal work on counterterrorism and American foreign policy, "no single approach makes an effective policy" (Pillar 2003). Using the example of highway safety policy, Pillar highlights the need for an array of well-coordinated policies—ranging from speed limits, seat belt laws, and car safety standards to police patrols and road maintenance—as necessary elements of good policy.
2. *Inclusive* and *multidisciplinary:* Actively involve governmental and nongovernmental actors with practical expertise on issues that are not confined to traditional counterterrorism—the military, law enforcement, and intelligence fields—that are too limited to address the complex phenomenon of violent extremism on their own. A wide array of other critically important actors also has to be involved including anthropologists, psychologists, educators, experts on delivering development aid, community leaders, communications specialists, community health workers, and

others, and they have to be diverse to bring perspectives that reflect and understand gender and age as well as cultural, historical, and other local perspectives.

3. *Multilateral:* Cooperation and action at the global and regional level are necessary to sustain international support and ensure that norms and strategic aims developed at the United Nations are taken forward at the local level and that cooperation occurs across borders where terrorists increasingly operate (in person and online).
4. *Civilian-led while promoting and protecting human rights and the rule of law:* Put procedures in place, and implement those procedures to ensure that the state is not abusing its power in the name of countering terrorism and undermining efforts to build trust with communities who are critical to prevention efforts. Strict adherence to this last point in particular is what distinguishes law-abiding citizens and their leadership from terrorists, who have no respect for criminal justice, the rule of law, and other essential elements of human rights norms and good governance.

The following section examines the extent to which these principles are being followed in practice by the United Nations and its member states.

THE UNITED NATIONS

Taking proactive steps to help the international community create and implement effective counterterrorism policies in accordance with the other aforementioned principles, we worked with the United Nations and many member states to contribute to the development of the UN Global Counter-Terrorism Strategy in 2006, which has become a blueprint for regions and states when developing their own integrated, whole-of-government actions to prevent and respond to terrorism. In 2008, we implemented an international convening process on a regional basis with dozens of governments to enhance the capacity of states to address terrorism without an undue reliance on military force. That process eventually led to the development in 2011 of the Global Counterterrorism Forum (GCTF), an intergovernmental body devoted to supporting civilian capacity-building initiatives under the normative framework of the strategy.

Through our work with policy makers and experts all over the world, we have developed a deeper understanding of contemporary terrorism as a dynamic and diffuse threat. Some terrorists exploit structural conditions, including inadequate development, poor governance, and other long-standing socioeconomic grievances, to garner support and attract recruits. Other terrorists emerge spontaneously, whether alone or in small groups, motivated by extremist ideas. The lines among criminality, conflict, and terrorism are increasingly blurred, making it difficult to develop responses to terrorism in isolation from other security and development threats. Greater attention is being focused today on the prevention of violent extremism, which requires integrated approaches that link security with development, good governance, and greater international cooperation.

Multilateral counterterrorism efforts have evolved over the past twenty years, but it has not been a straight, upward trajectory of continual progress. The United Nations, for example, has achieved some enduring and positive results on issues related to countering terrorism, but as I will note at the end of this chapter, there have also been some serious setbacks that have strayed from a principled, rule-of-law based, whole-of-society approach to the problem.

Over the past decade, my colleagues and I have regularly conducted interviews with UN and government officials as well as civil society and other experts well placed to take the pulse of the United Nations' efforts and offer reflections on the United Nations' counterterrorism program on what has worked and what needs to be improved.

The United Nations' norm-setting authority has provided a valuable international legal framework for combating terrorism—via the adoption of terrorism-related treaties adopted by the General Assembly and UN agencies and a number of legally binding resolutions adopted by the Security Council. However, the United Nations, driven by its member states' interests, has largely failed to establish a treaty-monitoring mechanism, similar to what is common in the human rights field, to monitor and/or put political pressure on states to join and implement them.

Furthermore, the defining feature of the United Nations' counterterrorism effort has been its reactive nature, adopting declarations or treaties or establishing committees or programs in response to individual attacks, without developing a coherent and coordinated response. Thus, even when states consented to be bound by the obligations contained in the treaties, the General Assembly had limited means to put political pressure on them to actually implement the obligations. Neither the General Assembly nor any other part of the United Nations offered technical assistance to help states draft the necessary laws to join and implement the treaties. Prior to September 11, 2001, therefore, it was not surprising that most states had not signed on to these instruments and that many had failed to implement them.

The General Assembly's inability to reach agreement on a definition of terrorism after nearly thirty-five years of discussions in one form or another—with the unfortunate continuing relevance of the phrase "one man's terrorist is another man's freedom fighter"—has limited the impact of its counterterrorism efforts and remains a stumbling block.

Nevertheless, in spite of these setbacks, by 2005 there was a positive shift toward "prevention" with more emphasis on soft power rather than hard power and civilian rather than military efforts, which makes the UN role in generating and leveraging political legitimacy all the more relevant and appropriate.

The unanimous adoption of the UN Global Counter-Terrorism Strategy by the General Assembly in September 2006 presented a plan that on paper at least is consistent with all four of the principles I outlined earlier in this chapter. The strategy calls for a holistic and inclusive approach to counter-terrorism. It includes not just law enforcement and other security-related preventive measures, which have been the Security Council's focus since September 2001, but also gives priority attention to addressing underlying conditions conducive to the spread of terrorism, such as poverty, lack of good governance, and social and economic marginalization. This gives it broader appeal than the Security Council's counterterrorism program, which has generally focused on law enforcement and other security-related issues. The strategy is also clear about the imperative for respecting human rights and promoting the rule of law across every element of the document and throughout its implementation. One of the strategy's achievements is that for the first time the United Nations' global membership has agreed that addressing conditions conducive to the spread of terrorism is an essential part of an effective and comprehensive strategy to combat and prevent terrorism. By elaborating a broad range of counterterrorism measures, underpinned by the commitment to uphold the rule of law and human rights, the strategy reinforces what many terrorism experts have long felt, namely, that an effective counterterrorism strategy must combine preventive measures with efforts to address both real and perceived grievances and underlying social, economic, and political conditions.

Part of the strategy's significance lies in the fact that it was adopted as an "instrument of consensus" on an issue where consensus has been difficult to achieve at the global level. Although it does not add anything not already contained in existing UN counterterrorism resolutions, norms, and measures, the strategy pulled them together into a single, coherent, and universally adopted framework. By focusing on the "softer," longer-term side of counter-terrorism, the strategy offered states a framework through which to promote a more holistic response to the threat. It represents a conceptual shift away from a primarily law enforcement/military approach to this "softer," more holistic one, which might be characterized as a "human security" approach to counterterrorism. By doing so and by reflecting the views of the UN General Assembly (and its universal membership), the strategy has helped move the counterterrorism discourse at the United Nations closer to regional and national perspectives. If this conceptual shift is going to succeed in practice, however, states, as well as donors, need to reflect this change of emphasis in their policies. Donors and the United Nations need to emphasize the development pillar of the strategy and in particular target disaffected and marginalized groups and others who are potentially vulnerable to recruitment by violent extremists.

While positive on the whole, the increasingly broad scope of the United Nations' counterterrorism programs and initiatives also resulted in the unintended negative consequences of overlapping mandates, turf battles, and duplication of work. Information sharing and other forms of cooperation between and among over thirty UN entities that claim to be working in this field have been inadequate and often redundant, which has inhibited the overall contribution. In conducting research for our report issued ten years after the 9/11 attacks, we heard in our interviews "that the United Nations can do more to provide political leadership to guide and encourage international cooperation against terrorism." We then offered a set of recommendations for improving the United Nations' architecture with the appointment at a minimum of an overall coordinator appointed by the UN secretary-general to oversee this broad effort and to ensure that the United Nations is fit for the purpose to facilitate the implementation of a holistic approach to prevent and counter violent extremism.

FROM PAPER TO IMPLEMENTATION?

In February 2017, the UN General Assembly finally considered this long-overdue proposal to establish a UN coordinator, but it proved to be more of a setback than a step forward. It ended up with too much focus on traditional counterterrorism with scant mention of preventing violent extremism. It thus creates the impression that the United Nations has not evolved according to the research and practical experience that has been amassed over the past fifteen years around preventing violent extremism (PVE) and its close corollary, countering violent extremism. This problem is likely to be further exacerbated because the coordinator appointment has been given to a Russian who comes from a country with a track record of policies that are inconsistent with the values outlined in the strategy and former secretary-general Ban Ki-moon's 2016 PVE "Plan of Action," which sought to amplify prevention but was unable to sustain the level of support that the strategy received ten years earlier (Ki-moon 2015). I am concerned that this will lead to further diminished respect for fundamental human rights and cooperation with civil society actors and communities when it comes to tackling violent extremism.

The responsibilities for the new under-secretary-general should reflect more balance and emphasis across all four pillars of the strategy and be mindful of the strategic message they send. They need to reflect and promote a whole-of-society approach to countering terrorism and extremism and draw on the expertise of the United Nations on a wide variety of issues, including development and education.

Without a coherent plan that ensures that all of the elements of the strategy—including addressing underlying conditions, taking serious steps to addressing grievances, and promoting and protecting human rights—it is unlikely that a principled approach to countering terrorism will take shape where it matters most: on the ground at the national and local levels.

In essence the United Nations has done a good job of articulating a counterterrorism strategy that is based on the fundamental principles noted at the beginning of this chapter, but the follow-through, in terms of implementation, has been limited at best.

Throughout its seventy-year history, the United Nations has been working on development, education, conflict prevention, and other fields that are now acknowledged as essential ingredients for preventing as well as countering violent extremism. Unfortunately, in practice there are few who are willing to resist political pressure to get involved in near-term crisis situations that distract from attaining longer-term goals. This approach is at the heart of the comprehensive approach outlined in the strategy and reflected in the ideas set out in the PVE "Plan of Action." It is not only essential to the success of multilateral counterterrorism and P/CVE efforts but also to ensuring the relevance and credibility of the world body as states and citizens grapple with the need to preserve international peace and security, promote inclusive and tolerant societies, and reaffirm their commitment to the norms outlined in the UN Charter.

The benefits of the United Nations remain clear when it can help to garner consensus around issues and develop useful norms, but the lack of coherence, internal turf battles, opacity of process, and inability to translate words into action are not only making it difficult for a growing number of member states to invest their time and effort into the United Nations' counterterrorism program but also too easy for the member states to favor much less principled counterterrorism in practice in their own countries.

Some countries have made an effort to amplify the message the United Nations preaches in the strategy. For example, the Obama administration undertook a concerted effort to promote a principled approach to preventing violent extremism. This included a White House summit on the issue in 2015, which brought leaders from all over the world together to extol the virtues of reaching out to communities and working alongside development experts and other nontraditional actors on prevention (White House 2015). President Obama also followed up by leading sessions with his counterparts at the United Nations. This helped to encourage other presidents and prime ministers to include references to the need for prevention in their speeches. The US Department of State also followed up with a comprehensive "Plan of Action" presenting a set of recommendations for improving research on and policies for engaging youth and women and others at the community level (U.S. State Department 2015). With the change in administration in the United States, it seems unlikely that any of the ideas presented at the 2015 summit and its follow-on documents will be implemented.

WHAT ARE THE PROBLEMS?

There are numerous obstacles to member state implementation of the UN Global Counter-Terrorism Strategy. My colleague, Eric Rosand, and I examined this question in an article for *Just Security* (Millar and Rosand 2016). We offered the following recommendations to address the disconnect between rhetoric and reality when it comes to implementing a principled strategic approach to the problem of violent extremism. First, we identified the ongoing problems:

1. *Lack of resources:* The lion's share of financial support is still channeled to the military and intelligence, while there is *ad hoc* and insufficient funding and other resources from the public and private sectors to support community-level P/CVE programs.
2. *What works and what does not?* A lack of knowledge of "what works" to prevent and counter violent extremism is a fundamental problem, leading not only to underfunding but also to inefficient use of finite resources, and potentially counterproductive interventions to address violent extremism built on perceived wisdom and politicized assumptions.
3. *Too many stakeholders, too little coordination:* Insufficient coordination and collaboration among the diversity of key stakeholders that includes traditional security and development actors, national and municipal government officials, as well as civil society, whether small community-based organizations or large international NGOs.
4. *An unmet need for innovation and experimentation:* A reluctance among donors to embrace the kind of innovation and experimentation needed to support locally owned solutions.
5. *Where's the trust?* Lingering trust deficits between governments, in particular, the police, and the relevant communities, which can generate grievances that can make individuals more susceptible to violent extremism recruitment.
6. *Limited vertical and horizontal cooperation:* Continued insistence of too many national governments to view national security issues like violent extremism—which require locally driven solutions—as being the exclusive policy domain of the capital or even single ministries (e.g., Interior).

7. *It's not just the message:* There is a tendency to place a disproportionate emphasis within the wider P/CVE world on efforts to counter the message being promoted by ISIL and other violent extremist groups, without a commensurate focus on changing behaviors and structural conditions, or offering alternative courses of action for those who are being recruited or mobilized.
8. *An international architecture that's fit for purpose:* The international architecture for addressing terrorism and violent extremism continues to be driven by the interests and needs of national governments and has yet to heed calls to be more inclusive of civil society and other subnational actors. These stakeholders are the ones most likely to notice the early signs of radicalization and be most effective in steering an individual away from violence, including by developing programs that offer alternatives to alienated youth, for example, (Rosand 2016).
9. *Balancing tactical, short-term counterterrorism priorities with strategic, medium to long-term P/CVE objectives:* Too many national governments continue to double-down on authoritarian policies and practices (often with direct or indirect support from partners in the West). These are geared to protecting the regime and the status quo—and ultimately do more in the long run to create grievances that can spur radicalization to violence—rather than providing security and liberty to the people they are meant to serve.

WHAT NEEDS TO BE DONE?

Although the impediments to achieving a more principled approach to countering terrorism are manifold, they are not insurmountable. Here are a number of steps that are required to overcome these obstacles.

1. *Promoting a more dynamic and complete set of policies and programs, and involving a more diverse set of actors, in particular at the local level, to address the complex nature of the threat:* National P/CVE strategies and action plans that embody the inclusive, "whole of society" approach championed during the White House CVE Summit and enshrined in the UN "Plan of Action" should be developed and properly resourced. These strategies must include a role for local authorities, as well as public health, mental health or social services providers; parents; researchers; teachers; businesses; or women, religious, and youth leaders.
2. *Leveraging (although not co-opting and certainly not securitizing) a wide array of efforts—including development, peacebuilding, good*

governance, gender equality, and public health—that can contribute to P/CVE by helping to address some of the grievances that fuel the spread of violent extremism and build resilience among core stakeholders.

3. *Recognizing that how governments treat their citizens really matters when it comes to preventing and countering violent extremism and terrorism:* In many respects, the broader aim of strengthening the relationship between the state and its citizens and building trust between all levels of government and local communities lies at the heart of the P/CVE agenda. More urgent attention is therefore required to address the issues that damage the government–citizen relationship and are among the most prevalent drivers of violent extremism: marginalization and alienation, poor governance, and state-sponsored violence.
4. *Deepening investments in P/CVE from governments, the private sector, and private philanthropy:* Despite the increasing rhetorical importance that leaders from around the globe now attach to P/CVE, specific programming and funding for these efforts continue to lag. The lion's share of counterterrorism resources continues to be directed to support short-term, tactical military efforts.
5. *Making the strategic case for P/CVE:* Political leaders and national security professionals must do more to refute the false dichotomy between "hard" and "soft" measures and to make the strategic case for a more nuanced approach to P/CVE to national parliaments and at all levels of society, as part of a spectrum of counterterrorism approaches that include a strong prevention element.

CONCLUSION

This brief chapter has reflected on the work that my organization has done over the past fifteen years to identify the fundamental principles of effective counterterrorism. Focusing on the work of the United Nations at the multilateral level, it is clear that a lot of progress has been made when it comes to articulating a coherent strategy for preventing as well as countering the threat of terrorism in a manner that is in keeping with all of the four core principles that I identified. The UN Global Counter-Terrorism Strategy is holistic. It promotes inclusivity, including ascribing roles for civil society. As a creation of the United Nations, the strategy is of course multilateral. And last, but most certainly not least, the strategy is abundantly clear about the importance of promoting and protecting the rule of law and human rights when it comes to implementation. Unfortunately, there has been much less progress when translating the strategy from a paper document into action on the ground. The obstacles are clear, but they are not insurmountable. The steps outlined earlier can and should be taken to implement and sustain a principled approach to preventing and countering violent extremism. It will require leadership at the United Nations and within its member states to more effectively meet this immense challenge to international peace and security.

Chapter 12

Overcoming Violent Extremism in the Middle East

Lessons from the Arab Spring

Sverre Lodgaard

Violent extremism (VE) thrives in failed states, where national governance has ceased to exist. The Middle East has many of them: Iraq, Syria, Yemen, Libya, and partly Egypt (Sinai). In Iraq and Libya, VE emerged on the ashes of foreign intervention. In Syria and Yemen, VE has been prolonged and enhanced by foreign intervention. In Sinai, VE drew weapons and inspiration from the region's other conflicts to become the strongest branch of Islamic State outside Syria and Iraq.

In all of these cases, VE gained strength by liaising with groups that had something to revenge: in Iraq, with Sunni members of Saddam's dissolved army and Ba'th Party; in Syria, with majority Sunnis who had been hard hit by father and son Assad's repressive and violent rule; and in Libya, with Qaddafi loyalists in his home city Sirte and elsewhere. In Sinai, Islamic State is piggybacking on the long-standing conflict between the Bedouins and the government in Cairo. In Yemen, Al-Qaeda on the Arab Peninsula (AQAP) has advanced in the turmoil of civil war and in the shadow of the fight between Houthis and Saudi interventionists. Nowhere is AQAP stronger than in Yemen. If Raqqa (Syria) is the headquarters of the IS, Makulla (Yemen) is that of AQAP.

In order to come to grips with VE, developing well-functioning states is therefore of the essence. This calls for a wide variety of efforts by diverse actors in government and civil society at the community, national, and international levels. Since no two cases are alike, they must be tailored to each specific case. The central task in all of them, however, is improving *human security*, defined as freedom from fear, mainly—but not only—of physical violence. The individual is the unit of account. In operational terms it means the rule of law, public order, and the peaceful management of conflict. A time dimension must be added: a sense of security, strong enough and long enough for development aid projects, foreign investments, socioeconomic development, and other nation-building efforts to take place (Lodgaard 2004).

This chapter[1] examines one slice of the problem: the role of external powers. What did external powers—the United States and the European Union (EU)—do or not do during the Arab Spring to help Egypt, Libya, and Tunisia build better functioning and more stable political systems? The Arab Spring seemed to offer ample scope for development of more inclusive and more robust governance, but only Tunisia developed for better. What can we learn from the failures and from the Tunisian success?

THE ROLE OF THE UNITED STATES AND THE EUROPEAN UNION

Experience shows that when strong national and regional interests work against the objectives of extra-regional powers, there is not much they can achieve—except to destroy states by the use of force, leaving societies in shambles. In Iraq and Libya, the only upside of the military interventions was the removal of the tyrannical top leadership. In Afghanistan, the jury is still out; but will the objectives—whatever they were, be it fighting the Taliban, stabilizing the country, introducing democratic practice, promoting women's rights or various other worthy ideas—be achieved? The Western world has worked for a two-state solution to the Israeli-Palestinian problem—but, except for a few months under Prime Minister Rabin's leadership, Israeli settlements have continued to expand. Today, developments on the ground point toward a one-state outcome with different rights for different groups of people. US secretaries of state have gone to Damascus for meetings with Assad, father and son, and returned empty-handed. Sanctions and military threats did not stop the Iranian nuclear program—the sanctions worked as intended only when realistic prospects for lifting them emerged, with the right constellation of governments in Washington and in Teheran that appeared in mid-2013.

When the Arab Spring erupted, the United States and the EU acted on the basis of their own values and experiences, as opposed to those of the countries in question: it does not seem to have occurred to any of them that there was anything wrong in doing that. The experiences and preferences of the countries in question were largely ignored. The European Union announced new institutional arrangements and additional funds to support political reform in the Mediterranean neighborhood. Different from the United States, the EU had no military-to-military relations to draw on: its military leg is not sufficiently well established to nurture such bonds. Its main foreign policy tools are economic, the Union being the world's largest trading bloc by far.

But, as with the United States, there was an implicit assumption that the more the neighboring countries on the other side of the Mediterranean could resemble the EU, economically and politically, the better it would be for all parties. Here, Americans and European suffered from the same blind spot.

Egypt

Ever since independence in 1952, Egypt has been ruled by the military. In January 2011, Mubarak was sacrificed, but the Supreme Council of the Armed Forces (SCAF) kept the reigns. The young, liberal activists who spearheaded the revolution were soon marginalized by the military and the Muslim Brotherhood, who won the parliamentary elections in 2011/2012 and the first-ever presidential elections in June 2012. With hindsight, however, it is clear that the Egyptian military never abdicated. They simply waited for an opportunity to hit back at the Brotherhood and retrieve the reins.

Egypt's new general-*cum*-president, al-Sisi, took repression to new heights. He did not distinguish between jihadists and Brotherhood supporters—they were all terrorists. Jihadist activities increased, primarily in Sinai, where the government lost control but in other parts of the country as well.

The United States and Egypt

The democracy promotion of U.S. NGOs and the State Department, which funded them, was well intended but conducted in a manner that made it vulnerable. The NGOs pushed for democracy based on the rule of law—but in Egypt, they themselves disregarded local laws that regulated the activities of foreign organizations. They did not register in Egypt, they transferred money illegally, and they recruited locals without work permission. They probably felt they had no better choice, but they obviously failed to understand the situation well enough to take care. At the end of 2011, SCAF put an end to their activities.

The NGOs helped to move Egypt out of the Mubarak era—but, by overlooking the strength of religious movements, they opened the door to the only organized contender for power: the Muslim Brotherhood and their Salafi allies, who had no interest in promoting Western-style democracy. The National Democratic Institute (NDI), the International Republican Institute (IRI), the Middle East Partnership Initiative (MEPI), the Project on Middle East Democracy (POMED), and other NGOs acted in good faith, but their strategies on the ground were unconvincing.

NGOs and foreign governments operating in South Africa under the apartheid regime circumvented national regulations too, transferring money and working with locals illegally. However, in South Africa the foreign agents cooperated with the African National Congress (ANC), the majority movement of the country, whereas in Egypt the secular youth who spearheaded the uprising were a small minority and a rather disorganized one at that. Moreover, the foreign anti-apartheid activists probably had a better understanding of the landscape in which they were operating. Above all, the ANC's conception of democracy was rather similar to the Western one. The Brotherhood's was not.

The Pentagon also did much to shape the US footprint in Egypt. It had well-established relations with the Egyptian military dating back to the Camp David Accords of 1979. The Pentagon is much better funded than the State Department; it is well represented at US embassies; its military representatives are trained independently of the State Department, and they report to their military superiors. They promote US interests as seen by the military establishment.

Since Egypt had two main contenders for power—the Brotherhood and the SCAF—it made sense, from the point of view of national interests, to have relations with both of them, and the American political system naturally allowed it to do so and hedge its bets. The system was projected onto the Egyptian political landscape, not by design—that was unnecessary—and apparently without much coordination. The two streams of activity were incompatible, however, and tended to annul each other. After a while, Egyptian leaders and activists of all walks of political life had misgivings and were left with the feeling that the United States could not be trusted.

The European Union and Egypt

In their initial responses to the Egyptian uprising, EU officials declared their support for the democratic aspirations of the Egyptian people, warned against the use of force, and offered to engage in dialogue aimed at achieving a peaceful transition to democracy. The EU launched three new policy initiatives: the Partnership for Democracy and Shared Prosperity in the Southern Mediterranean (March 2011); the New Response to a Changing Neighbourhood (May 2011); and Support for Partnership, Reforms and Inclusive Growth (SPRING) (September 2011). None of these aimed at intervening directly in Egyptian affairs. That would have drawn criticism from the Mediterranean partners, and it would have been contrary to the ethos of democratic legitimacy.

So, the EU landed on the side of caution, consistent with its own norms and institutional setup. The cross-cutting principle was "more for more": the more democratic reform, the more economic support. The Partnership program stressed the importance of free and fair elections and pledged support for civil society, small and medium enterprises, and job creation. The SPRING program also emphasized reducing internal social and economic disparities.

Initially, the EU had difficulties connecting with the new contenders for power, loath to take sides in what was supposed to be a transition to democracy. Ideologically, it sided with the secular moderates but moved to recognize the Brotherhood victories in the first elections. However, to make up for its previous indulgence of dictators, Union support was made more conditional than in the past, thereby punishing the newcomers for the sins of their predecessors.

Another problem, inherent in the EU institutional setup, was the slow disbursement of funds. Whereas wealthy Arab states gave money immediately, the EU would not allow unaccountable disbursements to any regime. Prompt delivery of economic support at critical moments can do much to promote desired change, even if the amounts are modest, but here the EU was ill equipped. As events unfolded fast and interlocutors changed quickly, these institutional shortcomings became particularly noticeable. As with many other donors, the EU's economic support fell short of the commitments that had been undertaken.

Libya

The United States and Libya

On February 26, 2011, when violence had erupted, the UN Security Council imposed sanctions on members of the Qaddafi regime. On March 17, the council adopted Resolution 1973, which imposed a no-fly zone over Libya and allowed for the use of force to protect civilians. Two days later, the air attacks on the regime's military assets began. The United States took the lead because nobody else was ready to but was happy to leave the command to NATO and the Europeans a little later and careful not to put new boots into combat. The Obama administration was set to lower the US military profile in the region. Sometimes it was nevertheless drawn back into conflict—the world being what it is and the United States being the number one military power—perhaps against its will.

The EU and Libya

On February 28, the EU approved a package of sanctions against Qaddafi and his closest advisors, including an arms embargo and bans on travel to the EU. Beyond this, there was no consensus on what to do. Only four EU members took part in the bombing campaign, and only two of them—France and the United Kingdom—attacked Libyan regime targets. The German government opposed military intervention. Italy found itself in a bind, having invested heavily in Libya and being dependent on Libyan oil. The EU was not able to coordinate evacuation of its nationals, and two humanitarian initiatives came to naught. In the initial stages of the Libyan crisis, the Union was therefore largely irrelevant.

The EU pulled itself together to become an actor of significance only when preparations began for the post-Qaddafi era. At first it tried to build a multinational program for reconstruction—encouraging China, India, Brazil, and others to reengage—but there was scant response. The United Nations reduced its presence in Libya and did not provide leadership. The EU nevertheless went ahead with emergency aid, with support for the National Transitional Council in setting up an interim government, support for civil society, rebuilding of the health and educational sectors, and reintegration of militia members into civilian sectors. France and the United Kingdom were the most engaged. Gulf states were also asked to contribute. The Libyans themselves lost their main source of income. By the end of 2014, oil production was down to 355,000 barrels a day, from a prewar level of 1.6 billion barrels.

Through 2012, the EU operated on the assumption that development support could be delivered through the European Neighbourhood Programme (ENP) mechanisms. However, as Libya descended into civil war and Islamist cells emerged alongside tribal groups, concerns grew about the long-term viability of the programs. Nor could the nascent civil society movements demonstrate the desired capabilities and trustworthiness as development partners. There were no adequate institutions at the receiving end.

First and foremost, the Western contribution to the Libyan revolution was the air campaign that helped the rebels to get rid of Qaddafi. Subsequent reconstruction and development assistance could not stem the decay into civil war. The EU had the resources and the will to assist in creating a new state but was hampered by its own internal disagreements and slow procedures. Moreover, the window of opportunity—the time between the elimination of Qaddafi and the beginning of the civil war—turned out to be short, only a matter of months. The civil war made everything worse, and not only in Libya: neighboring countries were heavily affected as well. The only remaining gain of the revolution was the removal of Qaddafi.

Tunisia

Compared with Egypt and Libya, Tunisia was a remarkable success story—the one and only upside of the Arab Spring. There are two sets of reasons for that: structural and the approach that Tunisian leaders took to revolutionary change. External actors also played a constructive role, but their contributions appear marginal in comparison.

The structural factors include the country's geographical location, shielding it from the geopolitics of the Middle East. There was no oil to attract foreign interference. Tunisia was able to pursue its own business in relative calm and quiet. Equally important, its armed forces are small in size, they have a tradition of staying out of politics, and they have no significant interests in the country's economic life. The population is homogeneous: 98 percent are Arab and 99 percent are Sunni. The middle class is relatively well educated. The first modern Tunisian constitution was a liberal one that emphasized gender equality. The judiciary is strong, and although it was co-opted by Ben Ali, it was quick to make itself independent. All of this is important for understanding the Tunisian success story.

The political leaders went for a clean break with the past. The old regime was abolished—but without excluding its collaborators from political affairs. Inclusion was facilitated by the fact that the distance between political parties in Tunisia is less than in other Middle Eastern countries. Also, Tunisia was blessed with a strong civil society. In the summer of 2013, when the political process was in danger of collapse, four civil society organizations—the labor union, the employers' organization, the human rights league, and the lawyers' association—invited the political parties to a national dialogue that led to the adoption of a new constitution by a majority of 93 percent of the members of the Constituent Assembly.

Two more factors augur well for the long-term stability of the new democratic regime: no single party has enough support to overrun the others, and no extra-parliamentary assistance is available to any of them to tip the balance. The apolitical stance of the military and the independence of the judiciary do not leave any such options.

The United States and Tunisia

The U.S. NGOs that were active in Tunisia—largely the same ones that were active in Egypt—could therefore operate in a much less complicated environment. The Tunisians, on their part, were open to advice, realizing that the NGOs had no strong national or personal interest in the course of events other than promoting better governance. The Tunisians sought advice on their own initiative as well—from the United Nations Development Programme (UNDP), the Venice Commission (affiliated with the Council of Europe), and countries in Africa and Latin America. In this way, they created a context that allowed them to maintain local ownership of the democratic discourse. Local actors could shop for support.

It is hard to trace NGO influence to specific outcomes. The NGOs cannot take credit for the fact that Tunisia has held several free and fair elections in a row, but they did contribute to the development of a democratic political culture and can thereby claim a share of the Tunisian success story.

The European Union and Tunisia

When the Tunisian uprising began, economic reform under the ENP was already in progress. Tunisia had a competent bureaucracy, so aid and technical support could flow through existing structures. Funds for 2011, earmarked for economic recovery, civil society, and democratic transition, were doubled, and humanitarian assistance was made available to cope with the influx of refugees from Libya. In addition, there was a 60 percent increase in European Investment Bank (EIB) loans. Tunisia was the first country for which the EU set up a task force.

The EU did not have to choose sides since Ennahda, which won the first elections, opted to engage in national dialogue. EU representatives advised the parties in the constitutional drafting process and reportedly provided many inputs while respecting the locally set agenda. Human rights groups reacted somewhat differently, feeling that the EU listened less to them and more to political leaders and government bureaucrats. If so, that was in keeping with established practice favoring engagement with governments over civil society contacts. The question here is a matter of degree and not of inverse priorities, which would have been impractical and potentially detrimental to civil society itself.

The EU was correct in assuming a pragmatic role and deferring to the preferences of Tunisian leaders. In three respects, its performance was less satisfactory. Financial transfers were slow because of the Union's bureaucratic procedures; the funding was doubled but still not on a significant scale; and paradoxically, the conditionality criteria were more strictly applied to Tunisia than to Morocco.

CONCLUSION

The Egyptian political landscape did not open up as much as seemed to be the case when Mubarak fell. The generals never abdicated. The "deep state" resisted democratic change, sabotaged Mursi, nurtured popular discontent, and waited for an opportunity to hit back. In a superficial reading, the proposition that there is not much that extra-regional powers can achieve if strong local forces are set against their objectives seems corroborated.

On closer analysis, however, the proposition was not put to much of a test. Ideally, both the United States and the EU wanted to see democratic change, but US policy was ambiguous and EU actions feeble. The United States hedged its bets, encouraging the revolutionaries while maintaining relations with the military. In a sense, there was strong logic in the EU's policy of more support for more democracy, but Egypt resisted calls for democratic practice and the EU was hampered by its own institutional shortcomings. It sympathized with the secular moderates and recognized the Brotherhood's election victories but ended up accommodating to the military.

The United States part of the story reconfirms another familiar thesis: big powers cannot be expected to play a constructive role in the promotion of democracy unless it happens to be in their national interest. Being an imperial power, the United States tried to preserve its influence in the region even while stepping down militarily. In the end, governance issues became secondary. The EU had no comparable imperial interests and encouraged revolutionary change by economic means, but in the case of Egypt, it ultimately sided with the United States and recognized the military takeover, without employing punitive measures. At that point, national interests seem to have trumped governance priorities. Quite possibly, an examination of the role of leading EU member states would have shown that more clearly.

In Libya, the United States was drawn into action but without much enthusiasm. Once Qaddafi was out of the way, the EU applied its economic instruments through the ENP mechanism but achieved almost nothing. Actually, neither the United States nor the EU did much to build a new Libyan state, and "more" is unlikely to have helped, for the odds were heavily tilted against it. Unlike Egypt and Tunisia, the Libyan revolution was militarized from the beginning, and under the impact of political power play in the international community and the multitude of conflicts among Libyan tribes, clans, and militias, the country fractured. To revert to the second part of our proposition, the big extra-regional actors had it in their power to destroy the state, leaving society in shambles. In this case, however, an important qualification is needed: unlike Iraq, where the US occupation of 2003 bears heavy responsibility for the calamities that followed and the growth of VE, in Libya the role of the extra-regional powers was secondary to that of the Libyans themselves.

In Tunisia, where structural factors and able leadership put the country on a distinct path to democratic governance, the United States and the EU were happy to render advice and provide economic support. Fortunately, the Tunisian leaders maintained local ownership of the political process: otherwise, the process might have been chaotic, for the many well-wishers were poorly coordinated. EU economic support was helpful, but slow in coming and modest in scale. Had the process been more fragile, it could have disintegrated for lack of timely and more substantial assistance.

Two lessons are particularly worth noting. First, the importance of civil society, which brought the political process back on track in the autumn of 2013, and second, the failure to support in any major way that was moving for the better but that remained vulnerable and could have fallen apart for lack of international support. Clearly, preventive action depends on strong leadership—for, when things seem to be going well, there is usually no public pressure to push decision makers into action.

Generally, the extra-regional powers acted on the basis of their own experiences and values, assuming that the more the Arab states could resemble them, the better. They paid much attention neither to national and regional specifics nor to the various dimensions of governance and how these dimensions could best be sequenced and promoted. With a view to future opportunities for change, there is ample scope for improvement in this respect.

Chapter 13

Civil Society Engagement to Prevent Violent Extremism

David Cortright

One of the less known effects of the tragic 9/11 events and the subsequent Global War on Terror is the chilling impact counterterrorism measures have had on civil society and citizens' agency. While the phrase "war on terror" is no longer used officially, US counterterrorism policies remain heavily militarized and employ repressive measures that curtail the operational and political freedoms of civic organizations worldwide. The development, human rights, and peacebuilding groups affected by these measures are working to address the political grievances, socioeconomic injustices, and power imbalances that are among the root causes of violent conflict. Understandably, these groups do not want to label their work as counterterrorism, but their activities are exactly what is needed to counter violent extremism. A policy that hinders the ability of these groups to prevent conflict and address human needs is counterproductive.

This chapter[1] places the closing of civil society space in a wider global context of counterterrorism wars, restrictions on civil society, securitization of aid, and increasing violent threats to civil society. It describes the persistent shift in international cooperation policy from sustainable development as an intrinsic public good to development as an instrument for national and geopolitical security and economic goals. The UN Global Counter-Terrorism Strategy is considered to be a legitimate anchor for the international community and civil society alike to work on civil society engagement, particularly in the areas of development, conflict prevention, and human rights. The overriding conclusion is that security policies in general and counterterrorism measures in particular are making the threat of violent extremism worse when they are developed and implemented without civil society participation and civic agency.

THE ROLE OF CIVIL SOCIETY

The growth and development of civil society is "one of the greatest accomplishments of our age," according to a World Bank study (Willebois 2010). The UN secretary-general's Panel of Eminent Persons on United Nations-Civil Society Relations defines the term "civil society" as encompassing associations of citizens (outside of families, friends, government, and businesses) entered into voluntarily to advance interests and ideas. The definition encompasses professional associations, social movements, indigenous people's organizations, religious and spiritual bodies, women's organizations, academic centers, and NGOs that operate in individual countries or transnationally (UN General Assembly 2004, 13).

The Centre for Civil Society at the London School of Economics describes civil society as "the arena of uncoerced collective action characterized by shared interests, purposes, and values" (Howell et al. 2008). NGOs are a distinct part of civil society as formally registered organizations, some membership-based, which engage in development, humanitarian relief, policy advocacy, poverty reduction, and other forms of nonprofit activity. Some organizations adopt an empowerment-based approach to development and human rights. They work in partnership with marginalized communities to shift power relations so that the previously excluded have a voice in political decision making and can gain access to resources and assets needed for autonomous development.

From a state perspective, some government officials view civil society organizations merely as assistance providers and implementing agencies for service delivery, capacity building, and technical assistance. This instrumentalist approach does not reflect the diversity of civil society in which many groups prefer to operate independently through bottom-up rather than top-down programs.

Citizen movements and NGOs have become major players in public advocacy on a range of social and economic issues and have articulated moral and political standards that in some cases have crystallized into policy. Civil society groups have been prime movers of some of the most innovative initiatives for dealing with emerging global challenges. Examples of significant civil society movements include the Nobel Prize–winning campaign to ban land mines and efforts to advance the role of women in international peacemaking through the implementation of UN Security Council Resolution 1325. At times civil society may rise up in mass resistance to tyranny, as in the historic 2010 democratic revolution in Tunisia. Less well-known but important civil society initiatives have been created for early warning and conflict prevention in West Africa and for human security and security-sector reform in Latin America and the Philippines (Cortright, Greenberg, and Stone 2016).

Civil society organizations can play a significant role in helping to resolve armed conflict and address conditions conducive to violent extremism. They provide advance notice of potential conflict and in many settings have served as election observers and human rights monitors. Civil society groups often have a wealth of knowledge concerning the human rights and development situations in specific countries and may be better informed than governments and intelligence agencies about the causes of armed conflict. Too often, however, civil society actors are limited in their ability to serve as mediators or interlocutors because of legal prohibitions against contact with groups designated as terrorist groups (Jahangir and Azzam 2005; OSCE 2007).

Some political leaders, especially in authoritarian regimes and "managed democracies," are hostile toward independent civil society groups. They distrust CSOs that work among marginalized populations, suspecting them of supporting political opponents. Governments sometimes create ersatz NGOs, dubbed "GONGOs," which serve to reinforce official positions and often obfuscate the authentic voice of civil society (Howell et al. 2008, 82; Naim 2007, 96). Organizations and movements that challenge the abusive policies of unaccountable governments inevitably arouse the ire of those in power, but in the past decade, pressures against such groups have mounted as policy makers have appropriated the language of counterterrorism to intensify their attacks against civil society–based critics.

COUNTERTERRORISM: THE GOOD, THE BAD, AND THE UGLY

Counterterrorism embodies a wide range of measures with differing impacts, which can be loosely characterized as the good, the bad, and the ugly. Good measures are those that enhance international cooperation and encourage support for equitable development and human rights, as recommended in the UN Global Counter-Terrorism Strategy. In the bad and ugly categories are counterterrorism measures (CTMs) that overemphasize security and distort development and aid priorities and that lead to extrajudicial killings, greater state repression, and increased human rights abuse. Repression against civil society activists has intensified in dozens of countries. According to Freedom House, annual ratings of political freedom have steadily eroded in recent years, making this the longest period of consecutive worldwide setbacks for freedom in nearly forty years (Abromowitz 2018, 1). Overly restrictive counterterrorism measures constrain the social, political, and operational capacity of civil society actors and impede the work of groups promoting improvements in governance, human rights, and development.

In the name of fighting terrorism, governments have curtailed political freedoms and imposed restrictive measures against human rights defenders and civil society activists in many countries. Repressive counterterrorism measures have undermined civil liberties and contributed to a climate of suspicion and hostility toward nongovernmental groups. Many of the organizations that work against violent extremism by promoting human rights and sustainable development are themselves being labeled extremist and are facing constraints on their ability to operate. The positive work of civil society to alleviate social and political marginalization helps to reduce grievances that can lead to political violence. Measures taken in the name of counterterrorism that limit the political space of such groups have the ironic result of inhibiting work on the ground to address conditions that fuel terrorism.

The proposed categorization of good, bad, and ugly is figurative and not meant to suggest absolute judgments about particular policies. The range of counterterrorism measures is extremely wide, and specific policies can have differing impacts in varying conditions and settings. Strengthened law enforcement efforts are good when they prevent attacks and bring perpetrators to justice, but these same measures can be bad if they lead to abuses and increased repression. Efforts to prevent the financing of terrorism are positive, yet programs intended to interdict such funding often have negative implications for nongovernmental groups and charities seeking to overcome oppression. The evaluation of particular counterterrorism measures depends greatly on context and the way in which specific actors implement policies. Judgments about particular policies should be based on the degree to which they contribute to genuine security and democratic governance while also upholding the rule of law and protecting the work of peacebuilders and human rights defenders.

Waging war to counter terrorism and insurgency is inappropriate and ineffective. Overcoming political violence requires a combination of diplomatic, economic, and social responses that go beyond and in many cases are incompatible with the use of armed force. Security specialists have long recognized that counterinsurgency is primarily a civilian task. Success depends on diminishing sociopolitical sources of support that enable militant groups to operate. The classic study by David Galula calls for a struggle that is 80 percent nonmilitary (Galula 2006, 63). The US Army 2006 counterinsurgency field manual, coauthored by General David Petraeus, echoed the need to prioritize civilian efforts. US operations in Iraq and Afghanistan have been exactly the opposite. A May 2009 Congressional Research Service study reported that some 94 percent of all US funds for the wars in Afghanistan and Iraq were spent by the Pentagon, with only 6 percent devoted to foreign aid and diplomatic operations (Belasco 2009, 4). Empirical evidence confirms that war is not an effective means of countering terrorist organizations. A 2008 RAND

Corporation study, "How Terrorist Groups End," shows that terrorist groups usually end through political processes and effective law enforcement, not the use of military force. An examination of 268 terrorist organizations that ended during a period of nearly forty years found that the primary factors accounting for their demise were participation in political processes (43 percent) and effective policing (40 percent). Military force accounted for the end of terrorist groups in only 7 percent of the cases examined. Terrorist groups end most often when they trade bombs for ballots and join a political process or when they are suppressed by local law enforcement agencies. Policing works best when law enforcement officials are rooted in local communities and have the confidence and trust of local residents that enables them to penetrate criminal networks (Jones and Libicki 2008, 42–43).

War policies are not only inappropriate, but they are counterproductive as well. When Western nations invade and occupy Muslim countries, this has the unintended effect of validating the ideology of extremists who claim to be saving Islam from foreign infidels. A widely accepted narrative now pervades much of the world. It is a story of invasion and military occupation; abuses at Abu Ghraib and other prisons; torture, water boarding, and extrajudicial killings; drones raining terror from the sky; the inevitable killing of civilians—all broadcast by Arab and Muslim media. Polls in Muslim countries have shown 80 percent agreement with the view that Western military interventions are directed against Islamic society, and that they are a war against Islam itself (Kull 2007; Scheuer 2008). As long as these attitudes prevail, there will be no end of recruits willing to blow themselves up to kill foreign troops and their supporters.

Most governments and international officials have emphasized the necessity of cooperative law enforcement to counter transnational terrorism. Especially effective are programs that emphasize community policing and respect for the rule of law and the rights of citizens. International police cooperation and intelligence sharing have been successful in thwarting attacks, perhaps most dramatically in foiling an alleged plot to bomb flights from London to the United States in August 2006. The head of the Crown Prosecution Service in the United Kingdom said, "The fight against terrorism on the streets of Britain is not a war. It is the prevention of crime, the enforcement of our laws, and the winning of justice for those damaged by their infringement" (Dyer 2007).

The repercussions have been felt most keenly by civil society actors in the developing world. Over the decades, NGOs in the global South have multiplied in number and assumed growing importance in defending human rights, promoting development, and mediating conflicts. When civil society actors attempt to reform policies or hold government leaders accountable to human rights standards, they may face criticism and repression. In some countries governments have imposed regulations and conditions that are disproportional to the threat and restrict the operational space of independent citizen groups. Repressive counterterrorism policies have added to these restrictions and created a climate of suspicion, especially toward groups that challenge social exclusion and unequal power relations. Many who work against extremism by promoting human rights and development are themselves being labeled extremist and are facing constraints on their ability to operate.

SECURITIZING AID AND ITS IMPACT ON CIVIL SOCIETY

The global trend toward using aid and development funds for military purposes has accelerated. This approach subordinates traditional goals of mitigating poverty to the agenda of counterterrorism and defeating insurgency. It blurs the analytic boundaries between security and development while politicizing both and detracting from efforts to improve the lives of the world's most disadvantaged communities. The process works in two ways: a growing proportion of the aid budget is channeled directly through military institutions and funds are allocated increasingly in support of military operations.

In the United States, Department of Defense's (DoD) development-like activities aimed primarily to serve security goals accounted for a quarter of U.S. development assistance funds (Tarnoff and Lawson 2016). Donor states provide a high proportion of development assistance toward countries in conflict zones such as Afghanistan and Egypt. Aid policies increasingly serve selective security purposes rather than the universal goals of overcoming global poverty and empowering marginalized communities. Development advocates recognize the connections that exist between development and the prevention of armed conflict, but they oppose the diversion of aid funding to serve the security interests of governments in the global North rather than the human needs of people in the global South.

The January 2010 report by humanitarian agencies in Afghanistan summarized the dire consequences of militarizing aid:

> More and more assistance is being channeled through military actors to "win hearts and minds" while efforts to address the underlying causes of poverty and repair the destruction wrought by three decades of conflict and disorder are being sidelined. Development projects implemented with military money or through military dominated structures aim to achieve fast results but are often poorly executed, inappropriate, and do not have sufficient community involvement to make them sustainable. There is little evidence this approach is

generating stability and, in some cases, military involvement in development activities is, paradoxically, putting Afghan lives further at risk as these projects quickly become targeted by antigovernment elements. (Action Aid 2010)

Direct attacks on aid workers have increased over the past fifteen years according to the annual Aid Worker Security Report—a total of 288 aid workers were killed, kidnapped, or injured in 2016, compared to 85 in 2002. This increase not only reflects a greater number of aid workers operating in insecure areas but also results from an apparent rise in politically motivated attacks (Stoddard, Harmer, and Czwarno 2017). Subordinating humanitarian assistance to military purposes is a violation of the International Committee of the Red Cross (ICRC) Code of Conduct, which provides for a strict separation of humanitarian assistance from any military or political agenda. Separation is necessary to safeguard aid workers and the communities they serve and to uphold the principle of prioritizing humanitarian assistance according to need (Krähenbühl 2011; ICRC 1994).

PROTECTING CIVIL SOCIETY

In December 2010, UN secretary-general Ban Ki-moon dedicated the annual observance of International Human Rights Day to the many human rights defenders around the world who are attacked and threatened for their efforts to protect and promote political freedom. He reminded governments of their obligations under international law to protect human rights advocates and uphold fundamental freedoms of expression and assembly (Ki-moon 2010). The following rights, derived from UN conventions by the International Center for Not-for-Profit Law, are the essential requirements for assuring political freedom and protecting the operational space of civil society:

- the right to associate and form organizations;
- the right to operate without unwanted state interference;
- the right to free expression;
- the right to communicate and cooperate freely internally and externally;
- the right to seek and secure resources; and
- the right to have these freedoms protected by the state.

Through their efforts for development, conflict transformation, and human rights, civil society groups are working to dry up the wells of extremism from which violence springs. Civic organizations address political grievances, socioeconomic injustices, and power imbalances that are among the root causes of armed conflict. This work is not labeled counterterrorism, nor should it be, but it is exactly what is needed to counter violent extremism. International policy makers must recognize and protect this vital civil society mission and take action to eliminate counterproductive CTMs. In the global struggle against terrorism, civil society groups should be welcomed as friends, not hounded as foes.

Many of the policies carried out in the name of counterterrorism are making the terrorist danger worse. An overemphasis on security measures has eroded civil liberties and human rights in many countries and diverted attention from the policies needed to counter the complex challenge of transnational terrorism. Preventing terror attacks requires not only improved security but also better efforts to address the underlying conditions that give rise to violent extremism. Resolving conflicts, ending foreign occupations, overcoming oppression, eradicating poverty, supporting sustainable development, empowering the marginalized, defending human rights, promoting good governance—all are vital to the struggle against terrorism, yet addressing these challenges is made more difficult by repressive counterterrorism policies.

Civil society groups themselves must engage more actively in the counterterrorism debate and take necessary steps to strengthen their role in eliminating conditions conducive to violent extremism. Independent citizen groups must stand together to protect their operational space and assert their right to serve community needs free of state interference. CSOs can respond most effectively to repressive counterterrorism measures by continuing to expose and challenge abuses and by building public support for more accountable governance based on the rule of law. They can contribute to the struggle against global terrorism by pursuing their core mission of human rights and economic empowerment and by emphasizing that development, freedom, and security are indivisible.

Chapter 14

Six Principles for Enabling State Responses

Lena Slachmuijlder

Search for Common Ground (Search) believes that "enabling state responses" is an important way of responding to violent extremism. Because violent extremists pose a security threat, it is naturally, yet not exclusively, the responsibility of the state to ensure the safety of its citizens. This involves the mobilization of the security forces, intelligence agencies, prison, correctional services, and overall law enforcement organizations.

The *opportunity* is to enable state responses that tackle the root causes of violent extremism, to create societal buy-in across diverse stakeholders toward a common goal, and to demonstrate respect for both the rule of law and the equality of all citizens in the process. State-led initiatives have the power to deploy a diversity of tactics, beyond the pure, hard-force security tactics of arrests, interrogation, and imprisonment to support healthy and resilient societies.

The *risk* is that state responses, when emphasizing hard-force approaches, can abuse human rights, inappropriately profile certain communities, and alienate those who otherwise could be allies to state-led efforts. This risk is often accentuated when human rights organizations do not collaborate well with security agencies and instead develop a competitive and adversarial relationship with these bodies.

By building a sense of shared interest, open dialogue, and a complementary approach among security agencies, civil society groups, the media, and the community at large, peacebuilders can empower countering violent extremism (CVE) efforts to be holistic and effective.

IDENTIFY, RESPECT, AND SPEAK TO THE NEED OF EACH STATE SECURITY AGENCY PARTNER

Within prison services, legal offices, or counterterrorism units, the entry point for building collaborative relationships starts with recognizing the needs of each government partner. These agencies are accountable to ministries, parliaments, and the public and also have both individual and institutional reputations at stake. When we enable them to feel more effective through improved tactics and dialogue with nonstate actors, their openness to collaboration will grow. Remember that these agencies often face the brunt of adversarial media coverage or finger-pointing by human rights and other civil society organizations (CSOs). The peacebuilders' approach to these agencies recognizes their needs and seeks to build a partnership toward serving those goals.

For example, in Indonesia, reintegrating offenders required collaboration between corrections officers, the National Bureau of Counterterrorism, the police task force, and CSO partners. Initially, Search found that state agencies at the national and local levels had very different ways of working, including local-level ministry officials. Search also had to learn better tactics for engaging national-level state actors in the process of empowering parole officers to coordinate reintegration. To build credibility and buy-in, Search Indonesia staff worked to clarify roles and expectations among stakeholders at the national and local levels. Over time, the groups worked together to determine the needs of prisoners at each stage of the rehabilitation process and what each group could bring in a complementary fashion.

Identify, Respect, and Speak to the Needs of the Various Nonstate Actors Who Are Involved in Responding to Violent Extremism

Civil society organizations have often been highly critical of state-led responses to violent extremism. At times, they have mobilized to denounce human rights abuses or unfair profiling of certain ethnic or religious groups. These civil society groups have clear constituencies, and in seeking to facilitate a relationship between them and state-led agencies, it is essential to first recognize and respect the needs of these civil society actors. Only when they see that shifting their relationship with state agencies toward greater collaboration will be in their interest will they agree to engage in the process.

In Indonesia, Search created and chaired a working group that brought together various stakeholders working in the broader CVE sphere. In creating this group, Search wanted to bring together not only legal, human rights, and secular-oriented groups but also the broad network of tens of thousands of Islamic boarding schools that played an important role in the country.

Build Trust Gradually among Stakeholders, Using Both Informal and Formal Initiatives

As peacebuilders, we know that trust deficits between state and nonstate stakeholders can create hesitation for formal and/or public engagement, particularly if they have an adversarial relationship. Stakeholders may also not see it as in their interest to publicly collaborate with other actors in the process, at least initially. Therefore, forcing a formal process too early can also harm the credibility of each actor among their constituents and within the community. Recognize that trust building can additionally be achieved through informal channels. Remember that saving face is an important cultural consideration, both for high-profile civil society groups and for those in the government who have a public image to manage.

In Indonesia, Search led an initiative to build collaboration between the country's leading counterterror force, Densus 88, and the most prominent human rights groups. This collaboration benefited from an extended period of informal engagement. The purpose of the collaboration was to create a dialogue around how counterterrorism operations could be done in a way that respects human rights and avoids triggering further support for violent extremist movements. In facilitating this process, it was important that Search avoided making either Densus 88 or the civil society partners that had been brought in feel exposed. Each group needed to feel in control and in agreement throughout the process so that they could frame their engagement appropriately for both their own constituents and the general public. To support such a process, Search undertook a number of informal, back-channel discussions to ensure that each side understood why they were being encouraged to meet with one another—entities they had previously viewed with trepidation and suspicion. This reduced the stakes for each side while allowing trust to grow and the identification potential avenues for collaboration to occur.

Engage a Wide Spectrum of Government and Civil Society Actors, Including Religious Groups

The durability of a peacebuilding process depends on ownership and buy-in of all who have a stake in the problem and its eventual solution. While some CSOs may have taken a strong (and sometimes public) stance, it is valuable to expand the civil society stakeholders beyond the most well known to include diverse perspectives. By enabling civil society actors to discover shared interests among themselves, across dividing lines such as secular-religious, or across ethnic or geographic lines, this can strengthen the potential for collaboration with state actors.

In Morocco, Search collaborated with the Rabita, a group of Islamic scholars with a mandate from His Majesty the King of Morocco to articulate and translate the work of senior Islamic scholars down to the tens of thousands of imams operating mosques at the community level. This collaboration brought imams into ongoing programs working on the disengagement of violent extremists in prisons. The Rabita also became a core part of an initiative that works with youth councils and organizations to shift the narrative around religion and violent extremism.

Remain Impartial and Inclusive throughout the Process

It is important for peacebuilders to recognize inherent biases within individuals and organizations. There may be risks in sharing or gathering sensitive information. Other may ill-perceive or misunderstand the purpose of reaching out to security agencies. The perception of impartiality by all stakeholders will be a critical key to your ability to strengthen collaborative relationships.

In Kyrgyzstan, Search created the first ever multi-stakeholder platform for countering violent extremism in the country. Peacebuilding staff brought together high-level actors from several government ministries, security and intelligence agencies, religious institutions, academia, and civil society to work to create trust at each step in the process. It was especially important for each actor to feel that Search understood their unique concerns and ideas to keep them on board. Finally, Search had to delicately balance these individual relationships with an awareness that once all groups were brought together, they would realize that Search had been cultivating similarly close relationships with everyone else. In this case, maintaining impartiality meant not only focusing on how to structure and guide the process (setting the agenda, ensuring all parties are heard, and creating transparency throughout) but also maintaining caution about how developed relationships with each actor would affect overall perceptions of impartiality.

Contrary to Other Peacebuilding Activities, Visibility and Publicity Must Be Tailored to Avoid Risks to the Stakeholders

It is common for peacebuilders to communicate publicly when they reach important milestones. Engaging state actors requires a more sensitive approach. In some instances, it best serves our goal to enable parties to work discreetly together and to contribute to a joint policy, program, or initiative without publicity. Be sensitive to security agencies' need for ownership over the process, their public reputation, and lines of accountability. Similarly, some CSOs may face resistance from their constituencies if they are perceived as working too closely with certain security agencies. It behooves peacebuilders to consult with them about how and when to use publicity. Collaboration with the media also needs to be grounded in a shared interest with journalists about how CVE efforts are portrayed, as coverage can both help and hinder efforts.

Handling publicity delicately also builds trust in the collaboration process. In northeastern Nigeria, Search trained and brought together various community leaders to serve as focal points in a violence early warning program. The purpose was for participants to collect and share information that would eventually reach security forces who could respond in the interest of public safety. Search staff understood that this type of program requires sensitivity to ensure that focal points would not become targets for retaliation. As a result, they were mindful in mitigating the risks of danger, both physical and reputational, in how and whether they announced their activities. Search avoided radio announcements, a public launch, and other common peacebuilding outreach tactics. They also sought to clarify to stakeholders that the platform they had created was to remain confidential, and successful prevention efforts would remain private unless deemed appropriate to share publicly.

What Are the Risks Involved for Peacebuilding Programs within the Countering Violent Extremism Arena?

Search's approach to transforming violent conflict (TVE) faces a variety of challenges. These include the following:

Losing Impartiality and Credibility

First, the very definitions of terms like "extremist," "terrorism," or "insurgent" are a reflection of both local and global power dynamics. State authorities—both Western donor governments and governments in the countries where we work—often have the greatest authority to choose which groups receive these labels in a way that may or may not coincide with our peacebuilding values. This is particularly sensitive when there are extremist ideas underpinning the majority party in power. Often, such labels can be quite harmful to our peacebuilding goals, such as when governments desire programs that exacerbate dividing lines through stigmatizing certain groups, curtailing human rights, and limiting freedom of expression.

In many contexts, the dominant political narrative of the state frames political opposition as treasonous or terrorist in nature. At best, this can make it difficult for peacebuilders to find the right political space for their programs, and, at worst, peacebuilders can be seen as colluding with "terrorist" groups. The adage that one group's "terrorists" are another group's "freedom fighters" is especially true in the CVE space, where we maintain our integrity and impartiality by working with all types of groups and communities.

Secondly, we risk being perceived as standing in opposition to certain viewpoints, including those labeled as "radical." Our ability to connect with all stakeholders rests on reassuring them that their values, beliefs, and identity are not under attack. In the area of CVE, radical ideology and violent tactics are often seen as going hand in hand. Within extremist groups, an emphasis on rationality, social disconnect, and narrow and exclusionary doctrines is intentionally intertwined to encourage members to commit violence. Alternatively, governments or other powers threatened by extremist groups may seek to associate challenging ideologies with socially reprehensible behavior in order to preserve their own credibility. Ordinary citizens, caught in an environment of insecurity, inflammatory media, and social instability, can be easily swayed to adopt this association.

Thirdly, taking on a large volume of programs labeled as CVE can inadvertently align us with domestic political figures or movements, which leaves our work exposed to abrupt changes in funding or strategy when political circumstances change. The threat can be further exacerbated when, as funding for CVE starts and stops unpredictably, our programs are then unable to deliver evidence of meaningful change. Even worse, politicians and funders can use this failure to justify abandoning peacebuilding work in favor of hardline approaches.

Finally, the way we frame our work as CVE affects our funding, staff, stakeholders, and organizational mission. Determining how and when to be explicit about our CVE goals as opposed to general peacebuilding goals requires flexibility and thoughtfulness. Confusion around CVE framing not only risks misleading our stakeholders. It also can distract ourselves from our organizational mission. There are additional risks around CVE framing regarding whether or not we can get buy-in for programs from both donors, who have their own political agendas, and our own staff, who may be concerned about potentially being endangered.

To address these challenges, peacebuilders should ensure that our spoken and written language should reflect an understanding that extremism can exist in all ideological spaces, whether religious, political, or otherwise. We choose also not to use words like "terrorist" that may cast aspersions on a particular political or religious viewpoint. Instead, we stress the values of ideological diversity, political pluralism, and peaceful means of activism and conflict resolution. These ideals are included in our social media presence, staff recruitment efforts, outreach to new partners, and our convening role when we begin and implement official programs. We use language around our goals, beliefs, and aspirations that emphasizes the importance of separating ideology and tactics. Additionally, in selecting role models to spotlight through our media and public engagement efforts, we look for individuals of all ideological backgrounds who represent a commitment to peace and a tolerance for diversity. Taking this approach is not without additional risks. Many CVE contexts are so politicized that the choice of not being in opposition to a radical group is perceived as being tacit supporters. Again, by highlighting our roles as facilitators, conveners, and interlocutors, we can promote understanding around our purpose and activities.

Relationships and Information Sharing Endanger Stakeholders

Search strives to engage partners who are sensitive, thoughtful, and credible. In conflict settings, the changing interests of each of our partners create risks that they might use relationships and information they receive through our efforts to exacerbate conflict. In conflict environments, where the state has a reputation for repressive tactics, our efforts may inadvertently aid government agencies in expanding the scope of their abuses. As we build inroads between state partners and local communities, we allow states to increase both their reach and authority in communities. If they may later seek to harm these individuals or communities through violence or oppressive surveillance in the name of public security, we may also risk being seen as either endorsing or collaborating with such state behavior. This level of risk not only harms our organizational credibility. It threatens to exacerbate tension and mistrust within a community.

On the other hand, our work at the community level involves working with groups and individuals who may be drawn into recruitment by violent extremist groups. Finding a way to hold that space while maintaining trust can be challenging, particularly in contemplating at what point to collaborate with security agencies in reporting high-risk individuals for the sake of public safety.

Risk management begins with transparency around the core intention behind our work. As peacebuilders, we have a responsibility to our stakeholders to be clear about our purpose of convening different groups and enabling them to collaborate more effectively while also reminding them that we do not control, influence, or condone the behavior of the groups that we engage. By being open about our purpose and scope, we support each of our partners in making informed decisions about when and how to engage with one another. We can also be clear with our stakeholder participants what aspects of our program activities are confidential, which are not, and where exceptions can be made so that we avoid exposing ourselves and our stakeholders to risk.

In Morocco, for example, Search's youth councils invited an influential Salafi imam to visit a Catholic church as part of a national day of tolerance and reconciliation. The visit received substantial press coverage, and the imam, who was very active on social media, shared his trip with his thousands of followers. Shortly after, this imam received hate mail and death threats from many of his followers who believed he was selling out on the "true Islam" he claimed to preach. Because the imam had by then been exposed to Search programming around tolerance, dialogue, and conflict resolution, he reached out to the lead individual behind the threats and learned that this person had himself been radicalized through extremist, disaffected Muslims living in Europe. Together, the two reached a point of reconciliation, which was shared publicly with the imam's followers in Morocco and abroad.

In Nigeria, Search has organized monthly coordination meetings for state security agencies and local CSOs to share updates on conflict dynamics and violent activities around the area. This collaboration has enabled local actors to feel confident that local threats will be heard and appropriately addressed by the police and intelligence services, but also creates a risk that those same responders will use repressive tactics that drive communities apart. To mitigate this risk, Search worked for a long time to build a culture of trust and honest information sharing among participants. Each group who attends these meetings and their constituents understand the purpose of participating.

Incomplete or Uneven Resources with Overpromised Outcomes Damage Credibility

Funding for CVE programs can be inconsistent. Political affairs in our donor and project countries can shift rapidly. Security challenges are ever changing. Although peacebuilders aim to develop CVE programs that are thoughtful, innovative, and contextually responsive, the aforementioned factors can derail success. When that happens, we risk not only convincing donors that our work is ineffective but also our stakeholders that nonviolence is a false opportunity. This is particularly true when our programs require long-term engagement to deliver results, but funding cycles last only one or two years and have rigid expectations. For example, if we develop youth programs to teach entrepreneurship skills, but then lack funding to help them launch new businesses, our participants can feel misled and could even turn to harmful activities instead.

At the political level, we can advocate for increased, long-term funding for both peacebuilding programming and evaluation. Through our role as experts and advocates, we can use our field experience to remind policy makers and donors that there is no one program strategy or approach that works quickly. Preventing violent extremism requires sustained investment in real community issues. One way to do this is to highlight change indicators from other areas of peacebuilding that identify relationship changes, collaborative action, accountability measures, and social shifts toward inclusivity that model needed changes.

Peacebuilders also face challenges with the emergence of CVE as a formal and separate field. While the challenges around violent extremism are not new to peacebuilding, we see a significant movement in Western countries who feel threatened by violent extremism to create a whole "new" field of international engagement around these themes. Governance and development work should not all be directed to serve the purpose of CVE, as it disorients us from the need to focus broadly on grievances and dividing lines. In the Sahel, for example, communities struggle with real challenges around economic opportunity, child marriage, and gender-based violence in addition to the violent presence of Boko Haram. As peacebuilders, our mission is to bring people together in collaborative responses to these problems and avoid derailing this focus in the name of combating violent extremism. Our program design should avoid raising unrealistic expectations aimed simply at gaining buy-in from donors and participants.

Root Causes of Injustice and Structural Violence Are Ignored or Smoothed Over

Individuals commonly join violent extremist movements out of feelings of frustration, marginalization, and a legitimate dearth of opportunities to address very real and pressing problems in their communities. Working to change their tactics without discussing their underlying grievances can lead partners and stakeholders to feel ignored or manipulated. Initiatives that promote tolerance, for example, without tackling the root causes of inequality, can end up backfiring on our credibility.

There are several risks involved in placing too much emphasis on counteracting the work of a particular extremist group in the short term while ignoring the long-standing grievances and social divisions that have fueled the current violent situation. In Yemen, for example, the majority of Western foreign assistance in recent years had focused on trying to uproot Al-Qaeda in the Arabian Peninsula (AQAP), yet the challenges of social cohesion of integrating the disaffected Houthi community in the post–Arab Spring national dialogue process require working across multiple dividing lines throughout the country. To address this challenge, peacebuilders should focus not only on educating vulnerable communities about the value of nonviolent conflict transformation but also on educating governments about the importance of giving regular citizens a greater role in shaping the laws and practices that control their daily lives.

Chapter 15

Legal Restrictions and Counterterrorism

Kay Guinane

Laws passed to protect national security can also undermine national and human security objectives—or in the parlance of systems theory create "negative feedback." In the United States this is the case with two laws that effectively limit civil society's ability to engage nonstate armed groups on terrorist lists in programs aimed at resolving conflict, limiting its impact on civilian populations or intervening to bring individuals out of the fight. These are the criminal prohibitions on material support of terrorism and economic sanctions laws. While these laws were not designed to limit peacebuilding or preventing/countering violent extremism (P/CVE) programs, they have had that effect.

Without a change in the legal environment, efforts to prevent or counter violent extremism will continue to be hampered. US authorities have resisted change, fearing that bad actors would somehow take advantage of legal safe space intended for legitimate nonprofit organizations (NPOs). However, it is possible to craft legal mechanisms that limit that risk and allow the benefits of peacebuilding and P/CVE work to flow. The objectives of protecting national security and peace-oriented work of NPOs are not competing or contradictory. Instead, they form interlocking pieces of a whole that can form a healthy ecology for effective counterterrorism P/CVE programs. This chapter will describe the laws involved and their impact and then suggest a new approach.

THE MATERIAL SUPPORT PROHIBITION AND THE HOLDER VERSUS HUMANITARIAN LAW PROJECT CASE

The material support prohibition is part of the Antiterrorism and Effective Death Penalty Act (AEDPA), which Congress passed in 1996. It gives the secretary of state authority to designate Foreign Terrorist Organizations (FTOs) and prohibits knowingly providing material support or resources to them, regardless of the character or intent of the support provided (Antiterrorism and Effective Death Penalty Act of 1996). The definition of material support is broad, including providing "training," "services," and "personnel." As noted in a 2015 report, "The scope of activities prohibited under US material support and counterterrorism laws are the broadest of all the jurisdictions examined and have led to widespread concerns being voiced by peace and humanitarian organisations" (Boon-Kuo et al. 2015).

In 1998, the Humanitarian Law Project (HLP) filed suit in the federal District Court for the Central District of California challenging the constitutionality of the material support statute on First (free speech) and Fifth (vagueness) Amendment grounds. HLP wanted to train two organizations designated as FTOs on how to use the United Nations' conflict resolution process and other nonviolent means to resolve their disputes. The court granted an injunction in favor of HLP, holding that the terms "personnel" and "training" were impermissibly vague under the Fifth Amendment, thereby denying due process. However, the court rejected HLP's First Amendment speech and association claims. In 2003, the Ninth Circuit Court of Appeals upheld that ruling.

After the 9/11 attacks in 2001, while the HLP case was pending, Congress passed the PATRIOT Act, which expanded the definition of material support to include "expert advice and assistance." In addition, President George W. Bush issued Executive Order 13224, which aims to disrupt the financial networks or terrorist organizations through sanctions, including asset freezes. The order established a list of designated terrorist groups and authorized the secretaries of Treasury and State and attorney general to designate additional groups or individuals that pose a terrorist threat, along with "their subsidiaries, front organizations, agents, and associates." The criteria for designation incorporate the material support prohibition, by authorizing designation to those that "assist in, sponsor, or provide financial, material, or technological support for, or financial or other services to or in support of, acts of terrorism or individuals or entities designated in or under the Order." The practical effect of this and subsequent Executive Orders that use similar language is to make the nontangible support involved in "training" and "expert advice and assistance" illegal under sanctions law and expose violators to potential penalties, including being placed on the list as a supporter of terrorism.

Antiterrorism and Effective Death Penalty Act has a very narrow exception. Basic necessities such as food and shelter are tangible properties within the meaning of this statute. This prohibits use of an FTO as part of the aid delivery chain, even if the ultimate beneficiaries are civilians. The terms "training," "expert advice and assistance," and "personnel" suggest that "material support" could include anything from medical treatment to conflict mediation projects. In 2004, Congress passed the Intelligence Reform and Terrorism Prevention Act (IRTPA) to provide greater clarity to the following three terms (Intelligence Reform and Terrorism Prevention Act of 2004 n.d.):

- *Training:* "Instruction or teaching designed to impart a specific skill, as opposed to general knowledge."
- *Expert advice or assistance:* "Advice or assistance derived from scientific, technical, or other specialized knowledge."
- *Personnel:* When a "person has knowingly provided, attempted to provide, or conspired to provide a foreign terrorist organization with one or more individuals (who may be or include himself) to work under that terrorist organization's direction or control or to organize, manage, supervise or otherwise direct the operation of that organization. Individuals who act entirely independently of the foreign terrorist organization to advance its goals or objectives shall not be considered to be working under the foreign terrorist organization's direction or control."

Antiterrorism and Effective Death Penalty Act gives the secretary of state the power to exempt such nontangible forms of assistance when, with the concurrence of the attorney general, he or she determines that the assistance cannot be used to carry out terrorist activity. However, this power has been used rarely, if at all.[1]

In 2003 HLP filed a second suit challenging the definition of "expert advice and assistance" as overly broad and vague. The two cases proceeded in a series of rulings and cross appeals until 2009 when the court of appeals held that the material support statute is not overbroad as to free speech rights, but that the definitions of "training," "expert advice and assistance," and "service" are unconstitutionally vague. Both HLP and the government asked the Supreme Court to review the case, and it agreed to do so. In June 2010, the Supreme Court ruled, by a 6–3 majority, that Congress can constitutionally prohibit the activities HLP proposed. The lack of a requirement that the support be intended to further terrorist activities is acceptable, the Court said, because the law requires that a person know the group is listed. As a result, intent to support peaceful resolution of conflict or turn a person away from violent extremism is not a defense in the event a criminal charge is filed, if training or specialized knowledge is involved.

IMPACT OF THE HLP DECISION

Although the Court said its ruling only applied to the HLP and the facts presented, the decision has had a broad impact on peacebuilding work, as well as the emerging field of P/CVE. This is because the very nature of many peacebuilding and P/CVE activities requires direct, knowing engagement with listed nonstate armed groups. Concerns about vagueness on what is and is not allowed, combined with harsh penalties called for in AEDPA and sanctions law, have created a chilling effect on many peacebuilding organizations.

There are many forms of peace-oriented training, expert advice and assistance, and services that, absent legal restrictions, could be provided to listed groups in a manner that manages and mitigates risks. Traditional mediation and back-channel diplomacy that can lead to peace talks are only a few of the ways in which peacebuilding organizations work. For example, the Swiss-based group Geneva Call works directly with nonstate armed groups, including some on terrorist lists, to train them in international humanitarian law and other topics. Its goal is to have groups sign Deeds of Commitment pledging to adhere to principles and practices that protect civilians. In March 2016, it signed an agreement with the Kurdistan Workers' Party (PKK) in Turkey, one of the groups HLP had sought to train, banning sexual violence and gender discrimination (Geneva Call 2016). It has been invited to help demobilize child soldiers in the Revolutionary Armed Forces of Colombia (FARC) as part of the peace process aimed at ending a long-running conflict in Colombia. It also works with groups on banning use of land mines. After the HLP decision, it became illegal for US groups to do this kind of work with armed groups on US terrorist lists. It is also illegal for US grantmakers to fund such work.

The decision has international impact, due to the extraterritorial jurisdiction provision in AEDPA. This means that if peacebuilders based outside the United States engage in prohibited activity, they can be prosecuted for it upon entry into the country, whether or not they are US citizens and regardless of where the work is done. The decision also limited peacebuilding approaches to violent extremism just at the time that interest in P/CVE was emerging. This has inhibited development of the field at a time when more strategic options for dealing with terrorism and violent extremism are needed.

There is a growing consensus that laws prohibiting support to listed entities "have contributed to a 'shrinking space' for those seeking to establish the conditions conducive to peace." The report *Building Peace in Permanent War: Terrorist Listing and Conflict Transformation* finds that terrorist listings "shrink the space" for international peacebuilding work in these conflicts by criminalizing third-party mediation and negotiation support (Boon-Kuo et al.

2015). The report says the Global War on Terror has "transformed the way in which political violence and armed conflict is understood and managed. At the heart of this transformation is the freedom for governments to apply the terrorist label to groups and individuals on the basis of very broad definitions of what 'terrorism' entails, or in the absence of any meaningful criteria at all—leading to a glut of terrorist designations." The result is reduced engagement with listed entities and compromised neutrality that erodes a focus on addressing the root causes of conflict.

REACTIONS TO THE HLP DECISION AND CIVIL SOCIETY ADVOCACY TO LIFT RESTRICTIONS

The HLP decision was widely criticized, including editorials in the *Washington Post* and *USA Today*. The *Post* said the decision went "too far," noting that "Congress was right to criminalize the donation of money and tangible goods to terrorist groups; such resources can be used to further violent ends even if donors mean them for legitimate purposes. The same cannot be said of the kind of services the Humanitarian Law Project intended to provide" (*Washington Post* Editorial 2010).

Civil society has pushed back, seeking exemptions and legislative fixes to the limits on peacebuilding. For example, AEDPA gives the secretary of state power to grant exemptions for activity involving training, expert and advice, and assistance and personnel when to do so does not threaten national security. In a May 12, 2011, letter, a bipartisan group of eighteen organizations and twenty-seven peacebuilding and foreign policy experts asked secretary of state to use this exemption power to make conflict resolution and other peacebuilding activities legal. The letter noted the importance of multitrack diplomacy, saying, "For many years, U.S. organizations and private individuals have paved the way for peace by helping to bring fighting factions together and providing alternatives to violence as a means of redressing grievances. We know that these initiatives can be the key to success in resolving conflicts" (Peacebuilding Exemption Letter 2011).

The letter included proposed text for an exemption to permit specific types of peacebuilding activities that are "designed to reduce or eliminate the frequency and severity of violent conflict, or to reduce its impact on noncombatants." Such activities include:

- Expert advice or assistance that facilitates dialogue and promotes opportunities for parties to armed conflict to discuss peaceful resolution of their differences and protect civilians pursuant to international humanitarian law and the logistics necessary to support such dialogue.

- Training, including in-person, written, and virtual presentations, aimed at demonstrating the benefits of nonviolent methods of dispute resolution and providing the skills and information necessary to carry it out.

Although State Department officials met with Charity & Security Network (CSN) members to discuss the proposal on several occasions, no exemption or program resulted. When Senator John Kerry became secretary of state, the effort was renewed by thirty-eight former government officials, academics, foreign policy experts, and religious leaders, including former president Jimmy Carter. They sent a petition to Kerry on June 20, 2013, asking him to "open the door for professional peacebuilders to fully engage in helping to end armed conflicts and suffering around the world, while making the U.S. safer" (Expert Letter 2013). When no action was taken, peacebuilding advocates turned their attention to Congress.

Some members of Congress had expressed concern about the impact of the ruling. In August 2011, Senator Patrick Leahy (D-VT), then chair of the Senate Judiciary Committee, wrote to Secretary of State Hillary Clinton and Attorney General Eric Holder expressing concern that peacebuilding groups "are unduly constricted" in their efforts. The letter urged Holder and Clinton to facilitate a dialogue between the administration and affected organization to produce "a set of guidelines that remove the uncertainty with the scope of the material support law, and the establishment of a process by which actors may seek exemptions" (Leahy 2011). As noted earlier, dialogue with the State Department did not produce a resolution of the issue.

In 2013, a bill introduced in the House of Representatives offered a legislative fix to the problems peacebuilding groups face, as well as constraints on delivery of humanitarian assistance. The Humanitarian Assistance and Facilitation Act (HAFA) of 2013, introduced by Representative Chris Smith (R-NJ) and cosponsored by Representatives James McGovern (D-MA), Jeff Fortenberry (R-NE), and Randy Weber (R-TX), proposed to lift restrictions on "engaging in any speech or communication with a foreign person that is subject to sanctions under this Act to prevent or alleviate the suffering of a civilian population, including speech or communication to reduce or eliminate the frequency and severity of violent conflict and reducing its impact on the civilian population" (Humanitarian Assistance Facilitation Act of 2013). Although HAFA did not pass, interest in its approach continues to grow.

With legal reform stalled, the CSN sought to clarify what that US government believes is permissible by scrutinizing its statements to the Supreme Court in the HLP case. In its brief and in answer to question in oral argument, then solicitor general Elena Kagan cited some clear examples, which are now summarized in the publication "Permissible Peacebuilding Activities" (CSN 2014).

AN ALTERNATIVE: THE RISK-BASED APPROACH

To date the legal environment for NPOs that wish to carry out peacebuilding and P/CVE programs has been a "strict liability approach," placing an absolute ban on a vaguely defined set of activities that, after the HLP decision, are considered "material support." At the same time enforcement policy has taken a relatively narrow view of what will be prosecuted. The Obama administration noted that it "has never prosecuted an individual or group for a legitimate effort to persuade others not to engage in violence" (DoJ 2017). It is not clear how the Trump administration will view these issues, so many view work in any "gray areas" as increasingly risky.

The result is similar to the "Don't Ask, Don't Tell" policy the US military had on sexual orientation, with similar pluses and minuses. While some activities in gray areas go forward, government maintains the flexibility to crack down if it wants to. Meanwhile, programs that could reduce terrorism and violent extremism and armed conflict remain limited in what they can do.

In defending this strict interpretation of the statute, the Obama administration justified its position by citing the risks, accepted by the court with little scrutiny, it said are associated with peacebuilding programs. What the court failed to consider is whether these risks can be managed or mitigated.

In the realm of anti-money laundering and counterterrorist financing (AML/CTF) regulations, the international standard is now a risk-based approach. This could provide an alternative to the "strict liability" approach to the material support prohibition. This approach was adopted in 2012 by the Financial Action Task Force, an intergovernmental AML/CTF body that sets AML/CTF standards globally. Its standard on nonprofit organizations (Recommendation 8) was revised in June 2016 to urge governments to "apply focused and proportionate measures, in line with the risk-based approach" (FATF 2016).

The risk-based approach is a step-by-step process that requires first and foremost that actual (not hypothetical) risks be identified and that laws and standards then be reviewed to determine whether risks are addressed in a proportionate manner. In the end FATF says restrictions should not disrupt or discourage legitimate nonprofits.

In the HLP decision the Supreme Court cited four primary risks of peacebuilding engagement with listed armed groups to justify the absolute prohibition on engagement. These are:

Risk 1: Terrorist groups may use negotiations to gain legitimacy and skills, which facilitate the organization's ability to recruit, raise money, and ultimately persist in its terrorist activities.

Risk 2: Resources gained by participation in peacebuilding processes may free up other resources to use for violence.

Risk 3: Terrorists may pursue peaceful negotiations as a means of buying time to recover from setbacks, lulling opponents into complacency, and ultimately preparing for renewed attacks.

Risk 4: Programs of US peacebuilding groups may constrain the US government's relationships with its allies, undermining cooperative efforts between nations to prevent terrorist attacks.

A risk assessment of peacebuilding and P/CVE projects would ask the following questions about the proposed activities:

1. What is the actual danger that risks 1–4 cited previously might happen?
2. In what circumstances is the risk of this happening higher than normal? When is the risk lower?
3. How do peacebuilders make that assessment?

The next step is risk management and mitigation, which ask, "What steps can be taken to reduce the risk?" If risk can be reasonably managed or mitigated, then the benefits to be gained by going forward with the activity outweigh the potential harms. If this approach can work for terrorist financing, which involves tangible resources that might arguably be more risky when diverted to terrorist groups, then it can work in the realm of peacebuilding and efforts to prevent material support of terrorism.

CONCLUSION

It is past time for the US government to move beyond the zero-tolerance approach taken to the material support prohibition, and for it to recognize that peacebuilding by civil society organizations is vital to addressing the root causes of conflict and terrorism. While there may be risks that something may go wrong in a civil society program, the larger risk is allowing the conditions that breed violence to continue. Government (and the military) cannot solve this problem alone. Instead, it must engage with civil society to find ways to take advantage of the full scope of what peacebuilders can offer while mitigating and managing risk. To do otherwise is to resign the world to endless war.

Chapter 16

Proscribing Peace

The Impact of Terrorist Listing on Peacebuilding Organizations

Teresa Dumasy and Sophie Haspeslagh

The work of nongovernmental organizations (NGOs) in the prevention of violent conflict and in support of efforts to build peace is more relevant than ever. The number of armed conflicts—forty in 2014—is the highest recorded figure since 1999. The multiplicity of armed groups engaged in intrastate conflict has increased, as have the range of groups and the internationalization of conflict through them. These factors call for the resources and influence of a broad range of actors, beyond national governments, the United Nations, and other multilateral organizations, to find ways to address underlying drivers of conflict and further any opportunities for peace.

For international NGOs (INGOs) and local civil society actors and communities, engaging with armed groups for peaceful ends carries immediate risks to physical security (both from the group and from state actors if suspected of collusion) and to reputation, given the political sensitivities of the task. Likewise running peacebuilding programs in conflict contexts where armed groups operate is complex and high-risk. If the group is on a terrorist list, then these risks only multiply.

For INGOs working with the full range of groups and individuals involved in conflict, relationships of trust built on independence, confidentiality, and impartiality are essential. Maintaining those principles and complying with the law have become harder since 9/11 and over the past five years as counterterrorism (CT) legislation has tightened its focus on international aid.

In 2010 the US Supreme Court ruled in the *Holder v. Humanitarian Law Project* case that "material support" for listed groups, including training and advice designed to facilitate negotiations to end conflict, is illegal. The impact of this decision and of the vagaries of CT legislation regimes on principled humanitarian action has been well documented. However, such impact analysis has not yet been applied to the peacebuilding, conflict prevention, and mediation field.

This chapter, based on a briefing paper of the same name, therefore sets out some of the risks facing this sector in relation to working with listed armed groups or in contexts where they operate, as well as the direct and indirect impact of proscription on organizations and their work.[1] Its purpose is to help find ways to mitigate the negative effects of listing and associated legal regimes and regulatory frameworks and to ensure that peaceful ways to end violent conflict can operate unhindered.

In the United Kingdom, humanitarian, peacebuilding, and development NGOs and related umbrella groups have come together to raise the attention of the government and regulatory bodies to the problems facing NGOs as a result of terrorist listing. A dialogue process is emerging between NGOs and relevant government departments, which may provide a channel through which issues may be discussed and solutions found to some of the problems outlined. The chapter is based on informal discussions and interviews with fifteen Europe-based organizations as well as evidence presented in published research reports and articles (Carl and Haspeslagh 2010; Dudouet 2011; Stock 2012). The examples do not attribute impact exclusively to one listing regime or jurisdiction unless specified. The findings are by no means exhaustive, and more evidence needs to be uncovered, in particular about the direct and indirect impact of terrorist listing on local partner organizations in conflict settings. Indications suggest that these organizations and individuals can often bear the brunt of the "criminalization" of their activities, including by their own national government.

Terrorist listing regimes in the United Kingdom, Europe, and beyond:

The basis for the terrorist listing (proscription) regime in the United Kingdom (UK) is the Terrorism Act of 2000. Under this Act, the Home Secretary may list an organisation if they believes it is "concerned in terrorism" (Home Office 2015). According to David Anderson QC, the UK's Independent Reviewer of Terrorism Legislation, (2011–2017) "The UK's definition of terrorism is in significant respects broader than those of other comparable countries". 64 armed groups are currently listed as "international terrorist organisations" under this Act. Groups such as Boko Haram, al-Qaeda, al-Shabaab, the Basque Homeland and Liberty (Euskadi Ta Askatasuna, ETA), LTTE, PKK, military wings of Hamas and the Hezbollah. (Home Office 2015)

The United Kingdom also applies the European Union (EU) listing regime born out of EU Common Position 2001/931/CFSP, which has two sublists, one for groups operating within the EU and one for groups' operation outside in non-EU member state countries, and the United Nations (UN) Security Council Resolutions 1267, 1988, and 1989 in relation to the Taliban and Al-Qaeda.

All these listing regimes are aimed at disrupting listed groups' fund-raising activities and travel and are mainly focused on asset freezes and travel bans. So, for example, they all criminalize financial transactions to these groups. But they differ when it comes to how explicitly they criminalize contact with listed groups.

While the EU and UN listings do not mention this, the UK regime allows "genuinely benign meetings." In November 2015, as a result of NGO engagement, the government clarified its interpretation of the law to state that such meetings are those "at which the terrorist activities of the group are not promoted or encouraged, for example, a meeting designed to encourage a designated group to engage in a peace process" (Home Office 2016).

The US legislation, on the other hand, explicitly criminalizes meetings with listed groups. The June 2010 US Supreme Court ruling, mentioned earlier, made it illegal to provide "expert advice," "service," or "training in human rights enforcement or peaceful conflict resolution" to a listed group. This applies to US nationals and is extraterritorial in scope.

In the United Kingdom, if a charity is suspected of having links with terrorism, it will first be investigated by the Charity Commission. The Charity Commission is an independent regulatory body, which monitors and investigates UK-registered charities. It has the power to take over or close charities. The Charity Commission has a "compliance toolkit" with a chapter on CT legislation and operational guidance (Anderson 2014; Charity Commission 2013). To ensure charities do not provide direct support to a listed organization, the UK Department for International Development (DFID) includes special clauses within its memorandum of understanding with partner organizations in areas deemed high-risk. This is done at the discretion of heads of DFID country offices. Australia, Canada, and the US governments insert specific CT clauses in all levels of funding agreements. These obligations are then passed on to all implementing partners.

THE IMPACT ON INTERNAL DECISION MAKING

Don't Ask, Don't Tell

The absence of prosecutions of peacebuilding and mediation organizations in the United States, United Kingdom, or EU member states is neither reassurance of protection under the law nor proof that terrorist listing and associated legislation are not having a negative impact. David Anderson QC stated in his 2014 review of the terrorism acts that uncertainty about the law can itself be damaging. "It is not sufficient to rely on the restrained exercise of very wide discretions by prosecutors (or by the Attorney General) in circumstances where trustees need to be satisfied that NGOs are not exposed to the risk of criminal liability. A prudent approach to such risks may thus result in NGOs discontinuing or not embarking upon necessary or useful work, even in circumstances where prosecutions are unlikely" (Anderson 2014).

The lack of clarity in terms of what is and is not permissible in relation to contacts with listed groups creates confusion and uncertainty for peacebuilding organizations interpreting legislation. This is compounded by the multiplicity and complexity of CT regimes and broadly depends where an organization is registered and the nationalities of its staff. In an effort to get clarity, a number of organizations have taken legal advice in the United Kingdom, EU, and the United States on their liability and risks.

Several of these requests were deliberately made in oral form to avoid a paper trail. Peacebuilding organizations say that CT legislation and frameworks create an atmosphere characterized as, "Don't ask the question if you don't want to know the answer." Some organizations refer to an approach involving "calculated risks" within uncertain legal and political parameters.

In one case, a peacebuilding organization asked its lawyers what would happen if its staff were to engage with Hamas or another listed armed group. The advice suggested that, as no funds were provided (only incidental expenses) and the organization was acting in good faith for conflict resolution ends, the risk of prosecution was low. In another case, after consulting US lawyers, an organization developed a specific policy for US national employees, under which the employee signs a document saying they comply with US CT legislation. The organization also concluded that for non-US citizens, the risk was more political than judicial. The threat of potential future prosecution is real, and the liability of peacebuilding organizations is serious. It inspires the "prudent approach" referred to by David Anderson QC in a field of work that inherently demands the taking of calculated risks.

Undue Diligence

Interpreting CT legal norms in order to operate within the law can require legal expertise in order to navigate the complexities of jurisdictions and regulations. Added to that, the legislation and regulations governing engagement with listed groups are often tied up with anti-bribery and corruption (ABC) regimes. The cost of compliance for organizations is steadily increasing across the charity sector. One telling example is the case of two leading UK-based charities, Oxfam and Islamic Relief Worldwide (IRW), documented by the Overseas Development Institute (ODI) in 2015:

> IRW and Oxfam, are instituting increasingly robust risk management and due diligence procedures based on professional standards for preventing fraud and money laundering, as well as more specifically related to counterterrorism measures. These and other organisations have begun screening staff, partners

> and even beneficiaries against lists of proscribed individuals or entities. Using databases/software provided by a range of suppliers, often at significant cost, some INGOs are able to screen against lists provided by inter-governmental bodies such as the UN and the EU and national governments. (Metcalfe-Hough, Keatinge, and Pantuliano 2015)

If the costs of such measures to large and established charities like Oxfam are high, then they will be disproportionately so for smaller organizations, particularly civil society partner organizations in-country, who have limited resources and capacity to navigate the complexity of funding requirements. One organization supporting local women's peacebuilding organizations related how they struggle with the growing administrative burden of complex and time-consuming procedures, which they felt to be out of touch with the operational reality involving modest numbers of staff and volunteers operating in challenging environments. Moreover, these core operational and compliance costs are increasingly difficult to cover from restricted donor grants, where the predominant trend is toward projectized funding seeking specific and tangible in-country results.

Liability is being delegated from donors to INGOs and then further down the chain. The 2015 report *Building Peace in Permanent War: Terrorist Listing and Conflict Transformation*, published by the International State Crime Initiative and Transnational Institute, made the point that peacebuilding NGOs are themselves outsourcing risk to their partners in certain contexts. In Somalia, one organization reported that it chooses to work through Somali partners as it "lessens our exposure by not having to make those decisions ourselves" (Boon-Kuo et al. 2015). A participant in a Chatham House discussion on this topic noted, "Donors have shifted risk onto NGOs in order to protect themselves."[2]

Another area of growing concern is around access to financial services. Organizations refer to difficulties in opening bank accounts and in transferring funds. In one reported case, despite following advice from the British Banking Association that developing a constructive relationship with the account manager would be sufficient to secure approvals for transfers, the organization's difficulties continued. Another organization based in Europe was refused a second account by a major national bank when the bank learnt that the organization was working in the Middle East and North Africa (MENA) region, even though the grant for the work was coming from the donor government.

These cases chime with similar developments in the humanitarian sector; a recent ODI report cited an INGO which "had foregone £2 million in donations in the preceding 12 months as a result of funds being blocked and had had to return funds to a donor because it was unable to get them through to their intended destination overseas" (Metcalfe-Hough, Keatinge, and Pantuliano 2015). Worryingly, in terms of transparency and the ability to track funds, a number of peacebuilding organizations admitted to resorting to "informal bank routes" and services such as Western Union for money transfers.

Information versus Reputation

Nervousness about liability and the permissible parameters of the law is resulting in information, as well as money, being conveyed in more informal ways. This mirrors a similar development among humanitarian agencies. A report exploring the impact of CT frameworks on humanitarian agencies found that sectoral transparency had deteriorated due to fear of the consequences of divulging information (Mackintosch and Duplat 2013).

Officials from donor governments are sometimes the ones keen on discretion, an implicit recognition that knowledge also requires accountability. Yet, in so doing liability is again conferred on to the NGO. One donor government asked an organization to report orally to avoid written records. Another made it clear that they were reluctant to see a list of participants for an event, clearly aware that the list contained names of those linked to listed groups.

These informal arrangements with donors rely on high levels of trust. Yet, organizations are also aware that by giving less information to donors and by watering down how much information goes into the public domain, their public-facing communication looks uninspiring and the value of their work is underrecognized, with consequences for their ability to attract political and donor support.

The partial disclosure of reporting, with some sections of reports not being made public, can also be in tension with the government's transparency requirements. Another UK-based peacebuilding organization, which has had the same charitable objectives for the past twenty-five years, reported that they were reluctant to attempt to revise them in the current climate as they were concerned that it would invite increased scrutiny from the Charity Commission.

THE IMPACT ON THE EFFECTIVENESS OF PEACEBUILDING WORK

Ben Emmerson, former UN special rapporteur on counterterrorism and human rights, notes that "many of the international and national measures aimed at countering terrorist financing and the provision of material support have also had a direct and chilling impact on public interest groups, restricting the ability of entirely lawful organisations to secure funding or to operate effectively" (UN Office of the High Commissioner on Human Rights 2015).

Diminished Understanding of Armed Groups

Effective peacebuilding requires an understanding of all stakeholders in a conflict, including armed groups, whether on a terrorist list or not. This understanding should include not only who they are, where they come from, and what they want but also how they see violence, how they see themselves and their adversaries, their relationship with their constituency, and whether they can envision peace. This kind of information is crucial to exploring options for peaceful resolution of conflict, but it is being affected by the extent to which peacebuilding organizations feel able to be in direct and regular contact with members of armed groups. The director of a conflict resolution NGO notes, "Our principle is that it is important to have the opportunity to talk to everybody. So, once you start classifying certain groups as 'terrorists' it complicates this and makes engaging certain groups in peace negotiations more difficult."

Certain organizations have also highlighted the dilemma they face in deciding whether to share their analysis of armed groups with officials in governmental or multilateral organizations, especially analysis carried out by local partners: "if we share it the risks are obvious to us, if we don't share it their [policy-makers/donors] analysis might be wrong."

Academic research on armed groups is also an important source of knowledge for people working to resolve conflict. But research on listed groups is being increasingly discouraged by ethics committees in UK universities, less fieldwork is being done, and funders are increasingly wary of supporting this type of work. In one reported case, a PhD student wanting to do research on the Basque group Euskadi Ta Askatasuna (ETA) was tipped off by the university authorities to the local police. Another student conducting research on the Kurdistan Workers' Party (PKK) was encouraged by the university to destroy his interview materials and change the focus of his thesis. However, another university deemed research by a PhD student on the Revolutionary Armed Forces of Colombia (FARC) as acceptable as the FARC is not on the United Kingdom's terrorist list.

The risk-averse nature of many research councils in the United Kingdom and the United States compounds the problem. One academic working on the Middle East conflict said that without Norwegian and Swiss funding for research over the past six years, there would be very little by way of research on Hamas by Westerners.

Changing Where We Work and With Whom We Work

Counterterrorism legislation is having a qualitative impact on the work of peacebuilding organizations, their choices and freedom to choose where they work and with whom. This is not only due to a combination of restrictions in funding, deliberate decisions not to take funds from particular donors, particularly US donors, but also due to self-censorship to minimize perceived legal or reputational risks.

The number of neutral locations for meetings with listed groups has become more limited. Organizations who want to organize meetings involving listed groups cannot do so in the United Kingdom, because of visa issues and the lack of clarity over what the law permits. Similarly, due to European CT legislation (mainly travel bans), meetings in other EU countries are also excluded. Instead, organizations typically organize training workshops and meetings in Switzerland and Norway, who have opted out of the EU's CT regime, or Turkey.

Working in certain high-risk areas and regions is also becoming increasingly problematic and limited, in particular in the Middle East and North Africa, but also Pakistan, Sudan, and the Horn of Africa. While the UK government has listed only the armed wing of Hamas, the EU list applies to the whole organization, and the United Kingdom, as an EU member state, in turn complies with the EU regime. In June 2007, the Quartet (UN, EU, Russian Federation, and the United States) established a "no-contact policy" with Hamas, and since 2009, the United Kingdom has been instructing NGO partners that contact should happen only "at a technical and lowest possible level" (Haspeslagh 2013). This has led the peacebuilding NGOs who have chosen to remain engaged in the region to lower their level of contact with the listed group. One US NGO has stopped training the Hamas leadership in conflict resolution, for example.

Furthermore, terrorist listing and related legislation are influencing whom peacebuilding organizations choose to work with, either avoiding those carrying the most legal and reputational risk for the organization, working through elected representatives or proxies, or with members of listed groups in prisons in order to minimize risks to themselves. "In South-Central Somalia one organisation said it had to refrain from carrying out a project that could have been strategic in reducing violence. This organisation made contact with 300 Al Shabaab fighters in the Bakool region of southern Somalia. These fighters said they wanted to defect and traditional elders from the relevant sub-clans had agreed to reintegrate the fighters, but UK and European donors shut down the initiative" (Boon-Kuo et al. 2015; Chatham House in collaboration with Conciliation Resources 2010).

It should be noted that the limitations on space for peacebuilding and mediation are not felt equally across the peacebuilding sector. NGOs feel more or less restricted depending on the nationalities of staff and where the organization is registered. Some NGOs feel greater security than others because of the status and standing of senior members of the organization or board of trustees.

THE IMPACT ON THE PEACEBUILDING ENVIRONMENT

The Direction of Political Winds

Due to the inherent difficulty and nature of their work, peacebuilding and mediation support organizations can tend to be seen as guilty by association. To mitigate this risk, beyond establishing adequate internal due diligence processes, they develop relationships of trust and confidentiality with officials and governments. Staff who feel that their work operates in a gray area of the law, ensure they brief ambassadors, senior officials, or in some cases heads of donor governments directly. However, most NGOs do not enjoy this level of access, particularly smaller and local organizations in conflict contexts. The degree of official support and legal and political protection are also dependent on the direction of the political wind at a given time.

Loss of Independence

The embedding of CT frameworks in donor contracts through disclosure clauses and partner vetting for work in certain regions has added to existing fears that NGOs are increasingly being cast as subcontractors of government policy. As local partner organizations are linked both contractually and by association, their work can also be stigmatized.

In the United Kingdom, concerns were expressed about developments in some funding programs implemented under the Conflict Stability and Security Fund (CSSF). These include more intrusive monitoring of activities. "In one case the donor reserved the right to sit in on any meetings, which would make the NGO's work, based on trust, impossible. The organisation concerned was considering turning down the funding, equivalent to two years' worth of funding and activities."[3]

Peacebuilding organizations' impartiality in the eyes of all stakeholders to a conflict is core to their effectiveness, yet the framing of funding streams, proposals, or analysis can compromise this. Project proposals from major donors dealing with violent actors are often pitched in a way that prejudices the conclusions of the work. One UK-based organization decided not to bid for a research project looking at countering violent extremism in Kenya as it felt that the project excluded a thorough interrogation of the role of state forces.

Finally, the effects of terrorist listing and associated legal frameworks on impartiality are not felt by NGOs alone. Staff in UN agencies have commented that the broader CT framework is having an impact on the perception of the United Nations' impartiality, crucial to their ability to engage with armed groups (Conciliation Resources 2012).

CONCLUSION

Peacebuilding practitioners, not least those in closest proximity to violence and conflict, are acutely aware of the risks and threats posed by armed groups, whether listed as terrorists or not. They share a common desire to prevent conflict and support efforts to build lasting peace.

The chapter presents a snapshot of the ways those engaged in efforts to build peace, support mediation, and better understand conflicts are adapting to the direct and indirect constraints and risks associated with terrorist listing and CT legislation. A picture emerges of resilience and adaptability in the face of legal and political uncertainty surrounding their work. In certain contexts, particularly the Middle East, North Africa, and the Sahel, the impact is felt in more tangible ways, and evidence suggests that those organizations who may be losing out the most, such as local women's organizations working on peace and justice, are those whose roles may be not only the least visible but also the most valuable in forging more peaceful societies. As noted in the Chatham House discussion, "Policymakers must take into account the consequences for mediation and political settlements when crafting counter-terror legislation. Finding a balance between immediate counter-terror measures and long- term strategic plans for conflict resolution is difficult but crucial" (Chatham House in collaboration with Conciliation Resources 2010).

WAYS FORWARD

Don't proscribe contact: In conjunction with humanitarian and development organizations, peacebuilding organizations should collectively explore with donor governments the potential for legal exemptions, which allow contact that supports peaceful change, peace processes, and the delivery of life-saving humanitarian support to populations in need.

Make the public case for conflict prevention and peacebuilding: Governments funding the work of NGOs in conflict settings should communicate a more robust public defense of the need for and value of conflict prevention, peacebuilding, and mediation, including the constructive engagement with nonstate armed groups.

Better understand the impact of terrorist listing on civil society in conflict contexts: Support or commission research into the impact of UK, EU, and UN listing regimes, including mirror CT legislation introduced by national governments in contexts of conflict or political instability, on local civil society organizations and communities and their contributions to peace.

Reassess the effectiveness of terrorist listing: Policy makers should initiate a critical examination of the effectiveness of terrorist listing regimes in incentivizing shifts away from violence, as well as in obstructing and containing it.

Clarify the intention of the law through government-NGO dialogue: Through standing fora for UK government and international NGOs, the government should agree on a clearer articulation of the intention of UK CT legislation and terrorist listing, and consider and agree, on an ongoing basis, the range of permissible and necessary activities by international NGOs and conflict researchers.

Section IV

THE ECOLOGY OF PREVENTING/ COUNTERING VIOLENT EXTREMISM (P/CVE)

Section IV

Introduction

This section explores the pros and cons of preventing and countering violent extremism (P/CVE) programs. Elizabeth Hume and Laura Strawmyer offer a foundation for this section in their chapter 17, "The Evolution of Countering Violent Extremism Policy," which outlines the origins and development of the P/CVE approach. Humera Khan and Adnan Ansari then provide a chapter (chapter 18) providing a "Countering Violent Extremism Framework" that outlines the practical areas of work related to P/CVE being done by their Muslim-based organization Muflehun.

Taking a more critical view, Arjun S. Sethi's chapter, chapter 19, explores the negative impacts of P/CVE in "Countering Violent Extremism in the United States: Unscientific and Stigmatizing National Security Theater." Mohammed Abu-Nimer echoes these concerns in his chapter 20, "Islamization, Securitization, and Peacebuilding Approaches to Preventing and Countering Violent Extremism."

In chapter 21, "Countering Violent Extremism; Disarmament, Demobilization, and Reintegration; Social Capital, and the 'Women, Peace and Security' Agenda," Dean Piedmont and Gabrielle Belli describe the challenges of working within a CVE context to implement disarmament, demobilization, and reintegration (DDR) to reintegrate women from violent extremist groups given the "Women, Peace and Security" mandate from the United Nations.

Chapter 17

The Evolution of Countering Violent Extremism Policy

Elizabeth Hume and Laura Strawmyer

For almost fifteen years, policy makers and development practitioners have struggled to define and implement counterterrorism (CT) and countering violent extremism (CVE) programs and policies. In the national public discourse, the overarching narrative has correlated military strength with safety, and since 9/11, the US government's (USG) response to the threat of terrorism and violent extremism has overrelied on the use of force. However, investing heavily in militarized CT efforts has failed to contain violent extremism and even inspired terrorism.

As the military approach proved insufficient to reduce terrorism, policy makers turned to the development sector. The notion that preventing terrorism and violent extremism requires a comprehensive approach involving programs designed to address the root causes of violent conflict reaches across sectors. Even military officials have stated that we cannot fight our way out of violent extremism. US general Allen stated that

> the lesson that the U.S. has learned . . . is that solving in a comprehensive and in a collaborative way with our partners these underlying social, economic, and political subcurrents, that the underlying causes which take hope from large segments of the population, that give large elements within countries no access to the institutions of government, no hope for a decent job, no way to bring their children up, no hope for education. Getting to the far left of the point of radicalization, which we're living with every day. That's why we're fighting. . . environment where people can be easily radicalized, become extremists, and ultimately join a terrorist group.

As it became clear that CT was more than a military issue, people working in the field of conflict resolution and peacebuilding began to consider a development-focused, "softer side" of CT that would be more focused on preventing the social, economic, and political grievances that drive violent extremism.

The first iteration of a development approach for combatting terrorism rested on the assumption that economic growth and greater access to jobs would reduce extremism. In 2005, the Trans-Sahara Counterterrorism Partnership (TSCTP) was established as a multifaceted, multiyear strategy implemented jointly by the Department of State, the US Agency for International Development, and the Department of Defense to assist partners in West and North Africa to increase their immediate and long-term capabilities to address terrorist threats and prevent the spread of violent extremism. In addition to training and equipping security forces to more effectively combat terrorist threats, TSCTP targeted groups in isolated or neglected regions that are most vulnerable to extremist ideologies. The strategy focused on youth employment, strengthening local governance capacity to provide development infrastructure and improving health and educational services.

Many in the development sector found that they had to engage with security and law enforcement extremely carefully, as empowering state security forces risks state abuse of power and may undermine the aims of the development programs. These programs, albeit development focused, were still within the CT frame of directly deterring those who were already radicalized and on the brink of violence. The peacebuilding field continued to advocate for prevention-centered programming that would affect individuals earlier on in the process of radicalization and began to understand that the problem was not just poverty and lack of jobs. In 2009, USAID put out a report that found

> an emphasis on the so-called "root causes" of violent extremism usually overstates the role of push factors (those characteristics of the societal environment that are alleged to push vulnerable individuals onto the path of violence). By the same token, they often underestimate the potentially critical role played by such pull factors as the appeal of a particular leader, self-appointed imam or inspirational figure, or the material, emotional or spiritual benefits which affiliation with a group may confer. (USAID 2009)

This report became a critical piece of research that showed there was not a one size fits all model for violent extremism and that there was an overreliance on programming that focused on jobs.

During the Obama administration, countering violent extremism (CVE) became the official terminology to address those who "support or commit ideologically-motivated violence to further political goals" (Office of the President 2011). However, CVE under the Obama administration was still closely aligned with the security objectives from which it developed.

In July 2015, over forty humanitarian, development, and peacebuilding organizations put out a statement on the US Global Countering Violent Extremism Agenda shortly after the White House CVE Summit in 2015. These international nongovernmental organizations and civil society actors stated that they appreciated the increase in political commitments to address the drivers and enablers of violent extremism. For example, they highlighted that the emphasis on community-led prevention at the February 2015 White House CVE Summit and, in the post-Summit, 9-Point Action Agenda was a welcome shift in US efforts to balance proactive and reactive responses to the instability and violence that take human lives, reverse development, and disrupt societies. However, they were concerned that this CVE strategy risked repeating the same mistakes as other post-9/11 stabilization initiatives. Their concerns included the following four points:

1. Civilian-led development, prevention, and peacebuilding that support locally led solutions to the root causes of insecurity are chronically underfunded, especially in relation to military efforts.
2. Subordinating development assistance under a CVE approach risks undermining the effectiveness of US foreign assistance. There is already too much linkage between development and security operations, damaging crucial trust and buy-in from local stakeholders. US security interests and foreign-aid effectiveness are better served when the boundaries between development assistance and security assistance and operations are clear.
3. Efforts to reduce extremism within communities are not being accompanied by sufficient progress or coordination on governance reforms, social inclusion, and accountability by governments and institutions.
4. The overreliance on military or aggressive security responses to threats when social and political solutions are needed can fuel grievances, encourage violence, and undermine CVE objectives (NGO Letter 2015).

The CVE framework remained controversial throughout the Obama administration. The peacebuilding field never agreed with the CVE terminology, and many still consider the concept of "countering" to elicit a militaristic approach rather than a peacebuilding one (Lyons-Padilla et al. 2015). Civil society believes that CVE should be understood as a community-building approach rather than a law enforcement tactic. In order for the programs to be effective, government must maintain mutual trust with the communities it seeks to protect and rely on through its CVE programming, both domestically and abroad. Many organizations chose to ignore the terminology and continue working in the peacebuilding sector to address the drivers of violent extremism. However, many other organizations pushed back on the CVE term and preferred to use the term "preventing violent extremism (PVE)" or preventing political violence. Prevention was a preferred frame because it refers to dealing with the drivers of violent conflict, understanding that extremism is a symptom of the larger epidemic of violent conflict. Many private donors believe that CVE is solely a national security priority, and it appears to prioritize the interests of the United States rather than the beneficiaries of international development programs. Subordinating development assistance under a CVE approach, some argued, risks undermining the effectiveness of US foreign assistance, which relies on relationships with local communities. There was already a strong linkage between development and security operations, which risks damaging crucial trust and buy-in from local stakeholders.

As CVE policy and programming evolved, prevention became an important area of work. Many development organizations continued to work in this space during the Obama administration, and many wrestled with the fact that their initial hypothesis that jobs were the answer to CVE did not correlate with the reality of those attracted to violent extremism. Many people who became violent extremists did not suffer from poverty. As it became clear that economic factors may not be the most important factor, and certainly not the only factor, pushing terrorist recruitment, the development community and the USG began to research the push and pull factors that drew people to violent extremism. The goal was to counter conventional wisdom with research and ensure that these findings correlated to policy and programmatic changes.

Practitioners, the government, and academia ramped up research on the drivers of violent extremism. Contrary to conventional wisdom, the primary motivating factors of violent extremism are not economic grievances, such as unemployment and poverty. These factors can play a role, but social and political factors are generally more powerful, including perceptions of marginalization and injustice, existential identity, a history of discrimination, feelings of isolation and oppression, lack of governance and state legitimacy, and a desire to right the wrongs one sees in the world. There is no profile of a violent extremist, even within specific movements, but these factors are generally shared across cases and can intersect to drive attraction to violent extremism (USAID 2009).

Even with a greater understanding of what drives violent extremism, development practitioners face numerous challenges to implementing CVE programs. Human rights are often subverted when the approach to fighting violent extremism is dictated by fear and short-term thinking. Violations of human rights increase the grievances of individuals and communities at risk for radicalization, which may in turn push individuals toward violent action. These injustices are more likely to drive violence than the general problem of poverty. Corruption by public officials can spur anger, while joblessness is accepted as a matter of luck. Without respect for human rights, CT policies are counterproductive. Human rights abuses can even be inherent in the CT approach, which may rely on surveillance and other violations of free speech.

Practitioners also face a challenge to address perhaps the most confounding driver of extremism, the perceived sense of injustice and marginalization. This develops from the experience of seeing a world that one thinks is broken and oppressive and developing a desire to right its wrongs. This factor is specifically related to CVE policy internationally and perpetuates itself when CVE is conducted as a version of CT. Recruitment material from violent organizations like Al-Qaeda and ISIS often highlights and depends upon this feeling of marginalization as a motivating factor. It invokes the suffering and humiliation of Muslims around the world, often at the hands of Western governments, and presents their organizations as agents of change (Lyons-Padilla et al. 2015). Violent extremist organizations like these posit themselves as a route to significance and a chance for potential recruits to change the world. This serves as an intoxicating idea for those who feel marginalized and victimized in their own communities.

At home, the disproportionate focus on Muslim American communities and CVE policy's checkered history of using its programs as a justification of surveillance and coercion has made Muslim communities throughout the United States suspicious of CVE programs. Members of these communities in turn feel victimized, alienated, and marginalized when they hear that CVE programs are implemented only in Muslim communities and are often misused by the Federal Bureau of Investigation (FBI) and other organizations to falsely implicate people who otherwise would not have engaged in violent extremist activities. Officially, under the Obama framework, "violent extremism" could apply to any type of extremism, including white nationalism. However, there is special concern about the potential to conflate the concept of "extremism" with Islam. During the Obama administration, the USG never explicitly defined CVE as a Muslim issue in its policy framework, yet its domestic programs focused almost exclusively on Muslim communities.

Because there is a tendency to view conflict through a political lens, development practitioners have difficulty embracing national security–based programs within their missions to be nongovernmental actors. There is still concern among international development practitioners that CVE programs, especially those branded as such, may even put their beneficiaries in danger. Even organizations without ethical reservations about engaging in CVE work may be hesitant because of legal limitations. In the aftermath of the Supreme Court's 2010 decision in *Holder v. Humanitarian Law Project*, peacebuilding organizations have been uncertain as to what communications with Foreign Terrorist Organizations (FTOs) remain permissible under 18 USC 2339B. This law threatens fines or imprisonment for anyone who provides "material support" to a known FTO, without defining what constitutes "support."

Peacebuilding organizations have stated that the decision has created a chilling impact on peacebuilding activities, inhibited constitutionally permitted speech and association, and reduced the kinds of contacts that might help them work on programs that would reduce violent extremism.

Countering violent extremism work is further limited by a lack of resources. Civilian-led development, prevention, and peacebuilding that support locally led solutions to the root causes of insecurity are chronically underfunded, especially as compared to military efforts. Billions spent on security operations are coupled with relatively minor investments in development, governance, or humanitarian activities. Even under the Obama administration, the vast majority of CVE funds went to law enforcement activities rather than community development programs. The peacebuilding field believes that investing in resources to prevent the onset of violence and war is far more effective than intervening after violence erupts; research shows every one dollar invested in peacebuilding carries a potential $16 reduction in the cost of armed conflict (Institute for Economics and Peace 2017).

The myriad challenges practitioners faced in the Obama era will now be compounded with the shift to a new policy under a new administration. In the early weeks of the Trump administration, the new leadership made it clear they intended to keep their campaign promise of prioritizing American national security, with little regard to maintaining positive relationships with the Muslim communities in the United States and abroad. There were rumors the Trump administration would change the Obama CVE framework, albeit itself controversial, to allow for an explicitly Muslim-focused "Countering Islamic Extremism" or "Countering Radical Islamic Extremism" initiative. The Administration announced that the USG would rescind funds promised to community groups to address far-Right white extremism (Washington Post Editorial 2017). The change in terminology also came with the announcement that the USG would rescind funds promised to community groups to address far-Right white extremism. The possibility of a shift to a more militarized approach greatly amplifies the concerns of the prevention community.

A year into the Trump administration, these early concerns began to start appearing in policy documents. The 2017 US National Security Strategy (NSS) offers the Trump administration's "America First" view of national security. The strategy is consistent with its predecessors on some matters: every NSS issued to date has affirmed that America must employ a range of means to prevent conflict. However, the use of "radical Islamist terror groups" and "jihadist terrorists" in the document to describe the general issue of violent extremism mischaracterizes the role that religion, in particular Islam, plays in violent extremism and risks alienating allies or undermining US efforts. Violent extremism is driven by many different factors, and the role that religion plays in motivating adherence to these groups is largely emotive rather than theological. By insisting on the naming of "radical Islamic extremism" as an enemy, there is an implicit conflation of all Muslims with violent extremism. For many organizations working in this field, the change of name is a red line; many will refuse to work in this sector. This change will also remove any efforts to understand and undermine the radicalization of violent extremists in other parts of the world outside of Muslim countries, especially white supremacists, who are significantly more likely to carry out violent attacks in the United States.

The silver lining in this new administration is that President Trump has appointed experienced military officers who understand the causes of violent extremism and the limitations of a military approach. Throughout this past decade, those in the military have been some of the strongest allies and advocates for development and peacebuilding programming that focuses on PVE. Unfortunately, the military budgets continue to go up while the peacebuilding budgets get reduced, making it difficult to develop and implement whole-of-society approaches.

Obama administration's 2011 strategy for CVE represented a positive shift from early CT programming because it more explicitly called for nonmilitary engagement at the local community level to address grievances fueling extremism. It focused on developing research that identified actual grievances instead of simply offering traditional development programs. However, this approach was still flawed in its emphasis on countering extremist narratives, the linking of development and security objectives, and the USG's strong focus on the use of military force. Policy makers and donors are increasingly educated and interested in innovative CVE programs, especially as lessons emerge from the Iraq/Afghanistan wars and the violent conflict in Syria. Looking ahead, it is unclear how much civil society will be able and willing to engage with the current USG on violent extremism given its leaning toward a more militarized approach and labeling violent extremist groups "radical Islamic Jihadists."

In conclusion, the policy recommendations from the joint humanitarian, development, and peacebuilding organizational statement on CVE to the USG remains relevant to the United States and global policy community (NGO Letter 2015).

1. *Announce robust financial commitments to civilian-led prevention and development:* Investments should be multiyear and include research and learning budgets and adaptive management structures to advance the evidence base for effective approaches. Sustained commitments should also be made to increase USAID's resources, both staffing and programmatic, to give prevention strategies a chance for success.
2. *Ensure that security operations do not work at cross-purposes with development and peacebuilding efforts.*
3. *Reverse cuts to democracy and governance programming and advance new monitoring and evaluation frameworks for measuring governance improvements across bilateral and multilateral assistance programs:* To

successfully address grievances, including those that may lead to violent extremism, community-level programming must connect to meaningful reforms around the particular motivating grievance, which often lie with a state.

4. *Uphold commitments to rights-based governance in all bilateral assistance:* US security assistance to other states to counter or prevent violent extremism must emphasize and ensure the protection of human rights, citizen security, and equal justice under law.
5. *Reform CT laws and regulations including material support laws that prevent humanitarian, development, and peacebuilding organizations from being able* to work with communities and individuals. The evidence since 1968 indicates that most terrorist groups have ended through political process and local policing. Military force has rarely been the primary reason for the end of terrorist groups. Therefore, an emerging body of evidence argues that domestic governance capacities are more effective than increased military capacities. However, in the US development partners are prevented by material support laws which prohibit providing any type of assistance to groups classified as terrorists. This prohibition prevents organizations from working with these communities to address the grievances that could ultimately lead to a political process (Jones and Libicki 2008).
6. *Commit to establishing voluntary guidelines for implementing the CVE agenda through joint USG and NGO dialogues that include local community stakeholders.* Parallel to existing Civil Military Guidelines, the CVE Guidelines would include a clear delineation of expectations and standards for USG engagement with nongovernmental actors, consistent with local priorities.

Chapter 18

Countering Violent Extremism Framework

Humera Khan and Adnan Ansari

Muflehun is an independent nongovernmental organization at the nexus of security, society, and technology. As a resource center focusing on preventing and countering hate, extremism, and violence, it researches and analyzes current social challenges and pilots impactful, scalable, and replicable programs to build the capacity of civil society actors, governments, and law enforcement. Muflehun is a regular policy advisor to governments and multilateral institutions.

As part of its countering violent extremism (CVE) solution portfolio, Muflehun has developed a five-sector framework for programming that includes Prevention, Intervention, Mitigation, and Rehabilitation, within a Policy and Strategy context, which is adaptable to any geography at the micro, meso, and macro levels. This framework, presented next, has been used for training practitioners and informing decision makers in over fifteen countries.

The field of CVE arose from the morass of need as traditional counterterrorism (CT) approaches have been demonstrably ineffective in preventing the mobilization of individuals toward violence. Indeed, evidence suggests that traditional force–based methods such as drones for targeted killings are actually used to recruit even more people, and in some contexts government actions that resulted in the death or arrest of friends and family members were the tipping point for up to 70 percent of individuals joining violent extremist groups. Inconsistency between government actions and messages about values has provided further fodder for extremist recruiting narratives. Governments have reluctantly been admitting that "we can't arrest our way out of this problem," and for sustainable long-term success CVE will be "more important than our capacity to remove terrorists from the battlefield" (White House National Security Council 2015).

What has finally shifted now is the recognition of the need to address the ideological, emotional, intellectual, and psychological aspects (Samuel 2012) that are bundled under CVE, plus the essential role of narratives in undermining the ideology and recruiting mechanisms of extremism as highlighted by the UN Security Council Resolution 2354 (2017) (UNSCR 2354 2017) and the role of civil society actors in various aspects of CVE (UNSCR 2178 2014; UNSCR 2354 2017; UNSCR 2396 2017).

BACKGROUND

Over the years many frameworks were developed to explain how individuals might be indoctrinated toward violence and radicalized toward terrorist actions. These have ranged from simplistic processes that flagrantly profile religious groups (Silber and Bhatt 2007), theories that explain the path to violence across a spectrum of extremist movements (McCauley and Moskalenko 2011), narrowing staircases toward terrorism (Moghaddam 2005), and more recently two pyramids separating opinions and actions (McCauley and Moskalenko 2014), models around significance (Kruglanski et al. 2014), and "devoted actor" theoretical frameworks describing the willingness to commit violence for sacred values (Atran 2016).

On the converse side, the nascent field of preventing and countering of radicalization toward terrorism, and/or the mobilization toward violence (P/CVE), is plagued with inconsistent definitions, vague concepts (National Security Critical Issues Task Force 2016), and few established response frameworks. Further complicating this endeavor to understand radicalization, develop definitions, and solution frameworks is that "for any given individual or group, the path to de-radicalization is not necessarily the reverse of the path to radicalization" (Moghaddam 2010), and there has been unprecedented backlash from community stakeholders and civil rights groups due to the profiling of communities, stigmatization of religious groups, lack of trust between stakeholders, securitization of transactional relationships, insufficient training for implementers, politicized and hidden agendas, and systemic lack of resource alignment (Khan 2015; Romaniuk 2015).

"Countering violent extremism" has consequently become a politicized and toxic term for many civil society actors in multiple geographies, even though differing opinions prevail on the definitions, concepts, terminology, frameworks, methodology, and tools.

An attempt to provide clarity and distinguish CVE from CT was made by the coinage and popularization of the term "preventing violent extremism (PVE)" by several UN agencies; however, as stated in the UN Plan of Action to Prevent Violent Extremism (2015), the document "pursues a practical approach to preventing violent extremism, without venturing to address questions of definition." The approach taken by the UN General Assembly toward not defining violent extremism or CVE or PVE but by describing the types of activities that should be included in the programming is akin to the UN approach of not providing a universal definition of terrorism but by describing terrorist acts.

The UN Security Council has similarly not provided a definition of CVE but describes in Resolution 2178 (2014) that countering violent extremism in order to prevent terrorism includes "preventing radicalization, recruitment, and mobilization of individuals into terrorist groups and becoming foreign terrorist fighters." The resolution goes on to describe measures that should be included, such as "empowering youth, families, women, religious, cultural and education leaders" and "promoting social inclusion and cohesion" (UNSCR 2178 2014); however, this approach fundamentally skews the arena as it makes assumptions about the drivers of violent extremism and also limits the scope of necessary solutions.

The UN Development Program (UNDP) makes a distinction between CVE and PVE by stating that CVE is "focused on countering the activities of existing violent extremists" whereas PVE is "focused on preventing the further spread of violent extremism" (UNDP 2017). It simultaneously adds that PVE-relevant interventions are "most usefully defined as those that seek to address the structural drivers of violent extremism" and PVE-specific interventions become synonymous with CVE as "seeking to disrupt the radicalization and recruitment process and to reintegrate individuals who have already actively joined a violent extremist organization." The ambiguity of using the term PVE-specific instead of CVE, at odds with their own internal descriptions, is indicative of the challenges faced by the industry writ large.

Civil society organizations that deal with multiple funders and political actors will sometimes use PVE as a shorthand for all types of preventative programming and CVE for all other aspects. Without being supportive or dismissive of the debate, this chapter uses the term "CVE" as defined next to include all PVE and CVE elements and approaches the field from the practitioners' perspective.

WHAT IS COUNTERING VIOLENT EXTREMISM?

In order to effectively communicate with practitioners, policy makers, and communities, Muflehun considered it essential to use a common language and frame to scope the problem (violent extremism) and constrain the solution landscape (CVE) in compliance with international human rights principles. It thus developed a practical definition of CVE to guide its own work and inform the rest of industry.

> Countering violent extremism (CVE) is the use of non-coercive means, to dissuade individuals or groups, from mobilizing towards violence, and to mitigate recruitment, support or engagement in ideologically motivated or justified violence, by non-state actors, in furtherance of political objectives. (Muflehun 2012)

This multilayered definition answers the questions of how CVE is different from CT, what types of activities are included and excluded, and what is the nature of violent extremism itself. In other words, the definition includes both the scope of the problem and the scope of the solution that can be met through CVE activities.

To start, the difference between CT and CVE is highlighted through the use of "non-coercive means." Unlike CT, CVE effectively excludes all kinetic and coercive actions. This also excludes military information support operations (MISO, previously called psychological operations or PSYOPS) that include deceptive, coercive, or manipulative tactics.

The objective of CVE is to dissuade individuals or groups and not to force behaviors—in other words, CVE is focused on changing the motivation or intent of engaging in violence rather than about limiting the means to act. Detection and disruption of violence and plotted attacks are part of standard law enforcement and CT activities; however, they are not a part of CVE. CVE efforts focus on mitigating all aspects of involvement, including recruitment, support, participation, and mobilization toward violence, However, once an individual has started planning violence or engaging in criminal activity, he or she will be subject to interdiction through CT operations until the person is in custody (if captured alive) and prosecuted. Once a person has left a conflict theater or is already in prison, there is an opportunity in some cases to help the individual reenter society at a later stage in life.

Violent extremism refers to the form of extremism where the ideology itself motivates or morally justifies aggression and violence toward the outgroup. Individuals might or might not join an extremist group because of their ideology; however, the group itself has an ideology that considers violence an essential practice and not just an opportunistic tactic. These actions are carried out by nonstate actors for political ends, thus excluding state-based terrorism. There are multiple existing international legal standards that govern hostile actions taken by states, and CVE does not aim to replace any of them. The end goal of violent extremism is always political. Violent extremism is thus a form of political violence; however, not all political violences are violent extremism.

Keeping these characteristics of violent extremism in perspective, it is important that for CVE to be effective, the ideology of the involved violent extremists needs to be understood and undermined. Second, there are many types of crimes and violence that occur in every society; however, not all of them are extremist in nature. Hate crimes as an example are not necessarily considered violent extremism if they do not have a political goal. Hate is often a precursor that is used to incite violence; however, not all hate crimes are committed by violent extremists.

Two additional concepts that are important to note are *CVE-relevance* and *CVE-specificity*. CVE-relevant programs and approaches are those that address any factor that reduces the propensity toward violence. They are not exclusive to risk reduction for violent extremism. CVE-specific programs and approaches specifically address the issue of violent extremism and are a lot more targeted in their focus. They are a lot more localized and require dedicated resources over extended periods of time. During implementation these distinctions can blur. However, it is important to keep the characteristics in perspective to inform the holistic design of the program and for developing appropriate metrics for monitoring and evaluation. Every involved community and society will need both specific and relevant CVE programs; the balance will depend on factors such as the context, urgency and prioritization of the threat, trusted relationships within the community, and resource availability.

COUNTERING VIOLENT EXTREMISM FRAMEWORK

One of the challenges in the CVE industry has been to decide which approach to take toward conceptualizing and designing solutions. The approaches that compete in this space are national security, public safety, human development, peace building, and most recently, public health and education, which have also joined the milieu. The selection of national security over public safety appears to be impacted by the geographic origin of the grievances and violent extremist ideology (if they are local/indigenous or imported from elsewhere); if the group has cross-border operations or funding; the relationship with neighboring countries; the role of the military within the country; the national surveillance apparatus; the budgetary priorities of the country; the civil liberties environment; the legislation; the scope and scale of the threat; the training and resources allocated to law enforcement; the robustness and independence of the judicial system; and political will among many other factors. With the other approaches, yet more variables need to be factored in, including the role of civil society; the funding mechanisms available; the quality and accessibility of health care, especially mental health; minority

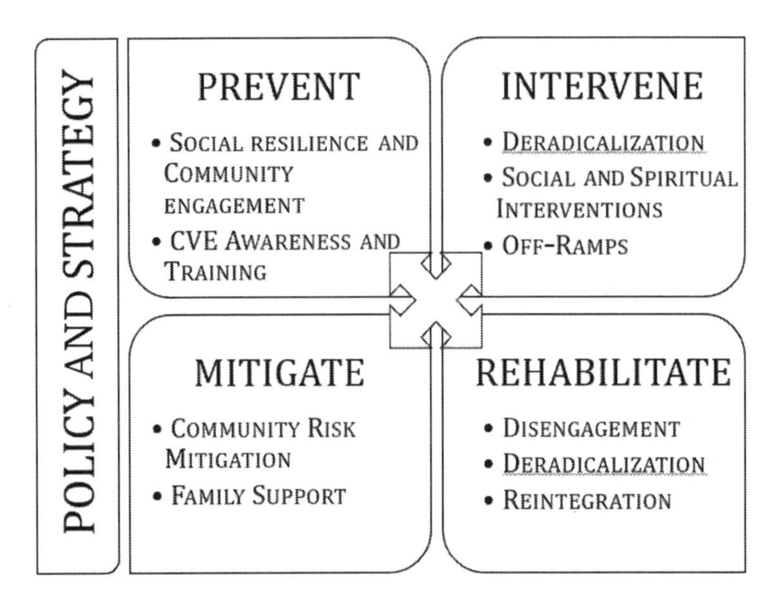

Figure 18.1. Muflehun's Five Sector CVE Framework

rights; media freedom; freedom of religion; social and cultural norms; quality and accessibility of the education sector; role of clergy and religion; secularism; and governance and governments.

What should be readily apparent is that given the diversity of factors, no one approach is sufficient. The assumption that a single approach to CVE will be consistently relevant and effective reminds us of the words famously immortalized by Maslow: "I suppose it is tempting, if the only tool you have is a hammer, to treat everything as if it were a nail" (Maslow 1966).

For CVE practitioners and implementers, a new hybrid framework combining elements is most effective. Rather than retrofitting CVE into frameworks designed to explain other phenomena, a hybrid framework based on its objectives, the audiences, and the stakeholders, while drawing from existing validated approaches, allows for localization and customization based on contextual priorities rather than approaching CVE strategies as off-the-shelf products.

A comprehensive CVE framework needs to include Prevention, Intervention, Mitigation, and Rehabilitation, within a larger Policy and Strategy context, adaptable to any region (at a micro, meso, or macro level). Each will meet the needs of a different audience and will require different stakeholder involvement.

Figure 18.1 illustrates the suggested CVE framework, inclusive of all primary components that need to be addressed to effectively identify the needs of society and policy makers and to design impactful programs to focus on the relevant risks of violent extremism.

Each sector of the CVE landscape has to address both the behaviors and as the ideas space and not just attend to one aspect to the detriment of the other.

An essential consideration before using any CVE framework, including this one, is to understand how to segment the audience based on behaviors and extremist ideological beliefs rather than misconstruing factors such as race, religion, religiosity, and political conservativeness as indicators of radicalization. Each audience type needs different types of programs. The balance of programs and audience will be assessed contextually. The suggested framework allows appropriate segmentation of the audience, matching them to relevant programming.

PREVENTION

The objective of Prevention programs and activities is to raise the barriers to entry to prevent support for extremism from taking root. At this prevention stage, individual has not been indoctrinated in any way and has not committed a crime either; thus, programming that reduces the propensity toward violence (not just extremist violence) will be important. One essential lesson to be learned from the public health approach to primary prevention is that the *whole* society (general public) is the audience.

Society can be further segmented into individuals and groups that are resilient and are able to actively resist the draw of extremist actors and violence; those that are unaware of the nature of the risks and might be unprepared on how to respond if faced with the situation; those that are vulnerable to the ideas or are accessible to the extremist social networks. The needs of society are best met through prevention, both CVE-relevant and CVE-specific. This includes shifting the naïve populations to resilience to effectively immunize them. In the same way, the at-risk cohorts have to be shifted at minimum to neutrality and at best toward resilience.

From a public health perspective, CVE-relevant prevention programs would be considered primary prevention and CVE-specific programs for a vulnerable population would be considered secondary prevention.

As the body of research into the psychology of violent extremism and terrorism has grown (Horgan 2014), the question of the role of ideology comes up often. Models describing the process repeatedly indicate that ideology is not the starting point; however, it is a crucial component in reducing inhibition toward violence (Kruglanski et al. 2014). However, once a person has been socialized into the extremist network, he or she will be indoctrinated toward the ideology, and sacred values are invoked to mobilize toward violence (Atran 2016), which will be addressed in the following section on interventions.

An important implication for CVE-relevant prevention programs and activities is that they can avoid addressing ideology and still be effective. Whether they work toward addressing grievances, improving resilience, or reducing vulnerability, they can be conducted without marginalizing communities or stigmatizing individuals about beliefs and faith. This also validates the public health approach that primary prevention is aimed at the public and opens the door for education, mental health, and development approaches in PVE. Ultimately, this does not eliminate the need for CVE-specific initiatives to address ideological elements; however, it allows more nuanced and better calibrated programs.

As this sector integrates multiple approaches to building resilient communities, it creates a natural space for civil society to participate and lead in PVE. This includes but is not limited to communities, leaders, youth, clergy, health care providers, social workers, counselors, teachers and educators, families, and the private sector.

An example of a CVE-relevant Prevention program designed by Muflehun is ViralPeace. ViralPeace is an interactive workshop for youth activists, change makers, and young leaders to learn strategies to push back against hate, extremism, and violence. Participants of the workshop learn to identify narratives that are used to incite hate and manipulate people toward violence, create their own narratives, and strategically use social media and networks for content distribution. They are taught to use design thinking to develop projects and campaigns to serve their own communities and stand up for their identified cause. Young influencers in several countries have been mentored in this workshop and have also run their own workshops after going through additional training of trainers. Some of these include youth groups in the United States, Germany, Indonesia, Jordan, Malaysia, Maldives, Norway, the Philippines, Singapore, and Sri Lanka, where this program has been implemented.

An example of a CVE-specific Prevention program designed by Muflehun is *Fiqh or Fiqhtion* (*Fiqh* in Arabic means jurisprudence and *Fiqhtion* is a play on words to indicate fiction). This interactive true-or-false-style quiz checks if youth can distinguish violent extremist ideology from normative religious theology by identifying verbatim quotes from violent extremist recruiting propaganda as fiqh or fiqhtion. One lesson learned from running pilots with students was that those who receive religious instruction through weekend and part-time schools were easily able to distinguish extremist ideology from theology as the value sets promoted in each are so different. Additionally, these Fiqh or Fightion sessions became an opportunity to have a dialogue in a safe space about other issues related to extremism that the youth were reluctant to discuss with their teachers or parents.

INTERVENTION

The second cohort we must address includes passive and active supporters of extremist thoughts or groups. In this case the individuals have not crossed the line into criminal or violent behaviors; however, they are indoctrinated to some extent and can be considered "at risk" individuals. Intervention programs are key in this space to stop the escalation from ideas to potential violent actions and to provide off-ramps for individuals who are already entrenched in the space. These programs focus on disengagement from the burgeoning extremist identity as well as deradicalization from the ideology. The distinction between disengagement and deradicalization is key (Horgan 2014), however, potentially less pronounced compared to cases where the individual has already committed violence.

From a practitioner's perspective, intervention programs are necessarily individually focused, and they deal with the particularities of each case. The role of counselors, mental health professionals, social workers, clergy, peers, families, mentors, victims, and even former extremists cannot be overstated. Depending on the context and legal systems, lawyers and law enforcement might also be involved. A common misconception is to consider these CVE interventions the same as secondary prevention from the public health lens—however, the basic characteristic of needing to be individualized rather than aimed at the general public renders that framework incompatible with Intervention, even though it has multiple overlaps with the Prevention space.

Interventions have to address the conditions that created the vulnerability in the first place to shrink the need for the extremist ideology. Additionally, the lure of extremist groups is not just in their actions or views, but it is also in the supportive social networks and surrogate families they provide to their in-group. Creating a new social network while deliberately limiting access to or reducing attraction to the previous peers is challenging and requires much willingness, effort, and persistence by the individuals themselves. Forcing a person into counseling for disengagement or deradicalization—as has been done by several government initiatives—is not sufficient in addressing the social dynamics and peer networks that have to be overcome. Similar to prevention, interventions are also conducted before an individual has engaged in criminal violent behavior; this arena benefits tremendously when civil society members are fully engaged as relevant partners to create realistic customized strategies for disengagement and deradicalization.

Depending on the context, government-led intervention programs dealing with ideology are often not considered legitimate and individuals associated with them lose their credibility. As violent extremism is a form of political violence, one of the "enemies" is often the government; it is unrealistic to expect that supporters will immediately turn around and trust the very institutions that they have grievances with. Instead, it is essential for the government institutions to enable legally safe space and facilitate access to resources for civil society members who can consistently provide long-term required services and monitor the progress of the individual(s) subjected to the interventions.

Muflehun launched a service called RampOff to provide information and early intervention support. RampOff helps family members and peers who have identified signs of behavior changes in their friends or family members; however, they lack sufficient understanding of what to do themselves or how to access community and professional support mechanisms to address the situation. RampOff fills this unmet need as a confidential, multichannel information and early intervention support service. Referrals into RampOff come in-person through the helpline and also through social media. Important lessons learned in this program are that such services need to be localized for greater effectiveness due to the customized needs of every intervention case and the accessibility of the professional support network.

MITIGATION

Irrespective of the resources and effort dedicated into preventing and intervening, we must be realistic and recognize that some cases will slip through the cracks of society's safety nets and proceed to participate in violence. Society needs to be prepared for such cases of failure and create conditions to minimize the damage done to society at large, support the victims, as well as immediate networks (including family and peer groups) of the individual committing the violent activity as needed.

Significant mitigation preparation in CVE can be conducted prior to the occurrence of a violent event, while customized damage reduction efforts occur postevent. Also, while all of society must be strategically prepared for undesired events of violence, communities and social networks at greater risk of repercussions need to be more aware and prepared for the consequences and backlash from violent events.

Significant mitigation efforts are mostly witnessed in law enforcement organizations where resources are channeled for trainings to cater to situations of violent events. However, the larger society is generally not prepared for such occurrences. Another sector that needs training is media to ensure that false reports, assumptions, and fear are not escalated in the immediate aftermath of incidents.

A major gap that still remains is in efforts to minimize potential damage to families and immediate networks of individuals committing violent extremist crimes. Families often face major repercussions due to being ostracized by communities, social isolation, bullying, harassment, in addition to the psychological damage incurred from individuals close to them. Families can never be prepared for such setbacks, but communities and social systems punish them for acts they were not responsible for. This additional marginalization places family members at a greater risk of seeking out extremism, which previously they might not have.

In addition, it is also observed in certain contexts, there is inaction to disengage individuals in the closest peer networks of the violent actor, who are already exposed to the extremist ideologies. This has led to additional individuals from the network following the path of those who have already committed criminal action. Had there been timely, relevant efforts made, such missteps may have been avoided. Systemic efforts to protect such vulnerable members of society are required for mitigation efforts.

Examples of mitigation support provided by Muflehun to communities have included liaising with law enforcement, assistance with media strategies to deal with journalists, facilitating training on reporting hate and bias crimes (including bullying in schools), and cultural competence training for law enforcement officers. In selected cases, Muflehun has provided advisory support to parents whose children have either joined extremist groups or have been arrested by law enforcement for the intention to recruit or join such a group. Such families were unaware of their loved one's involvement in violent extremism and are always unprepared to deal with the consequences. The support to each family varies per case, ranging from guiding toward relevant legal support, pastoral care, and counseling.

REHABILITATION

All individuals who participate in any aspect of supporting or engaging in terrorism must be brought to justice (UNSCR 1373 2001); however, we cannot assume that there is no more opportunity for them to change or that there is no benefit in supporting them. Even those who are incarcerated will need rehabilitation as they will need to reintegrate into society after serving their sentence, and they can also radicalize or recruit others who are serving sentences for other crimes in the same facility.

Indeed, each member state of the United Nations is called on "to develop and implement comprehensive and tailored prosecution, rehabilitation, and reintegration strategies and protocols" (UNSCR 2178 2014) "in accordance with their obligations under international law, including with respect to foreign terrorist fighters and spouses and children accompanying returning and relocating foreign terrorist fighters" (UNSCR 2396 2017), where foreign terrorist fighters (FTFs) are "individuals who travel to a State other than their

States of residence or nationality for the purpose of the perpetration, planning, or preparation of, or participation in, terrorist acts or the providing or receiving of terrorist training, including in connection with armed conflict."

Rehabilitation has three essential aspects: *Disengagement* from the behaviors and the group, *deradicalization* from the ideology, and *reintegration skills* to help the individual be a productive member of society. In the case of individuals who are already incarcerated, ideally the multifaceted rehabilitation process would start before they are released instead of waiting for after. Once a person has been released after serving his or her sentence, finding social stability sooner than later is important to reduce the risk of recidivism.

For returning FTFs and their families, we cannot assume that they have changed their views about the ideology even if they are disillusioned by the life that they experienced or the group itself. A further complication for criminal justice systems is dealing with the returning juveniles who were taken to conflict zones without their consent. There is a spectrum of rehabilitation programs (both in-prison and outside) ranging from comprehensive programs in Singapore and Saudi Arabia to the Danish Aarhaus model that provides disengagement and especially reentry skills but not ideological deradicalization (Bertelsen 2015) to countries like the United States that do not have any federal rehabilitation programs for violent extremists.

It is important to note that disengagement and deradicalization rehabilitation programs will be more effective with public–private partnerships and must include civil society stakeholders, mental health professionals, educational and vocational training resources, as well as trusted partners to address the ideological aspects. For reintegration to be effective, not only will the perpetrators need to learn reentry skills, but the communities that they will return to will also need to accept them back. The reconciliation process to allow for effective reintegration thus must be planned, and society must be prepared for it. In many countries high financial costs, unavailability of trained human resources, legal barriers, lack of political will, and social risks combined with unquantifiable returns have been deterrents in significant progress toward establishing such programs. In this domain, Muflehun provides advisory services for individualized rehabilitation programs in collaboration with law enforcement, families, and legal defense teams.

CONCLUSION

In the context of CVE, the framework summarized previously addresses the complexity and interdependence of the problem space and allows for the emergence of contextual, localized, sustainable solutions. This comprehensive CVE framework provides an approach to practitioners to segment the audience and design programs for the relevant needs, that is, Prevention, Intervention, Mitigation, and Rehabilitation, within a larger Policy and Strategy context, adaptable to any region (at a micro, meso, or macro level). It is expected that as practitioners and policy makers address the problems of violent extremism and find relevant solutions, this framework will further evolve in depth and breadth.

Based on its experiences and lessons learned in designing pilots and implementing across the first four segments, Prevention, Intervention, Mitigation, and Rehabilitation, Muflehun has been an influential behind-the-scenes player in the fifth segment, Policy and Strategy. Muflehun has provided advisory services to government agencies (national, provincial, and local) and multilateral organizations in strategizing approaches to the problems and designing solutions and programs.

Experiencing the high frequency of such requests from policy makers, it is evident that direct experience in the implementation space is needed and valued for informing better decision making at the planning level. As issue-specific and context-specific experiences are essential to influence relevant decision makers, additional professional organizations catering to the geographically specific societal needs are necessary.

This is the rationale for Muflehun being structured as a resource center for other organizations to learn from its pilot experiences and to develop similar, localized programs and advisory services to provide solutions customized to the specific needs of their countries, cities, and communities.

In summary, for good policy decisions, local experience of unbiased, independent nonpolitical actors in each segment of the framework described earlier is an essential prerequisite for the benefit of society at large.

Chapter 19

Countering Violent Extremism in the United States

Unscientific and Stigmatizing National Security Theater

Arjun S. Sethi

In February 2015, the White House convened a three-day summit on countering violent extremism (CVE) in Washington, DC. The gathering brought together local, federal, and international leaders to discuss how to combat violent extremist ideologies and prevent youth from falling prey to terrorist recruitment. The White House emphasized an interventionist model focused on "community efforts to disrupt the radicalization process before an individual engages in criminal activity." President Obama reiterated this message in his concluding remarks at the summit, noting that "terrorists prey upon young impressionable minds," in particular Muslim youth.

Prevention and intervention should generally be favored over arrest and incarceration. However, CVE programming in the United States isn't interventionist at all. It's based on bad science, impedes and chills constitutional rights, and relies on abusive policing and intelligence collection techniques. It also deepens the criminalized relationship between law enforcement and Muslims exacerbating the culture of intimidation, hate violence, and profiling that characterizes their daily lives.

COUNTERING VIOLENT EXTREMISM PROGRAMMING IN THE UNITED STATES

Law enforcement and intelligence officials have engaged with Muslims in America in a multitude of ways both before and after the September 11, 2001, terrorist attacks. Their first official public foray into CVE programming occurred in late 2014. The Department of Justice, the Department of Homeland Security, and the National Counterterrorism Center selected three cities—Boston, Los Angeles, and Minneapolis—to be pilot regions for combatting violent radicalization. These cities were selected because of their large Muslim populations and their prior engagement with law enforcement (Attorney General 2015). The initiative emphasized information sharing among educators, mental and public health professionals, law enforcement, and community and religious leaders. Community and religious leaders played a particularly important role in this initiative because they were asked to identify youth likely to become violent extremists based on warning signs of radicalization and then provide those names to law enforcement. In the words of one senior Department of Justice official, "[t]he intent is to identify and confront radicalization and deter it at the earliest possible point" (Murphy 2014).

The Federal Bureau of Investigation (FBI) built upon these pilot programs by launching a first of its kind CVE website, "Don't Be a Puppet," in early 2016 (FBI 2016). The web portal uses games, quizzes, and videos to teach students how to identify and resist violent extremist propaganda. It also seeks the assistance of students, teachers, and educators to identify youth at risk of embracing violent extremism. The website has six major sections, including "Why Do People Become Violent Extremists" and "Where to Get Help." The former emphasizes how unmet "personal needs" and "fears and frustrations" can lead individuals down the path to violent extremism. The latter lists "conflict resolution tips" and specifies "when to report violent extremism" based on particular warning signs. The website is an entirely self-contained resource, and there are no accompanying training materials. It is meant to be shared and disseminated by teachers and educators and incorporated into school curricula.

While this website was being rolled out and shared with educators, the FBI was simultaneously beta-testing a new CVE program called "shared responsibility committees (SRCs)" (Hirsch 2016). SRCs are an intervention strategy in which a hand-selected group of local mental health professionals, social workers, educators, and religious leaders are requested by the FBI to help individuals who are at risk of becoming violent extremists. SRC members must sign a multipage memorandum of understanding with the FBI memorializing the terms of their service. An SRC is convened if the FBI determines that intervention can help an individual resist violent extremism (Sethi 2016). The SRC will then schedule a series of meetings and interviews with the person and recommend to the FBI that they either drop or continue the investigation. The FBI can either accept the recommendation or ignore it based on the SRC's findings or the FBI's own internal investigation. It is unknown how many SRCs have been created or in which cities they operate. The government has revealed only that SRCs were being piloted in certain, undisclosed cities. Although some believe that the program has been terminated, the government has never publicly acknowledged its termination (Khan 2016).

The federal government's latest thinking on CVE programming can be found in a strategic document released in December 2016 entitled "Strategic Implementation Plan for Empowering Local Partners" (Office of the President 2016). The government again emphasizes interventions and "alternative pathways or 'off-ramps' for individuals who appear to be moving toward violent action but who have not yet engaged in criminal activity." It purports to accomplish this objective by supporting "community-based multidisciplinary intervention models" and drawing upon already-existing community programs.

The intervention model contemplated appears to mirror SRCs, as the document describes the creation of local intervention teams consisting of behavior and mental health professionals, local law enforcement officials, and faith-based and other nongovernmental representatives. The existing community programs the government seeks to replicate, meanwhile, are likely the Build Resilience against Violent Extremism Program (BRAVE) in Montgomery County, Maryland, and the Recognizing Extremist Network Early Warnings Program in Los Angeles, California. These are two of the most well-funded and prominent local CVE programs in the country. The former, like SRCs, enlists the support of numerous stakeholders, including faith and community leaders, public officials, law enforcement, educators, social service providers, and civic activists to "create a network of trusted adults who can intervene in the lives of troubled individuals" (WORDE 2018). Although public information about the latter program is sparse, it appears to be an intensification of the pilot Los Angeles CVE program. The program asks community leaders to report individuals exhibiting early signs of violent radicalization to the Los Angeles Police Department's (LAPD) Major Crimes Division for investigation.

BAD SCIENCE CHILLS CIVIL LIBERTIES

The entire US CVE interventionist framework is built on the flawed premise that an individual's path to violent radicalization is predictable and discernible to an outside observer. Instead, empirical research has repeatedly shown that there is no identifiable terrorist profile and that an individual's progression to violent extremism is complex and nonlinear (Patel 2011). In perhaps the most famous study to date, the United Kingdom's security service MI5 found that there is no "typical pathway to violent extremism" and that terrorists "had taken strikingly different journeys to violent extremist activity" (Travis 2008). In another study, former Central Intelligence Agency (CIA) officer and psychologist Marc Sageman analyzed and catalogued more than 500 terrorist profiles and likewise found that there are no hallmarks of violent radicalization and that the pathway to violent extremism is complex and case specific (Sageman 2008).

Because there are no general warning signs of terrorist radicalization, law enforcement and the intelligence community have adopted overinclusive and sweeping indicators that have little correlation, let alone causation, to violent extremism. Speaking at Harvard's Kennedy School in April 2014, President Obama's homeland security adviser, Lisa Monaco, discussed "warning signs" of radicalization:

> What kinds of behaviors are we talking about? For the most part, they're not related directly to plotting attacks. They're more subtle. For instance, parents might see sudden personality changes in their children at home—becoming confrontational. Religious leaders might notice unexpected clashes over ideological differences. Teachers might hear a student expressing an interest in traveling to a conflict zone overseas. Or friends might notice a new interest in watching or sharing violent material. (Monaco 2014)

The list of indicators detailed in Don't Be a Puppet is also far-reaching. The list includes "talking about traveling to places that sound suspicious," "using code words or unusual language," and "studying or taking pictures of potential targets" (FBI 2016). The LAPD RENEW program is similar, and though details are scant, relevant documents describe a typical terrorist as an individual with "a strong need to belong to a social group" who has "trouble fitting into a social context" or one who has "outrage over US or Western foreign policies." The documents also list "feeling alone," "detached," and "disaffection" as predictors of violent radicalization (LAPD 2010).

These vacuous indicators impede and chill sacrosanct civil liberties (Civil Rights Group Letter 2015). Innocuous activities like deciding to pray five times a day, attending a fiery religious service, associating with Muslim advocacy groups, and condemning US foreign policy have become "warning signs" that are reported to police because of countering violent extremism programs. Many community leaders have stopped having political and religious discussions because they fear that law enforcement and their informants will misinterpret their remarks. In other cases, Muslims, Arabs, and South Asians who travel abroad to visit their families or holy sites in the Middle East, speak a foreign language, or take photos of US landmarks fear that they'll be construed as terrorists.

Local advocacy groups in impacted communities are now challenging these programs. In Boston, a prominent Muslim leader called the program a "cloak for surveillance" (Bender 2015). More recently, local Boston advocacy groups, like the Council on American-Islamic Relations Massachusetts Chapter and the Muslim Justice League, organized a rally in front of City Hall

Plaza calling CVE programming surveillance and racial profiling (Nguyen 2015). In Los Angeles, local groups signed a coalition letter expressing grave concern about the "civil liberties implications" of CVE programming (Civil Rights LA Group Letter 2014). Shortly thereafter, the Islamic Shura Council of Southern California, an umbrella organization of mosques and Muslim organizations serving the Muslims of Southern California, and the Muslim Students Association of the West Coast, voted to formally oppose CVE programming (CAIR 2015). In Minnesota, nearly fifty local Muslim organizations signed a coalition letter describing CVE programming as "stigmatizing, divisive, and ineffective" (Minnesota Group Letter 2015). Later, in September 2016, local organizations like Minnesotans against Islamophobia and the Anti-War Committee sponsored a protest challenging CVE, calling it a form of Islamophobia. National advocacy organizations and civil society have joined the chorus as well (Holmen 2016). In August 2016, the American Federation of Teachers wrote an open letter to the FBI on behalf of its 1.6 million teacher members condemning the Don't Be a Puppet program (AFT 2016). The union argued that the program would create a "broad based suspicion of people based upon their heritage or ethnicity" and lead to profiling and bullying of Muslim youth.

PRIOR HISTORY OF OVERREACH AND FRUITS OF A POISONOUS TREE

In addition to relying upon bad science and flawed warning signs, law enforcement has repeatedly failed to specify the criteria necessary for opening an investigation into a Muslim in America. Rather than meaningfully intervening and rehabilitating youth, law enforcement is likely overreaching and profiling innocent people. Take the suspicious activity-reporting program, which encourages local law enforcement to track and report individuals engaged in "pre-operational planning related to terrorism" (ACLU 2015). Authorities have used this sweeping program to investigate individuals who've placed large purchase orders for computers at Best Buy, researched video games online, and purchased pallets of water at Costco. In addition, the National Security Agency has monitored the e-mails of prominent Muslim Americans, including civil rights leaders and professors, absent any connection to wrongdoing (Greenwald and Hussein 2014). The terrorist watchlist program, meanwhile, is so expansive that an individual can be branded a terrorist based on a single social media post (Sethi 2014). Here, too, Muslims have been disproportionately impacted. Dearborn, Michigan, a city with a population of less than 100,000 and known for its large Muslim and Arab American community, has more watchlisted residents than any other city in the United States, except New York (Scahill and Devereaux 2014). Prior history shows that countless Muslims have been surveilled and investigated without any evidence of wrongdoing. There is little reason to believe that those targeted by CVE programming are any different.

The FBI has also refused to specify the techniques and practices they use to commence and further ongoing investigations. Thus, even when CVE programs target vulnerable youth, the investigation may be built on abusive policing and intelligence collection techniques. For example, the Department of Justice (DoJ) permits massive data-gathering programs to map Muslim American communities in connection with "an authorized intelligence or investigative purpose" (Nicole and Yu Hsi Lee 2014). This language sanctions operations like the New York Police Department (NYPD) Muslim spying program, which tracked where Muslims lived, worked, shopped, and prayed. After more than six years of spying, eavesdropping, and infiltration, the NYPD Demographics Unit didn't generate a single terrorism lead. The DoJ has likewise sanctioned the use of confidential informants to snoop on Muslim Americans and infiltrate mosques absent any evidence of wrongdoing. Law enforcement and the intelligence community have also used expansive programs like National Security Agency (NSA) data collection, watch lists, suspicious activity reporting, and social media monitoring to both open and intensify investigations into Muslim Americans and their businesses, nonprofits, and houses of worship. The ends don't justify the means.

CLOUD OF COLLECTIVE SUSPICION

Muslims in America live under a cloud of collective suspicion in part because of programs like CVE. These programs abandon time-tested principles like the presumption of innocence and evidence of wrongdoing—embracing instead guilt by association, race, and faith as proxies for crime. They likewise turn community leaders, mental health professionals, educators, and even students into an extension of law enforcement. They're asked to draw dangerous inferences based on the innocuous behavior of Muslims in America, including what they say, with whom they associate, and how they express their faith. In some Muslim communities, the relationship between community leaders and youth is tenuous or broken. Youth increasingly see their elders as the eyes and ears of law enforcement rather than their own.

In addition to chilling constitutional rights, these programs lead to racial and religious profiling by law enforcement and the American public. They contribute to "flying while brown," and the deplaning of Muslims, Arabs, South Asians, and others for speaking a foreign language, scribbling notes, or even being nonconversational. They contribute to international incidents like the arrest and suspension of Ahmed Mohamed, the young Muslim teenager who was wrongfully detained and punished for bringing a homemade clock to school. Programs like CVE generate a hypersensitivity to everything Muslims do.

These programs also foster popular bias against Muslims in America because they reinforce deeply embedded notions of privilege and prejudice. If the government treats Muslims as a suspect community, so will everyday Americans. This popular bias can lead to harassment, discrimination, and even hate violence. It also contributes to a negative feedback loop. Muslims who experience bias often withdraw, making them more likely to be retargeted by bias and recriminalized by CVE. Moreover, as they recoil, they are less likely to cooperate with law enforcement. Those who mistrust the police are less likely to partner with them.

LOOKING AHEAD

Countering violent extremism programming isn't about preventing violence. It's about deepening the state's control over Muslims in America and further criminalizing a community easily scapegoated by law enforcement and the intelligence community, lawmakers, the media, and the American public. The resources devoted to CVE aren't even commensurate with the threat posed by Muslim violent extremism. Americans are many times more likely to be killed by a white, right-wing, violent extremist than a Muslim and immigrant, and many, many times more likely to be killed by gun violence than violent extremism generally. CVE is more about national security theater and political expedience than protecting Americans and actionable threats.

And yet, CVE programming in its current form will likely endure because Muslims will continue to be an easy target. They'll also have to wrestle with law enforcement's urge to predict crime. As African Americans and immigrant communities can attest, for decades, law enforcement has been afforded extraordinary deference to stop and surveil based on little more than intuition. In ordinary criminal justice matters, an officer is permitted to stop and interrogate a person if there is reasonable suspicion to believe that he or she may commit a crime. Just like CVE, the warning signs are broad and expansive. Avoiding eye contact with an officer, making too much eye contact, traveling alone, and traveling late at night all satisfy reasonable suspicion. And just like CVE, this sweeping standard has led to profiling and predictive policing of communities of color, including stop and frisk and "driving while black." In its latest incarnation, predictive policing uses big data to calculate "hot spots" and "threat scores" to predict the likelihood that a crime will be committed in a particular area by a particular suspect. CVE may follow a similar path, as police may be tasked to mine and analyze Muslim youth's social media posts and browsing history to predict the likelihood that they'll embrace terrorism.

Predictive policing is to the war on crime what CVE programs are to the war on terror. Both afford law enforcement immense discretion to intervene in American life based on little more than bias and intuition; both seek to anticipate crime with little regard for civil liberties and civil rights; and both quietly and quickly ensnare minority communities into the expansive, discriminatory, and abusive criminal justice system.

Chapter 20

Islamization, Securitization, and Peacebuilding Approaches to Preventing and Countering Violent Extremism

Mohammed Abu-Nimer

Preventing and countering violent extremism (P/CVE) campaigns are largely rooted in a response to Al-Qaeda, Boko Haram, Daesh, and many other smaller regional groups that claim Islam as their basis and manipulate Islamic identity and its components to justify exclusion, violence, and destruction against others (both Muslims and non-Muslims). Despite the fact that the overwhelming majority of the victims are Muslims in Muslim countries, the threat of these groups, particularly to European and American societies and interests, is seen as the primary motivation behind policy and priority change.

Muslim and Arab communities widely believe and discuss this assumption. In consequence, when international agencies refer to P/CVE, this is interpreted as a code for countering exclusively or primarily the discourse of groups affiliated with Islam and not Judaism, Christianity, Buddhism, Hinduism, or violent secular ideologies.[1]

This perception is confirmed by the sheer number, scale, and focus of P/CVE programs implemented by these international, regional, national, and local agencies in Muslim countries. While such programs exist, it is rare to identify or give wide media coverage and recognition to a program that addresses violent extremism (VE) motivated by the Jewish settlers in the occupied Palestinian territories, white supremacist groups in the United States, Sri Lankan, and Myanmar Buddhism, or Indian Hinduism in Gujarat or Kashmir.

Obviously, the threat and the scale of the terrorist groups motivated by their "Islamic ideologies" are being reported and portrayed as far more intense and widespread. Yet the fact that other forms of VE are not being addressed seriously by policy makers and donors reduces the legitimacy, credibility, and trust in the intentions of the message and messenger.

The Islamization of P/CVE is also evident when policy makers and media fail to distinguish between genuine Islamic teachings/values and the negative/

destructive interpretations espoused by the VE groups. Many mainstream media and politicians, especially in European, American, and even in some Muslim contexts, have consistently and systematically utilized certain VE framings that generalize and stereotype Islam and Muslims (Ali et al. 2011; CAIR 2016). The most discussed question in such media outlets is, "Does Islam support VE and terrorism?" At the same time, the attacks on Muslims and Islam are often neglected or marginalized in Western media. Such an approach has directly fed into the growing Islamophobia in the Western Hemisphere.

In general, public de-Islamization of P/CVE approaches is an essential step toward a more effective and credible response to the threat posed by groups that promote violent extremism in the name of Islam. The de-Islamization approach can include various elements:

> To an outsider, jihad is often interpreted as "religious war", whereas jihad means "struggling or striving". In the Quran, jihad has many meanings, not at all associated with war but rather with an individual striving in the path of God, in other words the personal struggle to live according to principles of faith (see Quranic verses 49:15, 9:20, 9:88).

First, avoid linking Islam as a religion or Muslims as people and communities with P/CVE campaigns, for example, by avoiding the use of terms like "Islamic terrorism," "Muslim terrorists," "jihadists," and so on. This can help delink Islam from VE.

Second, systematically provide examples and illustrations that most, if not all, other major religious and faith traditions have had groups within them, which manipulated their faith and tradition by justifying violence and exclusion. Members of these groups are also not representative of these faiths and traditions and the vast majority of their respective adherents. In fact, massive atrocities have been committed by misusing religions (including Christianity, Judaism, Hinduism, and Buddhism) throughout modern history. This does not mean providing legitimacy for the acts of violence but making sure they are put into historical and theological perspective.

Third, delink religion from the P/CVE debate by focusing the primary analysis not on religion and religious actors but on the root causes that produce structural violence in any given context. These root causes include the nature of the governance system, institutional corruption, social class divides, gaps between have and have nots, tribal divisions and loyalties, security/military structures and operations, weak educational systems, social norms and structures that support all forms of exclusion (gender and patriarchal), basic human rights violations, and so on.

When P/CVE programs are implemented in conceptual and practical isolation from the above factors, their effect can be limited and unsustainable. In many of these contexts the problem is generated by various drivers and requires a multilayered and multistakeholder approach, not further segmentation and sector-based divides such as those that arise when P/CVE programs are focused only on youth, women, or religious leaders but neglect to engage other sectors in the community. In fact, the exclusive religious framing of VE can contribute to the preservation of the status quo, the same order that produced it. When explaining problems in Lebanon, Iraq, Syria, Somalia, Yemen, Palestine, and so on as primarily religious or sectarian, international agencies are de facto supporting the internal structures that generate political and social violence. P/CVE programs that neglect these factors and exclusively focus on launching initiatives to revise Quranic interpretations, training imams on values of peace and conflict resolution, issuing public denunciations of violence, and so on are unable to gain legitimacy in the local communities. Instead, participants in these programs react by stating that the problem is not religious and "religion has nothing to do with it." Yet the implementers insist on religious framing of the problems in the community.

Other beneficiaries of these programs have voiced the suspicion that linking violence in the community and country to religion is in fact contributing to the intractability of the conflict and preventing genuine change. Such hypotheses have been confirmed by studies and analyses of fragile state systems, in which the problem lies not in the religion or religious interpretation but rather in symptoms of a weak central state that does not provide services to its citizens (OECD 2016).

INSTITUTIONAL RESPONSES TO PREVENTING AND COUNTERING VIOLENT EXTREMISM IN A MUSLIM CONTEXT: LOCKED IN SECURITIZATION

Similar to European and American contexts, policy makers in Muslim countries have joined the global P/CVE initiative campaign. This is reflected in a growing number of special centers and initiatives launched by many of these governments. In addition, policy makers and security agencies have mobilized religious leadership and institutions (religious endowments, ministries of religion, Dar al-Ifta, religious education institutes such as Al-Azhar, Al-Azytouna, and Al-Akhawain) in the fight against Daesh, Al-Qaeda, and Boko Haram. As a result of this mobilization, we have witnessed significant increases in the number of religious fatwas (decrees), conferences, and statements that denounce acts of terrorism carried out by these groups.[2] The security motivation reflected in the design, media coverage, and so on has cast a significant shadow on these meetings. Some religious representatives whisper: "Are we an extension arm of the security apparatus?"[3]

In Afghanistan, Iraq, Syria, and Niger, there are root causes that will continue to generate violence and exclusion even if all religious actors and agencies in these countries are converted to the discourse of pluralism and diversity and nonviolence.

Additionally, new centers have been established to this end, such as Sawab (True), a center sponsored by the Foreign Ministry of the United Arab Emirates that focuses on the fight against Daesh. Its programs aim to strengthen the capacity of media, social media, women, youth, and so on and to counter Daesh's recruitment efforts. Al-Marsad (An Observer) is another media monitoring initiative supported by Al-Azhar, one of the leading Islamic theological educational institutes in Egypt. Their aim is to monitor VE messages issued by Daesh and other groups in eight languages and to selectively respond to Daesh's religious interpretations by setting the record straight in terms of authentic Islamic theological discourse. A third example, Hedayah (The Right Path) Centre based in Abu Dhabi, was created as an International Government Organization (IGO) to focus on counterterrorism. Similar to other organizations in the field, it has also moved to focus on CVE research and training in various parts of the world.

There is no doubt that these organizations launched by and operated through Muslim governments are much needed to support the public discourse of antiexclusion and to counter the manipulation of religion to justify violence. Nevertheless, they remain focused on the securitization of P/CVE campaigns rather than a human security framework. Their approach is not far from other P/CVE operations that have failed to delink religion from their P/CVE analytical framework. In fact, some continue to link religion with violence and look at the community solely as a source of data and intelligence gathering to help security agencies' work to ensure order. The sustainable development community approach is certainly lacking in such operations. Additionally, since none of these centers deal with root causes of VE, their target audience and effect might also be limited.

Although Muslim formal governmental institutional responses continue to be overwhelmingly rooted in the securitization approach, there are a few examples that also reflect the potential role that religious agencies and actors can play in this context. Such examples aim to spread a culture of peace and promote religious diversity and pluralism, such as the newly launched Mohammed VI Institute for the Training of Imams Morchidines and Morchidates (male and female spiritual guides) in Morocco (Morocco on the Move n.d.), geared toward training imams in CVE by instructing them in values of openness and tolerance. However, similar to P/CVE programs, these interreligious initiatives are still not organically or systematically linked to the grassroots and remain under the general auspices of the governments and their political agendas. Additionally, they struggle in their efforts to delink their operations and methodologies from the "security-oriented" or "defensive Islam" P/CVE approaches. Another example is the Forum for Promoting Peace in Muslim Societies, which started under the leadership of Shaykh Abdallah Bin Bayyah in 2014. The forum has attracted high-level Muslim leaders and is committed to promoting the peace idealist paradigm despite pressure from policy makers and governments, who continuously push the P/CVE agenda.

The King Abdullah bin Abdulaziz International Centre for Interreligious and Intercultural Dialogue Center (KAACIID) is an example. The International Dialogue Centre is the only IGO governed by a multireligious institution, a board of directors representing Buddhism, Christianity, Hinduism, Islam, and Judaism. Using dialogue as its methodology, the center builds its interreligious peace and reconciliation programs on the assumptions that there is a gap between policy makers and religious agencies and that religious actors have a positive role to play in contributing to solutions to challenges facing the world today.

A PEACEBUILDING RESPONSE TO VIOLENT EXTREMISM: AN ALTERNATIVE APPROACH FOR BRIDGING THE GAP

The above-mentioned limitations to P/CVE approaches and public perception within Muslim communities in particular constitute serious challenges for peacebuilding practitioners and agencies. For peacebuilding in general and interreligious peacebuilding in particular, there are certain challenges, limitations, and implications to adopting P/CVE approaches, terminology, assumptions, and methodology on a community level, as well as in larger social and political contexts of peace work.

Peacebuilding as a field emerges from the "Idealist" rather than the "Realist" power paradigm (power politics or Realpolitik) that dominates international diplomacy and international relations. Its values and methodologies in responding to conflicts are thus based on human relationships, justice, compassion, collaboration and cooperation, mutual recognition, nonviolence, and emphasis on the role of nonstate actors. A "Realist approach," by contrast, is based on the assumption that the world is anarchic and only a power balance establishes order and stability; that states and individuals' primary objectives are to pursue and preserve self-interest, state sovereignty, competition, and force; that states are the only legitimate entity for representation; and so on (Jervis 1999). CVE is based on the "Realist" paradigm. It sees security and order as the end outcome; is developed by the state to serve the state's interests; and pays little attention to justice, cooperation, nonviolence, and so on.

Thus, when peacebuilding and interreligious dialogue practitioners uncritically adopt P/CVE language and methodology, they, by default, operate against their own "idealist" paradigm. Realism's pragmatic approach does not change the hearts and minds of people and communities; rather, it aims to restore the asymmetric situation present prior to the violence. The framework of such interventions does not include conflict analysis or nonviolence peace mapping, which requires identification of the drivers of violence: governance, corruption, foreign intervention, North-South dynamics, and possible nonviolent community-based responses. The language of relationship building, compassion, forgiveness, and reconciliation are not part of the design, leaving out the "human" aspect so integral to community ownership of such programs. Such values are an integral part of intervention programs even when the focus is on development, relief, or capacity building for local stakeholders.

Another dilemma with CVE programs for interreligious peacebuilding is the lack of spirituality or faith. Interfaith dialogue, when carried out by the "Idealist" paradigm, is rooted in faith and spiritual values of the community and participants. While many P/CVE interventions focus on the mechanics of peacebuilding and interreligious dialogue, the language of faith is absent from these meetings, and the space constructed by the practitioner or the agency is often framed as a place for learning technical skills and for the individual to become an agent of change who works and protects the state and its government agencies.

These secular, security-driven P/CVE solutions have proved antagonistic to religion and religious identity in part by reflecting the assumption that VE groups and their communities are self-defined as theologically based. Moreover, when there has been engagement with religious leaders, it has often been problematic, like the above-mentioned instrumentalization of religious leaders, meant to show community engagement, but still excluding religious leaders from decision-making processes. Asking Muslim leaders for a blessing or to issue a fatwa in support of a policy and not including them in policy making is not community engagement. This reality is not lost on community members and religious adherents, who often look to their religious leaders for guidance and answers.

To bridge the gap between the secular and the religious and to increase the likelihood of finding solutions that will work, there is a mutual responsibility in which religious leaders and community actors must be genuinely involved in initiating alternative framing for the P/CVE approaches used in their communities, especially when they are externally imposed. Religious leaders and religious peacemakers not only have the well-earned trust of their communities, but they are also able to use their religious identity to positively shift perceptions along the conflict-peace continuum.

Peacebuilders should follow the principle of inclusivity in representation by insisting on multireligious and multi-intrafaith group designs. In any given conflict that has a religious dimension, there are many religious entities and representations in each region, which need to be included in the process. When interfaith and faith-based representatives and policy makers meet, they often like to emphasize a discourse of harmony based on the notion that there is or was strong and peaceful coexistence between religions in the context. This tendency to avoid discussion of controversial issues, especially those relating to national policies regarding religious freedom, self-determination, and so on, can damage the authenticity of the program for participants who are affected by the conflict on a daily basis.

When interreligious peacebuilding practitioners or organizations are engaged in P/CVE initiatives, there are various principles that can guide their work to ensure that the core values and assumptions are maintained without compromising their credibility. For example, several principles were integral in implementing a program by the Salam Institute for Peace and Justice in Chad and Niger to enhance the capacity of Quranic school teachers to integrate values of peace, diversity, and nonviolence. The principles were derived taking into account the sensitive context: the participants are under continuous threat from Boko Haram, affiliated groups, and other political and religious factions that oppose any foreign non-Muslim intervention in their context; participant schools are also marginalized and neglected by their governments, lack basic classroom amenities, and are misperceived and labeled as hubs for terrorism and VE. The teachers and their principles were highly suspicious of the program's intentions and motivations, so it was necessary to build trust. It is obvious that these principles are not new to participatory development or effective peacebuilding practices. Nevertheless, they were implemented with a commitment to empower the Quranic school teachers and with respect for their faith, providing a dialogical space that allows transparency, honesty, and critical thinking.

Principles used to guide peacebuilding practitioners in a Quranic school intervention in Chad and Niger included the following:

- Assurance that Islam and religion in general have positive values, especially that the main message is peace and justice.
- The Islamic peace education framework is the only relevant way to engage the madrassa system.
- Islam and Muslims are misperceived and misunderstood by non-Muslims.
- There is an intra-Muslim challenge that prevents or obstructs change.
- Building trust and rapport with the teachers is a necessary step that should not be compromised.

- Quranic school teachers are the experts in Quranic interpretations, not the external team of trainers.
- The trainers will not impose any change, but all the work will be done by the teachers themselves and any change will be made with the full agreement and consensus of the group.
- The intervention should include improvement of school infrastructure and conditions.
- Maintaining Quranic schools' framework and core curricula, while avoiding theological debates.

(Abu-Nimer, Nasser, and Ouboulhcen 2016)

CONCLUSIONS AND IMPLICATIONS FOR PEACEBUILDING AND PREVENTING AND COUNTERING VIOLENT EXTREMISM

Some peacebuilders argue that it is possible to engage with P/CVE programs and maintain, to some extent, the "Idealist" discourse of interreligious peacebuilding.[4] Many peacemakers involved in P/CVE programs indicate that in general, the majority continue to do the same work and use the same framing; however, for purposes of funding and security approval, they began labeling their work as P/CVE.[5] Policy makers, donors, and other communities of practice (development and humanitarian relief) have moved from denying and avoiding the inclusion of religious leaders and institutions to exploring the relevance and feasibility of engaging religious leaders in their operations.

Preventing and countering violent extremism has also evolved to become one of the main avenues that religious leaders and interreligious peacebuilding practitioners are expected to engage with. In the context of the mounting pressure from states, international donors, and IGOs, maintaining the core peacebuilding paradigm values and ethics (especially interreligious dialogue and peace) is a current challenge. Torn between further marginalization due to lack of resources, changes of donors' agendas, or loss of relevance among their constituencies, peacebuilding practitioners have to make hard choices in terms of their engagement with the P/CVE "industry."[6]

Chapter 21

Countering Violent Extremism; Disarmament, Demobilization, and Reintegration; Social Capital; and the "Women, Peace and Security" Agenda

Dean Piedmont and Gabrielle Belli

Countering violent extremism (CVE) has taken on increased salience since the meteoric rise of violent extremist (VE) groups operating in asymmetric settings where disarmament, demobilization, and reintegration (DDR) is being considered in ongoing conflict. The environment in which CVE is taking place is somewhat of a moving target. This chapter postulates that trauma, stigmatization, and the needs of people exiting violent extremist organizations (VEOs) and nonstate armed groups (NSAGs) have not fundamentally changed over the past fifteen years. Armed groups like the Lord's Resistance Army (LRA), Revolutionary United Front (RUF), and the Islamic State of Iraq and the Levant (ISIL) have applied their own unique tactics, however; all share common strategic methods that include forced recruitment, volunteerism, and coercion to expand their ranks, as well as predatory violence to forward their agendas. This chapter addresses the importance of social reintegration of persons coming out of VEOs through DDR programs and how legal prohibitions on proscribed armed groups inhibit support to women and girls.

Countering violent extremism settings characterized by "extreme violence" and ongoing conflict with VEOs provide a window of opportunity to advance well-established best practices and social investments such as community-based resilience and social reintegration efforts. In the recent past these have been de-emphasized in postconflict peacebuilding settings in favor of socioeconomic reintegration in the form of jobs and livelihoods, including for DDR. In part the focus on social reintegration is a function in CVE of evidence pointing toward marginalization, lacking a sense of belonging and an identity crisis as "push" and "pull" factors driving VE. Poverty, unemployment, and a lack of socioeconomic opportunities are latent, or enabling, conditions, rather than primary drivers of VE.

A FRAMEWORK FOR DISARMAMENT, DEMOBILIZATION, AND REINTEGRATION

Disarmament, demobilization, and reintegration of former fighters in the aftermath of conflict is as old as war itself, dating from the third century BC, and has featured in some form in virtually every conflict (Muggah 2014). In fact, a multitude of DDR initiatives have taken place globally since the UN and major bilateral engagement in the late 1980s as evidenced by the sheer number of programs and types of groups slated for DDR (Munive and Stepputat 2015). While most were launched in the wake of international or civil wars as part of an internationally mandated peace support operation, over the past decade, shifting conflict dynamics and emergent caseloads continue to alter the landscape in which DDR operations are mandated and implemented. Whether occurring in a humanitarian crisis or as an outcome of a peace accord, DDR represented a voluntary civilian-led nonviolent policy option for peacebuilding, and national reconstruction and reconciliation efforts, for the international community and state in which it was implemented (Piedmont 2015). Arguably all of these elements that have been considered prerequisites for undertaking DDR may be absent in contemporary CVE settings.

Typically, DDR targets persons in combatant and noncombatant roles from statutory armies and NSAGs. The codification of these practices is enshrined in the Integrated DDR Standards (IDDRS). It is not uncommon for DDR to serve as tool for security-sector reform (SSR) and transformation efforts aimed at downsizing, rightsizing, and legitimizing armed forces under civilian control (OECD 2008, 105; United Nations 2015). The integration of DDR under an SSR rubric explicitly recognizes the legitimacy of the state and the call for peace at a national level. In this regard, DDR is a unique policy tool that enhances the resilience of local, national, and regional actors by addressing various peace consolidation issues spanning the civilian and security sectors.

The first generation of DDR occurred in the wake of the Cold War. Typified by verifiable caseloads under unified command and control, these occurred regionally in Latin America and Southern Africa. In the mid-2000s a second-generation approach was developed, which was, in part, a response to the international community's perceptions that DDR, and reintegration specifically, was not achieving intended development aims. This led to a broad range of initiatives targeting communities and promoting social cohesion as a means to facilitate enabling conditions for DDR (UNDPKO 2010). This created a shift in DDR from supporting a state-building policy agenda largely focused on security-centric efforts, toward a security governance lens where peacebuilding and development were inextricably linked to national and human security issues.

Disarmament, demobilization, and reintegration is undergoing a third generational shift. The monetization of DDR is creating a cottage industry for former fighters traveling across international borders to rejoin armed groups as mercenaries. At the same time, peace operations are receiving DDR mandates in areas where conflict is ongoing, and insurgent groups slated for DDR are associated with "terrorist" organizations, complicating the legal and political environment (Piedmont 2015, 4). This shift has been one of state building, to treating the failed state, to addressing environments with VEOs that contest the legitimacy of the Westphalian model writ large. VE is permeating borders to the point that the state is severely restricted from effectively countering (addressing) them using the practices in first- and second-generation DDR, thereby undermining the legitimacy of the state itself. Originally intended as a civilian-led postconflict and peace-building tool, today, both DDR and CVE are being mandated in settings where VE takes place in ongoing conflict. This is the environment of concern for us—*the CVE setting*. Social reintegration, capital investment, and community-based reintegration (CBR), the aforementioned best practices for maximizing social impact and human security, yet are finding increasing space within CVE settings.

ASYMMETRIC CONFLICT AND SOCIAL INVESTMENT—A CASE FOR GENDER ANALYSIS IN CVE SETTINGS

For decades, reintegration often took place following a comprehensive peace agreement (CPA) with NSAGs. These groups were often terroristic in their methods, tactics, and recruitment patterns and were perpetrators of human rights abuses, inclusive of sexual and gender-based violence (SGBV). They committed war crimes and crimes against humanity, though were not often categorized as "terrorist organizations" in a formal way. The impact of predatory elements on women and girls' reintegration is detailed without a mention of "terrorist organizations" in foundational policies, including the IDDRS (United Nations 2015), the secretary-general's 2011 report on DDR (UN Security Council 2011), the Brahimi Report (United Nations 2000), and UN Security Council Resolution (UNSCR) 1325 on Women, Peace and Security (UNSCR 1325 2000). What has changed is the enactment of prohibitions on the provision of material support for these groups including, though not limited to, people "disengaging" from sanctioned terrorist organizations. Many so-called terrorist organizations are comingled within operating environments, operations, policies, and program approaches that govern responses to violence more broadly.

When violent NSAGs become sanctioned terrorist organizations, the international community is constrained from providing support to its members, including those seeking to "disengage," as stipulated in the governing counterterrorism normative frameworks that are populated by international modalities like the UN Global Counter-Terrorism Strategy (United Nations 2006) and national laws such as the US Patriot Act (2001). Therefore, former fighters and associated members exiting VEOs may not receive the support they would have otherwise received upon leaving unsanctioned NSAGs, as there are no appropriate "off-ramps" in place to support their unique reintegration needs upon "disengagement."

Taken from this perspective there is an artificial distinction between NSAGs sanctioned as terrorist organizations and those not classified as such in at least two regards: first, for persons attempting reintegration, their trauma, stigmatization, patterns of recruitment, and rejection by communities of return have not fundamentally been altered; and second, communities being asked to accept back former, or "disengaged" fighters do not make distinctions between predatory NSAGs that are not considered "terrorist" organizations, or VEOs that are considered "terrorist" organizations. For these communities, the violence and victimization is fundamentally the same. The distinction is made primarily at the international policy level, hindering the provision of programmatic support by civil society NGOs with a negative impact on vulnerable persons in need of reintegration, particularly women and girls.

Prohibitions on the provision of material support to terrorist organizations are pronounced when we examine its impact on women seeking to "disengage" and women-led NGOs supporting that process. This represents a constraint to the implementation of the "Women, Peace and Security" (WPS) agenda, which is the global framework that "recognizes that conflict has gendered impacts, that it affects women and men differently, and that women have critical roles to play in peace and security processes and institutions" (United Nations 2000).

Additionally, it is a direct contradiction to other UN instruments, including the Global Counterterrorism Forum's *Good Practices on Women and Countering Violent Extremism*, specifically Good Practice #10: "Develop gender-sensitive disengagement, rehabilitation, and reintegration programs that address the specific needs of women and girls on a path to terrorist radicalization or involved in violent extremism" (GCTF 2015, 6), and the *Secretary-General's Plan of Action to Prevent Violent Extremism* (UN Security Council 2015), which states that "more attention needs to be paid to devising efficient gender- and human rights-compliant reintegration strategies and programmes for those who have been convicted of terrorism-related offences as well as returning foreign terrorist fighters," further calling for enhanced disengagement and reintegration efforts.

Reintegration is mandated in all WPS resolutions[1] predating yet *not* including the most recent UN Security Council Resolution 2242 (United Nations 2015), while "violent extremism" and "terrorism" are discussed *only* in UNSCR 2242,[2] demonstrating that in spite of numerable policy-oriented actions and responses, corollaries between women and NSAGs and VEOs on the ground persist and only the language has changed. This is particularly salient as patterns of recruitment, trauma, stigmatization, and related experiences point to women and girls being the victims of both sanctioned and unsanctioned NSAGs and terrorist organizations. Without appropriate "off-ramps" or other support for the women seeking to reintegrate upon leaving a VEO on terrorist watch lists, the international community can expect a reversal of the advancements espoused by the WPS agenda.

A NORMATIVE FRAMEWORK FOR ENGAGEMENT

What changes can be realistically instituted and implemented to affect reintegration of "disengaging" persons in DDR and similar security-governance initiatives? On one level, recommendations should reflect a new policy paradigm that translates into programmatic approaches and responses. These should be premised on the change in conflict dynamics as underpinned previously. Second, since many constraints relate to promulgations from engaging with proscribed armed groups, the international community, including the US government (USG) and United Nations, should take advantage of legal instruments and norms in international customary law that are permissive.

This chapter in affect is a *call to increase coordination* among a set of actors as a preferred condition to advance policy for CVE and reintegration in this area. Efforts at enhanced coordination in terms of engaging VEOs in DDR efforts must take into consideration the operating environment—its risks and constraints, as well as the principles of impartiality and "do no harm" as paramount. Further, it is incumbent upon DDR stakeholders in CVE settings where VEOs are operative, to codify and transmit emerging practices that can serve as cutting-edge policy doctrine and program staples. Specifically, there is a need for a triad of actors to act on concert or through dedicated fora and consortiums. These include (i) the USG and United Nations; (ii) local NGOs and civil society organizations (CSOs); and (iii) think tanks and academia.

Each has comparative advantages lending themselves to a synergetic relationship. In the case of the USG and United Nations, these entities can drive, and fund, significant policy shifts. They are well positioned to leverage their political clout and good offices to create foundational shifts in the issuance and structure of DDR mandates for VEOs, as well as how these are affected in large-scale and complex peace-support operations. These can be buttressed with major bilateral support from such entities as the World Bank, European Union, and African Union where germane. Policies and programs that seek to merely replicate tried and tested peacebuilding approaches in the CVE setting may do more harm than good. Policy and programming decisions must be based on a combination of innovation and evidence if they are to be supported and gain traction, let alone be effective. Think tanks and academia are best placed to do so and can add rigor to evidentiary approaches. Lastly, though of critical importance, NGOs and CSOs have access on the ground where social capital and community resilience modeling takes place. They are the engines of programmatic innovation. In the current CVE setting, it is often the case that international NGOs, the USG, and UN staff have limited access in the field due to security concerns where VEOs are operating. By necessity, local NGOs and CSOs are developing and implementing innovative programmatic approaches that will serve as baselines for policy development, lessons learned, and best practices as the DDR and VEO environment further evolves. Coordination is required to capture and transmit these for further testing and research as a means to inform policy.

Taken together, these entities should operate under a new set of evidentiary assumptions that informs a working theory of change (ToC), namely:

i. Reintegration for DDR is a conflict prevention, not a postconflict tool, when preconditions for "classic" DDR do not exist.
ii. A military solution alone will not create the necessary preconditions to undertake "classic" DDR programming.
iii. Social reintegration is a necessary precondition for socioeconomic reintegration. Socioeconomic factors alone cannot affect successful DDR.
iv. Prohibitions to provide DDR reintegration support to (former) VE members are not sacrosanct; there are conditions where service provision can take place.

First, treating reintegration for DDR candidates as a tool for conflict prevention, rather than postconflict tool, explicitly acknowledging that certain preconditions for traditional approaches do not exist in CVE settings. These preconditions for engagement include a minimum guarantee of security, that is, an environment not characterized by active VEOs or NSAGs, and a CPA codifying the legal framework for peacebuilding and state building. Currently most cases in DDR do not have these preconditions, including Afghanistan, Somalia, Nigeria, Libya, South Sudan, Yemen, and Mali. If these preconditions were in place, a programmatic response would encompass a national response, such as a military solution or a state-centric process. That not being the case in contemporary VE settings, in order to be more effective and integrate best practices, reintegration should be processed as a preventative measure through providing DDR in areas that are accessible to peacebuilders and peacekeepers, rather than attempting to design and implement programmatic responses at national levels. Aims should include community resilience on CVE; "countering recruitment"; and "prevention of reoccurrence," remobilization, and recidivism.

Second, operating within a conflict context, CVE and reintegration practitioners, especially those supporting women and girls, must further acknowledge that an outright military solution is not a durable outcome. This means despite predatory behavior and tactics that persons and groups adopting VE tactics either have a legitimate root grievance or exploit a geographic and political space where one exists (Piedmont 2015, 2). This is instrumental as countries like Nigeria come to terms with the fact that a military solution to Boko Haram alone is not a tenable option. This discourse is taking place within the framework of DDR and implies that approaches accompanying community-based reintegration must tackle "structural" issues commonly associated with "push" factors for CVE, as well as "pull" factors relating to individual motivations and identity as in the case of Sudan. This brings home another issue of DDR practitioners becoming inadvertent parties to protracted conflict in cases like Somalia where both "push" and "pull" factors are not receiving adequate attention. The result, in part, is prolonged detention of suspected al-Shabaab members who are ensnared in the DDR process.

Third, knowing that causes for VE are, in many cases, identity-based, job creation and livelihood development should be viewed as enabling conditions that serve as both "push" and "pull" factors away from and toward VE. This is well demonstrated in Sudan, which has experienced three DDR efforts over the past decade. While the results of these DDRs are mixed at best, ranging from successful to abject failures, each had livelihoods and job creation as centerpieces of a programmatic response. This is juxtaposed with the current planning for CVE in The Sudan, where a recent study undertaken shows that in the urban areas of Khartoum state a majority of people joining VE groups are well educated, enjoy secure livelihoods, and are employed (UNDP 2017). This provides another CVE opportunity to displace economic reinsertion with social cohesion and community-based reintegration as a CVE centerpiece. Specific to girls, in Somalia, an evaluation of DDR in 2016 showed gender mainstreaming, without gender sensitivity. This dichotomy existed as girls were considered in livelihood training for socioeconomic reintegration, though registration occurred at fixed dates limiting girls' capacity to attend. A rolling registration model would have accommodated the needs of boys and girls; however, assessments taking into account social issues and community expectations, as a reintegration precursor, would have been needed.

Lastly, regarding legal dispositions, the focus on "girls" implies person under the age of eighteen. In these cases, the law is clear and calls for the immediate release of children that includes their safe return home and the provision of reintegration support. For DDR this is inclusive and does not necessitate a child be in possession of a weapon or serve a particular role. Promulgated in international humanitarian law (IHL) and raised to the level of customary law, there are no exceptions or provisos exclusive to children that have been affiliated with VE groups or "terrorist" organizations. Leveraging the Convention on the Rights of the Child (CRC) and office of the Special Representative to the Secretary General (SRSG) for Children Associated with Armed Conflict (CAAC), and calling attention to the United Nations General Assembly (UNGA) (2015), which pays specific attention to "child soldiers" as victims, provides inroads for boys and girls under eighteen for immediate release and differential treatment for those under eighteen who are deemed "terrorists." While reluctance by the United States to adhere to such standards may include not being a signatory to the CRC, increasing political will to exercise these options is demonstrated in the May 2016 US CVE Strategy, which calls for "strengthen[ing] the capabilities of government and non-governmental actors to isolate, intervene with, and promote the rehabilitation and reintegration of individuals caught in the cycle of radicalization to violence" (USAID 2016, 7).

Promise for effective change is represented by a combination of this legal "low hanging fruit" for women and children and adoption of innovative models where caseloads of nonviolent offenders to engage with are identified by communities. Somalia provides a good example. Beset by the VE group al-Shabaab, government institutions, including those rooted in the criminal justice system (CJS), are too weak to detain, rehabilitate, and/or prosecute all members or affiliates. As a remedial measure, nonviolent offenders that have not committed "terrorist" acts are released to the custodianship of their clan and community. Should former al-Shabaab affiliates remobilize or become a recidivist, the state retakes custody of the offender. Government sanctions, clan resilience, and decreasing vulnerability toward VEO and NSAG recruitment, at its essence, are preventing and countering VE.

CONCLUSION

Countering violent extremism, like DDR, is a practice, policy tool, and programmatic approach, though mostly a process. Opportunities to engage can also be pitfalls to do harm—analysis is needed! When treated and applied as if in a classic postconflict setting, policy makers and practitioners, especially those from the international community espousing best practices, run a risk of being perceived as a party to conflict at best and costing lives at worst. Risk assessments require periodic undertaking to inform conflict assessments in what will be a changing environment. There are practices that work and conditions where the international community needs to be bold in acknowledging that there are nonpermissive settings where program implementation may not contravene efforts aimed at affecting women and girls' protection and reintegration.

While most people would not advocate for providing reintegration support to persons formerly associated with terrorist organizations, few would deny such support to the Chibouk girls in Nigeria (Amnesty International 2017). In Somalia, the government is willing to contest IHL under the premise, or pretext, that some children and girls are a credible national security threat—this may or may not be true. The point is that this is of particular importance due to the myriad of dichotomies in play; civilian, military, and intelligence actors severely constricting and complicating *CVE settings* while also offering solutions.

For persons "off-ramping" or otherwise "disengaging" from VEOs, lessons learned from DDR programs can prove useful for CVE. To this end, having dedicated experts equipped to provide cutting-edge services, not captive to some antiquated notions of the IDDRS, should include an understanding that social investment in CVE is a precondition for gender-based reintegration. Expertise should be multidisciplinary, including those with practical field experience that are proven "thought leaders" and "advocates." As a first order, a paradigm shift must include a move from a purely national security agenda toward a human security agenda. Doing so places the community and civil society at the center of CVE initiatives. Displacing socioeconomic reintegration as a prime mover, with social investment strategies, is recommended. This not only increases community resilience but also mandates increased partnership between the USG, the United Nations, academia, and local civil society.

Legal expertise in DDR and CVE is needed as a means to identify and institute "off-ramping" opportunities. This means using the tools enshrined in international humanitarian, human rights, and customary law as enablers to engage, rather than inhibitors to act. A first step can be the explicit recognition that women and girls are often targets and victims of VEOs while not denying their roles as agents and perpetrators. Patterns of recruitment, trauma, and stigmatization should be combined with legal statutes and principles to compel engagement and services for women and girls. Isolation and limited access, as well as interventions in VE settings, carry risks. Among these are violations of the "do no harm" principle. Ironically, failure to act based solely on the legal prohibitions to engage proscribed armed groups and their members also risk violating this principle in the form of an abrogation of UNSCR 1325, a central tenet in the WPS agenda. By not engaging, women and girls will continue to be disproportionally negatively affected not only by VE and conflict dynamics themselves but also by the very legal and policy frameworks designed to enhance their protection and participation in preventing conflict and building peace in the first case. Arguably this is starting to occur by virtue of denying women and girl's access to post disengagement support services.

Even so, the reasons for concern can be tempered with emerging political will to engage. The call issued by the United States in its CVE Strategy in May 2016 citing the importance of reintegration while recognizing persons as victims of "radicalization" provides an avenue for agency and places communities at the center of CVE efforts that include women and girls. An example of political will realized for DDR is the recent case of peace agreement in Colombia with former Revolutionary Armed Forces of Colombia (FARC), characterized as a terrorist organization for decades. Women and girls will be part of the caseload, both directly as members of FARC and indirectly through victims' (and survivor) assistance and reparation efforts. Afghanistan shares the same promise with more need for caution. Through the most recent DDR effort, the government offers Taliban and other insurgent groups peaceful reintegration in return for the renunciation of violence. If the DDR caseload has girls and women that may benefit, the reintegration of the Taliban into Afghanistan's polity through a DDR possesses the potential to reverse gains made in the WPS agenda over the past fifteen years. Again, this underpins the need for analysis, caution, and coordination when addressing DDR and CVE for women and girls.

Section V

THE ECOLOGY OF PEACEBUILDING

Section V

Introduction

Peacebuilding is a longer-term effort to address the political conflicts, governance challenges, and structural root causes of violent conflict. While peacebuilding does not specifically focus on violent extremism (VE) or terrorism, it can prevent and respond to these challenges. VE-sensitive peacebuilding recognizes the dynamic ecology of VE and attempts to avoid unintended impacts.

John Paul Lederach begins this section with an exploration of how a peacebuilding emphasis on "engagement" differs from counterterrorism's focus on "isolation" in chapter 22, "Addressing Terrorism: A Theory of Change Approach." Next, a chapter (chapter 23) on negotiation and VE by I. William Zartman and Guy Olivier Faure explores the question in "Negotiation and Violent Extremism: Why Engage and Why Not?"

Next, the peacebuilding NGO Search for Common Ground describes its practical approach in a series of three chapters (chapters 24–26): "Peacebuilding Principles for Transforming Violent Extremism," "Peacebuilding Approaches to Working with Young People," and "Peacebuilding Narratives and Countering Violent Extremism."

A second chapter on the positive role of the media in curbing VE by Myriam Aziz and Lisa Schirch documents the challenges and opportunities in chapter 27, "A Peacebuilding Approach to Media and Conflict-Sensitive Journalism."

Maria J. Stephan and Leanne Erdberg from the US Institute of Peace describe the role of nonviolent action in preventing VE in their chapter, chapter 28, "To Defeat Terrorism, Use 'People Power.'"

In a chapter on "Preventing Violence through a Trauma-Healing Approach" (chapter 29), Veronica Laveta from the Centre for Victims of Torture discusses how working on trauma and resilience can contribute to interrupting a cycle of violence and put people on a more positive path.

Chapter 22

Addressing Terrorism

A Theory of Change Approach

John Paul Lederach

The 2010 *Holder v. Humanitarian Law Project* US Supreme Court decision has sharpened the debate about engagement with blacklisted groups and has directly impacted the wider communities where designated foreign terrorist groups operate. Antiterror legislation has consequences and relevance for peacebuilding organizations whose engagement with these local communities and midlevel leaders creates ambiguous but potentially significant legal ramifications under the recent Supreme Court decision. As a practitioner-scholar I have been struck by the lack of basic discussion on the assumptions and theories undergirding the "listings" policy and dearth of evidence-based research testing the theories around these pressing issues. An explicit clarification of the theories of change that purports to address violent conflict and terrorism is needed. To elucidate a theory of change is not an abstract endeavor. It requires commitment to specify assumptions and demonstrate how a particular activity and approach functions and unfolds toward desired outcomes.

In this chapter[1] I want to provoke the theoretical imagination to assess and evaluate the central strategies for responding to violent conflict and terrorism. Let me start by making two observations and clarifying one premise.

First, since 9/11 and even more with the *Holder v. Humanitarian Law Project* decision, we have witnessed a divide emerging between two competing theories of change. The designated foreign terrorists list proposes a change strategy based on isolation. Peacebuilding proposes a strategy of *engagement*.

Both terms merit a brief description. By "isolation" I do not refer to the classic use of the word in political science that delineates a strategy of not participating in international affairs, conflicts, or issues. Rather as connected to the policy of designating foreign terrorists, isolation essentially proposes a strategy of identifying, targeting, and limiting individuals and groups who espouse violence defined as terrorism. *Isolation* as a strategy legally limits material support, the interpretation of which increasingly includes contact, consultation, or dialogue with blacklisted groups, as these activities have been determined to contribute to their legitimacy and success.

"Engagement" is not used here in its military form, quite the contrary. "Engagement" refers to strategies that require contact, consultation, and dialogue. In particular, strategic peacebuilding suggests that engagement must happen with a wider set of people and stakeholders at multiple levels of society than is typically undertaken in official processes (Lederach and Appleby 2010; Schirch 2005). Peacebuilding operates within the wider civil society affected by violent conflict. Engagement suggests continuous contact, consultation, deliberative dialogue inclusive of all views, and development of processes with a focus on understanding accurately the sources of violence and addressing them through a range of nonviolent change strategies.

Second, proponents of isolation and engagement have not adequately described the theory of change underpinning their proposed approach. In particular little direct discussion exists as to how a particular strategy addresses and transforms the challenge of terrorism. I would argue that of the two, peacebuilding has offered more concrete discussion of the undergirding theory of change in settings of armed conflict and repeated cycles of violence but rarely in direct reference to terrorism (Darby and McGinty 2008; Fisher 2005; Zartman 1983; Zartman and Faure 2011).

On the other hand, the isolation approach has rarely clarified its formational theories of change but has had a powerful defining impact on the environment in which peacebuilding develops. Isolation carries the sanction of official policy and the legal backing of courts but has less clarity and explicit development of theory about how, as a strategy of change, it contributes to the reduction of violence or the forging of a more stable peace. In particular, proponents have offered very little theoretical clarification about how isolation of designated groups and individuals contributes to desired change process in and with the communities where the identified groups live.

Finally, I propose an operative premise for this chapter. I assume that these two competing strategies, *isolation* and *engagement*, share the laudatory purpose that their actions are aimed at reducing violence, increasing security, and improving the environment for a stable peace. I have framed these goals in a way that permits us to explore theories of change. From these observations and premise, several framing questions emerge:

- What are central theories of change that constitute the strategies of isolation and engagement?
- Do they actually unfold the way the strategy proposes in terms of the identified and desired outcomes?

- What unintended consequences do they bring?
- Do they vary by context?

THEORY OF CHANGE FRAMEWORK

A theory of change framework proposes that each strategy, isolation and engagement, takes up a challenge to articulate more clearly how their approach works in terms of the guiding theory by which desired changes are sought. This chapter will explore three elements relevant to this task: (1) suggest a theoretical construct that more accurately portrays the complexity of the context and issues in responding to terrorism beyond what now appears as two mutually exclusive approaches; (2) discuss the theoretical assumptions of how isolation and engagement as strategies of change contribute to violence prevention and stable peace; and (3) discuss a few of the theoretical frameworks that elucidate the challenge of connecting a particular approach with its proposed outcomes.

As a starting point we must take note that at official levels responses to terrorism almost exclusively frame the challenge under a political umbrella constructed by way of either/or choices. Quite commonly we hear key leaders affirm that they "will never negotiate with terrorists." This framing comes in the context of a highly charged political environment and an emotionally laden legacy that follows the aftermath of mass violence. President George Bush expressed this choice as defining global partnerships and alliances after the events of September 11, 2001, when, in one of his key speeches, he made it clear to the international community that "you are with us or against us."

The blanket refusal to engage and negotiate with violent organizations, even those listed as terrorist, does not match the empirical evidence that engagement and negotiations have often taken place over the past decades with designated terrorists (Jones and Libicki 2008; Neumann 2007). While counterterrorism responses certainly existed prior to 9/11, the "listing" of designated individuals and groups as foreign terrorists gained salience and prominence in the weeks and months that followed. For a decade this approach has marked and defined a strategy of isolation that grew exponentially to include more and more groups and had an impact on wider civil society and local communities in a number of key strategic geographies.

The approach to listing has had significant debate. The UN General Assembly 2005 World Summit Outcome document declared that the Security Council and the secretary-general should "ensure that fair and clear procedures exist for placing individuals and entities on sanctions lists and for removing them, as well as for granting humanitarian exemptions" (UN General Assembly 2005).

In 2009, Eminent Jurists Panel of the International Commission of Jurists described the listing and delisting procedures used by numerous nations and international agencies as "arbitrary" and discriminatory. It is a system, said the panel, "unworthy" of international institutions such as the United Nations and the European Union (EU) (International Commission of Jurists 2009).

Legal issues aside, the most difficult theoretical issue posed by designated listings, emerge in the bifurcation affecting whole populations. We live in a far more complex world than one divided into two cells. A starting point for any theoretical exploration requires a careful look at this complexity and the many settings where designated foreign terrorist lists exist as defined by the United States and Europe.

In particular, the listing of organizations rarely clarifies how far the net of affiliation may be cast. While there are many reasons for this ambiguity, a primary one has to do with the nature of these organizations. More often than not, they are organized on loose but highly effective networks. They function by way of smaller independent nodes of operation with unclear hierarchies of power, strategy, and decision making. They have highly protective and secretive communicative systems. Perhaps most important, they embed themselves around a wider set of affiliations and crosscutting relationships within the societies where they live. In locations like South-Central Somalia these listings by their very nature implicate entire geographies, human and physical, and create significant difficulty for distinguishing where exactly the boundary of relationships begins and ends, making it difficult to know with whom it is acceptable to relate. The impact of such listings results in a whole population effect, creating physical and human geographies that have less and less contact with the outside world.

Careful consideration of the many settings where designated foreign terrorist groups exist finds that their identity and membership boundaries are fluid, ephemeral, and difficult to fully appraise. Rather than a clean "two-cell" designation, we find something more akin to a *gray area* of social relationships. These relational spaces can include extended families, varied kinds of associations and affiliations, and just ordinary people who have to navigate relationships in order to survive. All this is compounded by network-based organizational structures created by those engaged in violence who themselves have fluid boundaries and carefully constructed layers of secrecy and protection.

Simply put, bifurcation into two clearly delineated groups does not exist. We do not live in a bipolar world of us and them. As such we are not well served by a theoretical construct that requires rigid bifurcation when such a bipolar distinction does not exist in the societies affected by their presence. We may be better served by understanding these contexts as a spectrum of fluid and complex relationships. If we place this visually in theoretical construct, we move away from a two-cell understanding toward a continuum (see Figure 22.1).

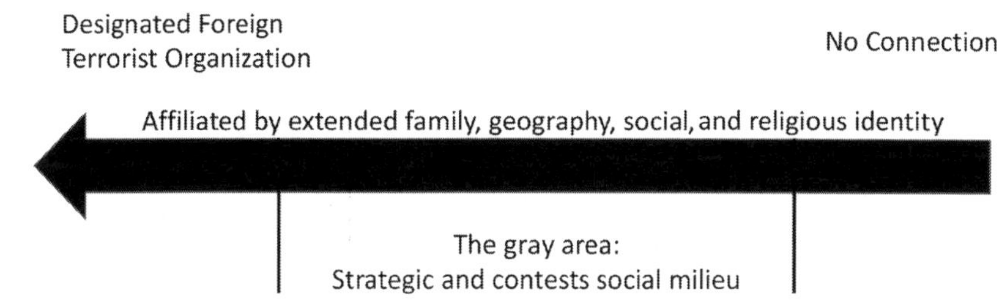

Figure 22.1. The Contested Gray Area: A Continuum of Social Relations

"Us/them" as a way to approach terrorism methodologically requires a capacity to clearly distinguish who would be placed in each category. In reality a spectrum exists that runs on one end from those who are activists in organizations that espouse terrorism and at the other extreme those who have absolutely no connection. However, in between and especially in geographies such as South-Central Somalia, we have *the gray area* comprised of people and organizations that have at a minimum some form of contact, connection, or affiliation with people and groups on the designated lists. This is often not by choice but simply because they live in a particular area, share a common religious background, or have extended family links, to mention only a few. After considerable years of experience in many of these settings, my own view is that this gray area may be much larger and harder to define than we understand. Yet in terms of violence prevention and stable peace, *the gray area is both strategic and contested.*

The expansion from bifurcation to complexity suggests that any theory of change, whether it articulates isolation or engagement, will need to carefully assess the assumptions that each brings to the complex challenge of *the gray area*, as it relates to the change they purport will emerge from their action. That careful extrapolation of theory of change has rarely been fully realized.

What we can delineate are the key effects, perhaps unintended consequences, the designated foreign lists have had on international humanitarian and peacebuilding organizations. In order to comply with the mandate of listings, the legally safe approach for international agencies and NGOs working in contested areas is to assume a wide net of implication. This translates into a preventative stance of guilt by contact and potential association for their activity, mostly any activity on the ground. As a result, the tendency has been to limit their presence on the ground and reduce their contact with local populations until communication and consultation stop. The fear is this: the wide swath of unpredictable association creates potential affiliation and may implicate them legally as supporting terrorists. The ensuing whole population effect results in entire groups of people finding themselves increasingly isolated from outside contact. The ultimate impact is clear: most international agencies and NGOs have chosen to slow down, if not completely stop, their activity in these areas.

Significant questions emerge at the level of theory of change in reference to the links between action and desired outcome:

- Is the intended consequence of designated lists to isolate whole populations?
- If not, in contested geographies, is it possible to isolate a particular group independent of the civil society where they operate?
- How does isolation as a strategy of change conceive and develop processes necessary to reduce violence and stabilize peace, if no contact, interaction, or dialogue can be developed with affected populations?
- When and how will movement from isolation to some form of engagement take place?

These questions lead to a more detailed exploration of theories of change that each strategy may carry.

ISOLATION AND ENGAGEMENT

Our purpose here is to provoke discussion and thought about how to increase a capacity to reduce violence and stabilize peace by looking more carefully at the underlying theories of change, which particular approaches suggest. My argument suggests that insufficient attention has been paid to the theoretical frameworks as responses to terrorism have emerged in the past decade. I suggest that two lenses may be useful. First, for illustrative purposes, provide an initial outline with a few theories of change that each approach might propose. And second, explore questions about how these theories address the strategic gray area of local and wider populations in affected geographies. I start with the engagement proposals.

Exploration of theories of change requires the formulation of how a set of actions relates to expected outcomes or in some cases unfolding processes. In its simplest form, it requires us to suggest how an activity will increase or decrease particular behaviors or outcomes. In a complex and multivariate context, this initial attempt will necessarily be reductionist. The purpose here is to provoke the imagination necessary to lift out what too often are implicit assumptions, an exercise that has been missing from much of the public, policy, and legal debates.

As illustration I will propose a few theories of change. I have divided these into two levels of engagement or isolation: approaches to gray area of civil society and approaches to people in positions of, or close to, leadership in designated terrorist groups.

Engagement

With reference to the civil society, the "gray area" with proximity to designated groups, increased engagement (contact, consultation, and dialogue) will:

- increase accuracy of assessment about key grievances and concerns leading to increased capacity to recognize opportunity and address issues in ways that respond to these grievances and diminish justification for violence;
- increase the consideration of alternative views of contested issues and history (thus encouraging views other than those as providing the justification for violence by dominant groups) opening potential for consideration and reconsideration of options that reduce violence;
- increase understanding of competing internal constituencies and varying perspectives and narratives existent within the wider civil society, affected by the violence that will lead to increased constructive dialogue and greater influencing of decisions, reducing the narrow control of internal decisions;
- increase the understanding of foreign concerns and interests, thereby reducing fear and increasing different views of threat and enmity;
- increase wider participation and influence the rise of alternative leadership; and
- increase capacity to identify opportunities for constructive change in the short term, initiating the social platforms necessary for long-term change, and increase capacity for dialogue and decrease violence as the defining approach.

With leadership of designated groups, engagement will:

- increase understanding of their key grievances, create potential openness to alternatives, and will augment capacity to identify opportunities for change resulting in increased potential to build alternatives to violence;
- establish key relationships especially among second-tier leadership necessary to explore and prepare early processes that shift from violent engagement toward dialogue and improving the potential to reduce violence and encourage nonviolent democratic processes;
- increase understanding of existing internal differences in the leadership; and
- provide opportunity to elicit alternative views of outside and foreign interests and concerns increasing accuracy of information. Increased accuracy of communication means greater potential for considering alternative and nonviolent processes.

Isolation

Increased isolation of terrorist groups and leadership will:

- reduce their economic and military capacity and thereby diminish their ability to engage violently;
- increase the capacity to identify, locate, and capture, or eliminate, key leaders and operatives, thus reducing the effective leadership of the wider movement;
- reduce the appeal and vibrancy of their relationship within their primary and secondary constituencies, a relationship they need and must sustain in order to survive. In essence isolation strangulates their political capital and reduces their social capital, driving a wedge between leadership and wider constituency, thereby reducing the likelihood and effectiveness of violence;
- reduce their capacity to recruit new members; and
- increase their desire and need to be accepted back into the international community and political mainstream and will thereby increase their willingness to end the strategy of violence.

Proponents of isolation often suggest key concerns about the pitfalls and unintended consequences of engagement. First and foremost, many express the concern that engagement represents a form of negotiating with terrorists that is politically unpalatable. Going a step deeper, the apprehension suggests that contact and engagement increase the legitimacy of these groups internationally, within their countries and key constituencies, and within their own self-view, providing them undue recognition. This serves to promote their standing and support, ultimately justifying the violence they employ against innocent civilians. As such, contact and dialogue with these leaders contribute to impunity and instability. This concern is coupled with a deep suspicion that contact and dialogue will be used tactically by violent groups and thus supports their strategic goal of harsher and renewed violence. Finally, in the eyes of many, including the Supreme Court, response to terrorism as a national security concern represents an area of legal responsibility that falls under the exclusive purview of governments. Engagement at other levels by nongovernmental actors reduces the effectiveness of official policy and may impede its success.

THEORY AND EVIDENCE

These competing ideas have considerable theoretical development and empirical evidence from numerous disciplinary lenses. The sociological literature on the dynamics of conflict escalation into violence provides some key observations and questions (Coser 1955; Kriesberg and Dayton 2009). What are the key dynamics and effects of escalating conflict and polarization? Several merit brief exploration.

As conflict escalates and polarization sharpens, social pressure increases significantly for people to define and join one side or the other, thereby reducing a middle ground. Increased outside threat to goals or survival creates a much stronger internal social cohesion. In highly polarized contexts people within a group have more contact and interaction with those who share their views and concerns and correspondingly much less direct interaction with those of differing perspectives.

This combination of dynamics, very common in polarized conflict, has a twofold impact. At times of polarization, in-group perspectives are viewed as accurately accounting for a complex reality with little room for alternative views of the complexity. This is coupled with a decrease in the available direct mechanisms for receiving and sharing information across differing views and results in people relying ever more on secondary and often inaccurate sources of information, in particular about the "other," often perceived as the enemy. This creates less accurate and less objective information on which decisions are made.

The decrease of internal debate and the interaction of differing ideas, perspectives, and interpretation of a complex reality carry significant effects. Among the most significant we find that escalated conflict creates greater opportunity for more extreme views to rise in prominence and solidify positions of leadership. Whereas prior to sharp escalation, these views may have been assessed as unrealistic, distant from reality, and incongruent, they gain in status as perceived and actual threat increases and violence emerges. Tolerance for and exploration of ambiguity reduce sharply in terms of group views. Little or no room exists for questions or the expression of alternative views. For the leadership, sustaining a clear and reinforced perception of outside threat sustains their status and position and reduces the need to deal with potential competing perspectives. Sustaining one interpretation and keeping "followers" far from contact with competing views and differing interpretations creates a monolithic, unquestioned, and highly cohesive internal constituency.

Here we find some of the most intriguing questions about the gray area and our two approaches. Engagement approaches would argue that the theory of change needed to transform the justification for violence and the support it may receive from geographically affected constituencies requires regular contact, consultation, and dialogue that both seeks the others' views and provides potential alternative views (Curle 1987; Lederach and Appleby 2010). In other words, contact and conversation create the mechanisms necessary to increase a level of ambiguity (people have the opportunity to interact with competing views of meaning rather than having one and only one correct narrative and interpretation).

This introduces and injects a dose of cognitive dissonance requiring exploration within diverse explanations of a complex reality. In turn the very existence of alternative conversations demands more of leadership than facile and monolithic explanations about why violence is needed and justified. On the other hand, isolation, though aimed at narrowing the space for operations of targeted leaders, in fact decreases outside contact and the introduction of alternative views when the outcome of this strategy creates a whole population effect. The net result may well strengthen the capacity of control of extremist leadership within their constituencies rather than reducing their sphere of influence (Cortright et al. 2011).

A careful exploration of theory of change requires empirical evidence. In particular, isolation as a change strategy needs to be more explicit as to how it interacts with the contested and strategic gray area and will need to establish why and how diminished contact and conversation within the wider affected population contributes to the desired change it purports to accomplish.

Empirically, if indicators were established to measure impact, several would shed light on the theory. For example, what if capacity to recruit people into terroristic acts were an indicator of desired change? In essence, here we would seek to measure whether a particular strategy of change increased or decreased the ability of leadership to recruit active followers and bring them into acts of violence. If the isolation strategy works according to its theory, leaders of these groups should have less capacity to recruit, and eventually their numbers will desiccate.

Little empirical evidence seems to exist that this holds true. In fact, in a number of locations the impact of isolation coupled with outside violence has led to increased capacity for recruitment. What accounts for the appeal and legitimacy these movements seem to enjoy? How does the impact of having little contact, consultation, and engagement with their views contribute to the ability of leaders to sustain a narrative that holds sway among a significant constituency?

One could argue that a more fine-tuned theory would be important in reference to specific ways in which isolation functions with an eye toward change. For example, Benjamin and Simon suggest this be approached with two concentric circles (Benjamin and Simon 2005). A small inner circle represents key leaders and those directly involved in terrorism. A much larger outer circle describes something close to the gray area, the contested population from which recruits may be found or from which may emanate pressure to shift the strategy away from violence.

Their argument suggests that this requires a strategy with capacity to appropriately target isolation of the few while robustly engaging the wider population. As Cortright and Lopez argue, the goal must "isolate hard-core elements and separate them from their potential base. This requires a political approach that addresses deeply felt grievances, promotes democratic governance, and supports sustainable economic development" (Cortright and Lopez 2007). Such approaches narrow the focus of isolation toward core leaders and encourage robust interaction within the wider civil society. The blanket approach that isolates whole populations in order to isolate leaders does not, at least as currently defined, have a clear theory of change and may have produced totally unintentional and undesired consequences.

If we move from the gray area discussion to challenge of more direct engagement with leaders or people close to leadership within these movements, another set of approaches, theories, and evidence can be explored. The most useful comparative literature emerges from more than three decades of research on how violent conflicts end, how negotiations begin, and what may be required for sustaining a change process from violence to nonviolent political process (Darby and McGinty 2008).

It is important to distinguish between a formal negotiation and the informal spaces, conversations and interactions that are necessary prior to a decision to officially and more publicly "negotiate." Evidence over many years suggests that the movement from violence to dialogue and peaceful engagement requires careful preparation, what many identify as "pre-negotiation." This phase often passes through contacts and openings that include a range of people, good offices, and processes that help create conditions to consider and explore avenues for ending the violence. They require a commitment to conversation, consultation, and dialogue. Formal negotiations or other kinds of alternatives can then be defined. While the political and ideological demands are repeatedly expressed publicly, such as "we never negotiate with terrorists," evidence suggests otherwise. The RAND Corporation in its study on how terrorism ends suggests that more than 80 percent happens by way of policing or political process. Less than 5 percent end by way of military victory (Jones and Libicki 2008).

Isolation as an approach emerges from the political goal (though with significant military influence) for responding to and weakening a foreign enemy with military threat and capacity. Isolation does not provide a clearly stated theory of exit, that is, how the strategy of segregating and secluding a group will create the conditions that bring their first- or second-tier leadership toward ending the violence, except by some form of elimination or military victory. For example, after surveying twenty years of peace processes, Darby and McGinty posed the question of whether it is possible to reach a more sustainable outcome if militants, often designated as terrorist leaders, are not included. In response, they note, "The reality is that total inclusion is never possible. There are always zealots who will not compromise. The more numerous and compromising the moderates, the greater the likelihood that the extremes can be marginalized" (Darby and McGinty 2008).

The challenge, in reference to our theory of change discussion, is how does a process of change achieve a growing set of moderates without some strategy of engagement. If in fact a low percentage of success comes by way of military victory and a much higher percent by way of policing and political process, then the isolation strategy would need to develop greater clarity in how, when, and with whom the potential for change is promoted. In other words, isolation as a theory of change would need to diversify its end-game scenarios.

Engagement, on the other hand, suggests that the process of change begins with understanding the concerns and perspectives of those involved, including higher-level leadership and their constituencies. It advocates a process of conversation and dialogue that introduces trustworthy communication and exploration of alternative narratives. Among the intriguing and complex paradoxes, we find in the comparative literature of how peace processes initiate and the interdependence of official and unofficial processes (Fisher 2005). Governmental leaders with highly visible public profiles can rarely afford the image of direct interaction with those whom they have indicated they will never talk. In many cases a combination of quiet, off-record, and unofficial explorations is happening simultaneously with public pronouncements that indicate the contrary. These unofficial spaces, more often than not, initiate with and through people who have the connections, relationships of trust, and understanding of dialogue, but who are not formally or officially tied to any government.

This activity is highly relational. It requires years of commitment and conversation. It often initiates with key second-tier leadership in environments of extreme distrust and potential violence. Emergent in this body of comparative literature is the increased understanding that the shift from violence to stable peace requires multiple layers of conversation at differing levels of leadership, the careful preparation of process, and the preparation to enter into dialogue. Also required is the understanding of how prudent and painstaking development of early conversations can move toward officially sanctioned processes of negotiation. Engagement as a strategy suggests that this requires contact and conversation with a range of leaders and with a commitment to varied potential processes. Isolation, particularly when designed as a blanket form of control diminishing any contact, has not clearly articulated a theory of change of how movements espousing violence will change or how alternative leadership emerges without outside interaction and encouragement.

CONCLUSION

This chapter suggests that a more direct exploration of theories of change could create a more effective understanding of how best to approach and encourage constructive social change. The primary requirements are twofold: ask proponents to delineate their key theories of change in more specific ways and develop a dialogue based on empirical evidence rather than ideological preference or politically driven mandates. There may in fact be significant overlap and areas of agreement that could, particularly when applied to concrete geographies, result in far more effective and varied strategies and approaches.

I would make the case that isolation in the form of wide-ranging terrorist lists was driven by desire to control future acts of terrorism. But the approach has little, if any, clear projections of a theory of change that addresses the complexity around the different contexts where it has been applied. It seeks to control violence in the short term but does not suggest how as strategy it contributes to desired change in the mid-to long-term. Engagement as an approach includes concrete ideas about change over the mid-and longer-term but does not have within its purview specific strategies aimed at controlling or preventing a particular act of terrorism in the short term. Its purpose is not policing. Engagement strategies seek to change the conditions from which violence emerges, to locate and create the opportunities that make the change possible.

POLICY RECOMMENDATIONS

- Delineate with greater specificity the theory of change that supports terrorist listings with a particular focus on how it will meaningfully and strategically engage the affected populations. The assessment of the basic theory requires a careful compilation of evidence that assesses, in particular, whether it has increased or decreased a capacity to recruit, solidified or weakened more extremist leadership, and provided for shifts in the wider population toward nonviolent strategies of social change.
- Develop a clear end-game scenario for how geographies most affected or controlled by designated organizations will shift the justifying narratives and behavior from violence (and the use of terrorism in particular) toward

nonviolent processes. This requires a specific strategy for how isolation contributes to constructive shifts in the wider civil society most affected by the terrorist listings.

- Pinpoint how isolation of leaders (similar for example to policing approaches for criminal behavior) combines with robust engagement of local populations.
- Develop strategies that constructively impact the rise of second-tier and secondary leadership. Given that many of these movements rely heavily on youth, a strategy that strategically approaches the growth of new and alternative leadership requires significant and varied approaches to engagement. Isolation as a blanket policy seems to hold little, if any, strategy for how alternative or future leaders will be different.

Chapter 23

Negotiation and Violent Extremism

Why Engage and Why Not?

I. William Zartman and Guy Olivier Faure

> Fuad Ali Saleh, a radical Islamist head of a terrorist network, is about to be judged. Victims that have survived his bomb attacks are present, among them a woman on a wheelchair and another with her face horribly distorted by an explosion. The presiding judge begins the hearing by verifying the identity of the accused.
> —Your name is Fuad Ali Saleh?
> —My name is "Death to the West"!
> Paris: January 29, 1990, The Law Court
> *Le Monde*, January 31, 1998

Contrary to popular notions, negotiating with terrorist organizations is not talking with the devil. It is not soul-selling or evil pacting, nor does it require a surrender of goals and values that the parties have held dear. Rather, the challenge is one of making extremist movements negotiable. This means inducing moderation and flexibility in their demands, reshaping their ends into attainable reforms, encouraging and abetting where possible the emergence of moderate leadership and organization, and forcing an end to their violent means of protest while at the same time opening the political process to broader participation and more effective policies on the deeper problems of society and governance that underlie extremist organizations' protests. Without such movement on *both* sides, the horror of terrorism will not be overcome.

But there is more. Unless the extremist movement's tactics are shown to be counterproductive, they will not be abandoned. Dealing with terrorism therefore means both keeping its violent means in check, transforming its ends from destruction to participation, and undercutting the grievances on which it rides. These three elements are the ingredients of a policy of engagement.

Thus, confrontation and engagement are not just polar opposites; they are both the ends of a continuum and the elements in a causal relationship. Engagement may appear to constitute a sharp change from a policy of confrontation, but containment and isolation are the means of causing the moderation that makes the extremists engageable. Engaging extremists works as part of a broad policy that is complex in tactics, deliberate in balance, and, ultimately, necessary.

Let it be said from the start that this policy—like any—does not always succeed, and there are even terrorist organizations beyond its reach. These are absolute terrorist organizations (Zartman 2003). As long as the ends of the organization are millennialist dreams, globalist transformations, and activated worldviews that require terrorist means, there is no point in negotiating, no hope in engaging, and no one with whom to discuss. Certainly, as discussed next, they require contact and surveillance to detect any changes in ends, means, and personnel. For the category "absolute" is an attribute, not a permanent condition. However, to become engageable, the ends as well as the means—and probably the personnel—of the organization must be changeable. To cite names, that means that Al-Qaeda and Daesh in their present form are not considered here to be engageable, Hamas is, and the Taliban, more complex, are located in between. Others—such the Revolutionary Armed Forces of Colombia (FARC) and National Liberation Army (ELN) in Colombia, the Moro National Liberation Front (MNLF) and Moro Islamic Liberation Front (MILF) in Mindanao, Liberation Tigers of Tamil Eelam (LTTE) in Sri Lanka, the Coalition for the Defence of the Republic (CDR) in Rwanda, and Hezbollah in Lebanon—may be difficult to engage but are not absolutes or intrinsically unengageables as the Colombian and Philippine experiences show.

Political terrorist or extreme violent organizations include nationalist terrorist organizations (NTOs), which use terrorist methods to gain self-determination and independence for their territorial claims, revolutionary organizations that seek a change in government to accomplish deep-seated social changes, and also religious or millennialist organizations who belong to the fourth wave of modern terrorism and seek to overthrow and replace a government they see as impious and unjust (Rapoport 2006).

Although these same organizations are also sometimes called freedom fighters or resistants or national liberation movements or holy warriors or martyrs, the important distinction is not whether the observer favors their cause or not, but whether they use violent methods directly against noncombatant civilian populations for the purpose of influencing policy, essentially the US and UN definition of terrorism (UNSCR 1373; 18 U.S. Code § 2331 2010). Terrorism and terrorists are seen here as a phase in conflict by ethnic, religious, ideological, and other groups, rather than as a distinctly separate phenomenon with no background, antecedents, or resemblances with other types and stages of identity conflicts. Few terrorist conflicts start out as such; they begin with "lesser" means to their ends and escalate into terrorism when those earlier means do not produce progress toward their goals. This understanding allows the analysis to include relevant material from current understanding of other conflicts before they have reached the terrorist phase.

Negotiation and the broader policy of engagement, while ultimately necessary in the absence of one side's victory, run through enormous associated difficulties and paradoxes and depend much on timing and diplomatic skills. Engagement has its risk for both sides, which explains their reluctance to engage. If engagement were an obviously good thing, there would be no need to ask why, and one could immediately jump to *how*. But for many reasons, engagement is a risky choice. There are many arguments against negotiating with extremists, and many of the same arguments made by the state can be made by the extremists about negotiating with the state—a parallel that is important to understand from the state side. This is not to suggest that the two sides are mirror images, but that questions of engagement that are often regarded from one side only are in fact posed to both parties.

Thereafter, the questions of *when* and *how* come to the fore. If engagement is inevitable, why not do it early and save all those lives, including those of the many innocent civilian bystanders? Part of the answer certainly comes from the difficulty of reversing a policy commitment to confrontation, but another part comes from the need to await or create appropriate conditions for a policy shift to engagement. When these conditions, including the possibility of conducting a policy reversal, are assembled, the final issue is *how* to engage.

OBSTACLES TO ENGAGEMENT

Just as politics is the art of the possible, negotiation is the art of compromise. The basic question, therefore, is, what does engagement between states and extremist organizations seek to obtain, and what are the chances of obtaining it? Negotiations with terrorists to end hostage crises seek above all to save lives, both those of the hostages and those subject to the future hostage crises that negotiation might encourage (Faure and Zartman 2010). They are engaged between two parties who have something to trade—hostages in exchange for something else (demands, publicity, safety)—and who are looking for a deal. Negotiations with political terrorist organizations are much broader in scope. They involve national, not just personal, security, and the fate of friends as well as enemies. Unlike negotiations with hostage takers, they do not involve parties looking for a deal, who try to define a zone of possible agreement (ZOPA) and find appropriate terms of trade. Negotiations with political terrorist organizations seek to change the means that terrorists use but also, to some degree, the ends they pursue. If the terrorists' ends were immediately acceptable, the extreme means of terrorism would not be necessary.

Both the state and the extremist organizations face these questions. Generally, the few works on terrorist negotiations examine the state's choices, as if to assume that the terrorists are ready to negotiate if only the state will (Hughes 1990). While this may be true for terrorists as hostage takers, it is not true at all for terrorist political organizations, which often face the same sorts of questions as do states. In fact, the terrorist political organization lies midway on a continuum, between a state, at one end, and looser rebellions and individuals such as hostage takers, at the other. It usually develops an institutionalized structure, including a military and a political wing, a tax and service system, foreign diplomacy, and often actual territorial control (even if only at night), as well as a complex belief system—all of which can combine to make it a sort of protostate, lacking only state status, as seen with the FARC, Afghan Taliban, and LTTE. "You are not dealing with a political party," declared the LTTE chief negotiator. "We have a judicial system, various structures where civilians are participating. So you have to take us seriously" (Sivaram 2006, 178). Yet the relative clarity of state-to-state negotiations, even with all the two-level international and domestic complexity that it might cover, is absent (Evans, Jacobson, and Putnam 1993).

As a result, the process of arriving at an agreement is complex, time-consuming, and frustrating, and even when the parties get there, the result is unstable, unreliable, unencompassing, and unenforceable. Negotiations with terrorist organizations are notoriously difficult, as the long negotiations with the LTTE, the ELN of Colombia, or the Free Aceh Movement (GAM), the National Union for the Total Liberation of Angola (UNITA), the Sudanese Peoples Liberation Movement/Army (SPLM/A), and the various Darfur rebel groups, among others, have shown. Indeed, "organization" is usually a misnomer. Usually there are many organizations, of unclear structure, competing with each other, riddled with factions, torn over the tactical question of whether to talk or fight (Haas and O'Sullivan 2000; Zartman and Alfredson 2010). Over these "organizations," whether territorial or millennialist, often hangs a maximalist goal sanctified by an absolute, all-justifying religious or ideological mandate. Beneath the "organization" often lies a substratum of tribal, ethnic, and traditional groups and allegiances, increasingly mingled with or replaced by criminal elements as time goes on. The ethos of both states and terrorists' mandate permits temporary agreements and justifies their rupture.

To begin with, engagement and negotiation carry with them the recognition of the terrorist organization (and, for the terrorists, the recognition of the state). Recognition confers a degree of legitimacy and status, and an implication that the party speaks for the client population it claims. For the state, engagement gives the terrorist organization legitimacy that overshadows its illegitimate tactics. For the terrorists, recognition of the state empties their own claim of exclusive legitimacy. Even for the mediator, recognition of the terrorists weakens its state-to-state relations with the terrorists' opponent (the state) and its own moral standing against terrorist tactics. No side can expect the other to give up its existence, general goals, and claims of representation, whatever the deal finally struck in negotiation. Regime change may come about, but for the moment, the terrorist organization makes its deal with the enemy state. Terrorists may moderate, but for the moment, the state makes its deal with the illegal terrorist organization. And the mediator deals with both as "unsavory characters," in President Jimmy Carter's characteristic phrase. Since terrorist groups, like any rebel group, seek above all status and representational recognition, engagement carries them a long way toward their goal.

In sum, recognition weakens the position of the state and strengthens the terrorist group—something the state does not engage in without some initial payment or expectations of a later one. Since reciprocity is the expectation, state engagement actually compromises the terrorist group as well, particularly if it has not actually beaten the state into submission. Thus, engaging extremists raises problematic implications, setting up precedents for future encounters, rewarding extremist methods, and risking entrapment in a relationship that may elicit more and more concessions. The question of recognition of organizations termed terrorist paralyzed potential negotiations between the Algerian government and the Islamic Salvation Front (FIS) in the early 1990s, as it had between the French government and the Algerian National Liberation Front (FLN), and also those between Israel and the Palestine Liberation Organization (PLO) until 1993, as it does in the next round between Israel and Hamas. Negotiations in Mozambique and South Africa in 1990–1994, with the National Resistance Movement (RENAMO) and the African National Congress (ANC), respectively, were not carried out with the state but with the governing parties in order to avoid these problems and led to serious regime changes.

Deeper than the problem of status is the way the two sides look at each other. States (and their populations) and terrorist organizations tend to demonize the opponent (Faure 2007; Spector 1998; Staub 2010). Demonization is the characterization of individuals, groups, or political bodies as evil, for purposes of justifying and making plausible an attack, whether in the form of assassination, legal action, circumscribing of political liberties, or warfare. The purpose is to facilitate killing or destroying the demonized people and to rally support for the accusers. Demonizing is a double process, addressing first the psychological dimension by building upon the anxiety, and then the strategic dimension, by degrading the opponent to justify extreme policies against it.

Governments and media demonize the extremists by developing a Manichaean worldview with "us" facing the "Green Peril" (successor to the "Red

Peril"), by defining the Quran as a "war plan against non-Muslims," by referring to Muslims as "Islamo-fascists," or, indeed, by loose use of the label "terrorist." Terrorist groups demonize their enemies in no less caricatural ways. The United States is the Great Satan to Iran and the head of the snake to Al-Qaeda. Westerners are labeled *kuffar* (unbelievers, against whom strong action is encouraged); heads of moderate Arab countries such as Egypt or Jordan are "apostates," the world is in a state of *jahaliya*, or pre-Islamic ignorance and unreformed governments are lackeys of the United States. The moral disqualification of the counterpart on both sides is used to authorize behaviors that would otherwise not be countenanced, such as terrorism and torture, or, in a negotiation, lying, tricking, manipulating, and deception. The role of a negotiator is then viewed as a way to distract the enemies while the state or organization is preparing to attack them.

Beyond images, states and terrorist organizations differ fundamentally on policy, and so engagement signals a policy compromise. Almost universally, when engagement is sought, it is the state that does the seeking and thus is the *demandeur*—the technical term for the weaker position in negotiation. When the terrorist organization talks of negotiation, it means state surrender on policy (and sometimes totally), as in Iranian president Ahmadinejad's 2005 letter to President Bush, or Osama bin Laden's 2003 offer to the United States. Terrorists are the weaker party in the conflict, who overcome their weakness with high-cost means—the use of violence against civilians—to gain a stronger position. They seek to buy compromise on policy and sometimes on the very existence of the state, using unconventional violence as currency. Thus, engagement with terrorists can be seen as both admitting compromise on policy (and on the state's existence) and accepting unconventional violence as terms of trade. Since the terrorists' goals are considered unacceptable, there is nothing to engage or to negotiate.

Both sides are in the conflict to win, and attempts at conciliatory policy undermine the commitment to that effort. Even when victory is not imminent, part of a winning strategy is simply to hold out until the effects of failure sink in on the other side. Very often victory is achieved not by a single salient battle but by showing the opponents that their tactics are unavailing. To sue for peace is to destroy this effect.

Thus, dealing with terrorists demands a major policy shift, from total confrontation to a position admitting that the terrorists are at least engageable and that there is something in their position that can serve as the basis for a negotiated compromise. They are no longer the devil with whom one should not shake hands or the enemy against whom one wages a total confrontation. The same is true on the extremists' side. Of course, tactical shifts are part of any conflict, but potential damage to one's political support and career is a strong inhibitor of shifts too radical. President George W. Bush was criticized among his own supporters for his engagement in his second term with North Korea, a state classified as a supporter of terrorism, as was President Ronald Reagan for his constructive engagement with Angola and South Africa over Namibia. A shift to engagement may gain new allies, but it will certainly lose old supporters and credibility. It rarely occurs without an important change in leadership. Policy changes toward dealings with terrorists after the elections of Charles de Gaulle, Alfredo Christiani, and Barack Obama in France (1958), El Salvador (1989), and the United States (2008), respectively, are examples of the latter effect.

In any case, engagement may be rejected, leaving the engaging party with a hand extended in the void and weakened by the attempt. In fact, engagement is quite likely to be rejected initially, so the initiator will have to persist and insist, accentuating its position as the weaker *demandeur*. There are many reasons why the attempt to engage may face rejection, at least initially and possibly for a while: misperception; reactive devaluation; or issues of credibility, justice, or obligation, to name a few.[1] The party being petitioned may find it hard to believe the policy change and may suspect the change as a trick to disarm it and rearm the initiator. The new signals may be misperceived, particularly because of contradictory noise and old signals coming at the same time. The opening may be dismissed as a sign that the initiators are suffering, so why not make them suffer some more? Or it may be seen as something the initiators should be doing anyhow, so let them continue to move toward surrender. Finally, there is the known psychological reaction that devalues what the other part offers and overvalues what the perceiver offers, making satisfactory reciprocation difficult. Iran, North Korea, Cuba, and Venezuela's reactions to President Obama's extended hand in 2009 are cases in point. All these are common reactions to a conciliatory move by one party in a conflict and stand in the way of a mutually beneficial engagement and negotiation.

For many, terrorism is an economic and dignity issue, if not for a lack of resources then for control of resources: desperate at not finding satisfactory conditions of life, for themselves, their families, and their community, terrorists take refuge in extremist demands and millennial goals. To undercut these aspirations, the engaging state must provide measures to assure a better life, lest the terrorists return to their old ways. If territorial demands are involved, the states must provide development aid and call donors' conferences to underwrite the results of the negotiations. Engagement in Palestine, Kosovo, and Mozambique, to name a few conflicts labeled "terrorist," has been expensive and not particularly satisfying to donors and recipients. Engaging terrorists is ultimately as costly as fighting them, although in different terms. If the economic issue is control rather than supply of resources, satisfaction is only available through costly high-level negotiations, as seen in the oil crisis of the mid-1970s and the associated terrorism it unleashed.

On the moral level, the terrorists' choice of means—violence against civilians—makes engagement and negotiation unethical. The very act of dealing with terrorists, particularly with the status and equality that engagement and negotiation imply, tarnishes the state, since the state is supposed to represent the highest values of legality and legitimacy. No government wants to recognize a terrorist group of extortionists, civilian killers, and suicides as a legitimate counterpart. Its very tactics disqualify the terrorist organization from the recognition, status, and credibility that negotiation confers. Politics, as noted, demands compromises, procedural as well as substantive, but dealing with terrorist organizations compromises the very nature of the state, procedurally as well as substantively.

Beyond the unethicality of dealing with terrorists per se is the compounded moral problem that negotiation actually encourages terrorism. President Richard Nixon's statement on hostage negotiations that "saving one life endangers hundreds" can be expanded by orders of magnitude in regard to negotiations with political terrorist organizations. It is irresponsible to allow terrorists to shoot their way through civilian casualties into policy decisions; rewarding their blackmail only encourages others to do the same. Repeated negotiations with Charles Taylor's National Patriotic Front of Liberia (NPFL) spawned new rebel movements claiming a place at the table every time talks were revived, and negotiations in Darfur and northern Pakistan have seen the same effect. Thus, engaging terrorists in order to bring terrorism to an end carries the moral hazard of doing the reverse (Kuperman and Crawford 2006; Martin 2003; O'Brien 1996).

It also is a slap to one's allies, particularly those in the conflict area. Not only does a shift to engagement alienate former domestic support, but it also leaps over moderates in the region to extend a hand to their radical rivals. Undercutting the moderates is not only politically incorrect, but it also risks alienating significant parts of the population that the state seeks to bring into support. Engagement with Hamas undercuts Fatah of the PLO, engagement with Hezbollah weakens the moderate parties in Lebanon, and engagement with Euskadi ta Askatasuna (ETA) circumvents the democratic Basque parties in Spain. Thus, engagement tends to be counterproductive, in many ways undoing the very goals it purports to achieve.

THE BENEFITS OF ENGAGING TERRORIST ORGANIZATIONS

The preceding risks and objections are logically tight and telling. Yet there must be another side to the question, since engagement does take place and would not do so if no benefits were forthcoming. Many of these benefits incur to both sides, providing a positive sum outcome for engagement that itself can be useful in moderating the terrorist organization; others fall to one side or the other, so that they are of tactical use.

The least benefit of engagement is to gain information. Public statements by terrorists, usually for propaganda purposes, are an unreliable source about what they really want, think, believe, will accept, and seek to achieve. In fact, these ideas are often very unclear in their own minds, so a chance to articulate them can lead to more reasonable formulations and more realistic thinking. It can also raise internal doubts about the validity of arguments and beliefs (Staub 2010). Even before any negotiations are on the horizon, contacts and talks with terrorist organizations' representatives can bring out useful information. Such talks proved effective in successful cases such as Northern Ireland, Mozambique, and Kosovo, among others (Irwin 2005; Judah 2008). It also may also bring out differences of opinion among the representatives, laying the ground for internal splits, promising contacts, and appropriate tactics, as occurred with the LTTE in 2005 or the FARC in 1986 and 2012–2013. Incidentally, these benefits and effects may also come to light on the government side, sometimes in response to clarifications and differences on the terrorists' side, feeding on each other and giving rise to improved government and terrorist policy. Thus, talks can provide useful inputs into intelligence and eventually policy, on both sides.

Moreover, communication is a potential path to influence (Fisher, Ury, and Patton 1991). Negotiation is a mechanism for influencing other parties' decisions, and, given adverse or suboptimal circumstances, negotiation may be the best, if not the only, way of avoiding an undesirable outcome. The point, therefore, is not *whether* to negotiate but *how* to negotiate creatively (Zartman 2003). A decision to negotiate does not mean acceptance of the other side's behavior or values—means or ends. What one must accept is that the underlying humanity deserves due process and that the desire for recognition and dignity often lies at the bottom of terrorists' needs and drives.

At the other extreme, negotiation may be a necessity, the only alternative to defeat or endless, costly conflict. Holding out may be a way to avoid giving in, but the holdout must weigh the cost of such a policy. When stalemates hurt, it is rational for parties to look for ways to come to terms; if both are caught in the impasse, the conditions are set for negotiations to provide a way out that benefits each (Zartman 2000). This situation does not guarantee a positive result, but it does provide the minimal conditions for one. Thus, the benefits of engagement are not fixed but depend on the conditions of the conflict.

The greatest benefit of engagement is to end the conflict or at least its terrorist form. If the terrorists can be pulled away from their terrorist methods, the state can meet them by being pulled off its nonengagement stance. This initial exchange is the beginning of the process of further exchanges. This brings up a previous objection: that negotiating with terrorists only encourages other terrorists. But it is not the act of negotiation that encourages or discourages further terrorist blackmail; it is the terms of the negotiated agreement (Zartman 2003). If the terrorists win their goals in the negotiation process and give the state little or nothing other than the end of conflict in exchange, others will indeed be encouraged to follow the same course. Large-scale sociopolitical movements, such as the wave of colonial independence, illustrate this effect, and the numerous recent secessionist movements (e.g., in Sudan, Eritrea, Casamance, Sri Lanka, Euskadi, Kosovo, Western Sahara, Tamil Eelam, and Aceh) involve a struggle over precedent as well as the individual issues. The normal "deal" is abandonment of terrorist means in exchange for entry into the competitive political system, with some moderation of ends as well. This is the basis of agreements with the GAM in Aceh, the PLO in Palestine, Renamo in Mozambique, Sein Fein (IRA) in Northern Ireland, MNLF and MILF in Mindanao, the FARC and ELN in Colombia, UNITA in Angola, the NLA in Macedonia, reconciliation groups in Afghanistan, and the Sunni Awakening groups in Iraq.

Moreover, consideration of engagement brings a salutary focus to the understanding of various national issues and conflicts. The end of the Cold War has made it possible for politicians and analysts alike to examine "root causes" of protest movements that use terrorist methods, and to recognize that, unacceptable though the methods may be, they are a symptom of the fact that something is wrong. This is not to say that their cause, any more than their methods, is "right," but only that their activities are signs of a problem that needs—and indeed cries out—to be solved. Quite often, the extremists' protest echoes widespread public sentiment, even while at the same time eliciting strong disavowal of their methods. Research shows, strikingly, that every actual or threatened electoral or nonelectoral takeover by an Islamist movement—beginning with Iran in 1979 and continuing to Algeria in 1991, Afghanistan in 1997, Somalia in 2004, Palestine in 2006, and Egypt in the 2000s—was not the result of a mass religious revival movement but a protest vote against a corrupt and incompetent government. Thus, terrorist outbreaks are warning signals of a deeper problem, and a call for governments to pay attention before it is too late.

The broadest benefit of engagement is to reduce tensions as a general tone in international relations. "Reach out and understand" replaces "combat and isolate." Concrete results may be slow in appearing, but the approach puts the state on the high moral ground, gives it a positive image among the undecided populace, and ultimately sends the message that "he who is not against us is with us," rather than the reverse. In so doing, it can reach out to other states supporting the terrorists for their own purposes as well. To conduct operations, terrorist groups have to rely on foreign sympathy, support, and asylum. When the terrorists' base lies within a host's territory, the group is subject to the host's authority. A host with sufficient political capacity may thus influence a group's behavior and ability to operate (O'Brien 1996; Zartman 2003). Countries hosting or supporting terrorist groups are often labeled "rogue states." According to US intelligence, seven of them, Iran, Cuba, Iraq, Libya, North Korea, Sudan, and Syria, have recently been involved in state-sponsored terrorism, covering a wide range of actions including embassy bombings, suicide missions, and hostage taking. By controlling weapons supplies, funding, and political support, states such as Iran and Syria strongly influence terrorists' ability to operate (Ranstorp and Gus 1994).

Reducing tensions with sponsors also serves the secondary function of improving terrorist credibility in negotiation, thus enabling states to expect terrorists to implement an agreement once reached. The likelihood of negotiation increases if terrorists are constrained by a host state when the host has something to gain or to lose (Zartman 1992). While unconstrained terrorists may defect from agreements without cost, constrained terrorists face punishment from host states that have an interest in pursuing good external relations. Since host states can also be punished for their support of terrorists, hosts have incentives to resolve terrorist events peacefully. Such has been the hope, at least, in US engagement with Syria and Iran regarding the actions of Hezbollah. Thus, engagement is aimed as much at third-party states and populations as at the terrorists themselves, and it can provide a ripple effect of benefits.

To begin and pursue engagement, third-party mediation is generally necessary. It also serves to improve relations between the necessary mediator and the parties (Grieg 2005; Zartman 1992). The importance of relations with a mediator is not to be underestimated in international politics, and mediator pressure for negotiations was a decisive element in conflicts with terrorists in Kosovo, Indonesia, Macedonia, Angola, Sudan, Mozambique, and Palestine. Even if mediator pressure to pursue negotiations fails, as it did in Sri Lanka and Colombia, the state can at least point out that it tried before returning to the "tactical alternative"—the use of force.

Engagement also provides tactical benefits. Negotiations may split the terrorists' unity or facilitate divisions already latent (Cronin 2008, 2009). When moderates in the organization see that partial gains ("half a loaf") can be made or that costs can be lowered by coming to terms, they are encouraged to reach out to the engaging hand. Engagement frees the moderates from the constraints of internal unity under which they operated and allows them to argue that the state will meet them halfway. Extremists will continue to operate, but they will be in the minority, sidelined by the engaging movement, and can be more easily controlled, as in the case of the Jundi Ansar in Gaza in

2009–2010, Hamas in Palestine in 1993–1996, and Front Nord in Casamance in 2000–2004. There will be internecine conflicts as the moderates move to pull the mantle of the movement over themselves, but the need to cover the moderates will encourage the state to move further toward them. As in most instances of negotiation, these dynamics are reciprocal, even if not necessarily equally so, and each side's need for an agreement affects where "in the middle" the outcome will be.

Or the move can strengthen the formerly dominated moderates to the point where they can pull in the extremists and draw the mantle of unity over all the factions. Such was the effect of engagement with the National Liberation Army (NLA) rebels in Macedonia, bringing both the Albanian parties and the NLA together around a common moderate platform at Prizren in 2001, or engagement with GAM in Indonesia, uniting the factions around an agreeable "half loaf" in "self-determination." Properly presented, engagement can show that further confrontation is pointless and that the opponents can reach their goals by other means. Terrorism is, after all, the weapon of the weak and the tactic of desperation, in the absence of success with other tactics; when the weak see how weak they really are, how their tactics are only alienating both the state and the surrounding bystanders, and that alternative tactics are open to them, they can be brought to the engagement table. Thus, engagement can encourage and facilitate the evolution of the terrorist group.

Either way, negotiation is on the path to moderation, which is, in turn, the necessary condition for engagement. The circularity is obvious: moderation is both the result of, and the requisite for, negotiation and engagement. The terrorists' willingness to negotiate is a sign of the broadening or relaxation of their tactics, as it is for the state. But the state offers engagement and negotiation (since it usually is the initiator) only when it perceives enough relaxation of means—and, possibly, of ends—to indicate further movement in the same direction. The description clearly indicates the delicacy of the operation: the state has to elicit indications of moderation from the terrorists and encourage them in the same process. Moderation is the goal of engagement and the major benefit to be obtained from it. It aims at producing some agreement: the renunciation of terrorist means, in exchange for some concession that the state can provide, from either its own means or its ends.

WHEN AND HOW TO ENGAGE

The reasons against engagement outnumber the reasons for, but they do not outweigh them. Taken together, the reasons for and against indicate two things: that engagement and negotiation are difficult, risky challenges and that their opportuneness depends on evolving circumstances. While it is often true that the whole terrorist challenge might have been prevented if original grievances had been handled by "normal politics" in the petition phase, in many cases this is a frivolous suggestion: either the original grievances are beyond human capacity to meet (e.g., immediate economic development, total government benevolence, or restoration of the Golden Caliphate) or they are high goals, not to be met lightly and worth fighting for (e.g., independence or total revamping of the sociopolitical system). So the combat begins with the means at hand and continues to victory/defeat, continued escalating confrontation, or stalemate—the only possible outcomes. In the absence of the first outcome, the two parties edge warily toward the realization that engagement is the only alternative, that there are other ways to achieve goals than by terrorism, and that half a loaf now is indeed available.[2] There are ripe moments for engagement, as for any other negotiatory path. The challenge is to cause them, sense them, and seize them (Zartman and deSoto 2010).

In rational terms, the bargaining dynamics are simple and straightforward, as noted earlier. The state wants the extremists to give up their terrorist means; but in exchange for what? Ultimately, for a better chance by using other, "lesser" means to get less of what they had hoped to get. Those terms are scarcely appealing *unless* a new condition is introduced: the impossibility of getting all that they want by terrorist tactics. This means that the possibility for the extremists to achieve their current goals must be convincingly blocked and also that the possibility of achieving at least something of those goals by alternative means must be convincingly open. Any other terms are of too little appeal to bring the parties to the table.

Chapter 24

Peacebuilding Principles for Transforming Violent Extremism

Lena Slachmuijlder

Search for Common Ground defines "violent extremism" as the choice individuals make to use or support violence to advance a cause based on exclusionary group identities. The particular identity of the perpetrator of violence does not determine what constitutes violent extremism, nor does the nature of the ideology, even if some may consider that ideology radical. Rather, violent extremism relates to an individual or group's violent advancement of an exclusionary ideology, which seeks to eliminate the "other" group, culture, or identity.

Over the past fifteen to twenty years, we have seen many predominantly military approaches used to address symptoms, rather than the drivers, of violent extremism. In many cases, these actions have aggravated tensions and triggered more support for violent extremism, such as when they led to human rights abuses or stigmatizing an entire identity group based on the actions of small fraction of their members. These actions can further augment the appeal of violent extremist movements by justifying their own narrative of grievances and power relations.

There is an opportunity to reframe the challenge of countering violent extremism (CVE). Drawing from the tools and tactics from peacebuilding, state and nonstate actors can be equipped to (1) understand the dynamics that foment violent extremism, (2) identify a set of tools and approaches that prevent those dynamics from giving rise to violent extremism, and (3) ensure that responses do not aggravate and radicalize affected communities even further.

Transforming violent extremism recognizes that while violent extremism exists, the reasons and motivators leading to an individual being drawn to violent extremist movements can be transformed into a different type of agency or engagement. This is distinct from CVE that is reactive to extremist violence rather than aimed at altering the dynamics that motivate it.

Search for Common Ground has drawn on three decades of experience in transforming violent conflict in communities plagued by many of the same dynamics underlying violent extremism: frustration with weak, corrupt, or illegitimate governance; marginalization; fractured relationships; lack of voice and opportunity; and struggles with diversity. This experience gives us tangible insight into building communities that are resilient to the pull of violent extremist groups. They also aid in early detection, thus helping to prevent violent extremism before it happens. Our goal is to offer questions, insights, and general guidance to peacebuilders and policy makers who are stepping into this nuanced space while highlighting the value of peacebuilding practices in what has become an overly security-driven and militarized field.

We recognize that the political and operational space around work labeled as CVE is fraught with complexity and, at times, dangerous. As peacebuilders, we also possess a unique set of values, best practices, and analytical tools that are uniquely useful in preventing and unraveling violent extremist activity. By drawing on this skillset, we have the potential to empower states, civil society, and vulnerable groups to peacefully and proactively respond to the challenge of violent extremism while also enabling individuals with whom we engage directly in choosing constructive, nonviolent alternatives in conflict settings.

Since 1982, Search for Common Ground has been transforming the way the world deals with conflict, moving away from adversarial approaches and toward cooperative solutions. With programs in thirty-five countries across Africa, Asia, and the Middle East, we collaborate with governments, civil society, media, and the private sector to strengthen the capacity of communities to build lasting peace. With 80 percent of our global staff of 600 hailing from the countries in which they work, we adapt and localize our approaches according to the needs of each country or region.

We view conflict as a natural and normal part of our lives, with the potential to catalyze peace, prosperity, and justice. When we transform conflict, we enable parties in conflict to identify shared interests and work together toward collaborative, win-win solutions.

CORE VALUES

Five core values form the bedrock of how we seek to transform violent extremism.

First, through impartiality, we engage all sides of a given conflict in the communities in which we work, enabling us to build trust and communication between stakeholders, each with differing sets of lived experiences, prejudices, narratives, and institutional practices.

Second, by maintaining respect for all people, our initiatives can create an environment where trust and empathy grow, opening up new insights and understandings of the dynamics at play in and around violent extremist movements.

Third, believing in our shared humanity means that we see everyone involved as part of the solution. The processes that we initiate seek to enable everyone, no matter what role they have played in conflict to date, to regain their sense of interconnectedness on a fundamental human level.

Fourth, we strive for inclusivity so that aggrieved or marginalized groups are given equal voice and groups that are usually segregated from one another can learn to engage in a productive dialogue while working cooperatively together.

Finally, our firm belief, grounded in practical experience over thirty-five years, that transformation is always possible allows us to bring both hope and proactive solutions to even the most protracted and intense conflict settings. It also reminds us that while people may choose violent extremism at one point in their lives, they can make new choices later on, transforming themselves and their relationships as a result.

By drawing on these values, peacebuilders can be effective in bringing about enduring change when encountering violent extremism and avoid the panicked, fear-based reaction that often arises instinctively when we feel threatened or confused. Our efforts are adaptive, locally grounded, and perpetually seeking to offer new skills, relationships, and perspectives that stakeholders can use in shaping their own futures.

Our focus is on directing our resources and organizational authority to programs that provide positive alternatives to violence, emotionally engage extremists and their potential recruits, and highlight diverse, pluralistic voices in divided settings. Through this effort, we can help shift the tide in CVE away from hard-line, short-term approaches toward those that build resilient communities for years to come.

WHAT DOES "PREVENTION" MEAN AS A WAY OF RESPONDING TO VIOLENT EXTREMISM?

As peacebuilders, our efforts to prevent violent extremism aim to tackle the contributing factors behind an individual's choice to engage in violent extremism. Prevention efforts should understand the environment, which enables violent extremist groups to operate and recruit. They must also tackle the factors that make individuals and groups susceptible to enlisting in such organizations. Search for Common Ground uses four outcome indicators for its work to prevent violent conflict. These include the following:

- Real or perceived grievances are addressed through nonviolent channels.
- Marginalized groups participate equally in the community.
- Young people express agency and leadership through nonviolent means and are seen as partners in prevention by adults.
- New relationships are built across dividing lines that debunk stereotypes.

Each of these areas brings an important focus to prevention work, but certain ones are emphasized, depending on the environment.

The opportunity of prevention efforts lies in applying peacebuilding tools to address the number of factors that lead to violent extremism. By creating opportunities for relationship building, community dialogue, and public engagement, peacebuilders can give anyone living in communities threatened by violent extremism a transformative opportunity through nonviolent approaches to addressing their grievances. At a societal level, we can empower key institutions with the skills, knowledge, and capacity to mediate grievances and conflict in a way that gives voice to the needs of all citizens while debunking pernicious myths that allow extremism to take root.

The risks are that a failure to effectively apply preventive peacebuilding strategies will allow violent extremist movements to continue to recruit and grow their influence within the community. When we are unable to tackle the conflicts without communities resorting to violence, it opens the door for violent extremist groups to rally support for their ideologies and tactics.

HOW CAN PEACEBUILDING APPROACHES HELP TO DEVELOP ROBUST PREVENTION PROGRAMS?

Search for Common Ground (Search) has identified seven guiding principles for working on violent extremism:

Determine What Enables This Environment, Using Both Root Cause and Conflict Scan Analysis

Prevention analysis begins by first identifying the root causes that have allowed violent extremism to take root in a community. Speaking with returnees, fighters, and the families and friends of those who have been recruited helps to identify pathways of recruitment, build a psychosocial profile of someone who is potentially vulnerable to recruitment, and why they are drawn to it. By listening to vulnerable individuals who have not been recruited, we can also build a clearer picture of what drives individuals to feel isolated from their family or community and thus more likely to be attracted to common recruitment tactics of violent extremist movements.

Second, peacebuilders can use conflict scan methods to understand the prevention landscape at a societal level. Fleshing out the role of state agencies, religious groups, community leaders, the media, civil society organizations (CSOs), including women and youth groups, and other influential institutions builds a more nuanced image of what factors shape the conflict environment. Looking at community-level factors such as grievances, dividers and connectors, and social pressures also helps to define strategy and messaging in prevention programs.

While it can be extremely difficult to identify all causal factors and mechanisms, together, these two analytical approaches paint a more complete picture of the enabling factors for violent extremism at the micro and macro levels. In Kyrgyzstan, Search used this combined analysis through key informant interviews, a literature review, and community assessments to identify Kyrgyz migrant workers who left to work in Russia as a high-risk group for recruitment to fight in the Middle East. This finding shifted previous assumptions that religiously conservative Uzbek groups were the most at-risk for recruitment by violent extremist organizations. Search staff also uncovered that the official claims that violent recruitment of Kyrgyz citizens had ended were inaccurate and that families were instead underreporting the recruitment of individuals to avoid stigma and shame. Together, these efforts helped peacebuilders build and sustain more effective early detection and prevention programs.

Seek to Understand Not Only Why People Join Violent Extremist Movements, But Also Why They Choose Not To

As peacebuilders, we know from experience that the vast majority of citizens do not support or engage in violence. Even in communities plagued by violent extremism, this remains true. Only a small minority of people—many of whom feel strongly about the same real or perceived grievances—make the choice to engage in violent extremism. Just as conflict analysts strive to understand not only the dividers but also the connectors in societies, peacebuilders seeking to understand the drivers and enablers of violent extremism can understand the factors of resilience by seeking to understand why communities resist or reject violent extremism. For example, after it was discovered from which neighborhoods in Brussels the violent extremists who had carried out attacks had been living, peacebuilders undertook research in the same neighborhoods. One of their methods was simply having conversations with people in the community to gain insight into why other second-generation immigrants, living in the same neighborhood, facing the same marginalization, had resisted the potential allure of extremism. This approach aligns with several best practices of peacebuilding throughout the decades, where a "whole-of-society" approach to strengthening resilience, trust, and inclusion can be reinforced to mitigate the risk of violence being seen as the only alternative.

Understand the Channels of Communication and Influence in the Community

Mapping channels of communication and influence within communities can enable peacebuilders to understand both the reach and resonance of various narratives and perspectives. Channels of communication can range from social media and formal journalism to youth organizations, coffee shop chat, and social or religious centers. In volatile contexts, violent extremists will often leverage these channels to establish their presence, undermine the credibility of peaceful actors, and bring in new members. Through mapping these channels, peacebuilders can understand not only how violent extremist groups are communicating but also how other communicators and advocates are reaching the same target groups. This opens up opportunities to amplify the voices of those who are tackling similar grievances or speaking to similar needs through nonviolent means.

In Northern Morocco, research showed that mothers were among the most powerful forces in influencing whether their sons and husbands would leave the country to fight for violent extremist groups in the Middle East. Search therefore organized a series of women-led dialogue caravans to discuss the problem of violent extremism within their communities. Rather than direct messaging, the goal was for women to hold a convening space for dialogue among imams, youth, and men in the community. In this way, Search empowered women to use their familial roles to promote frank discussions about violent extremism and its effects on family and community.

In Germany municipalities offer youth at risk of recruitment into extremist right-wing movements opportunities to experience "heroic" leadership with programs that allow them to work with fire departments and police forces while the nongovernmental organization Exit works with martial arts studios and training programs to provide youth positive role models and shift them.

Coordinate and Share Information with Other Actors Working in Prevention

State agencies often use tools that assess overt security threats but may overlook more long-standing causes and dynamics favoring violent extremism, such as a breakdown of social fabric, demographic shifts, or a lack of economic opportunity. Similarly, their responses to these threats often deploy the tools that are most familiar to them, such as surveillance, arrests, or other securitized responses. By sharing an analysis of the drivers behind violent extremism with state security actors, peacebuilders can pave the way for a more holistic approach to prevention. These shared perspectives can also inform other international actors, multilateral organizations, UN agencies, researchers, global forums, relevant think tanks, as well as other international organizations in the development and humanitarian space.

For example, in Nigeria, the Search team forged relationships of trust between security forces and civil society actors. This ensured that an ongoing dialogue would gradually build a shared understanding of the security threats posed by violent extremist groups. These conversations also enabled the state and nonstate actors to understand each institution's role in both driving and preventing violent conflict.

Seek to Understand Deeper Human Needs Related to Agency, Identity, and Connection

Social marginalization; joblessness; and a lack of basic food, shelter, and security can drive support for extremist movements, particularly when some people have more than enough, and others do not. Recognizing these drivers should not override the need to satisfy many other less material needs. These include universal human desires, such as self-esteem, belonging, and a sense of empowerment through being part of something larger than oneself.

Even in the poorest communities, successful programs can enable agency among young people while incentivizing institutions to mediate rather than ignore or aggravate conflict. In northern Nigeria, for example, Search's work of convening "peace architecture" meetings with diverse state and nonstate stakeholders has reinvigorated people's sense of agency, countering the sense of powerlessness that many can feel in such resource-scarce environments.

See Religion as Part of the Solution, Rather Than the Problem

Throughout history, insurgent, separatist, and liberation groups have sought to profit from weak governments and fragile environments by exploiting people's sense of grievance—real or perceived—to mobilize them toward violence. Targeted individuals see violent extremism as a means to better meet their needs based on their lived experiences. By applying a peacebuilding lens, we see that it is not ideology that makes individuals vulnerable to extremist recruitment but a desire to meet deeper personal needs around visibility, empowerment, dignity, and identity.

Peacebuilders also understand that it is not the content of religious teachings that radicalizes people but rather offering aggrieved individuals a religious framework through which to understand and redress their grievances. To prevent people from choosing violence, we work to understand how the strength and weaknesses of their relationships with others might cause them to search for identity, dignity, recognition, and heroism through violent activity.

In Kyrgyzstan, the psychosocial profiles of returned fighters showed that many of them were not initially religious but became so when faced with socioeconomic or sociocultural vulnerabilities. The recruitment leaders who drew them into violent activities were not the leading muftis or ulemas in the community but rather independent religious figures or extremist leaders who were not connected with the mainstream religious community.

In Diffa in the southeast of Niger bordering Nigeria, Search observed that young people rarely joined Boko Haram because of the religious ideology underpinning the movement. Rather, it was due to the longing for the material rewards and associated status, including cash and a motorcycle that Boko Haram recruits were receiving. When Boko Haram fighters from Niger began to flee and return to Niger, local authorities sought to work with religious leaders so that the principles of Islam could help with their rehabilitation. Similarly, in northern Nigeria, Search has observed that oftentimes those most vulnerable to recruitment to Boko Haram are young people who are in poorly resourced religious boarding schools far from their families. They have viewed Boko Haram as better able to satisfy their livelihood and protection needs while giving them a sense of strength and purpose.

Be Attentive to Radicalization and Mobilization Risks Present in Refugee Communities

Search's experience in war and postwar conflicts has shown us the potential for radicalization among some internally displaced or refugee populations. This risk is heightened when they are forced to flee in ethnically or religiously homogenous groups, toward host communities that represent the "other." Similarly, host communities are vulnerable to forming stereotypes and prejudices when faced with an influx of refugees, which can serve to radicalize viewpoints within the host community. When peacebuilders recognize this dynamic, initiatives can seek to strengthen open and transparent communication channels within and between these groups. These efforts can be focused on dispelling rumors, collaborative problem solving, and encouraging them to recognize the humanity of the "other."

In Lebanon, Search has worked to bring together Syrian refugees and Lebanese host community members as a way of mitigating the sense of isolation, animosity, fear, and overstretch of public resources that have grown in recent years. Such polarization and radicalization can occur within both host and refugee communities, as both are vulnerable to manipulation through the propagation of rumors and stereotypes. In the Central African Republic, Search faced an environment where violence and extremist recruitment was rampant. Through targeted programs, Search enabled people to move away from extreme viewpoints by finding moments of safety where they could bring Muslims and Christians together for conversations around their shared needs, allowing them to see one another as people. Staff also produced and screened a film about the power of forgiveness and dialogue that featured former fighters.

Chapter 25

Peacebuilding Approaches to Working with Young People

Lakshitha Saji Prelis, Michael Shipler, Rachel Walsh Taza, and Lena Slachmuijlder

Today's generation of young people is the largest generation the world has ever seen. One out of every six people worldwide is aged between fifteen and twenty-four years and the median age of the global population was 29.6 years of age in 2015. Over 600 million young people live in conflict and fragile environments, where often the percentage of young people is even higher.

The majority of Boko Haram fighters are teenagers, the typical ISIS recruit is around twenty-six years old, and most Jemaah Islamiyah members are young and male. Real or perceived disengagement and marginalization leave young people vulnerable to recruitment. Other young people join violent extremist groups because they see the underlying extremist narratives as the best way to rectify real and/or perceived injustice or to feel part of something larger than themselves. Some feel coerced to use violence because of manipulation or fear.

The large youth population combined with their visible involvement in violent extremism (VE) has led many to see young people as a threat. But research shows that youth who participate actively in violence are a minority, while the majority of youth—despite the injustices, deprivations, and abuses they confront daily, particularly in conflict contexts—are not violent and do not participate in violence. Too often efforts around VE seek to understand solely the reasons why young people support or join these movements rather than learning about why it is that they are indifferent, resisting, or actively seeking to address the factors favoring VE in their communities.

Young women and young men have historically been dissatisfied with how their elders have tackled grievances. They have driven forward social movements, which advocate what seem to be radical ideas and approaches to long-standing social and political injustice. This "radicalism," in itself, is not the problem. The challenge is how to translate these radical ideas into positive, collaborative, and nonviolent action, which does not rely upon violent and exclusionary ideologies and tactics to be achieved.

In transforming VE, youth engagement is paramount. But rather than considering young people as either perpetrators or victims, young people must be engaged in programming as key partners in preventing violence and promoting peace. This means that their engagement is active through all stages of programming: analysis, design, implementation, learning and monitoring, and developing recommendations for the future based on lessons learned. This is now recognized best practice in peacebuilding work and is applicable to the challenges of VE as well.

Over the past ten years, Search for Common Ground has helped to build an architecture for this type of youth engagement. This includes the Guiding Principles on Youth Participation in Peacebuilding to the first Global Forum on Youth, Peace, and Security that produced the Amman Declaration on Youth, Peace, and Security (calling for a global policy framework on youth as partners in peace and security), the Youth Action Agenda to Counter Violent Extremism and Promote Peace (the first policy document where young people articulated what VE means to them, what they are doing to address it in their communities, and ways key stakeholders can engage young people as partners to expand and strengthen prevention efforts). These and other efforts led to the UN Security Council unanimously adopting Resolution 2250 on Youth, Peace and Security. This resolution calls on governments, international actors, and civil society to invest and engage this youthful majority as partners in peace.

ENGAGING YOUNG PEOPLE IN TRANSFORMING VIOLENT EXTREMISM

Search for Common Ground uses five guiding principles for engaging young people:

See Them as Partners for Constructive Change

In developing strategies and policies, avoid the conceptual trap that youth only constitute a risk factor. Programs with this underlying assumption are characterized by fomenting a sense of dependency, disempowerment, and entitlement.

Young people have a unique and critical perspective on VE, based on their understanding of what drives recruitment at the community level and the programs and policy necessary to address it. Their proximity to local realities, systemic grievances, and messaging that may lead to radicalization result in unique insight on how to effectively deradicalize those who have chosen to join extremist groups.

In Tunisia, the youth-led association Tunisians against Terrorism worked with the Ministries of Youth, Education and Interior, as well as members of the National Assembly, to develop a curriculum including critical thinking skills, analysis, and peaceful tenets of Islam. The association also worked on community policing initiatives, including training of police officers.

In Cameroon, the Association of Dynamic Young People in the north of the country held dialogue sessions in forty-seven municipalities of the country most affected by Boko Haram. These sessions brought together local government representatives, security forces, religious leaders, and other youth organizations to build confidence among these stakeholders and reflect inclusively on a collective response. The association also ran awareness campaigns aimed at communities vulnerable to recruitment as well as trainings to promote economic opportunities for young people.

In Bangladesh, the youth-led MOVE Foundation developed the first campaign on constructive narratives, in consultation with faith leaders and security experts and vetted by a diversity of youth, government, and law enforcement. Opposing political parties, including the ruling party and top Islamic parties in Bangladesh, also publicly endorsed the campaign.

Facilitate Collaborative Relationship across Dividing Lines

Systemic mistrust remains one of the most significant impediments to increased inclusion of young people in CVE programs. Tension, rather than trust, often characterizes the relationship between government and security forces and young people. Within government, a closed-door approach to security matters and the perception that youth either are troublemakers or are not credible or qualified counterparts may discourage otherwise champions from pushing for greater youth cooperation and partnership. In parallel, youth are wary of ulterior motives behind government engagement, particularly in environments with a history of domestic spying.

Youth organizations working with government may face backlash or a loss of credibility within their own communities if cooperation is perceived as government affiliation or undue influence over their priorities and objectives. In parallel, such dynamics of mistrust also discourage otherwise champions from within government from pushing for greater youth cooperation and partnership.

Many governments and their ministries continue to keep decision making around VE closed to youth, despite young people's insight into recruitment and the mechanisms by which deradicalization might be most effective, lasting, and respective of human rights. This may be the result of unwillingness or uncertainty on how to engage youth. Peacebuilders can enable governments at the local and national levels to create informal and formal channels for collaboration and coordination with youth on specific issues, such as education, entrepreneurship and job creation, social cohesion, rehabilitation and reintegration of prisoners or ex-combatants, countering extremist messaging, and implementation of national laws against terrorism.

Channels for input, collaboration, and partnership should be reliable, equitable, and transparent and could be pursued through:

- youth advisory boards at the local level;
- offices within municipal bodies, public administration, and school associations designated for youth engagement and collaboration across sectors;
- outreach by and access to representatives of relevant ministries and government agencies;
- youth parliaments at the national level; and
- funding mechanisms supportive of youth-led programs.

This will increase the relevance of preventing and countering violent extremism (P/CVE) policies and programs and ensure that partnership and collaboration are not pursued on a case-by-case basis. Equally important is to recognize that "youth" are not a homogenous block, and that the dividing lines—be it across ethnic, sectarian, or regional lines—run deep and long.

In Central Asia, Search facilitated the first-ever Central Asia Youth Forum with young people from Kyrgyzstan, Uzbekistan, and Tajikistan. The young people were able to understand the dynamics of VE in each of their countries and agree on a resolution, which put young people at the heart of initiatives across the region. A similar effort took place in West Africa between young people in Cameroon, Chad, Mali, Niger, and Nigeria.

Recognize Young People's Need for Respect, Dignity, and Agency

Research from development psychology, criminology, and sociology suggests that some adolescents may be more vulnerable to recruitment into armed groups due to their transitional stage of biological, psychological, and social development. While material incentives may contribute to young people's choice to engage in violence, research shows that "greed" is rarely a motivating factor in its own right and that various forms of "grievances" are more or just as important. Self-realization is not only about obtaining economic resources but also about gaining access to the respect, dignity, and status benefits associated with adulthood. When young men in particular face failure in front of social norms expecting them to be providers, or face with obstacles in accessing love and affection, they can seek out other avenues to satisfy these needs. The pressures of masculinity are far greater than simply material well-being and speak to young people's need to have meaning, value, and often valor in their lives.

Just as young people over time have joined gangs, many of the same factors are at play in the choice to join a violent extremist movement. It offers not only a sense of purpose but also the comfort of a shared sense of identity and a path to heroism or becoming a protector.

In Palestine, Search has produced two seasons of *The President*, a reality TV show modeled on *The Apprentice*, which puts young people through a set of challenges as they "campaign" to be elected "the President." This show, seen by 40 percent of Palestinians, has brought prominence, respect, prestige, and honor to the young people participating in the program. As the contestants have battled to find collaborative, nonviolent solutions to conflict, they have also promoted positive models of leadership and heroism.

Be Wary of Quick Fixes

When an analysis of grievances points to socioeconomic marginalization, programs are often designed to create jobs or build employment skills. Be open to engaging young women and men who are beyond the "usual constituency." Look for ways to move beyond the capital-city-based elite youth organizations toward associations of motorcycle drivers, or sports clubs, or associations linked with religious organizations.

Another quick fix can be to overlook the potential for young women to be at the heart of programs to transform VE. Just because young men may be more numerous as fighters, it does not mean that only men must be engaged in initiatives to encourage withdrawal. In fact, young women's initiatives can often be exactly what is needed to draw young men out of these movements. This is because women have shown to be powerful influencers in men's decisions to join, or not join, VE movements.

Research about the impact of VE programs points out that livelihood responses are not complete in tackling vulnerability. For example, International Alert's research about young people's involvement in VE in Syria suggests that the main factors that underpin resilience are:

- alternative and respected sources of livelihood outside of armed groups, which give individuals a sense of purpose and dignity;

- access to comprehensive, holistic and quality education in Syria and in neighboring countries;
- access to supportive and positive social networks and institutions that can provide psychosocial support, mentors, role models and options for the development of non-violent social identities; and
- avenues for exercising agency and nonviolent activism that provide individuals with a sense of autonomy and control over their lives, as well as a way to make sense of their experiences.

The sense of self-realization, the relationships of respect and dignity, and the potential to exercise agency are equally important as the needs for material well-being.

In Burkina Faso, Niger and Chad, Cote d'Ivoire, Lebanon, and Indonesia, Search ran a program where young people were equipped with skills to produce short films about their lives, their conflicts, and their aspirations. The pride of being able to tell their stories, use these films in public screenings, and then facilitate discussions responded to young people's need to feel relevant and powerful in their communities. From this space of pride, they were able to reach out across dividing lines, and toward local authorities, to facilitate dialogue and collaborative problem solving.

Be Comfortable with a Diversity of Viewpoints

In the age of social media, everyone is a broadcaster. Peacebuilders should not aim for young people to all speak with one unified voice against VE. On the contrary, it is the availability of diverse viewpoints and a plethora of tactics and approaches to tackle the grievances that make for a healthy and resilient society in which VE will find it difficult to gain traction.

While campaigns can be effective, they sometimes risk engraining the notion of "black or white" perspectives, rather than recognizing that most people's ideas are neither black nor white but rather different shades of gray. A campaign that seeks to demonize young people who have chosen VE fails to recognize that young people are always somewhere on the spectrum between positive engagement and negative, violent disruption. Such initiatives can also prematurely close the door for young people hoping to step away, or step out, of violent extremist movements.

In Indonesia, Search established youth-run radio stations inside the Islamic boarding schools. The students were trained and coached—not just to broadcast a radio drama series on tolerance but to hold discussions that valued all points of view, created a safe space for questions, and told stories of young students in all of their diversity.

In the Netherlands, a group of young people created "Dare to be Grey" as a way of "branding" the middle ground amid a polarized world. Dare to be Grey tackles this online polarization by creating a platform for the "gray" middle ground with its different views, room for listening, nuance, and countless personalities, anyone's opinion can become the focal point of tomorrow's debate.

Chapter 26

Peacebuilding Narratives and Countering Violent Extremism

Lena Slachmuijlder

Narratives are a set of ideas, facts, perspectives, and experiences that inform the way an individual or group perceives their place in the world around them. They often blend elements of historical truth with constructed storylines and can resonate deeply with people's sense of self and how they make sense of events in their own lives. As peacebuilders, we understand narratives can be positive or negative and function as a natural part of the human experience.

Within a society, it is common for different social groups to have dissonant narratives. For example, one group's national liberator may be perceived as an oppressor by another. Grievances, both real and perceived, often play a major role. Given their dependence on perception, information, and new experiences, they are constantly shifting how they are constructed and used. Rather than the specific context of a narrative, it is the way that narratives are constructed that mobilizes people to create real or imagined communities.

HOW DO NARRATIVES FUNCTION IN COUNTERING VIOLENT EXTREMISM?

People use narratives to identify friends and enemies and to establish their alignment across divisive issues and social conflicts. In this way, narratives are often used by extremist groups to seed resentment, disconnection, and violence in order to gain sympathy and draw in new members. Narratives are used to dehumanize opponents and justify brutality against them. Extremist groups also rely on propaganda and visceral images of their activities to wield influence in both their target community and around the world. Examining these narratives is therefore an essential component of countering violent extremism (CVE) efforts.

The media plays an especially important role in constructing popular narratives. Stories, photographs, and headlines shape what people believe and therefore what ideas they buy into and whom or what they support. They can also be exceedingly influential in how the public views different sides of conflict.

HOW CAN PEACEBUILDERS WORK WITH NARRATIVES TO PREVENT OR TRANSFORM VIOLENT EXTREMISM?

Search for Common Ground (Search) seeks not to deconstruct the facts, values, and storylines perpetuated by violent extremist groups but instead to create new perspectives and possibilities around acting on those beliefs that instead favor dialogue and acceptance. These initiatives can enable people to feel empowered and dignified in responding to their grievances through nonviolent means.

In exploring narratives, the opportunity lies in amplifying credible voices in a community that reinforce inclusive values and highlight peaceful avenues for change. By drawing from the innovative use of media, peer-to-peer outreach, and personal interaction, we can build increasingly resilient and pluralistic societies that reject violence.

The risk is potentially seeding disconnect and mistrust in our relationship with vulnerable communities by targeting their deeply held beliefs and values through counter-messaging. Our selection of voices and role models to empower must remain ideologically neutral and grounded in providing positive means to redress grievances, or we may unintentionally exacerbate conflict, lose credibility, or be dismissed as mere propaganda.

Here are four guiding principles for engaging with narratives:

Amplify Narratives That Reinforce the Power of Emotion and Human Connection

As peacebuilders, we have learned that counter-messaging can be ineffective challenging long-standing and sincere beliefs about history, relationships, and personal identity. Furthermore, extremist narratives are often based on feelings of marginalization or exploitation born of very real and very upsetting human experiences.

Instead of trying to change minds through new information, our goal is to rejuvenate an individual's sense of emotional engagement and self-worth that allows participants to empathize and identify with their broader society over isolated extremists. First, we can elevate the voices of regular citizens looking to address grievances through peaceful and constructive means. We can also highlight social role models that debunk stereotypes and constructively drain grievances of their narrative pull. Finally, we can use our work with the media to promote popular dialogue that encourages collaboration and empathy.

In Morocco, for example, Search observed three stages of narrative-based recruitment specifically targeted at youth. In the initial stage, extremist groups generate narratives that are similar to peacebuilding narratives and focus on ideas of friendship, brotherhood, and family within their ranks. Once youth have achieved some level of buy-in, recruiters employ a second stage focusing on philosophical discussions about the relative value of reason and emotion that is intended to elevate the power of reasoning and create distance between a recruit and their emotional bonds with family and community. Finally, once youth accept new narratives and identities grounded in extremist rationalism, they become emboldened to undertake gruesome acts that highlight their rejection of emotion using narratives of persecution and the meting out of punishment to remedy injustice.

From a peacebuilding perspective, the time between the first and second stages of recruitment can be the most useful entry point. We can amplify messages imbued with emotions, which highlight the value and potential of individuals, rather than framing targets of radicalization as marginalized or victims. These complimentary narratives can also provide people with dreams that they see as achievable for themselves and their own future. Within our own communication as peacebuilding organizations, it is also important to refer to vulnerable groups using language that highlight their value and importance rather than framing these groups as hapless targets or beneficiaries of programming.

Above all, face-to-face, personal interaction is key to countering recruitment or pulling people back from extremist groups. Evidence has shown that for groups like Al-Qaeda and ISIS/ISIL, members do not join merely because of videos and online propaganda, but because of interpersonal connections built with recruiters over time. Peacebuilders can rely on their deep community relationships and embedded local presence to reach vulnerable individuals in a personalized manner that builds trust and shows individuals that they are valued, included, and have a rightful place at home. By creating a sense of fellowship, family, and respect at the community level, we can weaken the appeal of joining a violent extremist movement.

Focus on How Narratives Are Constructed and Shared Rather Than Their Content

Peacebuilders should also think carefully about their use of media outlets, message frequency, and the messenger they choose to deploy. In our increasingly pluralistic world, violent extremists, civil society, and governments alike use social media, SMS, radio, television, and other methods to spread both a greater number and diversity of voices related to conflict. As peacebuilders, we can use these same channels to identify credible voices at the community level who can reach out to vulnerable individuals being drawn or recruited into extremism.

In Myanmar, for example, Search conducted a recent study on the triggers of violence in Buddhist extremism. Their approach focused on understanding the flow of information and key influencers within two specific communities rather than the specific messages of anti-Muslim bigotry. This allowed peacebuilders to understand the source of prejudices and stereotypes that were emerging and confirmed that when individuals had a personal encounter with someone they believed was the enemy, it was effective at shifting their perspective. These insights helped influence the design of peacebuilding efforts bringing Buddhist and Muslim communities together.

While discussions around narratives often refer to media and communication technology, peacebuilders understand that all areas of our work are an opportunity to work on narratives. Face-to-face conversations can be a particularly powerful channel for engagement, as they reinforce relationships, draw on emotion, and personalize new experiences. For example, peacebuilders can engage community leaders and role models to draw potential recruits away from the social media and online messaging preferred by extremist groups and into tangible, in-person relationships. By thoughtfully and intentionally crafting a narrative space around dividing lines and social connectors, peacebuilders can speak to the needs of vulnerable groups and offer tangible, credible alternatives to violence.

In Burundi, Search often organized solidarity events between Hutus and Tutsis. The purpose was to counteract the common media discourse that mutually demonized each group, which lived largely in separate ethnic enclaves. This approach complemented existing radio deradicalization programs by giving people the opportunity to know one another face to face. In this way, Search took narratives out of an exclusively media-oriented space and gave community members the opportunity to shape their own views and experiences in engaging with the opposite group.

Similarly, in northern Kyrgyzstan, Search organized a community fair for boorsok, a local fried food dish used to decorate tables. They invited local youth, journalists, atyncha (religious women), imams, and police officers to participate. At the event, groups that often struggled to interact peacefully shared a day of fun and socializing while tasting and judging each submission.

Choose Credible, Resonant Messengers

Choosing credible messengers is perhaps the most crucial strategy in the narrative space. We understand that as peacebuilders, our role is to listen to local communities and find opportunities to reinforce healthy relationships and nonviolent avenues for change. Given the daily bombardment of messages that citizens receive through peer-to-peer interaction and media (including social media) channels on a daily basis, breaking through the noise requires a careful selection of voices that will be perceived as compelling in all areas of our programming. Careful selection of messengers also ensures that our work is emotionally engaging and deeply rooted in on-the-groundwork with the communities we are hoping to engage with.

In Indonesia, Search worked with ten Islamic boarding schools (pesantren) in areas of the country where there had been attacks or suspected activity of violent extremist groups. The pesantren were popularly perceived as harboring terrorists and being behind intolerant forms of Islam as guilty for the attacks. To address this, Search undertook several levels of programming that enabled the young *pesantren* students to explore themes of identity, tolerance, and diversity. These included a curriculum-driven comic book series, founding community radio stations within the schools and training students to be broadcast journalists, and teaching students documentary filmmaking. Not only did this directly engage with these youth, but such programming challenged outside perceptions regarding these young *pesantren* students.

The films were particularly powerful. Students explored intimate topics around their identity, such as how to be a punk rocker and a Quranic student at the same time, or a Balinese dancer while still a Muslim. They ventured out of their comfort zones with the aid of the camera, learning about other religions and opening up with sensitive conversations around the perceptions of terrorism and their schools. The films were screened and discussed at both the community and national levels, allowing the *pesantren* students themselves to be the voice of tolerance and dialogue.

When choosing role models and community leaders to highlight through our programs, it is also important that we give visibility to a diverse range of ideological viewpoints. This approach not only builds a culture of tolerance and dialogue but also highlights that both hard-line and moderate individuals can benefit from engaging each other peacefully. Finally, amplifying diverse perspectives preserves our credibility as impartial peacebuilders and allows us to continue engaging groups across the ideological spectrum.

Choosing appropriate messengers can be particularly challenging in conflict contexts. Peacebuilders must choose whether and how to highlight former fighters, religious leaders, political figures, activists, and victims—all of whom can contribute to or detract from peace efforts in different contexts.

Amplifying the voices of ex-prisoners, for example, can give them a platform to expand or combat ongoing recruitment to violent organizations depending on the context. In Nepal, Search hired a former nationalist militant after a careful, informed decision to provide outreach to active members of armed groups. He was able to use the credibility and relationships he had built before defecting to encourage other young fighters to choose peace. The sincerity of this individual's personal transformation was essential to the success of his outreach and rewarded Search's sensitive selection effort. Similarly, outreach from families and loved ones can leverage the emotional connection and credibility between them to encourage peace and disengagement. In Colombia, for example, radio broadcasts of family messages reaching out to individual members of the FARC helped drive defection around holiday periods.

Caution is similarly vital when contemplating the use of victim narratives. In some environments, employing a victim-centered approach is fundamental to building empathy and breaking the narratives that justify violent extremist behavior. The narratives of victims can also be powerful in highlighting examples of people who transcend their suffering and publicly recognize the humanity of their perpetrators, as occurred around South Africa's famous Truth and Reconciliation Commission. In other instances, particularly where the notion of victimhood is deeply engrained into local culture, victim narratives can also be used to mobilize others into violence and justify continued cycles of violence. Beware of the sensitivity around these particular voices of victims.

Engage and Work with Professional Media Outlets to Equip Them with Skills in Common Ground Journalism

When journalists themselves are not convinced of the value and feasibility of peaceful solutions, they can prove harmful to the broader peacebuilding process. Alternatively, when journalists are empowered with the skills and understanding to transform conflict through their work, they can use their platforms to challenge violent narratives and create a space for peaceful dialogue.

Our work on Common Ground journalism is founded on two principles of journalism. First, journalists should be aware that when they cover incendiary topics like extremist attacks, the details of the event are not the only important news, but their portrayal of the event can also either generate or alleviate animosity toward the communities involved. Second, journalists have an obligation when covering conflict and extremism to widen their framework for understanding the problem in order to highlight where people are productively working together across dividing lines, rather than simply those who do so violently. This avoids exclusively covering grievances that legitimize the means that extremists use for recruiting.

Similar to our work at the community level, our work with journalists should rely on using local influencers and thought leaders to initiate discussions about peace and conflict issues in a way that is both trusted and organic.

Religious leaders, for example, can play a helpful role in listening to journalists' personal grievances, acknowledging their own viewpoints, and opening discussion about possibilities for productive steps forward.

Common Ground journalism magnifies diverse voices from the ground up without stigmatizing different groups with different labels such as "radical" or "moderate." This in turn allows citizens to feel that they have a regular, peaceful, and legitimized outlet for discussion and acknowledgment of their grievances. It also creates an environment where people feel comfortable reflecting on different viewpoints while touching upon underlying grievances and still offering respect to those with extremist views.

For example, Search's work with journalists in northern Nigeria helped to reshape discussions to highlight not only the devastation caused by Boko Haram but also local initiatives of people working to better their own lives after escaping or recovering from Boko Haram. Similarly, the HEROES program in Burundi sought to address the widely held belief that other people were responsible for each community's suffering. For five years, Search produced radio shows every week that told the story of someone whose life was saved by someone from the other ethnic group. The program helped debunk stereotypes and prejudices that enabled extremist views to take hold in each community.

Chapter 27

A Peacebuilding Approach to Media and Conflict-Sensitive Journalism

Myriam Aziz and Lisa Schirch

Media is the "oxygen" for terrorism. Without media, there are no reports of blown-up buildings or severed heads. There is no shock and awe for those who are not eyewitnesses. There is no fire without oxygen. There is no terror without a report.

Garnering public attention via mass media channels—including the range of official news media and informal Facebook, Twitter, and Internet chat rooms—is an essential element of terrorism. ISIS makes news with its attacks. ISIS also produces a wide range of media. Every day, ISIS averages three videos, fifteen photographic reports, 90,000 social media reports, and 46,000–70,000 pro-ISIS Twitter posts.

Military experts understand this. In March 2018, the Pentagon spokesperson pleaded with news agencies not to release footage of ISIS ambushing US soldiers in Niger. Colonel Rob Manning stated, "We ask the media and the public and all responsible entities not to aid these terrorists in recruiting efforts by viewing or bringing to attention these images, these videos. You are complicit in amplifying ISIS propaganda if you do that."

Psychologists studying media's influence on the public find the fear of terrorism far outweighs the actual threat. And the more people watch news about terrorism, the more depressed, fearful, and anxious they become. Control of journalist reporting is more than ever at the center of the battle between nonstate groups that use terror and governments trying to stop them. The battle does not just affect the radio and television waves, the newspaper and magazine pages, or the Internet sites. The battle comes down to the bodies of journalists imprisoned, kidnapped, and assassinated by both government forces and nonstate groups.

VIOLENT EXTREMISM POSES A "QUADRUPLE THREAT" TO JOURNALISM

There are a range of threats in this new age of mass-mediated terrorism. Journalists face threats from nonstate terror groups like Hamas or the Taliban, from states that see journalists as inciting terrorism, and from states that want journalists to contribute to their efforts to "counter violent extremism" (CVE).[1] In Afghanistan, journalists receive "night letters" from both the government and the Taliban threatening their execution if they publish negative news. In Gaza, journalists face repression from all sides. Hamas arrests and tortures journalists if they talk to Israelis or even the rival Fatah Palestinian leadership (CPJ 2017). Israeli rockets have killed numerous journalists in Gaza (Stern 2014). Israel arrests and imprisons Palestinian journalists for inciting violence (Kuttab 2016). Everywhere, journalists face economic pressures that limit their ability to do in-depth research and lack of resources for their security. And in most places, governments are pushing journalists to contribute to their CVE program.

Security Threats from States

In 2016, Turkey held over eighty journalists, editors, and producers in prison for "anti-state" incitement. The government shut down 100 media outlets (Beisar 2016). The 2016 World Press Freedom Index by Reporters without Borders signals a "disturbing decline in respect for media freedom at both the global and regional levels" (Reporters without Borders for Freedom of Information 2016). The report states the following "many laws have been adopted penalizing journalists on such spurious charges as 'insulting the president,' 'blasphemy' or 'supporting terrorism.' Growing self-censorship is the knock-on effect of this alarming situation. The 'media environment and self-censorship' indicator has fallen by more than 10% from 2013 to 2016" (Reporters without Borders for Freedom of Information 2016).

The Committee for the Protection of Journalists website makes available data on imprisoned journalists. It offers an interactive map, visual diagrams, and nuanced data based on countries, regions, and types of violence (imprisonment, missing, etc.). According to CPJ's website, 259 journalists were jailed worldwide as of December 1, 2016. "CPJ considers article 309 of Bahrain's penal code, like many other provisions criminalizing speech in the country, overly broad and ambiguous, allowing the government to arbitrarily apply the law to silence critical and independent voices" (Committee to Protect Journalists 2016).

Security Threats from Terrorist Groups

The Islamic State killed at least six journalists in Iraq and Syria in 2016. In the past decade al-Shabaab killed twenty-four journalists in Somalia. In 2009, thirty-two journalists and media workers were killed in one attack in the Philippines. In almost all of these cases, harm to journalists happens with impunity (Witchel 2016). In the past, "terrorists" maintained a relatively good relationship with journalists to use their platforms to express their grievances. Currently, social media provides easy access to platforms for terrorist groups to express those grievances. Journalists have thus become more valuable as hostages to gain leverage.

Economic Threats from the Media Industry

Journalists work in a challenging economic context where news producers compete with free online sources of news, and news outlets struggle to fund investigative, professional journalism. Too often, journalists and editors face time and space limits as well as economic pressure, contributing to an oversimplification of complex conflicts and superficial sensational coverage. Reporters capture the "he said, she said" facts of the case, but they fail to ask questions or do research to uncover why different stakeholders take the positions they do. Editors keeping an eye on company profit margins focus on flashy stories about gruesome attacks to grab readers' attention rather than deeper, more complicated, and "boring" issues that affect the public far more. In addition to the tyranny of time, space, and the need to make a profit, reporters in some parts of the world face restrictive press laws, demand for "patriotic" coverage reflecting a "my country right or wrong" approach, pressure from media owners, and lack of support from editors.

The changing economic landscape of journalism dictates cuts, which directly affect safety measures. CPJ's website features multiple stories of journalists who were killed, sentenced for blasphemy, or detained in Syria (Committee to Protect Journalists n.d.).

Large media companies controlling the media landscape also significantly contribute to the type and nature of the available information. In her article "Ten Global Advertising Trends That Threaten Independent Journalism," Michelle Foster argues that digital giants dominate the market: "They have consolidated under a number of powerful players with holdings in diverse areas that allow them to cross-market and leverage their holdings. Readily available branded media content now crosses borders and brings global and regional advertising with it" (Foster 2017). Their wide outreach and appeal make it difficult for local and independent journalists to compete, which in turn jeopardizes the availability of credible, independent, and rigorous news.

Threats from the Countering Violent Extremism Agenda

Increasingly, government counterterrorism and CVE officers are looking to the media to provide "counternarratives" of tolerance and peace to replace those of hate and violent radicalization (Ferguson 2016). Counternarratives (in the CVE context) are "being intentional and direct efforts to deconstruct, discredit and demystify violent extremist messaging, whether through ideology, logic, fact or humour" (Briggs and Feve 2013). The CVE world has developed a media-based theory of change that targets the ideology of VE. Journalists are asked to be agents of the P/CVE agenda by constructing counter VE communication narratives with a customized counter communication set of "counternarratives." However, this theory of change fails to acknowledge the core reasons for which a VE narrative is appealing in the first place. Subsequently, the design of the corresponding counternarrative is highly questionable since counternarratives do not address identity crises, underlying grievances, or global factors that may support an ideology-based VE narrative. The evidence body cannot offer substantive support for the effectiveness of counternarratives at decreasing the VE threat, nor can it sufficiently demonstrate a causal relationship between the employment of a counternarrative and a change in its target audience (Briggs and Feve 2013; Ferguson 2016; Schmid 2012).

Moreover, journalists face risks when tasked with promoting direct, reactive counternarratives. The current digital landscape had created new challenges for journalists by providing hostile parties with means to track journalists down and hurt them. While the changing economics of journalism has resulted in the collapse of safety resources, the responsibility for journalism is falling on local journalists operating in situations of total impunity.

Governments tasking journalists with CVE seem to assume that journalists are safe while doing their job. However, in a letter to the High Commissioner of Human Rights, the Committee to Protect Journalists states their concern that there is little distinction between VE and terrorism. This confusion leads to an "overly broad application of counter-terrorism measures, including against forms of conduct that should not qualify as terrorist acts." In Cameroon, for example, the government's new law silences legitimate opposition in addition to its supposed target Boko Haram (CPJ 2017). These journalists describe how UN programs to "Prevent Violent Extremism" are resulting in state repression of journalists who are charged with fostering "violent extremism" or even "nonviolent extremism." "While packaged as positive measures, many PVE initiatives have a significant potential to threaten the human rights to equality and freedom from discrimination, the right to privacy, and the freedoms of expression, association, and religion or belief" (Radsch 2016). CVE programs provide insufficient information and vague definitions on

VE, which subsequently results in the targeting and labeling of journalists as supporting VE when they are gathering information to report on a story. As a current buzzword, CVE is used as a smokescreen to control journalists' ability to report. CVE closes the civic space with increasing legislative pressure on journalists to restrain nonpopular political and social opinions. A thorough risk analysis is needed as general practice to help contain the ambiguous parameters of CVE projects.

CONFLICT-SENSITIVE JOURNALISM AND A PEACEBUILDING APPROACH TO VIOLENT EXTREMISM

Conflict-sensitive journalism offers a better peacebuilding alternative to address VE. Instead of efforts to counter narratives, conflict-sensitive reporting aims to *do less harm* in inciting violence and conflict and *do more good* in providing information that can inform and support ways of handling conflict

Table 27.1. Peacebuilding Principles for Conflict-Sensitive Journalism

1. *Interview diverse stakeholders* such as religious, academic, government, business, or other civil society groups that care about the issue or conflict. Drawing on multiple sources of information contributes to more accurate and impartial reporting and can prevent violent extremism by providing a public space for negotiation between competing interests.
2. *Frame a news story as a problem of conflicting interests* between diverse stakeholders rather than as a struggle of good versus evil.
3. *Identify grievances and interests* of diverse stakeholders, including violent extremist groups.
4. *Use images that show empowered people and treat victims with dignity and respect;* the camera guides how others will see victims.
5. *Choose language to be as specific as possible and avoid language that stereotypes,* or fosters hate toward whole groups of people or incites violence or revenge.
6. *Recognize that reporters are "first responders" in the midst of a tragedy.* Reporters shape how a community will tell its own story about a tragedy.
7. *Be sensitive to victim's needs.* Ensure that interviews do not emotionally exploit victims or cause additional trauma.
8. *Identify both differences and common ground.* Document multiple views to help the audience form a "whole" picture of the story rather than competing versions of the "truth."
9. *Foster audience involvement.* The news audience has the potential to play a central role in public issues. Democracies require an informed public.
10. *Document potential solutions, including both best- and worst-case scenarios.* Identify who is working and offering solutions to the issue. Include not only high-level attempts at negotiation or peace processes but also civil-society efforts led by community-level leaders including women and youth.

constructively. News reporters are not required to take a Hippocratic Oath. But the responsibility of reporters is just as serious as the physician's role in an operating room. How reporters choose and frame what makes the "news" can send ripples out into the world, either supporting peace or fueling violence and division.

Conflict-sensitive journalism is good, professional journalism that respects the core values of impartiality, objectivity, and confidentiality that professional reporters rightly cherish. Conflict-sensitive reporting requires a deep analysis of the competing interests of diverse stakeholders or groups involved in an issue or conflict. Then it requires a respectful telling of their stories and perspectives, with care not to exacerbate division but instead to foster public understanding of the issues and events from all side's perspectives. It is solution-oriented, documenting options for addressing key interests of all stakeholders.

Table 27.1 illustrates ten key principles of conflict-sensitive journalism. The framework provides a lighthouse to guide reporters for reporting in ways that do less harm and do more good to the societies they serve. A number of organizations, scholars, and practitioners have created similar frameworks (Howard 2009). This framework seeks to synthesize the best practices from this wide collection and bring it all together in one place.

CONCLUSION

Violent extremism poses severe threats to journalists, who face threats from states, nonstate groups, and the economic market place that limits on their resources for safety and ability to do their work. In the midst of these threats, the demands to participate in CVE pose new challenges to journalist safety and professional ethics. And CVE counternarratives have yet to yield tangible, empirical evidence of efficiency and effectiveness in positively affecting targeted audiences. Conflict-sensitive journalism presents an alternative communication strategy that could potentially provide alternative narratives that provide an understanding of the ecology of VE, enabling more effective state responses and public understanding.

Chapter 28

To Defeat Terrorism, Use "People Power"

Maria J. Stephan and Leanne Erdberg

Nonviolent citizens' movements are the missing piece of a global strategy against extremism. As governments and communities seek the right combination of methods to halt terrorism, one that we too often miss is nonviolent resistance. It's not that we haven't seen the power of protest movements that use mass marches, sit-ins, boycotts, and other forceful but nonviolent tactics. To the contrary, people worldwide have been moved by watching such movements sweep aside the walls of apartheid, the tanks of dictators, or the impunity of kleptocracies. But governments and civil society alike have failed to connect the dots—to promote nonviolent action that can help communities address grievances while absorbing the youth alienation upon which terrorist movements feed.

We understand the need to undercut extremist ideologies by strengthening the inclusiveness and justice of governance in conflict-afflicted societies. Thus, governments and peacebuilding organizations fund and support programs to redress injustices and alienation. Such programs may focus on strengthening the rule of law under corrupt or weak governments; others build the social and political participation of youth and women. Or they may strengthen communities through local dialogue initiatives and other methods of conflict resolution.

Those efforts are essential. Yet a piece is missing. Typical strategies to counter violent extremism fail to confront what we know is a paramount appeal to youth of terrorist groups: the attraction of belonging to a community that seems to be on a moral mission to resist injustices. As one strategy study of recent years noted, ISIS's powerful message for recruiting alienated youth is simply, "Join us and help build an ideal society where you will always belong."

MOVEMENTS OFFER YOUTH A MISSION

Any complete strategy against terrorism must beat this extremist offer to youth of belonging and mission. In the marketplace of ideas and emotion, the product that can beat it is "people power." It is no accident that, for decades, the faces we have seen in nonviolent, grassroots throngs—from South Africa's anti-apartheid campaigns to Tunisia's Arab Spring to East Germany's toppling of the Berlin Wall—are so often youthful. Grassroots resistance movements offer alienated youth a powerful group within which to press a moral cause, feel the validation of social bonds, and concretely redress the ills that energized them through collective action.

A first reason that nonviolent resistance can displace terrorism is that it addresses the kinds of injustice on which extremist ideologies feed. In Nigeria, Boko Haram began in part as an anti-corruption movement—and grew in strength and brutality on the fuel of Nigerian army units' indiscriminate attacks on civilians. In Iraq, ISIS was able to seize much of the Sunni Muslim heartland because it won support from Sunnis who felt marginalized and alienated by the central government. Both of those extremist groups, and many others, dramatize just such injustices in their recruitment campaigns and propaganda videos—and declare that only violent struggle can advance a righteous cause.

A second reason that nonviolent resistance can trump terrorism is that, as the hard data show, it is more effective than violence (Chenoweth and Stephan 2011). More than a century's worth of struggles worldwide have shown that peaceful resistance movements are twice as likely as armed struggles to achieve their objectives. And they are significantly more likely to produce rights-respecting and peaceful societies in the end. Campaigns of forceful but nonviolent action are especially valuable against tyrants: in recent decades, they toppled dictators such as Chile's Augusto Pinochet, Serbia's Slobodan Milosevic, and Liberia's Charles Taylor.

NONVIOLENT STRUGGLE WORKS BETTER

So to add this "missing piece" to our strategies against terrorism and extremism, a powerful step is simply to show aggrieved communities that nonviolent struggle works better. The stories and images of successful resistance against corruption and tyranny—from Gambia or Guatemala, Argentina or Afghanistan—can dilute the extremists' allure (Stephan and Beyerle 2015). Fortunately, many of these campaigns are well documented and just need to be popularized and adapted locally.

A third reason to promote nonviolent action is the healthier state in which it leaves societies and individual participants. Societies changed by nonviolent movements are more stable and the improvements more lasting. For individuals, the emotional effects of camaraderie and solidarity at sit-ins and marches can be powerful—in contrast to the psychological damage from killing people. In 2000, Serbian youth famously branded their antidictatorship movement, Otpor, with a clenched fist and made participation in their nonviolent activities cool, hip, and fun.

Even in the toughest cases, where extremists have achieved power, nonviolent resistance can weaken them. Under ISIS's brutal rule in Iraq and Syria, protests led by women or respected religious figures led to tactical victories such as the protection of cultural sites and the release of political prisoners (Stephan 2016). Resisters used comedy and satire to counter ISIS and similar groups in videos that animate the absurdity of their extremism (Rogers 2017). Community-led, nonviolent, collective action has resisted predatory armed groups in places like Colombia, Syria, and the Philippines, protecting civilians in the process.

So how can this effective "missing piece" be deployed to dissolve the roots of terrorism (Merriman and DuVall 2007)? Like dialogue and facilitation, strategic nonviolent action and movement building are skills that are transferable across cultures and contexts. For the most part, this work is done at a modest scale by nonprofit, nongovernmental organizations such as International Center for Nonviolent Conflict, Beautiful Rising, Rhize, and Nonviolence International. These organizations, along with the US Institute of Peace, specialize in training, education, and the building of peer networks among activists and movements. Equipping aggrieved, oppressed people with the knowledge and know-how to organize in their communities and build powerful movements to advance rights and freedoms is a powerful antidote to violent extremism.

In the end, that "missing piece" to defeat terrorism is not missing at all. It's in plain sight but must be expanded if it is to fulfill its powerful potential.

Chapter 29

Preventing Violence through a Trauma-Healing Approach

Veronica Laveta

Terrorism, war, and counterterrorism contribute to psychological trauma. The effects of trauma can be turned inward (destructive toward self), outward (aggression toward family, strangers, joining militant group, going back to home country to fight), or mobilized toward positive change and activism. This chapter addresses the traumatic impacts of violence and how these relate to the prevention of violent extremism. There are a multiplicity of causes for violence and violent extremism. Understanding these conditions and proactively creating new conditions that promote health and resilience of individuals, families, and communities can reduce or stop vicious cycles of violence, including violent extremism.

As an international services clinical advisor for mental health for the Center for Victims of Torture (CVT), I supervise and advise trauma rehabilitation programs in the Middle East and South Africa.[1] CVT is a service provider and human rights organization committed to rehabilitation of torture and war survivors and the prevention and elimination of torture as a practice. Our holistic rehabilitation and justice-related work contribute to violence prevention. Through our work, we have seen the horrible effects of violence on individuals, families, and communities. Although these traumatic experiences of extreme violence could theoretically increase someone's risk for engaging in violent behavior or joining an extremist group, we eschew any direct causal link between suffering traumatic experiences and turning toward violent extremism. Assuming a causal relationship is unproven and casts victims with a taint of suspicion and feeds into a larger biased narrative that casts Muslims (especially men and adolescent boys) as potential terrorists. This generalized suspicion can lead to harmful actions such as mass "preventative" detentions of those who have been victimized.[2]

Many intersecting conditions must be in place for a person to choose violence, and a history of trauma alone is not in and of itself sufficient. A narrow focus on how trauma "might" lead to people turning to violent extremism overlooks much more common harmful effects of unhealed trauma—self-harm and suicide, increased family violence, and increased sexual violence in the home and community.[3]

Furthermore, some who are traumatized from torture or war violence find meaning by committing to pro-social behaviors such as helping other people in the same situation, starting advocacy or rehabilitation organizations, and becoming human rights activists to speak up for others who are vulnerable. Frankel notes the critical role of finding meaning as a protective factor for those who have endured horrific experiences (Frankel 1956). We can hold two realities at the same time: acts of torture and war and resulting unhealed trauma can create the conditions for cycles of violence, including violent extremism *and* when properly supported people can tap into their strength and resilience to not just overcome trauma but to meaningfully contribute to their families and communities. Recognizing these two truths allows us to see the critical role trauma healing can play in violence prevention. Repairing and healing harm can go a long way to transform pain and shame, restore dignity and trust, and mobilize human qualities of connection and care for others.

HOW TORTURE, WAR, AND COUNTERTERRORISM CREATE CONDITIONS FOR FURTHER VIOLENCE

Torture and war survivors contend with many traumatic effects, including physical, cognitive, emotional, and behavioral symptoms. These include the debilitating feelings of pain and shame caused by being stripped of one's dignity through abuse and humiliation. Torture carried out in the name of either terrorism or counterterrorism purposely seeks to shatter the victims' dignity through forcing them to do things that go against their very integrity (e.g., making them torture another prisoner or rape a family member), using sexual violence to humiliate them, and systematically dismantling identity, leaving them stripped bare literally and figuratively. These practices rob victims of their power and dignity, leaving them with immense shame, hopelessness, and an acute sense of injustice. Many of our clients report not only being victimized in their own country but also while being detained trying to flee their dangerous situations. As fears have escalated about potential terrorist attacks in the United States and Europe, arbitrary counterterrorism border detention is often accompanied by harsh interrogation and torture against survivors who were tortured in their home country and were "on the move" trying to reach safety when they were detained. Regardless of how horrible the violence these survivors are trying to escape, they are presumed guilty by virtue of their religion, country of origin, and/or gender. In addition to the degrading violence against survivors fleeing war zones, conditions such as not being able to work in a host country, children being bullied in schools, discrimination from the host community, and being treated with suspicion by neighbors just because of their religious or ethnic identity increase these feelings of humiliation. Most of our clients present with multiple experiences of violence, injustice, and humiliation.

As Gilligan notes, "Once we have labeled someone as 'evil' there is often no limit to the cruelty and violence we can feel justified in administering to him" (Gilligan 2001, 14). Gilligan (1996, 2001) asserts that reactive violence is often an attempt to reclaim dignity and self-esteem, "The basic psychological motive, or cause, of violent behavior is the wish to ward off or eliminate the feeling of shame and humiliation—a feeling that is painful and can even be intolerable and overwhelming-and replace it with its opposite, the feeling of pride" (Gilligan 2001, 27). Shame is not enough on its own to cause someone to be violent but that other preconditions must be in place. Gilligan states, "Another precondition for shame to turn to violence is that they do not perceive themselves as having non-violent means by which to maintain or restore their self-esteem or self-respect" (Gilligan 2001, 37). Silove (2013) remarks on the negative effects of pervasive and cumulative injustices on psychological symptoms and behavior and that "social consequences of this pattern can be severe, with anger induced acts of aggression becoming ill-directed, resulting in adverse impacts on the person, the family and the community at large" (Silove 2013, 242). We can thus hypothesize that the extreme and ongoing ill treatment experienced by torture and war survivors creates conditions for the possible vulnerability to violent extremism.

Condition #1: Defending against Shame, Powerlessness, and Injustice

Anger and aggression are often a defense against feeling the intolerable shame, humiliation, and hopelessness fueled by thoughts of the injustices they have experienced. Migration and displacement strip people of their roles as they may not be able to work or have any opportunity to improve their situation. This combination of circumstances and traumatic effects may lead to desperate acts. With our clients, these acts might include harming oneself or family members (discussed next) or persistent fantasies to get revenge on those who hurt them or inclinations to join a rebel group. There is no conclusive research to draw a causal link from this humiliation and powerlessness to people joining extremist groups (as there are many causes and conditions that would result in this choice). Unhealed trauma creates a risk factor when people are not given any other way to reclaim their dignity and speak out against injustice.

Condition #2: Family Violence and Cycles of Harm

Despite humiliating conditions faced by torture and war survivors, few overtly express a desire to join extremist groups. Much more common harmful effects of untreated trauma include a significant rise in suicidal feelings and behavior and an increase in family violence. In the therapy groups, I observed in Jordan a majority of men and women reported that their unregulated anger from their ill treatment and powerlessness led to an increase in their own violence in the home. Most expressed shame over their behavior knowing it was wrong to hurt those they loved but still struggling to control their anger. Unhealed trauma increases the risk of child abuse and familial violence, and child abuse is a risk factor for future violence (Gilligan 2001, 110); if we want to prevent violence, including violent extremism, the intergenerational cycles of violence must be addressed.

As a supervisor, the clinical cases that were the most challenging and heart wrenching were those clients who had intrusive fantasies of killing themselves and their families in a desperate attempt to escape the unbearable pain and humiliation of their circumstances. They saw this as the only way they could save their families from pain. Here we see the devastating effects of ongoing conditions of powerlessness and humiliation where destruction of the self and family is seen as the only way to reclaim agency.

Condition #3: Hardening of Identities and "Us and Them" Thinking

"Us and them" thinking is a well-known driver of intergroup violence (Sen 2006; Volkan 2004). Religion-based identity classification feeds into the discriminatory response to global terrorism. Abusive counterterrorism strategies and detention practices are often justified through dehumanizing the victim as "other," as "terrorist." Many of our clients were targeted in their home country for being seen as "other," whether Sunnis persecuted by Shia militias or other minority religions such as the Yazidis persecuted by ISIS for their religious beliefs. Ironically no matter how brutalized the population, the survivors are still often cast as potential terrorists. Just by virtue of having been in ISIS territory, they are seen as collaborators, traitors, or terrorists and detained and mistreated, further destroying dignity and identity.

Furthermore, traumatic experiences trigger a generalized fear response that can be projected on to any member of the group who has harmed them. If a

Shia militia targeted you and your family, you may become fearful and angry at all Shias. This fear is adaptive in the short term for survival but maladaptive if the trauma is untreated or if negative leaders capitalize on this "chosen trauma" to justify violence against another group (Volkan 2004). Unhealed individual and community trauma results in the hardening of group identity based on victimization, thus reinforcing "us and them" thinking.

In our therapy groups, we see this dynamic play out in the first session as most of our groups in Jordan include Sunnis, Shias, Sabeans, or other minority religions. Feelings and projections about "others" in the group range from fear to anger to hatred. During the first group session, survivors are looking around with caution, as they see representatives from the group that harmed them. The fear is tangible, and trust building is a key first step to the group process.

Condition #4: Psychological Deterioration

Torture and war strip people of their dignity through shame and humiliation, resulting in feelings of hopelessness and powerlessness, unregulated fear and anger, hardening of "us and them thinking," thus creating conditions for the possibility of violent outcomes toward self, family, or others. Persistent, unrelenting traumatic symptoms and left untreated can result in psychological deterioration and functioning, including poor judgment and impulse control, impaired cognitive abilities to be able to accurately assess threat, and heightened reactivity.

By understanding these conditions, we can explore interventions that prevent violence and strengthen resilience to resist extremist messages. The next section explores how CVT's healing and justice-related interventions not only heal the effects of violence but also prevent violence by restoring dignity, strengthening families, disrupting "us and them" thinking, and ultimately breaking cycles of destruction.

CREATING CONDITIONS FOR PEACE: CENTER FOR VICTIMS OF TORTURE'S HEALING INTERVENTIONS

Center for Victims of Torture's intensive trauma rehabilitation programming helps create conditions that increase the likelihood for positive change and posttraumatic growth, prevents or reduces violence in the home, interrupts cycles of violence, and reduces risk factors that might lead someone toward extremism. Our main modality is a ten-week trauma-focused group model with parallel tracks of counseling, physiotherapy, and social work services. In 2015, I spent three months in Jordan directly observing ten different groups of all demographics as we implemented our new group counseling model. The client quotes illustrate the profound transformation that I witnessed when observing the groups in Jordan.[4] The name of our counseling group manual is "Restoring Hope and Dignity," which aptly reflects the transformation that happens in the course of the ten weeks.

RESTORING HOPE AND RECLAIMING PERSONAL POWER

Survivors come to our groups feeling powerless, with little hope for the future. Early in the group, we teach stabilization skills that help them start to have control over their bodies and reactions. When they learn how to control their emotional and physical reactions through a combination of relaxation skills, changing unhelpful thoughts, identifying and building on internal strengths and somatic movement exercises, they are able to arrest the vicious cycle downward and start experiencing positive feedback loops in their lives. For example, they learn to manage their flashbacks or fear, leave the house to find work, or reduce anger that is triggered by trauma. This helps them stop behavior such as hurting family members and have more control over themselves. This creates a sense of agency and control that had previously been stripped away.

In the early stages, the program aims to restore their dignity by helping them identify strengths that have allowed them to survive. This helps them see where they have power and where they can make positive changes in their lives. The survivors reflected that by actively working to change their thoughts and to make better choices about their behaviors, they significantly improved their well-being and felt empowered to change. They learn the Cognitive Triangle, which many groups rename as the "triangle of life," that helps them identify where they have control (over their thoughts, feelings/physical sensations, and behaviors/reactions).

One survivor remarked, "The triangle is always in my mind. When I have a negative thought, I call the fire brigade and put water on it straight away." Survivors are taking steps to improve their lives. "I'm taking action rather than sitting around and waiting." Others are controlling their anger so as to not hurt themselves or others and taking steps to improve their health. Several survivors noted that they began to rediscover their passions: "It is because of the group, I want to play music again. I am no longer drowning in negativity." Torture completely takes away power and agency, and these first sessions start to restore a sense of personal power, reducing the likelihood that they will turn to desperate acts.

Healing Shame and Restoring Dignity

The content and structure of the group is designed to heal trauma, restore dignity, and address shame, humiliation, and loss of identity. As people learn to control their symptoms and reactions to trauma, they feel increasing pride and agency as they start to reclaim their sense of self and inherent dignity. In the middle section of the group cycle, we use interventions to begin to heal intrusive traumatic memories that drive feelings of humiliation, powerlessness, and shame. Once group trust has been established, the survivors have the opportunity to process through their most difficult memories; they have often never shared these traumatic events with anyone. "Speaking the unspeakable" in front of other people is powerful. Afterward one participant said that "a burden has been lifted," and this relief was visible on many of their faces. They had been holding on to these shameful secrets and were terrified of being rejected if they ever shared them. Feeling the support of the other group members while sharing these painful memories can help heal their internal wounds allowing them to move forward. Learning that they are not alone in having experienced humiliating atrocities reduces the shame they felt about what happened to them.

After the trauma processing, the group addresses guilt and shame from what they were forced to do to other people, such as having to helplessly witness the rape or murder of a loved one. Airing these feelings openly and seeing the commonalities between group members can allow for the beginnings of self-forgiveness and reclaiming goodness in themselves.

After giving voice to the indignities and pain that survivors have suffered, the last sessions further help survivors reclaim dignity. We use the metaphor of a tree as a symbol of inherent dignity that remains despite broken branches and fallen leaves.

These sessions help them restore multiple aspects of their identity and strength as well as work on developing future-oriented goals. Survivors stated they are different people now that they rediscovered their identity and humanity. One man came to the group extremely discouraged, struggling with anger and depression. He recounted, "Before, I felt I was an animal. I just ate and slept. I didn't trust anyone and wouldn't talk to anyone, even my remaining family members. Now I talk to my sister. We walk together. My thinking has changed. I can be empathic to others and so can deal with people better. I have more energy." Another said, "At the beginning, I was nothing. Now I am a person I can be proud of." "This is a safe place to cry. I'm more compassionate now. My volcano of tears exploded, and no one judged me." Another man said, "I express myself and people listen. I haven't been able to cry. Here I was able to cry, and I feel better." These statements attest to the transformation in reclaiming dignity as a person worthy of respect.

REDUCING FEAR OF THE "OTHER" AND DISMANTLING "US AND THEM" THINKING

In addition to restoring dignity, our group model reduces generalized fear and dismantles "us and them" projections. Throughout the ten weeks, the group members experience the feared "other" differently and were able to see that they have more similarities than differences. By the end of the ten sessions, walls dissolved, and the group created an "us" as they saw their common humanity. Entering a group with people from other religions and nationalities was very scary for many survivors. Overcoming their own assumptions about the "other" was a theme we heard in many of the groups. One woman described her journey of transforming her fear and prejudice. "At first I thought she (another group member) was a terrorist! I was afraid of her and avoided walking with her after the group. Now I call her over as soon as I see her and give her a kiss. Imagine what a separation there was between us! Now we love each other."

Many participants acknowledged how much prejudice and hatred they held in their hearts before the group and how the group helped them heal their prejudices. One man used the "triangle of life" to change his negative thinking toward other groups. "I used the triangle to change my thoughts about Iraqis and Sabeans and this helped me cure my own discrimination and inability to cope with differences. We are Syrians and Iraqis, we are here together to support each other." He went on to say that he feels "free as a bird" now that he is less angry and distrusting of others, and he has redirected his anger into wanting to "strengthen the well of goodness in others." He expressed aspirations for reconciliation in the region, saying, "We want the Arab world to come together like before and for foreigners to see us other than terrorists." One participant said, "We want to separate from the evil that divides us and come closer to that which brings us together." In each group at the end of the ten sessions, people affirmed their common humanity as men, women, parents, people who like to cook, people who have been wounded, and people who have love and support to give. Repairing the social fabric in this way strengthens the resilience of individuals and communities, reducing the likelihood that an individual will choose a destructive, extremist path.

Reducing Family Violence

We have evidence that CVT's interventions reduce violence in the home and enhance the protective role of families.[5] Due to traumatic reactions, the stress of displacement, and changing gender roles, many survivors (men and women) spoke openly of their increased physical aggression toward family members and the guilt and shame they felt as a result. Parents talked about how they changed their behaviors and stopped hurting their children and spouses, thereby arresting cycles of violence. Several parents shared, "I want to raise my children right. I have been neglecting them. I want to understand them and give them my best instead of hitting them." By healing the parents' own trauma, giving them skills to regulate their emotions, and restoring dignity, they were able to change negative behaviors at home into positive attachment behaviors, such as playing with their children and practicing coping skills together as a family. This improvement in parenting and feeling connected again to their loved ones gives survivors a sense of pride and positive identity as parent and spouse. Furthermore, learning how to regulate their anger allowed them also to create a home environment that is healing and protective for their children. Remembering that child abuse is a risk factor for future violence, this type of family stabilization and reduction in child abuse is critical for stopping cycles of violence.

In addition to our adult groups, we have innovative child and family programming that reconnects parents to their children in healthy ways by strengthening attachment that often gets severely disrupted due to trauma and dislocation. This improves family resilience to cope. Having the family unit become a source of connection and belonging decreases the need to find this elsewhere (gangs, extremist groups). As the family is a key unit connecting individuals to community, the benefits ripple outward.

ADVOCACY AND ACCESS TO JUSTICE

Center for Victims of Torture believes it is important to provide options for survivors to speak out against the injustices they have endured as another way to reclaim agency. CVT brings survivors' voices into our advocacy work to end torture and to improve conditions related to dislocation. A report based on interviews with survivors in Jordan included concrete policy recommendations to help survivors with what they identified would help them the most, such as loosening the work rules in Jordan so they could support their families. Other projects are exploring giving survivors multiple options for documenting their stories for advocacy, community archives, memorials, or criminal prosecutions. We believe that meeting "justice related needs" is part of the healing process and that justice means different things to different people.

CONCLUSION

Psychological factors can perpetuate violence, and therefore, psychological interventions can prevent violence. At its most basic, violence begets violence, and if we let the effects of violence go untreated, we create conditions that can lead to more violence, including violent extremism. In spite of horrific violence that people have endured, a trauma-healing approach can arrest or reverse these cycles and repair the social fabric to prevent violence and violent extremism. Although survivors certainly continue to face challenges after CVT groups, the changes the survivors reported were truly transformative. Survivors regain their dignity and humanity, break cycles of violence in their homes, challenge their own prejudices, and reconcile with those whom they perceived as enemies. These changes and positive feedback loops create ripple effects of hope and healing through families and communities. Giving people options other than violence to reclaim respect and dignity strengthens communities and creates conditions for an ecology of peace and well-being.

Section VI

CASE STUDIES

Section VI

Introduction

This section explores the ecology of violent extremism through the lens of six different case studies. First, three case studies explore the ecology of violent extremism in Pakistan, Kenya, and Indonesia. Millicent Otieno offers a case study of the impact of counterterrorism on civil society's efforts to foster development, prevent violent extremism, and contribute to longer-term peacebuilding in her chapter 30, "The Ecology of Violent Extremism in Kenya." In chapter 31, "Preventing and Countering Violent Extremism through Empowering Women Economically and Socially in Pakistan," Mossarat Qadeem gives stories and examples from Pakistan. Chapter 32, "The Radical Muslim and the Radical Mennonite," by Agnes Chen, Paulus Hartono, and Agus Suyanto then illustrates how a peacebuilding approach works in practice in Indonesia.

Next, staff from three large peacebuilding and development NGOs, Mercy Corps, World Vision International, and Catholic Relief Services, reflect on the impact of the countering violent extremism (CVE) framework on their development and peacebuilding efforts. Rebecca Wolff and Keith Proctor identify their research on economic drivers of violent extremism with the NGO Mercy Corp in chapter 33, "What Works to Prevent Violent Extremism: Lessons from Employment and Education Programs." In chapter 34, "A Child-Focused Perspective on the Preventing and Countering Violent Extremism Paradigm," Matthew J. O. Scott describes the impact of violent extremism and P/CVE frameworks on World Vision International. Finally, Aaron Chassy and Nell Bolton describe Catholic Relief Services approach in chapter 35, "Putting Human Dignity at the Center: An Alternative Perspective on 'Countering Violent Extremism.'"

In closing, a final chapter, chapter 36, then summarizes the key lessons learned and policy recommendations that emerge from all the chapters in the book in "Toward a Synergy of Approaches to Human Security."

Chapter 30

The Ecology of Violent Extremism in Kenya

Millicent Otieno

Kenya has been a frequent target of terrorist and extremist attacks. In 1998, Al-Qaeda bombed the US Embassy in Nairobi killing more than 200 people. Soon after Kenya's October 2011 military intervention in Somalia, the extremist group al-Shabaab intensified its attacks inside the country. In 2013, the militants carried out a massacre at Westgate Mall in Nairobi, killing nearly seventy people. In 2015, al-Shabaab massacred 147 students and staff at Garissa University. Early 2017 saw an uptick in al-Shabaab attacks as the group tried to pressure the Kenyan government to withdraw its troops from Somalia. In July 2017, three days after engagements between the Kenyan forces and the militants, members of al-Shabaab reportedly beheaded nine civilians in the village of Jima, in southeast Kenya. These and other attacks also damage the Kenyan economy. Kenya's government is spending more on its security sector and less on health, education, and development and Kenya's tourism sector due to a reduction in tourism. The reality of violent extremism as an actual threat to the country has provoked academic, policy, and popular debate to discover solutions to the challenge.

Violent extremist groups that espouse fundamentalist religious narratives are growing across Africa. Some cite the boom in violent extremism as a result of colonial rule that fostered undemocratic and anti-Western movements in the Middle East and Muslim world. Extremist groups argue conservative religious rule is a cure to the injustice that followed colonialism. The transition from tribal authority to colonial authority to state elections was challenging. Ethnic divisions, high unemployment, fluid borders, corruption, and weak governance combined to create a situation ripe for violent conflict.

The links between national and international jihadist groups are also growing. Terror groups often base themselves in border regions where state security actors are scarce, local communities have few resources, and cross-border networking is possible (Buchanan-Clarke and Lekalake 2016). Local African extremist groups that began with local grievances are evolving into transnational organizations that increasingly link with a variety of different global terror groups. In 2012, al-Shabaab appeared to declare allegiance to Al-Qaeda, but recently, there have been infighting over whether to shift the allegiance to the Islamic State of Iraq and the Levant (ISIL).

There are many factors that influence violent extremism in Kenya. Some recruits to terrorist groups are looking for money, glory, and fame, possibly because they are unemployed. Some come from a radicalized religious environment and are influenced by cyber preachers and sheikhs. Some join terror groups to resist what they see as state repression and injustice. These factors interact with each other, making it difficult to prioritize a plan of action.

At the same time, the interventions to prevent and respond to violent extremism also interact. Counterterrorism initiatives overrely on force and punishment of the Muslim community, particularly Somali Muslims. The distrust bred by counterterrorism makes it difficult for communities to see CVE programming as legitimate or helpful. Counterterrorism laws make it difficult for Kenyan civil society to engage in peacebuilding, as some groups are accused of assisting terror groups without any basis or evidence. Instead of counterterrorism, CVE, and peacebuilding working together, there is considerable conflict between these approaches.

THE CYCLE OF STATE AND NONSTATE VIOLENCE

The Kenyan government initiated several measures to combat the imminent threats from al-Shabaab. These measures included deploying anti-terror police unit to border regions to increase border patrols, freezing assets of al-Shabaab sympathizers, and shifting government funding to the security sector (Megged 2015). But without a broader plan, these security measures have not had an effect or addressed the root causes of violent extremism in Kenya.

Kenya Defense Forces worked with Somali, United States, and other foreign military advisors when it invaded parts of Somalia to capture and kill members of al-Shabaab with Operation Linda Nchi (meaning to "protect the country" in Swahili) in 2011 (U.S. Department of State 2015). The 2013 attack on Westgate Mall was al-Shabaab's response.

After more terror attacks in Nairobi and Mombasa in April and May 2014, the Kenyan government launched Operation Usalama Watch with the goal of flushing out terrorism-linked foreigners in Nairobi and Mombasa. The Kenyan government issued a directive ordering the Kakuma and Dadaab refugees residing outside the designated camps to return to their respective camps or face the law. The government also deployed 6,000 additional security offices in Eastleigh to arrest foreign nationals residing unlawfully in the country as well as any individuals suspected of terrorism. Such actions were carried out in a manner that fed into community profiling. Police rounded up thousands of Somalis and put them in Kenya's main stadium. Amnesty International reported that the operation used collective punishment of Kenya's Somali population with arbitrary arrest, harassment, extortion, ill treatment, forcible relocation, and expulsion (Amnesty International 2014). The Kenya National Commission on Human Rights (KNCHR) released a report on their investigations on human rights abuses in the ongoing crack-down against terrorism (KNCHR 2015). The KNCHR documented multiple human rights violations and breaches of the law including extortion, arbitrary arrests, sexual harassments, illegal deportations, torture, arbitrary detentions, degrading and inhuman treatment, all committed by the government security agents against innocent civilians especially of the Muslim Somali community.

Despite the government's efforts, attempts to contain violent extremism have largely failed. Incidents of state violence are now relatively widespread. Kenya is now witnessing extrajudicial killings, which is an indicator of state violence and how state atrocities relate to violent extremism. The Kenyan government's reaction to terrorism by attacking Muslim leaders and mosques viewed as terrorist and radicals sympathizers indicates a cycle of violence, where the Kenyan state uses force in an attempt to prevent terrorism. The high-profile murders include that of Sheikh Aboud Rogo Mohammed, a radical Muslim cleric from Mombasa, businessman Jacob Juma, and lawyer Willie Kimani. Kiai (2016) states, "Year after year, bodies are found all over the country killed by the state security. Of course, one hopes that some of these killings are legitimate and are done to preserve the lives of others and of the police officers, but in the absence of clear statistics and procedure from the police after killing it is very difficult to discern which killings are legitimate or not."

Some see Kenya's counterterrorism policy as increasing rather than decreasing the appeal of violent extremism and the threat of terrorism. Hussein Khalid, the head of a Kenyan NGO, wrote this in the *Washington Post* article "Kenya's Wrongheaded Approach to Terrorism."

> I believe that a large motivating factor for al-Shabaab recruits is the actions of the Kenyan National Police, particularly the Anti-Terror Police Unit. This unit's human rights abuses contribute to a climate of fear so pervasive that people who may have useful information for the police's counterterrorism operations choose not to come forward for fear that they may become police targets themselves. (Khalid 2015)

The public demands the government do something in response to terrorism and al-Shabaab's attacks but at the same time many denounce state killings and question the strategy. Horowitz points out that "direct counterterrorism efforts in Kenya have been subject to widespread criticism for alleged human right abuses" (Horowitz 2013). Afrobarometer research data on violent extremism in the country show that the Kenyan people disapprove of the government's radical handling of terrorism. The survey findings indicate that Kenya government should allow empowering of civil society, curb police abuses, and explore developmental approaches to counter violent extremism and terrorism while at the same time not generating grievances among the isolated and vulnerable Muslim Somali community (Buchanan-Clarke and Lekalake 2015).

KENYA'S CIVIL SOCIETY AND COUNTERING VIOLENT EXTREMISM

The public's horror and the perceived failure of state violence to address violent extremism prompt support for development-oriented approaches, such as preventing violent extremism (PVE) and countering violent extremism (CVE) initiatives to address the root political and socioeconomic causes of extremism. Kenyan civil society is working through community centers, radio and cultural programming, as well as vocational training programs. Other CVE efforts in the country have been witnessed through USAID's programs addressing the country's increasing vulnerability to and penetration brought about by extremist groups and ideologies.

In Kenya, the work being done by the civil society to counter violent extremism is tremendous and crosscutting. Kenyan civil society is creating new methods of protecting civilians from terrorism, working to counter recruiting narratives, and challenging the ideology of violent extremism. An example is the ongoing efforts being made by the Kenya Community Support Centre (KECOSCE) aimed at empowering the Kenyan Coast communities to prevent and contest radicalization in the region through carrying out research, documentation, and building the capacity of the youth to increase resilience to counter violent extremism; create community organizations; and provide continuous space for dialogue among the communities with public institutions, local authority officials, politicians, and development actors to deal with grievances (Kenya Community Support Centre n.d.).

Other notable efforts include the Kenya Transition Initiative's (KTI) *Being Kenyan Being Muslim* (BKBM) intervention that aimed at CVE and other forms of intergroup conflict through the promotion of value complexity (Savage, Khan, and Liht 2014). The project was carried out in Eastleigh, Nairobi, with a group of twenty-four participants of Somali and Kenyan origin; eight of the participants were then identified as vulnerable to extremism while six were former al-Shabaab members (Savage, Khan, and Liht 2014). The enhancement of community understanding of violent extremism and the addressing of misconceptions about Islam have been achieved through existing community programs such as Kenya Tuna Uwezo and partnerships with faith-based groups such as the Supreme Council of Kenya Muslims, institutions, and scholars. Most of these initiatives are community-based and engage youth, community leaders, and women on how to counter context-specific drivers of violent extremism.

In January 2015, USAID commissioned a conflict mitigation and CVE Local Needs Assessment (LNA) that highlighted the heightened vulnerability of both males and females including from well-established families with graduate education to recruitment and radicalization to violent extremism. The *Yes Youth Can* initiative by USAID in the North Eastern Region (Wajir, Mandera, and Garissa counties) helped 16,028 youths from the region to organize into 610 youth-led *bunges* (Parliaments) that offered the at-risk youth the chance to join legitimate village and county-based organizations that provide a platform for dialogue between youth and county governance structures (USAID 2017).

In September 2016, Kenya launched its new strategy aimed at the prevention of violent extremism. President Uhuru Kenyatta vowed that this strategy would pool resources from government, civil society, and the private sector in support of counterterrorism efforts. The plan would emphasize deradicalization over military tactics. Martin Kimani, director of Kenya National Counter Terrorism Center (KNCTC), would lead the plan. Three county governments, Mombasa, Lamu, and Kwale, established their own CVE strategies as well (West 2016).

Civil society organizations expressed concern that the CVE policy would continue to unfairly target Muslims and limit the freedom of civil society. The KNCTC director responded stating that the new policy informs the police to allow the civil society organizations to "engage in responsible advocacy efforts in public interest while considering the sensitivity of violent extremism." He added the following to specifically respond to the concern for civil society, "Globally, established democracies are limiting their civil liberties to fight terrorism. In Kenya we've gone the opposite way, the Kenyan people have decided we are going to strengthen our democracy and we are also going to fight terrorism" (Muraya 2016).

The Supreme Council of Kenya Muslims took part in a CVE consultation with the KNCTC. The council's secretary general said this about CVE:

> Radicalization of youth to violent extremism is the epicenter of terrorism and terrorist activities in Kenya. . . . The recruitment and radicalization of vulnerable youth has spread throughout the country. This recruitment has taken advantage

> of the difficult historical circumstances facing youth that include real and perceived marginalization, grinding poverty, un-employment, drug abuse and manipulation by the political and religious elites. (Muraya 2016)

On March 27, 2017, Kenya announced the formation of a committee that comprised of all principal secretaries and the inspector general of police to spearhead CVE efforts. The committee would operate under the new CVE strategy to rally and unify national efforts to reject violent extremism ideologies and curb extremist recruitment. In September 2017, officers conducting a multiagency security operation in Linda Boni in Lamu discovered and destroyed three key al-Shabaab hideouts at Lango la Simba in Witu Division of Lamu West. These hideouts were being used by the militants to launch attacks on vehicles plying the Lamu-Gamba-Garsen road (Kazungu 2017).

In February 2018, a decline in the number of students joining the militant groups was realized with only fourteen being recorded in 2017 compared to forty-four in 2015 and 2016. This has been attributed to the counterterrorism strategies and initiatives by the Kenya nongovernmental organizations, religious organizations, and the government. News sources report that more than sixty al-Shabaab returnees, including former university students, are undergoing rehabilitation at undisclosed camps after surrendering to Kenyan security agents. They are undergoing intensive psychological and medical support before they are finally reunited with their families and reintegrated back into the society (Wabala 2018).

While there is real progress in developing a comprehensive CVE policy in Kenya, there are also considerable challenges. A study conducted in Kenya on the outcomes of CVE-focused prevention programs found that grantees and beneficiaries of donor funds can also face threats or violence from armed groups, which may see organizations working on CVE as "collaborating" with their enemy, the state. By forcing organizations to choose sides either pro-CVE or pro-terrorism, the CVE programs can further polarize communities, increasing their vulnerability from terror groups' intent on recruiting in the community. Labeling programs as CVE also forces communities to identify terror groups as the "problem" rather than allowing them to frame the problem in a different light that would include a focus on the state itself as part of the problem. CVE could potentially make communities less likely to pursue reform of the state (Khalil and Zeuthen 2014). Civil society organizations that work on human rights, sustainable development, and conflict transformation have been erroneously labeled extremists and terrorists themselves and have been confronted with serious constraints on their ability to operate (Tiwana and Belay 2010).

Corruption in Kenya is undermining CVE efforts. Some argue "the police corruption destroys trust in the government's ability to fight terrorism properly" (Dooley 2016). The issue of corruption is also at the center of Kenya's national elections. NGOs played a significant role in preventing the escalation of violence following Kenya's 2008 elections. But when the Kenyan government did not hold perpetrators of that violence to account, it was Kenya's civil society that pressed the International Criminal Court to become involved. And that move accentuated the tensions between the Kenyan government and civil society (Allison 2016). But Kenya's CVE policy was developed within a legal context that punishes and restricts civil society. In the context of extremism and the August 2017 general elections, the Africa Policy Institute (API) and the UN Development Program (UNDP) cohosted a high-profile forum in Nairobi in June 2017 to discuss the country's preparedness and overall strategy to insulate the 2017 general election against the threat of violent extremism and cybercrime. It was highlighted that challenges of violent extremism have immense potential to undermine public confidence and trust in the electoral process in general and the legitimacy of the election outcome in particular.

KENYA'S COUNTERTERRORISM LAWS

In December 2014, the Kenyan National Assembly passed the controversial Security Laws (Amendment) Act-2014 (SLAA), which amended sections of twenty security-related laws that were aimed at giving the security agencies more powers in combating terrorism in the country. This saw the opposition government (CORD) together with several human rights groups move to the High Court in an effort to challenge the constitutionality of the law. They successfully managed to have some of the sections that violated the provisions of the bill of rights and international law declared unconstitutional. These offensive clauses touched on the rights of refugees, the freedom of the media, right to privacy, fair trial, and arbitrary detention among others. These government responses have had an impact on the civil society efforts to counter violence extremism (KNCHR 2015).

Kenya's civil society is strong, with approximately 6,500 registered civil society organizations. The ability of civil society organizations to express their views and take part in the country's affairs is guaranteed under the current constitution. But counterterrorism laws threaten civil society organizations' ability to work.

In 2014, the Kenyan government's NGO Coordination Board deregistered 540 organizations for alleged noncompliance with the law accusing some for using their charitable status as an avenue for raising funds for terrorism (*Kenya Today* 2014). The board quickly reinstated 179 organizations after they proved they were in full compliance. Out of the deregistered organizations, fifteen of them were accused of links with terrorism and violent extremism. Other twelve organizations including Concern Worldwide, Adventist development, Medecins Sans Frontieres, Relief Agency International, and Centre for Health Solutions Kenya, among others, were asked to submit their audited accounts or risk deregistration.

Then in 2015, the Kenyan NGO Coordination Board deregistered 957 Kenyan organizations, including the Kenyan Human Rights Council (KHRC), if they failed to present audited accounts to the board within a fourteen-day notice period. Many were not able to meet this short deadline and lost their registration. A civil society petition to the Kenyan government read, "We are concerned that this attempt to deregister KHRC and other NGOs is part of a larger campaign of systemic legal or administrative measures to discredit, repress, and prevent independent civil society organizations from undertaking legitimate human rights work in Kenya" (NGO Petition 2015).

In 2016, the High Court had ruled against unwarranted attempts by the NGO Coordination Board to interfere with KHRC, concluding they were unconstitutional. Yet despite the court's ruling, and government promises for enabling civil society to contribute to Kenyan democracy and the challenge of violent extremism in its 2016 CVE policy, threats to civil society continue. Following the August 2017 elections in Kenya, the NGO Coordination Board raided and deregistered more NGOs, including the Kenya Human Rights Council and the Africa Centre for Open Governance (Cherono and Mwere 2017).

Nyiragira analyzes this trend, stating, "There are negative forces within the ruling class in the country that want to take it back to the days before the adoption of the African Charter on Human and People's Rights and the promulgation of the current constitution." Nyiragira further states that "even though there could be some entities and groups using the cover of the not-for-profit status for other purposes, the mass deregistration of more than five hundred NGOs portrayed a strong message to civil society actors that the Kenyan government was after their sector" (Niyiragira 2015).

CONCLUSION

Kenya still has a long way to go in addressing the economic, political, as well as social disparities and intercommunal conflicts driving violence, radicalization, and violent extremism. The Kenyan government knows the important role that the civil society plays in CVE, and it is impossible for the government to do the work of CVE or peacebuilding itself.

The Kenyan civil society has for long been one of the continent's bravest and most vocal as well as a model for the others; however, the civil society organizations and faith-based organizations (especially Muslim entities) are now finding it hard to perform their core functions of holding the government to account. The government continues to intensify its "effort to crack down on independent civil society organizations, from administrative harassment, legislative hurdle and a public campaign to tarnish their reputation" (Allison 2016).

There is need for concerted efforts from all civil society actors in the country to work toward ensuring that the fourth chapter of the constitution is protected because the government can easily silence the civil society actors, including the media. The CSOs should also ensure that they comply with existing laws, government laws, and internal procedures in an effort to avoid any room for government's false accusations and shut down in the context of shrinking spaces.

Chapter 31

Preventing and Countering Violent Extremism through Empowering Women Economically and Socially in Pakistan

Mossarat Qadeem

For decades the acts of violent extremism have taken a toll of human lives; destroyed infrastructure; and shattered key resources and affected communities socially, economically, and psychologically in Khyber Pakhtunkhwa (KPK) and Federally Administered Tribal Area (FATA) in particular and in the rest of Pakistan in general. Few countries in the world match Pakistan in its political, social, or economic complexities and security-related challenges. It is a country of 200 million people, from over a dozen ethnic groups, myriad tribes, and minority groups that coexisted peacefully for decades.

Preventing and countering violent extremism (P/CVE) is a new concept in Pakistan, although the country has been grappling with it for past fifteen years now. For most of Pakistan society, there is no conceptualization of a role for women in P/CVE efforts, nor for the civil society. Most people believe it is the domain of the security agencies to curb violent extremism and extremists using force.

In the traditional and conservative Pukhtoon society, women's mobility is quite restricted. Some women feel secure and protected within the four walls of their house. What compels these illiterate, semiliterate, and traditionalist women to join violent extremism, and how do they join? This chapter addresses how the widows, female victims, and survivors of violent extremism develop coping mechanisms and learn to identify what works better to prevent violent extremism.

PAIMAN ALUMNI TRUST

As a nonprofit Pakistani civil society organization, PAIMAN Alumni Trust (PAIMAN) is a pioneer in initiating a process of P/CVE since 2007.

PAIMAN's P/CVE programs work alongside our efforts to address economic marginalization and to provide education and support to Pakistani communities. *Paiman* means "promise" in Urdu. From the platform of PAIMAN, we research and interrupt extremist tendencies through community mobilization, active citizenship, and community empowerment for building social cohesion.

To create influence at the national level, PAIMAN organizes women to conduct advocacy activities such as peace rallies, radio/TV talk shows, round table discussions, and production and dissemination of publications on the impact of violent extremism on women and women's role in addressing it. PAIMAN's projects include various stakeholders—including elected representatives, government officials, clergy, teachers, journalists, youth, and female—from FATA and other conflict-torn areas as part of its conflict transformation and peacebuilding programs.

PAIMAN programs include holding conversations and seeking help from religious leaders and scholars to develop counternarratives to extremist narratives so as to promote better understandings of peaceful Islamic values and dispel misinterpreted ideologies. PAIMAN also facilitates dialogues with women and youth groups, madrassa and school teachers, political parties, and religious leaders, women activists of all faith to encourage dialogue about extremism and brainstorm solutions for how to address it in their communities. PAIMAN hosts television and radio talk shows with youth and women affected by conflict to draw attention to extremism's negative, and increasingly deadly, consequences. PAIMAN builds capacity of university youth in conflict resolution skills to mediate local disputes and prevent violence; works with mothers of extremists to deradicalize and reintegrate extremist youth in society; and helps extremist youth in positive transformation to become active citizens with positive thinking by providing them psychosocial support, life skills, and alternative job skills training. From the platform of Women's Alliance for Security and leadership (WASL),[1] PAIMAN connects the local with global by advocating around the inclusivity, pluralism, and issues of women peace and security.

As of 2017, PAIMAN has worked with 1,415 extremists and those who were vulnerable to extremism. In addition, we have trained 64,367 males and 43,600 female youth in the region. Once the youth and women receive training from PAIMAN, they become members of our peace groups called "TOLANA" working at the community level across the KPK and FATA to help promote practices of peace and countering violent extremism from within the community. Both male and female groups carry out community meetings to educate their respective communities on the impact of radicalization and mobilize them to work for peace and conflict transformation. They use negotiation and mediation to address conflicts in their region. PAIMAN also conducts surveys and research studies on the sociopolitical and economic dimension of conflict and the impact of violent extremism on youth and women in FATA and other parts of KPK.

PAIMAN offers information and education on violent extremism and how to address it on social and electronic media and by holding community sessions in schools, madrassas, and public places. PAIMAN developed an inclusive peace curriculum and trained 175 school and female teachers of religious madrassa to teach respect for diversity, pluralism, and nonviolence, using creative methods like sports, poetry, art, and interactive theater.

PAIMAN established the country's first center for conflict transformation and peacebuilding, reaching thousands of young people and women across the FATA and KPK province. PAIMAN also coordinates Aman-o-Nisa, a coalition of women leaders throughout Pakistan striving to moderate violent extremism and promote understanding among diverse ethnic, religious, and political groups.

Based on the experience of PAIMAN, this chapter presents the best practice of women addressing issues of violent extremism at different levels in Pakistani society and is mostly based on the author's own field experience in KPK and FATA, an area hard hit by violent extremism since 2000.

WHY SOME WOMEN SUPPORT VIOLENT EXTREMISM

Groups that embrace violent extremism exploit women in the name of religion. Some women raise funds for them and send their sons and those of their families and communities to work with and for extremists. Women supporting extremists also stitch suicide jackets, collect gold and money, act as informers, give shelter, and facilitate recruitment for extremist groups. These were unbelievable tasks that these women carried out but what made them do so is a simple story.

"My name is Mujahida and I wanted to fight against the enemy of Islam and that was the best way I can do as Jihad. My Quran teacher would always say jihad is the surest way to jannah (heaven) and she called me to help in raising funds, so the Taliban can fight the infidels[2] and I can earn heaven. I started going from one village to another collecting funds and convincing other women to join us in this movement," says Mujahida of Qambar village, Swat.

There were many like her who were convinced by the sermons of extremist leaders in Swat valley that they as mother, sister, wives, and daughters have a duty to contribute to war against the enemy of Islam. The normalization of violence and desensitization about acts of extremism along with poverty and oppression, lack of knowledge of Quran and Islam, as well as internal desires shaping motivations are some possible explanations for why these women become part of violent extremist groups. Many women wrongly viewed these militants as fellow Muslims and sons of the soil simply yearning for Islamic law. These women made us realize that women's natural disposition is not necessarily toward peace simply because they are women.

THE IMPACT OF VIOLENT EXTREMISM ON WOMEN

Women also are hurt by violent extremism. Women are widows, victims, and survivors, displaced and traumatized by suicide attacks, bomb blasts, and military operation against the extremist groups in some parts of Pakistan. If their male relatives are fighting or killed, women may be the de facto household heads, shouldering the responsibility of feeding; nursing; and sheltering the old, the young, and the injured (Khaliq 2010). The very fact that many of the menfolk in Swat were absent often heightened the insecurity and danger for the women and children left behind and accelerated the breakdown of the traditional protection and support mechanisms upon which the communities—especially women—had previously relied in the traditional ridden society of KPK and FATA. The breakdown or disintegration of family and community networks forced these women to assume new roles. Women who had never been out of their houses in their entire life suddenly were forced to go stand in queues to get rations for their families or find some jobs to earn livelihood. In the wake of military operations and Taliban's control in Swat, there were a high number of women-headed households that needed both economic and psychological support from the government and civil society.

Women's mobility, access to education and health facilities, and ability to fully care for their families were severely impacted. Nearly in all areas hard hit by violent extremism, women were being traumatized mentally and psychologically, and each has experienced a different form of violence. The beating, threatening, and, in some cases, killing of women by extremists had its long-lasting impact on women's physiological, psychological, and social well-being. The feeling of insecurity and uncertainty is another mental torture. "When my sons and husband would go out for prayers I would just wait in the door till they returned. I saw that Taliban killed my next-door neighbor while praying in the mosque on the plea that he spoke against one of Taliban's commanders. You never know when they would decide to kill anyone and why. We were living in a constant agony and it has made me mentally sick. Now I forget things and my memory has become very short," said Shazia, a school teacher in Charsadda (Shazia, interview with the author on April 2012).

For those whose sons were among the militants, the suffering is also profound. They were worried for their children's lives and suffered yet lived in communities that may shun and isolate them and even attack them for their familial associations. They had little or no recourse to protection.

WOMEN'S RESPONSES TO VIOLENT EXTREMISM

Our analysis and research on why some women support violent extremism and how Pakistani women are affected by it led us to the challenging and unthinkable solution to address this menace by engaging mothers of vulnerable, extremist, and radicalized youth and other women in those communities. PAIMAN realized that it is this innocent mother who needs to be sensitized and educated to counter the extremist's strategy as she was the last person to know that her son has become extremist, but the important aspect is that she didn't understand the negative impact of being extremist. People would only talk of those who joined Taliban openly, but no one would speak about the silent invisible extremists living within the community. We developed our strategy of engaging mothers with the belief that mothers shape the morals and values of their children and instill a sense of responsibility for creating positive human relationships in both family and community. We all know that mothers are their children's first teachers, but after meeting the extremist women, we realized that what they taught is not always peaceful and tolerant.

It was a gigantic task to take women and mothers out of the houses in the most conservative patriarchal Pukhtoon society and involve them in our P/CVE initiative. We started building relationship with mothers within each community and attracted them to learn livelihood skills to start earning some money for their families. At the same time, we held dialogues and built trust with community elders, influential and male relatives of women paving the way for them to come out of their houses. It worked. The politics of economics worked. Focusing on concepts of self-confidence, competence, and empowerment, we started our ambitious program of engaging mothers in phases.

In the first phase we gave them marketable livelihood skills as per their aptitude because they needed to establish a position of authority within their families; a child respects the mother only when her position is not challenged by her husband or friends or society as a whole. This helped in contributing to their family's income within a short time and infused a new confidence in these mothers.

In the second phase we equipped them with the necessary knowledge and self-confidence to become active players in their family and community. We built their capacity in critical thinking by using pictures, stories, games to interpret, analyze, evaluate, then reflect, and would relate all this to the situation in their area. We also educated them on the indicators of violent extremism in an individual as well in community as signs of early warning and ways of addressing it, dialogue, and community peacebuilding and made them aware of their potential in influencing and guiding their children's lives and in preventing them from engaging in extremist activities. In almost all cases the extremists used the text of the Quran to attract youth and communities toward the concept of jihad or convince them to act in an extremist fashion. We used the Quranic verses in its context to help transform the mindset of these mothers. The basis of our transformative methodology is Quran and Sunnah as Prophet Muhammad (PBUH) insists that the mother's role is vital in the upbringing of their children in accordance with the values of true Islamic teaching that does not preach hatred or violence.

"Talking to my son about extremism and extremists is impossible for me," said Zargula in response to our conversation about engaging her radicalized son in a dialogue. That was 2008 when PAIMAN embarked upon a program "Lets Live in Peace." One of the key aspects of this program was to empower mothers of extremists and other women in the community to help in prevention of radicalization. Zargula convinced not only her son but also two other boys from her community to join PAIMAN's program of positive engagement.

The transformation of mothers like Zargula was slow but steady and firm. The newly gained knowledge and economic empowerment gave them the confidence to communicate openly with their sons and help foster deeper mother–son relationships. Through these transformed mothers, PAIMAN approaches their sons who are then convinced to join PAIMAN's program of positive engagement and transformation.

The metamorphosis of mothers from celebrating their sons' martyrdom in suicide attacks to becoming the agents of positive change in the community was a tedious and uphill process. For mothers it was extremely difficult in a patriarchal and conservative society to convince other women and men about the negative impact of violent extremism or the exploitation by certain groups in the name of religion. After receiving PAIMAN's training, these mothers/women became members of PAIMAN's Mothers Peace Groups, called "TOLANA ("together" in Pashto) Mothers," and started reaching out to other mothers.

Today TOLANA Mothers holds community sessions with other mothers in their respective communities and teaches and preaches nonviolent ways of addressing the menace of extremism. TOLANA Mothers along with Youth TOLANA are instrumental in identifying vulnerable and extremist youth for PAIMAN's positive youth engagement and deradicalization program. They are actively involved in the challenging task of reintegration of extremist youth transformed by PAIMAN. Initially it was very difficult to speak about this issue publicly, so they would speak during social gathering like wedding functions and funeral and speak about the issue in a storytelling way. Later, they hold compound sessions within their communities, around the importance of prevention of violent extremism and the positive impact of the community's attitude toward reintegration of transformed youth. Today, it is these TOLANA Mothers who are bringing their communities together and are encouraging reconciliation through community networks, building connections, and sharing information. They have educated and sensitized 15,000 female community members of KPK and FATA to realize that they have a role to play in P/CVE in their area and hence sustain the whole process of community peacebuilding.

TOLANA Mothers keeps an eye on its surroundings and looks after early signs of violent extremism within the family and in the community. One such story is the exemplary courageous deed of PAIMAN's TOLANA Mothers' member Sheeba. She noticed that her younger brother Gul Zareef had started coming home late and had become very silent. She inquired repeatedly about his late coming and noticeable silence, but he refused to respond. Remembering early signs of behavioral changes in youth from her PAIMAN training, she started observing his movements and behavior. She followed him one night and found that he visits a house in the nearby street. She discussed the situation with women members and Youth TOLANA. Some members of Youth TOLANA started visiting the same house and found out about strangers coming and delivering lectures, luring in youth to join them in their mission. Sheeba along with others from Mother TOLANA reported this to the local police, who raided the house and seized negative extremist propaganda material and arrested three strangers who had already lured five young men from that community. This early warning by a women's community peace group helped in saving many boys of that area from becoming the prey of an extremist group. PAIMAN's Mother TOLANA walks into extremists' houses, talks to them, and tries to influence their mind-set (Allam 2018). In the process we have learned that continuous interaction, education, and sensitization help these women change positively.

WOMEN'S ROLE IN INTERFAITH HARMONY

In Pakistan, men dominate positions of leadership in mosques, church, temples and other religions and shape attitudes, opinions, and behaviors. In the same context female madrassa teachers, politico-religious female leaders, and non-Muslim activists have a large constituency of women and female youth; they also have outreach and networks, and they are credible to their constituents but remain unnoticed.

PAIMAN built the capacity of madrassa teachers, women activists of other faiths, and female leaders of religious political parties. PAIMAN has worked with 100 female madrassa teachers and 120 women activists of all faith in Pakistan and female leaders of religious political parties to form a coalition of "women of faith building social cohesion in Pakistan." The members of the coalition coordinate efforts to promote inclusion, equality, and interfaith dialogue in their communities, providing a platform for all voices to be heard, regardless of personal religious belief. These members also celebrate each other's religious festivals and support each other in case of any incident of violence against one or the other community. The group is based on women's ability to reach across lines of difference in tense environments, lead nonviolent protests, and mobilize communities, as well as their engagement with the theological aspects of gender roles in peace. Through this platform women belonging to different faiths overcame the three major obstacles to their participation in interfaith dialogue: the lack of access to religious education in other nonIslamic faiths, to representation, and to communication. Through sharing and discussions, they discover similarities and differences in their respective positions as women and as believers. The members of the coalition today are working to promote inclusion, equality, and interfaith dialogue in their communities, providing a platform for all voices to be heard, regardless of personal religious belief. They celebrate each other's religious festivals and support each other in case of any incident of violence against one or the other community.

Today PAIMAN's Women of Faith network have taken up crucial issues to mobilize communities, find solution, and advocate with authorities. The Lahore members amicably resolved a decades-old conflict between Shias and Sunnis of Rehmanpura, Lahore, where the Sunnis did not allow the Shias to hoist black flags and to take out Shia processions in that area during Muharram, resulting in violent clashes between the two sects. Through continuous interaction and a series of dialogue with religious leaders of the two sects of Rehmanpura, the issue is resolved.

Zareen is a member of PAIMAN interfaith group. Her son Adil was often involved in extremist acts against the Shia procession during the month of Muharram in Peshawar. She decided to transform her son. Zareen, with other members, decided to guard the Shia procession during month of Muharram so as to avert the attack planned by her son and his friends. After seeing their mothers, they left the place without harming anyone. Later mothers carried out dialogues with their sons and helped them in overcoming their prejudices against Shia. Today Adil is one of the most active members of Youth TOLANA and leads the campaign of interfaith/intersectarian harmony, tolerance, and social cohesion in Peshawar.

CONCLUSION

PAIMAN's successful engagement of women in preventing violent extremism reveals that women's roles as communicators of cultural knowledge and familial traditions are significant in its capacity to transform both within the private realm—through equal access to decision making and child-rearing—and in the public, and through a movement like TOLANA Mothers it has become a nonviolent social movement. PAIMANs programs are low-cost: about $100 per person for the training, coaching, and engagement to prevent violent extremism. This is a fraction of the profits made by those who sell weapons or who benefit financially from violent extremism.

PAIMAN has learned that women can be very effective in transforming conflict and addressing issues of violent extremism provided they are economically empowered, have knowledge of the issues, have skills to discuss, negotiate, and have strong support network like TOLANAs. Women's peace groups like TOLANA Mothers act as change agents by creating awareness, preventing radicalization, supporting other women, speaking out, and lobbying for the inclusion of women in key peace and security structures and committees, including those that influence laws and policies. We also learned that commitment and continuous campaigns and explanations are required to consolidate the minds of the women to be able to change mind-sets. PAIMAN TOLANA Mothers Peace Groups contributed to community reconciliation, trauma healing, and stabilization during the most difficult and uncertain time in our area because of the trust that they build within their communities. They work with school management committees, teachers, and parents in disseminating peace messages and organizing student peace groups in madrassa and schools.

PAIMAN's experience reveals that culturally relevant solutions are an important step toward increasing the efficiency of countering and preventing violent extremism, and this requires knowledge of local ways of living and gender roles in these societies without which any P/CVE effort is not sustainable. It is also important to remember that women are not a monolithic social group. Their potential and their power will be shaped by their self-perception, their social status, and how their communities perceive them. The government needs to recognize the role of women in countering and preventing violent extremism in Pakistan and must evaluate women's existing efforts and ways in which those efforts could be strengthened to have a larger impact on countering violent extremism.

Chapter 32

The Radical Muslim and the Radical Mennonite

An Interfaith Encounter for Peace in Indonesia

Agnes Chen, Paulus Hartono, and Agus Suyanto

In a world where counterterrorism and countering violent extremism (CVE) are the dominant approaches to violent extremism, engaging the violent extremist "other" through nonviolent, noncovert, and transformative ways remains a rare practice and is often made difficult by governmental restrictions and social taboos. Yet many communities around the world have implemented alternatives to mainstream approaches to violent extremism. Such a story can be found within a Mennonite Christian community in Central Java, Indonesia, and their journey of interfaith dialogue and engagement with a local Islamic paramilitary group, the Hizbullah Front.

The story started in Surakarta, a city also known as Solo. Despite Solo's positive reputation as a center of Javanese tradition and culture, it also has the unfortunate label as *kota bersumbu pendek*, or a "city with a short wick." Suyanto, Agus and Paulus Hartono. (2015)[1] Like a firecracker with a short fuse, a little political, ethnic, or sectarian friction could trigger a full-blown violent conflict in the city. From 1911 to 1999, Solo experienced twelve large-scale riots across ethnic, religious, economic, and political divides.

Moreover, while most Muslims in Indonesia espouse a moderate, nonviolent expression of Islam, serious concerns have been raised over the rise of militant Islamic groups starting in the post-Soeharto *reformasi* period. These groups have fiercely opposed Western military and political interventions in the Middle East and consider themselves the bulwark against a rising tide of immorality and values antithetical to their religious ideology. Although many Islamic militant groups in Indonesia are homegrown and typically focus on local or national sectarian affairs, they are increasingly connected with and influenced by global violent extremist movements such as ISIS.

Solo is known as a fertile ground for such violent extremist networks. These include *Jamaah Islamiyah*, an Al-Qaeda–affiliated network in Southeast Asia, as well as Islamic paramilitary forces involved in ethno-religious wars and violent extremist attacks across the country. The 1997–2001 Christian-Muslim conflicts in Poso and Ambon, the Bali bombings of 2002 and 2005, and the Marriott Hotel bombing in Jakarta all had connections to Solo-based Islamic fronts and networks (BBC 2016; Campbell 2017). While the Indonesian government's counterterrorist operations have weakened *Jamaah Islamiyah*, the rise of ISIS recruitment has the potential to mobilize and unite Islamic militant factions (Fabi and Kapoor 2016). Thus, once again there is concern regarding Solo's vulnerability for violent extremism recruitment.

Responding to the volatile dynamics of Solo and the nation, Mennonite Christians had a radical vision that their church would become an agent of peace and reconciliation. Mennonites, which historically splintered from the Protestant Reformation in the sixteenth century, have espoused pacifism, nonviolence, and active peacebuilding for nearly five hundred years years. Despite threats from Islamic militants and fearful hesitation from the Christian community, these peacemakers took the risk to engage with Islamic militants who have closed down Christian churches and participated in other acts of religious intolerance. These efforts included visiting the commander of the Hizbullah Front to build *silaturahmi*, or communal ties, partnering with the Hizbullah Front to rebuild communities in the aftermath of environmental disasters in Indonesia, and creating a civil society organization called Mennonite Diakonia Service to function as the service arm of an Indonesian Mennonite denomination and as a local platform to engage with the Hizbullah Front.

PRE-ENCOUNTER

Kalau tak kenal maka tak sayang is an Indonesian proverb that means that one cannot love what one does not know. The proverb rings true for members of the Hizbullah Front and members of the Mennonite Christian church in Solo, whose initial assumptions were based on stereotypes and a lack of understanding of each other.

The Hizbullah Corps "Battalion 99" Sunan Bonang Division, or the Hizbullah Front for short, is an independent Islamic paramilitary group in Solo that named itself after a historical paramilitary group that was prominent in Indonesia's pre- and early independence days. Under the leadership of Yanni Rusmanto, the front has grown to be a battalion of five hundred troops and has increased their influence into twenty counties and cities throughout Central Java (Solo Pos 2000).

The Hizbullah Front's goal to "live nobly or die as a martyr" for their God and country has motivated them to do a number of activities, ranging from conducting humanitarian actions, promoting Islamic solidarity and culture, and working with the Indonesian police to maintain order and stability in the region. However, the front's convictions also compelled them to engage in the Christian-Muslim conflict in Poso and Ambon and other acts of religious intolerance, such as closing down churches. The front is also known to be a fierce opponent of the U.S. foreign policy in the Middle East and almost deployed their troops to support the anti-Western movement in Lebanon and Palestine in 2006 (Rosyid 2006).

Indonesian Christians typically perceive groups like the Hizbullah Front as waging *jihad* and violence against them. Nearly twenty years ago, a Mennonite Christian pastor named Paulus Hartono would echo the same sentiments. Due to the legacy of colonialism that favored ethnic Chinese and Christian communities on economic and political terms, many Indonesian Muslims still consider Indonesian Christians who are ethnically Chinese as having double outsider traits. "As an ethnic Chinese, Christian, not to mention pastor, it wasn't easy for me to enter into the thick of a hostile group. People like me are prone to face discrimination and prejudice," Hartono explained.

Mennonite Christians trace their spiritual heritage to Jesus's teachings, particularly from the Sermon of the Mount, and to the Anabaptist movement that formed in sixteenth-century Europe. This particular stream of Christianity emphasizes nonviolence in all forms, including church- and state-sanctioned violence. Several centuries later, the Mennonite Anabaptist movement was introduced to Indonesia through Dutch colonial rule and missionary activity (Dharma 2013). Like other Mennonite leaders before him, Hartono has sought to continue the Mennonite spirit of peace and reconciliation by establishing interfaith allies to jointly respond to the needs of Solo.

Likewise, Hizbullah members also had their suspicions against Christians. They thought that the whole Christian mission was to exploit the poor economic conditions of Muslims and to convert them to Christianity. According to the Quran, Rusmanto said, Christians would always try to influence and convert Muslims until the end of age.

THE BEGINNINGS

Rusmanto and Hartono first met in the early 2000s as directors of their respective Islamic and Christian radio stations. When Rusmanto's Hiz FM had a bandwidth frequency dispute with another Islamic radio station, Manajemen Qolbu (MQ) FM, Hartono, as the director of the Christian radio Immanuel FM, mediated their conflict. Since then, Hartono began his attempts to befriend Rusmanto. For months, Hartono audaciously showed up at the Hizbullah headquarters to build *silaturahmi*, or communal ties, with the commander.

Yet the effort was not well received at first. "Anyone outside of the Islamic community and creed is a *kafir* [infidel]. You are an infidel! And because you're an ethnic Chinese, your blood is *halal*." These were the words Hartono received at the Hizbullah headquarters. In Islamic terminology, *halal* means lawful or permissible. "It is *halal* for us [Muslims] to kill you," Rusmanto explained (quoted in Al Qurtuby 2013). But Hartono shrugged off the commander's offensive remarks. "You think I'm an infidel? No problem. The real problem is that there is a lack of communication between Muslims and Christians in our city." Hartono's persistence proved to be fruitful. They continued meeting informally over tea for the next couple of years, in which Rusmanto became more acquainted with and trusting of Hartono.

At the end of 2004, Islamic paramilitary groups carried out church evictions and church bombings across Indonesia. Upon hearing the news, Hartono contacted Rusmanto. He asked whether the commander could meet and talk with Christian pastors in Solo specifically on why Islamic paramilitary groups, including the Hizbullah Front, were closing churches at an alarming rate. Rusmanto accepted the invitation.

That night, Rusmanto found himself in a dialogue with two hundred Christian pastors, along with Dian Nafi of *Nadhlatul Ulama*, one of the leaders of the biggest Islamic association in Indonesia, who served as the night's moderator. During this discussion, Rusmanto explained that the evicted churches lacked the proper permits. The pastors responded by explaining the challenges in processing church permits in their neighborhoods, especially compared to the process of gaining building permits for mosques and *mushollas*. This conversation challenged Rusmanto's perspectives and helped to mitigate the conflict over church evictions.

BREAKING GROUND: HIZBULLAH AND MENNONITES IN ACEH

The first opportunity for the Hizbullah Front and the Mennonite community to work together came following the Indian Ocean tsunami of December 26, 2004. Along with other hard-hit regions, the tsunami engulfed over 170,000 and displaced up to half a million people in Aceh. Indonesia declared a state of emergency. Relief groups poured into the region.

The Hizbullah Front also had plans to assist in Aceh's post-tsunami reconstruction. Rusmanto had already shipped two hundred volunteers to Aceh. A couple weeks later, Hartono called Rusmanto. He asked Rusmanto whether he would travel to Aceh and work with an interfaith group affiliated with *Forum Kemanusiaan dan Persaudaraan Indonesia* (FKPI—the Indonesian Humanitarian Solidarity Forum), with financial support from Mennonite

Central Committee, a global relief, peacebuilding, and development organization. Knowing that Rusmanto had skills in assembling radio kits, Hartono also asked if Rusmanto would be willing to teach communities how to assemble radio receivers in Aceh. Rusmanto's travel expenses would also be covered during this trip.

Rusmanto agreed to collaborate with the interfaith group and together they flew to Aceh. The Christian participants who flew with Rusmanto were secretly afraid when they first heard that they were to fly to Aceh and work with the commander of the Hizbullah Front. To make things worse, Hartono, the main bridge between the Hizbullah Front and the Mennonite community, was to join them in Aceh at a later date.

When they landed in Aceh, Rusmanto wanted to set guidelines for the trip. "We have ideological differences and our own set of beliefs," he said. "Do whatever suits your convictions and we (Muslims) will do the same." Afterward, Rusmanto created zones that were not to be trespassed by Christians; they functioned exclusively as Muslim prayer rooms and for Quranic teaching.

As per agreement, Rusmanto trained civilians how to set up radio receiver kits every morning and evening for ten days. Over a thousand radio receivers were assembled and distributed so that they may play trauma-healing programs for tsunami survivors. Rusmanto and the interfaith group saw that the radio kits were highly welcomed in communities that were in critical need of trauma healing and relief. When Hartono joined the volunteer group, he couldn't help noticing that Rusmanto was enjoying himself. Hartono even learned how to make a radio receiver kit from him.

The impacts were felt not only by the host communities but also among volunteers of Hizbullah and the interfaith group. Ten days were spent with Christian, Hizbullah, and other Muslim volunteers serving together, eating at the same table, and living under the same roof. In a few days, the volunteers were sharing jokes, experiences, and stories with each other. Rusmanto also noticed that the Christian volunteers did not proselytize the Muslim volunteers or the resident communities in Aceh.

Slowly Rusmanto too became at ease with the Christian volunteers. He was surprised when a Christian volunteer woke him up before the dawn to do his *sholat*, or Muslim prayer. Furthermore, the Hizbullah interfaith group also faced similar challenges to entering the region dominated by *Gerakan Aceh Merdeka* (GAM—Free Aceh Movement), an Acehnese separatist group whose wars with the Indonesian government had destabilized the region prior to the tsunami. At first, the local community of the region denied the interfaith group's entry because a Christian group once proselytized to the community. To resolve the problem, Rusmanto showed his Hizbullah membership card for the interfaith group to access the region. Rusmanto later confessed, "To be honest, I became comfortable with [the Christian community] and started trusting them during my trip in Aceh, not during the radio station days."

Before the ten-day trip ended, a delegation from the United States and Canada came to visit and evaluate post-tsunami relief program in Aceh. When they arrived to the scene, Hartono asked Rusmanto to share how he became involved with the interfaith humanitarian project as well as the progress of the relief efforts. Rusmanto began his presentation. After a few lines, however, he stopped in his tracks. He couldn't find the words to say what he had planned on sharing. Tears came out of his eyes. The delegation left in confusion and proceeded to other meetings.

A couple of days later, Hartono asked why Rusmanto broke down during the presentation. "How could I not cry?" he responded. "My mind flashed back to the horrible experiences I had in the Poso and Ambon wars. Now I have seen with my own eyes that Christians are not as militant as what I once thought. These Christians and pastors have come from far away and left their families to care for the needs of my brothers and sisters in Aceh. I have come to believe that I was being used as a tool by larger political bodies [in the Ambon-Poso wars]. It's dehumanized me. War has turned us into demons, the Ambonese, the Posonese, the Islamic soldiers. All of us." He added remorsefully, "Had I known you five years ago, I would not have gone to Ambon to fight the Christians there."

LESSONS LEARNED

The journey did not end with the Aceh joint mission. After a decade of observing members of the Mennonite church in Solo applying active peacebuilding, the larger Mennonite synod of *Gereja Kristen Muria Indonesia* (GKMI—the Muria Christian Church in Indonesia) established an agency called Mennonite Diakonia Service (MDS) to expand its ministries in disaster relief, peacebuilding, and environmentalism. It was through MDS and another local interfaith organization called *Lembaga Perdamaian Lintas Agama dan Golongan* (LPLAG—the Peace Institute across Religions and Groups) that more peacebuilding initiatives occurred in the region. In 2006, Hizbullah and Mennonite Christian youth worked together to clean up and rebuild houses damaged by an earthquake in Bantul, Central Java. In the following years, the Hizbullah commander was invited to talk on Christian campuses as well as radio shows in interfaith dialogue and peacebuilding. Hizbullah troops underwent conflict transformation trainings, co-trained by Muslim and Christian facilitators. In consultation with the Hizbullah community, MDS and LPLAG volunteers renovated Hizbullah members' houses that were located in the slum areas of Solo. Indonesian and international Christian delegations have met Rusmanto at the Hizbullah headquarters, which furthered interfaith understanding and allowed transformative moments to occur.

These efforts were conducted despite the costs to befriend the "other." Throughout the process, there remained internal misunderstandings that needed to be resolved between Hizbullah and Mennonite members. Islamic commanders and Christian pastors doubted Rusmanto and Hartono's interfaith efforts. Some accused Rusmanto of receiving bribes from the Christian community. Others viewed interfaith efforts as a form of betrayal to Islam. Yet Rusmanto maintains the value of these peacebuilding initiatives.

Several lessons about interfaith dialogue can be gleaned from this story. First, interfaith dialogue needs to involve all members—not simply those in the "moderate" camp and those in leadership positions. The efforts must go beyond formal panel discussions and enter the realms of relationship building and action. Furthermore, interfaith engagement needs not to water down the major tenets of any religion. To this day, Rusmanto and Hartono believe in the principle of *lakum dinukum waliyadin*, to you be your religion, to me my religion. Yet interfaith engagements must be done without a hidden agenda, for ulterior motives would set back the integrity of the engagement.

This journey also hinges on the belief that everyone has the capacity to become a peacemaker. Instead of merely serving and extending kindness to the "enemies," the Mennonite community invited the Hizbullah commander and troops as equal partners and indispensable agents of peace in the Indonesian society.

Throughout the process of Mennonite Indonesians' engagement with Islamic paramilitary members, Mennonite Indonesians have observed the ways in which global events and policies have impacted their relationships with their Muslim neighbors. In particular, they feel the brunt of Western counterterrorist operations that fuel Islamophobia and the grievances of Islamic militants. Instead of making it hard for these relationship-based processes to occur, Western governments should pay attention and learn from the model that Indonesian Mennonite community has shown in building bridges with the Hizbullah Front, through a contextualized interfaith engagement, a commitment to transforming oneself and the relationship, and an adherence to values such as openness, integrity, and trust.

Chapter 33

What Works to Prevent Violent Extremism

Lessons from Employment and Education Programs

Rebecca Wolfe and Keith Proctor

The crisis of youth is often depicted as a crisis of unemployment. An "economics of terrorism" narrative suggests that idle youth, lacking licit opportunities to earn a living, are a ready pool of recruits for the likes of the Taliban, Al-Qaeda, or al-Shabaab. Poverty, as a driver of conflict, combined with the booming population of young people in poor states, animates anxieties about the youth bulge, for which the guiding metaphor is, often, the "ticking bomb." Political violence is job seeking by another name. It is a narrative voiced in the editorial pages of the *New York Times* and the *Economist* and echoed by leading development officials, such as the president of the World Bank and the secretary-general of the United Nations.

In response, donors and governments have funded a range of both short-term and long-term economic reintegration programs: education initiatives, microbusiness lending projects, and vocational training programs with the implicit—and sometimes explicit—aim of expanding economic opportunity for the young and, in the process, dampening the appeal of armed militias and terrorists.

Unfortunately, there is little to commend such efforts. As the Overseas Development Institute (ODI) detailed in a 2013 report, there is a profound shortage of empirical evidence on the effect of employment creation on the stability of fragile states. Intervening years have done little to fill the evidence gap. While economic development is undoubtedly vital, and there is a rich body of research examining the negative impacts of unemployment on individuals and societies, the evidence linking unemployment to political violence—such as terrorism and violent extremism—remains limited. Indeed, the casual arrow may run the other way: violence may make people poor rather than poverty making them violent (Mercy Corps 2011).

Given the limited empirical evidence connecting employment and poverty to engaging in violent extremist movements, a question remained: What did drive young people to join these movements? Only by understanding this question, donors and implementers could better design programs to prevent violent extremism. Next we describe our efforts to understand the first question, which culminated in the report *Youth and Consequences*. In short, we found that the underlying drivers centered largely on grievances, particularly experiences of injustice. Since that report's release, we have focused on the second question: How can we reduce the lure of these violent groups? We end this chapter by summarizing recent research in Afghanistan and Somalia, two of the cases featured in *Youth and Consequences*, and provide some initial thinking about how to design programs to reduce support for political violence and violent extremist movements.

MORE JOBS = PEACEFUL YOUTH?

A growing body of evidence contradicts the assumptions driving bread-and-butter stabilization programs (Cramer 2010). In various contexts, studies conducted over the past decade have found little or no clear evidence that unemployment drives violence (Berman et al. 2011; Blair et al. 2013; Krueger and Maleckova 2003; Wolfe and Butichi 2013). In Somalia, for example, Mercy Corps surveyed youth as part of a baseline report for a USAID-funded secondary education program, which included elements of civic engagement, and found no relationship between job status and support for—or willingness to participate in—political violence (Wolfe and Butichi 2013).

We observed something similar in Helmand, Afghanistan, where a vocational training program that led to measurable and positive employment outcomes did not lead to significant changes in youth support for armed opposition groups. From 2011 to 2014, Mercy Corps implemented the Introducing New Vocational Education and Skills Training (INVEST) in Helmand program, targeting people aged fifteen to thirty-five. The INVEST program, funded by the UK Department for International Development (DFID), worked to increase youth employment by offering courses in technical vocational education and training (TVET) centers across the province.

Program evaluations suggest INVEST may have been the rare employment program that actually worked (Blattman and Ralston 2015). At the time of the evaluation, more than 22,000 students graduated from the program, including—remarkably—more than 6,500 young women. Most INVEST graduates—84 percent—found jobs.[1] Moreover, evaluations suggest that local markets have been pushed closer to equilibrium. For example, a shortage of motorcycle repairmen in the Lashkar Gah bazaar had inflated prices: it cost as much as 10,000 Afghanis—approximately USD 185—for simple repairs. According to locals, the addition of INVEST-trained repairmen has driven prices to a stable 2,000 or 3,000. This opened the market to new customers. And because 85 percent of INVEST graduates reported an increase in income, the demand increased for other services in the market.

However, according to surveys of program graduates, INVEST's employment successes did not translate into more peaceful graduates. Admittedly, stabilization was never an explicit goal of the program; rather it was part of the donor's overall strategy for Helmand. Nevertheless, the finding was striking in its contradiction of the assumptions behind economic theories of violence. Though most graduates were economically better off, INVEST did not result in a measurable drop in support for armed insurgents such as the Taliban.

NOT JOBLESSNESS, BUT INJUSTICE

During key informant interviews and focus group discussions conducted in Helmand and three regions of Somalia—Somaliland, Puntland, and South Central—in 2015, informants tended to cite noneconomic motives: to find meaning in a larger-than-self movement, to join a cause, to escape a humdrum existence, or to follow the example of an esteemed relative or friend. Among these informants, fighting was less a calculation of utility maximization. Rather, it tended to be more emotional, bound up in a desire for self-assertion or to prove one's worth. Often the decision appeared to be guided vengeance. "I did not join the Taliban because I was poor," said one former fighter, whose village mosque was destroyed during a Coalition bombing campaign. "I joined because I was angry. Because they (the West) wronged us."

According to informants in both Afghanistan and Somalia, joblessness alone is not what makes young people angry. Unemployment most could accept as circumstance, poor luck, the will of God. "Those are not things you fight against," said a young Afghan man. Corruption by public officials, however, makes them angry, as do discrimination and being cheated or humiliated. Early experiences of violence—being roughed up by security forces, for example—are associated with pushing young people into violent groups (Dahlberg 1998). Yet rarely is the choice to take up arms simply an economic one. Ideas and experiences appear to be more important. From El Salvador to Southeast Asia, studies found that a far more consistent predictor of political violence is injustice (Wood 2003). "Often you will hear people say joblessness is the biggest problem for the youth," said a young Somali woman. "And unemployment is a major problem, but underneath that is hopelessness and a belief that there is no fairness," she said. "Young people get angry and frustrated and look for something to do."

THE WOES OF WEAK STATES

Unfortunately, there is no shortage of injustice, unfairness, normalized violence, and corruption in the world's weak, fragile, and failing states, the exact places where violent extremist groups thrive (ICG 2016). Indeed, the drivers of political violence appear to be rooted in the social and political fabric of these places. The most marginalized youth describe being routinely cheated by unsavory employers or harassed by police, with no avenues for appeal. This marginalization is a persistent source of hostility. Though youth are a demographic majority in fragile states, they exist on the political and social fringe. Past research in Sierra Leone has found that young people who do not feel represented by a political party are two or three times more likely to take up arms (Humphreys and Weinstein 2008). Mercy Corps' analysis of Afrobarometer surveys in thirteen sub-Saharan African countries found poor governance, and specifically corruption, to be a consistent driver of violence (Tesfaye and Wolfe 2014). Similarly, DFID, in a twelve-country consultation with youth, found the single-most important issue cited by participants was governance (DFID 2013).

Both Afghanistan and Somalia sit at the bottom of international rankings of public perceptions of corruption. In Somalia, the children of elites study in foreign universities and cruise into posh government jobs, but most young people scramble to survive and lack the connections to do so. While al-Shabaab's radical turn, in recent years, has perhaps depressed its appeal, the group's rejection of clanism, with its aura of corruption, continues to resonate among Somali youth (Chatham House 2012; Puntland Development Research Centre 2013). Some Somali youth, dreaming of a better life in Europe, emigrate, making the long trek across the Sahara toward the Mediterranean's shores, risking death and enslavement on the way. Those who stay behind complain bitterly of systematic corruption, nepotism, and unresponsive government officials and clan leaders (Puntland Development Research Centre 2013). "We're outsiders in our own country," said one Somali youth. "We have no voice in Somalia, and therefore we have no future."

In Afghanistan, the perceived corruption of the central government provides insurgents the opportunity to play a familiar hand. The Islamists originally attracted popular support as a protest movement and state-building exercise. In the early 1990s, the Taliban imposed stability and rule of law after years of conflict among rival mujahedin. Animated by frustrations with a Tajik-dominated government viewed as both corrupt and anti-Pashtun, Talibs seized the capital, Kabul, in 1996 (Laub 2014). They are trying to do so again, and the Western-backed Kabul government, many believe, remains the insurgents' most effective recruiter. A 2013 survey of Afghans found corruption second only to chronic insecurity as the most frequently cited national challenge. According to Pashtun shura leaders in Lashkar Gah, the provincial capital of Helmand, bribery is a necessary part of accessing government services: getting their children a seat in school, for example, or accessing the formal courts, the Huquq. Even those who are no friends to the insurgents see national security forces as, at best, morally equivalent. "Troubled young men go in one of two directions," said one shura leader. "They either join the police or the Taliban."

FRUSTRATIONS: LONG-TERM INTERVENTIONS, NO SHORT-TERM OUTCOMES

The issues that drive young people to join these groups often require long-term solutions: addressing corruption and nepotism, improved security and protection, and discrimination. Systems and institutions are slow to change. Yet young people have needs now. While the vocational training programs and education programs mentioned previously are about helping young people with their futures, as well as good governance programs that look to increase transparency, accountability, and service delivery at various levels of government, these programs address few of young people's concerns in the present. On the other end of the spectrum are more humanitarian-oriented programs, like cash for work, that may help young people address immediate economic needs and do little to address the long-standing grievances they have that relate to their futures. Additionally, both these short-term handouts and long-term interventions may actually increase frustrations as expectations are not met. Short-term benefits often fade quickly; long-term interventions do not translate to real change soon enough.

MAKING MATTERS WORSE?

Admittedly, most vocational training programs do not aim to actually create jobs (in fact, the evidence that they do is quite limited) (Izzi 2013). Rather, in the anodyne language of development, they seek to boost "employability" by supplying vocational and skills trainings. But where demand for skilled workers does not rise in tandem with the increase in supply, such programs, in the words of one scholar, "serve as waiting rooms, not launching pads" (Hamilton 1994).

Where skills programs do not deliver, they may contribute to youth frustration. Hopes are raised and then dashed. Expectations matter. One theory behind the restlessness of many Arab youth is not simply that they are unemployed, but that widespread education raised their expectations about the future (Farooq, Bukhari, and Ahmed 2017). What may be important is not so much what people have, but the gap between what people get and what they expected. In some cases, poorly designed and/or poorly implemented employability programs may simply be making matters worse. A regional government official in Somalia's Puntland, who was critical of development programs raising unrealistic expectations, described it as "giving someone a glass to drink, but there's no water."

THE VOICELESS MAJORITY: CIVIC ENGAGEMENT PROGRAMS

The often-acute problem of frustrated expectations is not specific to vocational training or economic development programming. It is often endemic to other kinds of youth-focused development efforts. For example, it is also apparent in civic engagement programs, a staple youth engagement that seeks to ameliorate widespread feelings of political marginalization. NGOs train youth leaders in community mobilization, messaging, and leadership. Programs emphasize dialogue and community service while often throwing sports into the mix.

However, civically engaged youth are not predisposed to be passive or peaceful, particularly in societies suffering from widespread injustices, corruption, and experiences of marginalization. For instance, research among Arab youth found that attitudes toward political violence were not influenced, one way or the other, by political engagement (Kurtz and Gomez 2013). In Somalia, Mercy Corps surveys found that youth who were more civically engaged were more likely to have engaged in political violence, not less (Wolfe and Butichi 2013). These are the youth who want things to change.

In some cases, civic engagement programs—by providing an avenue for a political awakening among youth populations—may in fact be fanning the fire. A group of youth in Somalia, all part of a Mercy Corps' civic engagement program, praised the program. "It helped me find my voice," said a young woman. Many, however, were frustrated. Ossified political institutions—dominated by clan elders—were failing to integrate youth. "Young people are very angry," said a twenty-three-year-old young man, a village leader. He was appreciative of international efforts that gave him the tools to advocate for youth, but in the same breath he condemned the clan-dominated political structure. At the time, the Arab Spring—the mass youth-driven protests against Middle East and North African governments—was on his mind. East Africa hadn't experienced its Arab Spring yet, he said. "But we're getting there."

Critically, where programs are isolated from meaningful governance reforms, they are unlikely to reduce support for political violence. Indeed, such programs may be priming a confrontation. Traditional elites, in many places, will be unenthused about youthful "troublemakers" issuing demands, and lobbying for positions of responsibility, or improvements in youth services. Where existing political institutions lack the capacity—or the will—to incorporate new voices, youth empowerment may result in expectations outpacing changes in the status quo. Dissatisfied youth may seek alternative methods to express their frustration.

NOW WHAT?

A common refrain among policy makers is that while understanding what drives youth to join violent movements is important, what is truly critical is understanding how to prevent them from getting involved in the first place. Based on two recent program evaluations in Somalia and Afghanistan we are starting to have a clearer idea of how we might design programs to reduce young people's support and engagement in political violence.

Somalia

The data described previously were part of a baseline study of a USAID-funded project focused on secondary education and civic engagement of Somali youth titled Somalia Youth Leaders Initiative (SYLI).[2] Three years later we evaluated the program, first in Somaliland and then in Puntland and South Central. Based on that initial data, we adapted some of the project elements—specifically around civic engagement to address the concerns that not having an ability to use one's voice could have adverse consequences (Tesfaye 2016, Tesfaye, McDougal, and Maclin 2018). The civic engagement component included ways for young people to contribute to their community—a hands-on experience of influence, taking the advice from *Youth and Consequences* directly. For example, in Puntland, youth conducted culture and arts promotion events with assistance from Mercy Corps and the Ministry of Labor, Youth, and Sports (MoLYS). These one-day art and culture events taught Somali youth how to use art to support peace, revived the arts culture in Somalia, and used art and literature as a tool to build community cohesion. Government delegates, including Sanag governor, Baran and Eyl mayors, and members of Parliament, as well as other community members, attended these events.

Across all three regions, our main results were quite consistent: those who were in secondary school and participated in the civic engagement component were significantly less likely to *support* violence compared to those who did not participate in the project. In Somaliland, they were also less likely to *participate* in violence (we were not able to ask about participation in Puntland and South Central). For example, in Somaliland, those who were in this combined intervention were 13 percent less likely to engage in political violence and 22 percent less likely to support political violence. In short, combining education and civic engagement programs appeared to significantly reduce support for political violence, and, where we were able to measure it, participation as well.

Why was the combination of secondary education plus civic engagement more successful at reducing support for political violence than secondary education alone? In the earlier study, we speculated that the civic education component provided a way for youth to see that nonviolent change was possible. In the follow-up study, we asked a number of questions to better identify why. Was it due to learning about nonviolent change or something else? Our study found that the combined intervention increased confidence in nonviolent change, and this helps explain the relationship between the intervention and reduced support for political violence. The combined intervention of the program also reduced people's pessimism about their future livelihood opportunities, and this contributed to the reduced support for violence, as well. While these explanations also help us understand the education only results, these findings were stronger in the case of the combined interventions. Moreover, we see that the scope for this reduced support for violence resulted from both short- and long-term shifts, including changed attitudes about their immediate environment (i.e., beliefs in nonviolent change) but also about their future livelihoods (i.e., potential employment after graduation).

Afghanistan

Previously we discussed an impact evaluation of a vocational training program in Helmand that, while economically successful, did little to change attitudes related to political violence. We decided to replicate this study in Kandahar but added a twist—we wanted to compare cash transfers to vocational training to be able to disentangle the economic effects of training from other aspects of training (e.g., working with others, softer skills learned as part of the training). There is a growing debate on the value of cash over other types of interventions, including training (as people can buy training with cash if they need it) (Blattman and Ralston 2015). In this study, we had four conditions: vocational training, an unconditional cash transfer (one-time transfer of $75), both vocational training and cash, and control (Kurtz, Tesfaye, and Wolfe 2018).

As with the previous Helmand study, we found similar results with vocational training; while there were positive economic impacts of vocational training six to nine months post program, it did little to change support for political violence. Cash on its own swayed opinion in support of the government compared to armed opposition groups in the short term; yet after the one-time disbursement of cash was spent and there was no follow-on, there was a slight backlash effect—with support moving toward armed opposition groups. In contrast, in the combined condition, we found our largest change in support for political violence: a 17 percent reduction six to nine months post program. Despite fifteen years of conflict, and intimate knowledge of the warring factions, the people's opinions appeared to be remarkably responsive to programming.

As in the Somalia study, why did the combined treatment—in this case cash and vocational training—have both the most positive and robust effects? We found that perceptions of government, particularly local government, improved. However, this was only true in the combined condition. While the cash was not explicitly attributed to the government, other research has demonstrated that people credit their local governments for bringing aid to their community (Dietrich and Mahmud 2017; Evans, Holtemeyer, and Kosec 2018). However, a one-time cash transfer wasn't enough to sway opinions. Additionally, while the vocational training was in government schools, the benefits of the vocational training were not realized until six to nine months later. The combined interventions helped people with basic needs while also giving them skills for the future. It signaled that the government understood their needs, thus improving perceptions of government performance and responsiveness, while also swaying support from the Taliban to the government.

A PATH FORWARD: LESSONS FROM SOMALIA AND AFGHANISTAN

Pairing Short- and Long-Term Interventions:

In both Somalia and Afghanistan, the programs paired short- and long-term interventions. That pairing was more successful in reducing support for violence. Why is this pairing of short- and long-term interventions important? While understanding the underlying drivers is important to reduce support and participation in the long term, there are also more proximate causes that may prompt someone to join a violent group—such as financial incentives, food, security, and a trigger, such as a recent bombing or security incident. By focusing on the long term, we may never experience the security and stability needed for those interventions to gain traction and succeed. Development interventions are often best suited for preventing future conflict, not reducing existing violence (Zürcher 2017). However, short-term solutions are not sustainable. Once the intervention ends, we risk backlash effects, as we saw in the cash-only condition in the Afghanistan study. By pairing short- and long-term interventions, we stabilize a situation while addressing the long-term reasons for violence so that after the "band-aid" is gone, the additional reasons why people are drawn to support violence are addressed—or at least there is progress on those issues.

Interventions Must Be Multidimensional:

Not only do people have short- and long-term motivations for becoming involved in violence, but there are also a host of issues and concerns that may drive them to engage in or support political violence. These may be ideological, political, self-interested, and/or altruistic, such as the desire to protect one's community or identity group. Often, these motivations interact with one another and with people's identities to determine this support. Consequently, as the findings from this research confirm, interventions that focus on only one potential motivation for participating in violence are much less likely to be successful. Interventions to address violence therefore need to respond to multiple motivations. At the same time, while the reasons people participate in violence are multidimensional, it does not mean that the same interventions need to address all of them. Certain pairings of interventions may be more impactful than others. For example, in the Afghanistan study, both interventions were economic but addressed both short- and long-term reasons for becoming involved in violence. Other interventions may have borne fruit. For example, an intervention pairing a protection component with the provision of services—such as food, water, and economic support—could reduce an individual's physical vulnerability and exposure to a violent group while also reducing the basic needs that can make recruitment attractive in the first place.

Address Perceptions of Government:

A common finding across both studies was the importance of perceptions of government. In both studies, perceptions of government provide some explanation of decreases in support for political violence. In Afghanistan, people who received both cash and vocational training saw the local government as more effective and responsive; in Somalia, perceptions of government explain the reduction in support for political violence for those enrolled in secondary education. These findings align with our research in *Youth and Consequences*, which found that anger related to injustices and grievances was the preeminent reason people cited for becoming involved in political violence. Programs that shift these feelings of grievance, where governments are either directly or indirectly addressing concerns, are likely to have strong results. Moreover, it is clear that there are multiple ways of addressing perceptions of government.

An important principle of international aid is to promote local and national government ownership and visibility in the implementation of development projects. When development actors bypass governments to create alternative service structures, they undermine formal institutions and erode public confidence. Our research suggests that more indirect engagement by government can also work. Where government is not seen as the implementer and director of the aid, but as an effective agent and partner in an international effort to help their constituencies, the state can still gain credibility as a consequence of the interventions.

CONCLUSION

What these results illustrate is that there are successful interventions—largely in the development space—that can reduce support for violent extremist groups. And these results were realized in some of the most challenging environments where violent extremist groups have thrived for years. This provides hope; as we look to prevent violent extremist groups from taking hold, there are lessons on which to draw on for designing programs.

In particular, these results may demand that development practitioners be more deliberate in designing multifaceted approaches. Sometimes layering programs can have an additive effect, as we have seen. Addressing short-term needs can create the space for long-term effects to gain traction and, importantly, to stick—ideally, measurable change should be observable months later, not simply immediately post-program. In some cases, behavioral change requires more than new knowledge but tangible and near-term opportunities for participants to practice new roles, shift perspectives, and gain confidence in fragile state institutions.

While a multilayered approach can create the space for positive effects to take hold, we need to be thoughtful about how such approaches are designed. It is not always true that "more is more." Multipronged approaches may cancel each other out. Furthermore, the effects that we do observe may not simply reflect the intended result. An economic intervention may have a political effect, as we witnessed. However, while programmatic theories of change tend to assume spillover effects of this kind, they should not be taken for granted. Sometimes we get them, sometimes not. This demands a critical approach to design. Particularly in funding environments of shrinking aid dollars, we need to avoid a kitchen-sink mentality to design interventions on the basis of a robust, evidence-based rationale. The work presented previously provides some initial thoughts for how as community we design and develop that evidence base for how to prevent violent extremism and a road map for how we continue refining our understanding of what drives people to join these groups and how we stop them.

Chapter 34

A Child-Focused Perspective on the Preventing and Countering Violent Extremism Paradigm

Matthew J. O. Scott

The preventing and countering violent extremism (P/CVE) discourse has preoccupied the foreign policy and security sectors for decades, largely avoiding the international humanitarian and development communities. This discourse suffers from the lack of a universally accepted definition. Despite the fact that the term is included in many international policy directives—including UN Security Council Resolution 2178—there is little consensus or clarity to define it.

Many bilateral donors, including the United States and the United Kingdom, approach the problem of P/CVE while holding several unhelpful presuppositions. The first assumption is that young people are *the problem*. So many violent extremists are young, so the theory goes; therefore, the majority of young people must either be violent extremists or be vulnerable to recruitment. Promoting deradicalization becomes the main preoccupation with this assumption. The available data suggest, however, that an emphasis on the violence of a few while overlooking the nonviolence of the majority risks further endangering peaceful actors. The majority of young people in conflict-affected contexts reject violence actively on their own, without influence from outside actors.

A second unhelpful assumption is that young people are more vulnerable to recruitment and extremist organizations when they lack livelihood alternatives. Because there are so few jobs, so the theory goes, young people have few alternatives but to join organizations that exalt violence. If idle hands are the devil's workshop, then give young people work and you will crowd out malevolent actors. The available data suggest, however, that poverty is not a principal driver of extremism. The data also suggest that livelihoods programs alone will do very little to disrupt the recruitment of violent extremists and in some cases may do harm (Mercy Corps 2015).

Most nongovernmental organizations (NGOs) working with young people in conflict-affected contexts for the past several decades have not considered intersections of their work with the global P/CVE agenda until recently. In 2017, however, geopolitical trends and in particular the security considerations of the largest aid donors are locked into a collision course with humanitarian and development principles.

World Vision is a child-focused, community-empowering, Christian NGO working in dozens of contexts affected by violent extremism. In many of those contexts, World Vision empowers children and adolescents as positive-change agents within their communities. Whether through social accountability or livelihoods programming or empowering children and adolescents as peacebuilders, World Vision's peacebuilding objectives have a clear focus. The organization's priority is helping communities weave a fabric of resilience throughout a community, so they can resolve their own conflicts, build capacities to heal broken relationships, and nourish more just systems and structures. In all projects, programs, and advocacy, World Vision aims to integrate conflict-sensitivity and peacebuilding and provide significant contributions to community-based peacemaking in selected operational contexts (World Vision 2008).

World Vision's own evidence and other organizations have identified contributing factors that can move individuals or groups from grievance to mobilization, often shaped closely by local and contextualized dynamics that create a permissive environment for extremist groups. A complex interaction of sociopolitical inequality, underemployment, family security, and social marginalization can be exploited by extremists who recruit followers by wielding compelling narratives as well as material and social incentives. For example, Mercy Corps recently identified in research in Jordan that a desire to protect families and communities was a much stronger driver of extremist violence than religious doctrine (Mo'alla 2016). Extremist recruiters often mix together gender power archetypes, criminal intent, and distorted religious narratives not limited to a single faith.

A community-focused approach to peacebuilding is mindful of these factors but assumes a human security paradigm. Community-based peacebuilding rejects criminality and violence as viable options but does not aim at improving state security. While there may be good governance goals embedded in community-based peacebuilding, these efforts are usually aimed at improving local and sometimes informal governance structures. The informal or ad hoc governance structures may in some contexts be populated by people advocating violence, whether motivated by criminal or religious intent. In these contexts, most organizations working with young peacebuilders are committed to empowering young people to design and implement programming that promote a culture of peace and disarm any dominant culture of violence through persuasion rather than coercion.

Adding a further layer of complexity, most multimandate international NGOs like World Vision are also committed to upholding International Humanitarian Law (IHL). Principle 3 of the Code of Conduct for the International Red Cross and Red Crescent Movement and NGOs in Disaster Relief reads: "Aid will not be used to further a particular political or religious standpoint" (ICRC 1994). World Vision is a signatory to the similar SPHERE standard, and internal organizational policies likewise forbid proselytism and promotion of political views.

These twin commitments—to the well-being of local communities in their own terms and to IHL—put many international NGOs in a difficult dilemma. Bilateral donor funding is often directly or indirectly tied to P/CVE strategies and objectives. Sometimes these donors are the only substantial sources of financial support for peacebuilding programming. Some NGOs refuse such P/CVE "tainted" funding on principle, pursuing funding instead raised directly from private individuals. Other NGOs accept P/CVE-related funding while maintaining a loyalty to the communities where they work rather than a Western government's security objectives. Many communities do not care for or do not have time for such nuance. Many also resent their communities being labeled as potential extremists or "terrorists." Most grassroots peacebuilders are grateful for any investment in peace in their community regardless of what apparent strings are attached by the donor agency.

On the horns of this dilemma, many international NGOs (INGOs) strive for a kind of "principled pragmatism" that is less about balancing competing stakeholders and more about maintaining a laser focus on the desired end result, namely, more peaceful communities. Some INGOs, including World Vision, ensure their alignment to community peace objectives by investing deeply in context analysis and using guidelines that calibrate programming to the security particularities of the local context.

In World Vision's case, the organization has trained thousands of staff in the "Do No Harm" framework and generated several tools to carry out conflict analysis (World Vision International n.d.). Most INGOs working in contexts of violent extremism invest in understanding their local programming context in considerable detail.

World Vision also developed a tool to understand the security tradeoffs of certain contexts where armed violence is prevalent. World Vision's HISS-CAM tool guides humanitarian and development workers through a deliberate weighing of the considerations that inform any project activity in a complex security environment:

- *H*umanitarian imperative
- *I*mpartiality and independence
- *S*ecurity and protection

- *S*ustainability
- *C*ompelling aim
- *A*ppropriate adaptation and adequate information
- *M*inimal negative impact

Although the conflict analysis tools and HISS-CAM were not designed to deal with the dilemma presented by P/CVE funding, they currently function as proxy decision filters for World Vision on whether or not to pursue such funding in the first place, and if so, how to implement programs in a way consistent with the organization's policies. World Vision's forthcoming P/CVE policy will seek to translate some of the above-mentioned foundational positions and principles into guidance for funding offices, field offices, and staff.

In addition to these principled policy commitments, World Vision brings the field experience and impact evidence of working with child and adolescent peacebuilders. Contrary to the dominant donor theory of change, the field evidence points to the overwhelmingly positive yet unrecognized force that youth exert toward peace in their communities.

A 2015 multiagency evaluation of youth peacebuilding efforts in Colombia, Nepal, and Democratic Republic of Congo (DRC) found four clear areas of impact and eleven enabling factors (McGill and O'Kane 2015). The same research identified three important recommendations for donors and practitioners to support youth peacebuilders. Peacebuilders between the ages of fifteen and thirty:

- became more aware and active citizens for peace,
- increased peaceful cohabitation and reduced discrimination,
- reduced violence in communities, and
- increased support to all vulnerable groups.

Eleven different factors can hinder or enable the impact of child and youth peacebuilding efforts:

1. Attitudes, motivation, and commitment of children and youth and their organizations
2. Capacity, knowledge, skills, and experience of children and youth
3. Family attitudes and support
4. Cultural attitudes, beliefs, and practices
5. Key stakeholders' motivation, commitment, and support
6. Awareness raising, sensitization, and campaigns among key stakeholders
7. Culture, theater, arts, and sports engaged for children and youth
8. Existence and implementation of government laws, policies, strategies, and provisions

9. Financial and material support
10. Income generation for marginalized groups
11. Conflict, political instability, and insecurity

The overarching recommendations of that evaluation were to:

1. engage children as peacebuilders from a young age to ensure continuity and increased impact;
2. encourage multipronged and multistakeholder efforts supporting children and youth peacebuilding to multiply and amplify peacebuilding impact; and
3. engage with children and youth as partners in formal and informal governance and peace structures in a wide range of contexts, not only those affected by armed conflict.

This body of evidence runs against the dominant assumptions of the P/CVE narrative outlined in the beginning of this chapter. In addition to the recommendations from the Nepal, Colombia, and DRC examples, World Vision is committed to several important principles when working with children and adolescents vulnerable to the allure of violent extremism:

- Life skills, vocational training, and other livelihoods programming must include peace skills training, including empathy, tolerance, conflict resolution, and social cohesion.
- Young people should be treated as both current and potential leaders for peace rather than (potential) violent extremists.
- Children under the age of eighteen are prohibited from participation in armed forces of any kind.
- Peace programs should not discriminate by assuming that any one religion or culture is inherently more violence-prone than others.
- The best ideas to counter violent narratives within a particular group come from young people themselves.
- When working with faith leaders, INGOs must avoid instrumentalizing them for their influence but rather regard them as equal partners in pursuit of peace.
- Fostering collaboration and alliances between civil society and faith-based groups within countries and transnationally is essential to multiplying peace impact.
- Advocate against overly broad counterterrorism or materiel support measures that impede life-saving operations or risk falsely criminalizing the legitimate humanitarian and peacebuilding work of INGO staff at risk of criminal prosecution if assistance is diverted.

The humanitarian principles and human security paradigm on which many INGOs base their work are important departure points for World Vision from many of the core assumptions of the still-vague world of P/CVE. The evidence of what works is another. Together these form a series of considerations for donors wanting to support the empowerment of young people seeking peace in places wracked by violent extremism:

- Poverty alleviation, especially for the most vulnerable in the most difficult places, is still the dominant paradigm in the world of aid. Relabeling or diversifying aid funds toward P/CVE objectives has a strong potential to undermine the integrity of the entire global aid enterprise.
- Clarify the intent and meaning of P/CVE or counterterrorism legislation and the intentions of their funding and the conditions under which they expect partners to implement. Many restrictions have negative impact on NGO operations in terms of operating space, ability to access, get funding, ensure staff safety, and manage security risks, local partners, and communities. Without guidance on how to handle sensitive issues (e.g., dealing with proscribed groups), INGOs avoid uncertainty or subjectivity around interpretation and application. The net effect of the growing body of P/CVE legislation is risk aversion and a stifling of innovation.
- INGOs should be given leeway to steer away from certain donors in certain contexts. INGOs and their partners already assume risk in contexts affected by violent extremism. Mitigating risks includes conducting due diligence to assess CVE available funding and whether it has the potential to compromise humanitarian principles, operating safety, and the safety of our beneficiaries.
- Dialogue with NGOs on P/CVE is vital to understand our operating environments and concerns and to constructively work together towards solutions. The humanitarian imperative should override all other concerns where possible.
- Healthy interdepartmental dialogue within donor governments on P/CVE helps avoid inconsistency and duplication.
- Open political space is essential to explore and address challenges and share practical experiences and examples/dilemmas faced by INGOs. The ability to share program evaluations publicly without being concerned about the consequences of future restrictions in funding or having a reporting obligation is very helpful.

There are encouraging signs that the international conversation on P/CVE is becoming more nuanced and overcoming some of the unhelpful assumptions about young people in particular that have framed the debate. UN Security Council Resolution 2250 (UNSC 2015) represents an important policy recognition of the case made here. Among many recommendations, the resolution encourages UN member states to "engage relevant local communities and non-governmental actors in developing strategies to counter the violent extremist narrative that can incite terrorist acts, address the conditions conducive to the spread of violent extremism, which can be conducive to terrorism, including by empowering youth, families, women, religious, cultural and education leaders, and all other concerned groups of civil society and adopt tailored approaches to countering recruitment to this kind of violent extremism and promoting social inclusion and cohesion." Resolution 2250 includes twenty-one other operative paragraphs that make a strong case for a more positive, holistic, grassroots, and youth-focused approach to the problem of P/CVE. The available data suggest that this empowerment paradigm is much more successful in addressing P/CVE, particularly when it does not bear the P/CVE label.

World Vision does not yet have a P/CVE policy in large part because the organization defines security in terms of the well-being of children, their families, and communities. This focus on children in communities lays aside many of the state-centric security assumptions of the P/CVE paradigm in favor of a human security approach. World Vision is committed to a youth peacebuilding approach to the problem of violent extremism on principle and because the evidence suggests it is the most effective.

Chapter 35

Putting Human Dignity at the Center

An Alternative Perspective on "Countering Violent Extremism"

Aaron Chassy and Nell Bolton

Since its founding during World War II in 1943, Catholic Relief Services (CRS) has confronted violence perpetrated under the banner of many ideologies and causes, by states as well as nonstate actors. Since 2014, for example, CRS has reinforced the resilience over 758,000 rural West Africans by, among other things, strengthening the institutional capacity of local governance, the degradation of which has been a major driver of religious extremism and violent conflict in the region. Our response remains consistently guided by a commitment to safeguard lives, uphold human dignity, and promote integral human development, which is the ability of *each* person and *all* people to realize their full potential.

Guided by these principles, CRS and our local partners seek to nurture a just peace: building and restoring healthy relationships while also pursuing transformation of inequitable institutions and systems that are the drivers of violent conflict. In Central African Republic, for example, the CRS-led Interfaith Peacebuilding Partnership forges a foundation for sustainable peace by engaging key institutions and individuals in building social cohesion within and among different identity groups, addressing economic disparities through mutually beneficial livelihoods programming, and seeking to end the cycle of violence through provision of peace education, trauma healing, and gender-based violence prevention.

In practice, a commitment to human dignity of all people and the common good of all communities means honoring and supporting the voice and agency of the people we serve. Perhaps nowhere is this more relevant than in work with young people: youth are often perceived as being easily manipulated by state and nonstate actors to participate in political violence, yet CRS views youth as agents of change rather than simply as potential perpetrators of violence. Such an approach has achieved significant results at the individual, relational, and structural levels:

- In the West Bank and Gaza, over eighty youth ambassadors for nonviolence have worked with local civic organizations to promote peace by producing their own youth-led contextual analysis reports, leading creative initiatives to address identified conflict issues and influencing municipal government leadership to focus on addressing high priority issues.
- In Bosnia, young leaders are carrying out nearly 100 interethnic community initiatives, visiting one another's houses of worship, listening to and grappling with one another's group narratives of the war, and serving on municipal working groups for reconciliation.
- In Northern Ghana, young peace ambassadors used a variety of creative methods to mobilize and influence their peers—including those most likely to act as agitators—to promote peaceful elections and to contribute to conflict early warning systems.

CRS developed these principled approaches after a long period of reflection following the Rwandan genocide in 1994 when, like many other international organizations, it realized only too late the full scale of the horror that eventually unfolded. Recently, however, CRS has found its approaches to be in tension with the rise in recent years of the prominence of programming, which has been designed not so much to address root causes of violent conflict, improve social relationships, or maximize human development, but to "counter violent extremism" (CVE). While preventing and reducing political or ideological violence is indeed of grave importance, particularly to the poor and vulnerable residents of conflict-ravaged countries that bear its heaviest costs, CRS has been reluctant to adopt the CVE-influenced programming approaches, for reasons that will be described next. In this chapter, we first provide an introduction to the key principles, framework, strategies, and approaches used by CRS to prevent and reduce violence. Through this prism, we then analyze and critique CVE as a preferred programmatic response for many international donors operating in conflict-prone environments.

CRS'S APPROACH TO PREVENTING AND REDUCING VIOLENCE

The Foundation: Guiding Principles

The *dignity of the human person* is one of several principles of Catholic social teaching (CST) that guide CRS's work. Others include the promotion of the *common good*, or the social conditions—"economic, political, material and cultural"—that affect people's ability to realize their full potential and human dignity; the common good calls for all actions to be made with the welfare of the whole society in mind. At the same time, CRS adopts a preferential *option for the poor*, or a "weighted concern to the needs of the poorest and most vulnerable . . . in every economic, political and social decision" (CRS 2008). That is, CRS gives particular attention to promoting the dignity and rights of those people who are most marginalized in a given society. The principle of *subsidiarity*, meanwhile, states that no higher-level authoritative institution should intrude in lower-level initiatives to the point of overtaking them or corroding the capacity of actors at the lower level to address those challenges. After all, the people who are closest to a problem have the greatest interest in solving it and the best understanding of how it should be solved.

CRS also adheres to international humanitarian principles. *Impartiality* allows CRS to provide assistance on the basis of need alone, regardless of origin, race, creed, ethnicity, or political affiliation. CRS also must retain its *independence* in order to conduct development programs and humanitarian response in a manner consistent with our guiding principles and our mission to alleviate human suffering. As a signatory to the Code of Conduct for the Red Cross and Red Crescent Movement and NGOs in Disaster Relief, CRS endeavors to avoid acting as an instrument of government foreign policy.[1] Impartiality and independence are the basis of CRS's acceptance by local communities.

Particularly during violent conflict, CRS strives to *do no harm* or minimize harm by identifying ways CRS and partners can strengthen local capacities for peace, rather than allowing assistance to inadvertently exacerbate the conflict.

The Framework: Integral Human Development

CST inspired CRS to develop the Integral Human Development (IHD) framework which promotes the good of the *whole* person and of *all* people (Heinrich, Leege, and Miller 2008). CRS' approach to justice and peacebuilding uses the IHD framework to prioritize indigenous nonviolent approaches to conflict transformation and reconciliation. This approach responds to the root causes of violent conflict, including unjust relationships and structures, consistent with IHD. In fact, IHD informs all of CRS's programming so that taken together, it contributes to achieving the goals of CRS's Global Strategy: "(to increase) marginalized communities' . . . access and have more influence on the systems and structures that facilitate greater social equity and inclusion."

The Strategy: Social Cohesion + Social Justice Produces a Durable Peace

As described earlier, CRS's justice and peacebuilding programming strengthens *horizontal* social cohesion while also transforming *vertical* social cohesion, or the quality of the relationship between people and their governments. Working along both of these axes directly addresses the marginalization, exclusion, and injustices that drive violent conflict. For CRS, social cohesion and social justice are mutually reinforcing. They form a "virtuous circle" in which greater horizontal equity, or social justice, among different identity groups improves horizontal social cohesion. Similarly, healthier relationships among groups improve their willingness to work together to pursue mutually beneficial aims.

As citizens find common cause in issues that connect them (e.g., increased access to public information, resources, and decision making), they are more willing to collaborate in influencing decision makers to respond to their demands. Decision makers are more likely to respond when these groups have formed a critical mass, a constituency for the desired social change, which gives them more power to make such demands. As decision makers become more willing to respond to citizen demands, the quality of governance increases, which, in turn, improves vertical social cohesion. More effective governance, in turn, mitigates social tensions among different groups.

CRS's signature "3B" approach (binding, bonding, and bridging) improves both horizontal and vertical social cohesion by progressing strategically through changes at the individual, relational, and, potentially, the sociopolitical or structural level as follows:

Binding

The first B, binding, creates space for personal reflection and self-transformation. It includes a focus on strengthening emotional resilience through healing and support for recovery from trauma already endured as well as activating personal leadership capacities (Brakarsh 2009; CRS 2016). Drawing on spiritual resources, this work often engages religious and traditional leaders, whose influence and moral authority then attract others from their respective identity groups.

Bonding

Bonding strengthens relationships and fosters mutual understanding among members of the same identity groups (Colletta and Cullen 2000). In the relative safety of a single-identity setting, they are able to examine critically their narrative around the violent conflict and their grievances. They reflect on (i) what happened, (ii) how it affected them as a group, and (iii) what they are willing to do to resolve the conflict and to prevent it from reoccurring. CRS recognizes that there is great diversity even within a single identity group, making it all the more important to recognize and motivate the marginalized to find and use their voice.

Bridging

Bridging provides opportunities for conflict groups to collaborate on issues of common concern (Colletta and Cullen 2000). Conflict groups codesign and coimplement connector activities to build, restore, or reinforce healthy relationships while prioritizing the role of the marginalized in these activities. Connector activities enable them to transform their "right attitudes" into "right action," putting into practice the principles of mutual tolerance and acceptance. Here again, when working with religious communities, CRS fosters greater mutual understanding of one another's sacred traditions and joint discovery of spiritual resources for peace. Intergroup dialogue shifts the focus on the causes of conflict so that they are perceived more as concrete, resolvable issues than historical, intractable ones.

The 3Bs can also advance social justice. Increased levels of intergroup cohesion allow group leaders to mobilize their respective members to work together to influence key actors, addressing grievances that may (re)escalate into violent conflict if ignored or if instrumentalized by state and nonstate conflict entrepreneurs. As a constituency for social change, they can leverage their political power and use their collective voice to:

- increase the political will among key actors to design and implement more effective, equitable public policy;
- create more meaningful opportunities for civic participation, which reinforces healthy relationships among the constituency's different identity groups; and
- improve institutional performance by government structures so that they are more accountable, transparent, and responsive.

Thus, for example, the thousands of men, women, boys, and girls engaged in 3B activities through CRS programming in Mindanao, southern Philippines, reported changes not only in their own attitudes and in their intergroup communication but also in the functioning of local conflict resolution processes. In this project, mobilizing traditional and religious leaders resulted in the resolution of thirty-five land conflict cases, as well as the creation of four municipal networks and interagency working groups to increase coordination within municipalities pursuing durable policy solutions in response to shared challenges (Bolton and Leguro 2016).

In Bosnia, CRS has successfully engaged the leadership of over 30 percent of the country's municipalities, along with key influential parliamentarians and political party leaders, to commit publicly to working for reconciliation. CRS is now working with these municipalities' mayors to ensure that their action plans and budgets include concrete initiatives to advance this commitment. Such initiatives include, for example, housing and livelihoods support for return of minorities to their prewar communities and integration of interethnic collaboration in economic growth strategies. This progress builds on a broad and deep foundation of engaging citizens in critical self-reflection, intra- and intergroup dialogue, and joint action. Project activities support war victims as they work through their trauma, understand one another's narratives, and speak out together in favor of reconciliation. Activities also help young people address their secondary trauma, build relationships across divisions, and embrace a collective future.

The template for achieving social change, rooted in IHD and driven by social justice, reinforces both horizontal and vertical social cohesion while also increasing equity. It underscores the importance of recognizing that peacebuilding and good governance serve both as important means and as ends to preventing violent conflict.

Key Approach: Integrate Youth Voice and Agency with Economic Opportunity

CRS's guiding principles and commitment to nonviolent conflict transformation—transforming unjust systems and practices, reconciling communities, and promoting healthy societal relationships—apply also in our programming with youth. In 2015, there were 1.2 billion youth aged fifteen to twenty-four years[2] globally, accounting for one out of every six people worldwide. Over 88 percent of these young people live in developing countries, and, in many places, they represent between 30 and 50 percent of the population. As such, their concerns and aspirations are particularly relevant to realizing a just and sustainable peace.

Since 2007, CRS has implemented more than one hundred youth-focused or youth-serving projects. These programs are rooted in IHD and use the ecological framework, which recognizes that individuals live within families or kin, who live in communities that exist within a wider social system. To maximize both the level of impact and the likelihood of sustainability, CRS and its partners work with key stakeholders at all levels: the youth themselves, their household and community, service providers, the private sector, and structures in the political and cultural environment. CRS's youth programming gives careful consideration to the transitions that mark the milestones in youth development: from childhood to adolescence, from adolescence to adulthood, and from school to the workforce. As well, CRS youth programming addresses the systems and structures that affect youth in these transitions: legal, socioeconomic, and political systems; cultural norms; health and educational institutions; and religion.

Guided by these frameworks and principles, CRS works with youth in the following three programming pathways, which have constructively channeled the energies of hundreds of thousands of youth who previously felt they had little control over their environment or their future:

Economic Strengthening

Recognizing the daunting livelihood challenges facing youth. There are 71 million unemployed youth worldwide, and 169 million young workers are living in poverty (ILO 2015); in the next ten years, over a billion youth will enter the labor market worldwide, yet only 40 percent of these are expected to be able to enter currently existing jobs (Goldin 2015). CRS in Central America has adapted a highly successful model originally developed in Harlem, New York, in the late 1970s known as YouthBuild to reach young people, ages fifteen to twenty-four, from highly violent communities who are not in school and/or are unemployed (CRS 2017).

The YouthBuilders program provides life and job skills training, vocational training, school reentry, job placement, entrepreneurship training, and social services for at-risk boys and girls. The model uses community projects to help young people acquire critical leadership, service, and job-preparedness skills while working on projects in their communities.

CRS piloted YouthBuilders in Central America between 2009 and 2011. Since 2011, the program has continued in El Salvador, reaching more than 5,000 young people with documented results—by the end of the program, 80 percent get a job, start a business, or go back to school. In addition, CRS has developed a youth-specific focus for Savings and Internal Lending Communities—or SILC—and emergency disaster–risk reduction and is beginning to incorporate youth-friendly approaches in agriculture value chains.

Youth Learning

While livelihood opportunities are critical for youth, CRS also recognizes the importance of supporting youth to realize their full potential and develop their beliefs and values. As illustrated in the YouthBuild example, CRS integrates life skills capacity building in its youth programs to help them make appropriate life choices. While often characterized as "soft" skills—for example, leadership, negotiation, appropriate behavior in the workplace—these skills require the most significant shift for youth: from attitudinal to behavior change. They are key for youth to develop and maintain healthy relationships, as highlighted next.

Peacebuilding and Good Governance

Peacebuilding with youth is based on the fundamental premise that youth, even in the poorest and most violent contexts, have the power to change the direction of their lives and that of their communities. CRS's work addresses underlying causes of violence and creates the conditions for greater equity and social cohesion, supporting at-risk youth to:

- transform their *relationships* with peers, family, and community;
- influence their *environment*, including policies, institutions, and governance;
- develop the *knowledge, skills, and attitudes* necessary to serve as change agents; and
- replace the *motivating factors* behind negative behaviors with practical and positive experiences.

These programming pathways are mutually reinforcing: a study with a sample of the out-of-school adolescents participating in CRS economic strengthening and life skills programming across twelve districts of Zimbabwe found that self-efficacy ($p < .001$), self-esteem ($p < .01$), and hope ($p < .01$) were measured to be significantly higher than for a small sample of adolescents who did not participate in CRS's SILC. In CRS's work in El Salvador, described earlier, participants not only acquired employment or started small businesses, but they also donated over 200,000 hours of community service. And, school-aged children in coastal Kenya have led dozens of advocacy initiatives against child marriage, complementing and spurring efforts to address the economic, cultural, and structural drivers of this issue.

WHY COUNTERING VIOLENT EXTREMISM (AND MILITARIZATION, MORE BROADLY) IS A CONCERN

A significant challenge for CRS in the past sixteen years has been the increasing militarization of US foreign policy and of foreign assistance in particular. The military has expanded into the space traditionally reserved for humanitarian and development actors while capturing an increasing share of scarce funding resources. Funding for US democracy, human rights, and governance programs, for example, has declined 38 percent since 2009 (Igoe 2015; Shane 2015). The results have been predictable: an overreliance on using militarized approaches to respond to complex crises, particularly ones involving violent conflict.

In this landscape, CVE programming is designed primarily to support military or political objectives, such as mitigating risks to the United States and preserving regional "stability," rather than protecting local populations, never mind strengthening their resilience or addressing their development priorities. And yet, CVE is increasingly prevalent in US Agency for International Development (USAID) and similar programming, especially in countries with fragile states. When integrated with humanitarian response and development assistance, CVE's security objectives overshadow the aims of alleviating human suffering, addressing poverty, and building peace, in ways that we find deeply problematic.

Compromising to Our Core Principles

First, the CVE enterprise, as conceived, funded, and implemented, stands in contrast to CRS's commitment to upholding human dignity. Domestically and internationally, CVE programming focuses nearly exclusively on *Islamic* extremism—despite the fact that, for example, in the United States since 9/11 and through 2015, white (Christian) extremists have killed twice as many Americans as Muslim extremists have—and on young people as potential or actual participants in violent extremism (Shane 2015).

The CVE lens thus reduces people to whichever aspect of their identity—age, religion, socioeconomic status (more on this later), national origin—brands them as being "at-risk." This is, to an extent, a continuation of the actual or perceived "presumption of guilt" inherent in USAID's post-9/11 global vetting system, ostensibly designed to prevent terrorists from receiving "material support." In CRS's peacebuilding programs in the Middle East, some local partners have simply refused to participate in USAID-funded projects because they are offended by this presumption. One former CRS chief of party for a USAID-funded peacebuilding project lamented that he spent 60 percent of his time assuring compliance with the USAID global vetting system requirements, leaving little time for assuring program quality.

In CVE, community members are engaged not for their potential contribution to local development and governance but for their strategic value to the CVE mission. CRS starts with a completely different premise, viewing youth, for example, as potential agents of peace, willing and capable not only of changing their own lives for the better but also of transforming their societies.

Second, CVE contradicts our commitment to subsidiarity and to the "option for the poor." Services provided under CVE programming are not pursued as goods unto themselves—education for the poor, job training for young people, infrastructure for community development—but to support security objectives. One recent education program in the Sahel, administered by USAID but funded by the U.S. military, would have required the implementing agency—not CRS—to report on which families were sending their children to state-run public schools and which were attending Islamic *madrassas*.

The military's objective, of course, was to identify potential recruits for radical religious groups operating in the region. In addition, because militarized forms of assistance are often designed for "quick impact"—a key tactic in the battle to win "hearts and minds"—they are rarely designed with meaningful community input and may not reflect local priorities, strengthen local capacities, or promote local decision making. The cumulative effect of such projects is to instrumentalize community participation and delegitimize development programming.

Finally, while reduction of violent extremism should serve the common good, in practice the current global preoccupation with CVE is used by authoritarian regimes as a justification to narrow the space for civil society, delegitimize those who criticize the government and its policies by labeling them "extremists," and violate human rights and democratic norms. For example, Sustainable Development Goal target 16.a, with its emphasis on strengthening national institutions to prevent violence and combat terrorism, is reportedly being used cynically by some states to divert development resources to militarism or suppression of civil society. Participating country governments in the New Deal international policy framework have regularly asserted their need for repressive policies and practices, many of which contradict the New Deal's lofty guiding principles, to eliminate violent extremist groups.

Increased Risk to CRS, Partners, and Communities

Such approaches also increase the risk of doing harm. Blurred lines between civilian and military actors undermine principles of independence and impartiality, to the detriment of all those operating in this sphere. Actual or perceived relations with military actors in a CVE project can cause unintended harm by heightening insecurity for staff, partners, and project participants. For example, they risk being viewed and targeted as informants and foreign agents if they are understood to be gathering and sharing intelligence. CRS has encountered just such a dilemma in its USAID-funded programming designed to strengthen capacity of communities in border areas of Central African Republic to protect themselves from potential attacks by the Lord's Resistance Army (LRA). The CRS-supported communities' early warning system has been tracking the movements of the LRA and sharing this information with members of the "international community," which includes the US government and, one can only assume, the US military.

Tactical Shortsightedness, Grave Consequences

Some of the most popular strategies for CVE include efforts to interrupt the process of "radicalization"—often through "messaging" to counter radical religious teachings and extremist groups' propaganda campaigns—and provision of vocational training to provide alternative livelihoods. "The (FY 2017 budget) request includes $187 million across several accounts for the purpose of countering violent extremism, a category that has not been highlighted in previous budget requests. The request is more than double the $92.2 million attributed to this purpose in FY2015" (Eppstein, Lawson, and Gill 2017). Yet, the evidence suggests that the political violence represented by violent extremism is not strictly or even primarily generated by radical beliefs and values nor by poverty and unemployment. A growing body of evidence indicates that young people do not turn to violence simply or even primarily because they lack access to jobs; most do so because of their experience of injustice, disenfranchisement, and marginalization (Mercy Corps 2015). Without equitable access to public resources, and a voice in shaping their and their communities' future, they become vulnerable to recruitment by groups that offer them the chance to become a part of something greater than themselves, even when such offers involve participation in violence.

Instead of addressing symptoms, effective strategies for addressing violent extremism require the political will to address underlying causes and conditions of poverty and violent conflict. Indeed, more than 74 percent of global terrorism victims in 2015 were from only five countries, all of which were immersed in violent conflicts[3] (Global Terrorism Index 2017). The root causes of violent conflict and the expression of violent extremism are inextricably linked. Both are fueled by the abuse of power, the misuse of resources, and the repression of civic participation.

Prioritizing and expanding the reach of CVE approaches that treat symptoms rather than root causes, along with other militarized policy interventions by the United States and other bilateral partners, signal support for the repressive policies described previously. It provides both tacit and explicit support for nondemocratic regimes, who then feel emboldened to use CVE as a pretext for consolidating power by reducing the space for civil society, restricting political competition, and disregarding the rule of law (Ginsburg and Moustafa 2008; Patel and Koushik 2017).

Such practices push potential agents of peace out of the civic arena, reduce their willingness to use nonviolent conflict resolution, and unwittingly plant the seeds for violent conflict and instability—setting in motion a vicious cycle that exacerbates the very issues CVE was designed to address. Indeed, an Australian government–commissioned study on CVE revealed that it often undermines its stated goals of peace and stability: "strategies for countering violent extremism can erode democratic principles and social cohesion, increase radicalization and incite conflict and violence" (Patel and Koushik 2017).

CONCLUSION

CRS aims to integrate justice and peacebuilding throughout all its programs with the overall goal being to transform society by building (or restoring) healthy relationships and promoting social justice (Rogers, Chassy, and Bamat 2010). CRS's embrace of IHD and commitment to justice and peacebuilding bring people together across different races, religions, ethnicities, and places of origin. This is more than just a "best practice." It enables CRS to put in practice its guiding principles, working in solidarity with those whom it serves for the common good and to protect the dignity of all. We believe this approach is also good stewardship; in the long run, it is a more effective means of preventing and responding to violent extremism. It also stands in stark contrast to CVE, which instrumentalizes humanitarian and development assistance and subordinates it to achieving geopolitical objectives. As outlined earlier, CVE places staff, partners, and project participants at risk of physical harm; compromises our and our partners' credibility to work with communities; and paradoxically sets into motion a vicious cycle that works against CVE's stated aims of peace, development, and stability.

Even when such efforts might be well intentioned, allowing a CVE lens to supersede guiding principles and core values inevitably leaves the marginalized and most vulnerable worse off while doing little to change the underlying power dynamics that drive the root causes of poverty and conflict. Such changes take time, often longer than the typical three- to five-year project cycle. Rather than using ethically flawed, dubious programming approaches to achieve such changes, policy makers would do better instead to heed Pope Francis's exhortation:

> Violence is not the cure for our broken world. Countering violence with violence leads at best to forced migrations and enormous suffering, because vast amounts of resources are diverted to military ends and away from the everyday needs of young people, families experiencing hardship, the elderly, the infirm and the great majority of people in our world. (Pope Francis I 2017)

Chapter 36

Toward a Synergy of Approaches to Human Security—Policy Recommendations

Lisa Schirch

A human security approach to violent extremism and terrorism places emphasis on the safety of civilians, the protection of democracy and civil liberties, and the economic trade-offs for how to invest public and private money to maximize public goods. In order to address the complex ecology of factors that correlate with violent extremism (as summarized in Table 2.1 in chapter 2), we need to coordinate interventions that recognize the interplay between different stakeholders and approaches to preventing violent extremism summarized in Table 3.1 in chapter 3 and detailed in the other chapters of this book. Based on this vision, this chapter summarizes the key recommendations and principles for creating a synergy of approaches to violent extremism and terrorism.

RECOGNIZE THE FULL COSTS AND BENEFITS OF EVERY INTERVENTION STRATEGY

A human security framework for preventing violent extremism and terrorism requires calculating the full costs and benefits of each strategy within the entire "ecology" or system. These ecological costs include the following:

- The cost in human lives, including all civilians, regardless of their citizenship, who die in both terrorism and counterterrorism operations;
- The economic costs, including the costs of terrorist attacks, the costs of counterterrorism, preventing and countering violent extremism (P/CVE), and peacebuilding interventions, and the trade-offs of money not spent on

other societal goods such as transportation, education, or environmental protection

- The social and political costs to civil liberties, human rights, and democratic freedoms that are restricted because of terrorism as well as counterterrorism
- The strategic costs in terms of whether the intervention is effective or unintentionally exacerbates violent extremism and terrorism in terms of broader national interests, which include geopolitical and economic goals

The current policy emphasis on counterterrorism methods has exacted high costs in terms of human lives, civil liberties, and the sheer costs of wars aimed to stop terrorism. A smarter approach to counterterrorism would ensure a human rights–based approach. New efforts to P/CVE include a jumble of positive and negative impacts. A smarter approach to P/CVE would emphasize community-led efforts divorced from targeting specific groups and intelligence gathering and spying on community members. While far fewer resources are invested in peacebuilding, evidence suggests these efforts should be increased to address the political conflicts and structural challenges that correlate with the rise in violent extremism and terrorism (GPI 2017).

DESIGN INTERVENTIONS TO PREVENT AND STOP VIOLENT EXTREMISM AND TERRORISM THAT DO THE MOST GOOD AND THE LEAST AMOUNT OF HARM

An "ecological approach" requires a synergy between the three main paradigms of interventions to address violent extremism and terrorism. These include:

- Use peacebuilding processes to address the underlying political and governance factors and to build the resilience of the whole system to prevent and respond to violent extremism.
- Use a rights-based, community-led approach to P/CVE to address specific problems that appear to be driving violent extremism, and rehabilitate and reintegrate former members of violent extremist groups.
- Use human rights–based counterterrorism intelligence and policing to stop individuals and groups preparing for terrorist attacks.

TAKE A MULTIDISCIPLINARY APPROACH TO ADDRESS FACTORS THAT CORRELATE WITH VIOLENT EXTREMISM INCLUDING INDIVIDUAL IDENTITY, COMMUNITY GRIEVANCES, NATIONAL IDEOLOGICAL, AND GLOBAL CONTEXTUAL FACTORS

Address Individual Identity Factors

In an increasingly complex world, investing in social structures and programs that support individuals can address some of the factors that correlate with violent extremism. Involving all sectors of society, including women and youth, in civic engagement, migrant transition, education, and work opportunities can improve self-esteem, counter feelings of humiliation and disrespect, increase a sense of group belonging, and provide alternative paths to glory, adventure, and heroism while improving life in the community. Psychosocial support, trauma recovery programs, and gender awareness training are also efforts that can prevent violent extremism. Investments in preventing these factors correlated with violent extremism will also address a host of other problems, such as depression and suicide.

Address Community Grievance Factors

Marginalization and disenfranchisement are felt as some feel a sense of relative deprivation at the economic, social, and political privileges enjoyed by some groups while others suffer exclusion. The state-society relationship is fragile in many countries, where communities view their state security forces as predators rather than protectors, and state actors represent some groups but not others. Efforts to improve the state-society relationship through supporting a robust political democracy, a sustainable economy, public safety, justice and the rule of law, and social and cultural well-being can each contribute to preventing the grievances that correlate with violent extremism. Supporting nonviolent civic resistance movements and comprehensive peace processes can help address the grievances that correlate with violent extremism and terrorism while at the same time preventing other forms of violence such as civil war.

Address National and Ideological Factors

Leaders of violent extremist groups can mobilize grievances in support of an ideology that promises to address those grievances. A variety of efforts can help to channel grievances into nonviolent efforts. These include human rights and peace education, nonviolent civil resistance movements, deprogramming efforts that challenge violent beliefs, and building support for democratic values and tolerance toward others. This can include dialogue and relationship building to break stereotypes and rehumanize people.

Global Contextual Factors

At the global level, interventions can address broader contextual factors. Some efforts aim to stop the cheap and unregulated flow of weapons that terrorist groups can use to carry out attacks. Other efforts support conflict-sensitive journalism that recognizes the significant impact media coverage plays in reporting on terrorism and helping the public understand root causes and potential solutions. Efforts to mitigate and adapt to climate change through environmental diplomacy and sustainable development can address some of the triggers that seem to correlate with the rise of violent extremism.

STRENGTHEN CIVILIAN LEADERSHIP OF CITIZEN-ORIENTED STATES TO ALIGN SHORT-TERM SECURITY GOALS AND LONG-TERM HUMAN RIGHTS AND CIVIL LIBERTIES

Of all of the factors correlating with violent extremism, the Global Terrorism Index and UN Development Program (UNDP) found that state abuses against society and political violence strongly correlate with higher levels of violence extremism and terrorism (GTI 2017; UNDP 2017). A state that orients its power and resources toward the needs and interests of its population is most likely to be seen as legitimate and to enjoy relative freedom and human security. In a citizen-oriented state, an active civil society partners with government both to provide public services and to hold government to account for transparent, good governance. One of the most important principles of a human security approach to violent extremism is to ensure civilian leadership that protects human rights and rule of law and prevents abuses of power from states and their armed forces (Human Security Collective 2013).

IMPROVE THE QUALITY OF THE STATE–SOCIETY RELATIONSHIP BY INVOLVING THE WHOLE OF SOCIETY IN A MULTISTAKEHOLDER APPROACH TO EVERY INTERVENTION

No one group can achieve human security on its own. Individuals and groups affected by insecurity have a “stake” in human security and are "stakeholders." Every intervention should include women, youth, and diverse sectors of society and aim to improve the state–society relationship.

Counterterrorism (CT) interventions are state-led, but civil society can play important roles in civilian oversight and accountability. Human rights organizations can help to shape CT approaches. Community organizations can provide feedback on the impact of CT approaches to provide corrective feedback to avoid antagonizing communities.

P/CVE should be community-led and should primarily support local solutions to prevent, educate, and support the resilience of communities. P/CVE initiatives to improve police–community relations are examples of how P/CVE can improve the state–society relationship.

Peacebuilding includes both community-led and state-led efforts to address the political conflicts and structural issues that contribute to community grievances, such as political, economic, and social exclusion and discrimination. Peace processes are most effective when they include all levels of society, including government, midlevel, and grassroots leadership (Lederach 1997).

EXPAND MULTISTAKEHOLDER COORDINATION

Different stakeholders need to coordinate with each other through joint processes that enable them to work together. States need to coordinate and act multilaterally to address these challenges that cross state lines and require international cooperation. States also need to coordinate with civil society to support human security. Coordination improves coherence and effectiveness. Multistakeholder coordination avoids duplication or unintentional harm to other groups, uses resources more efficiently, and maximizes the potential that interventions to prevent and stop violent extremism and terrorism will interact synergistically, adding up to better outcomes than any one intervention on its own. Civil society and the state can coordinate in five areas (Schirch and Mancini-Griffoli 2016)

Joint capacity building: Joint training, coaching, and support can build relationships and develop a common set of skills, concepts, and processes for working together to support community resilience and human security.

Jointly assess human security challenges: Joint conflict assessment can include jointly designing research questions and data collection methods and jointly analyzing data to identify factors driving violent extremism and supporting community resilience.

Jointly plan human security strategies: Jointly determining appropriate programs and strategies to support human security and determine relevant theories of change related to violent extremism.

Jointly implement human security strategies: Jointly implement a project together to prevent violent extremism, such as organizing a dialogue between police and youth, providing work opportunities and grants to communities from the state, or addressing trauma in local communities.

Jointly monitor and evaluate security sector performance in oversight mechanisms: Joint institutional oversight mechanism to identify the baselines, benchmarks, and indicators for monitoring and evaluation of programs to prevent violent extremism and how each type of intervention affects the "ecology" or community and developing recommendations for the future based on lessons learned.

PROTECT CIVIL SOCIETY AND MEDIA SPACE TO ADDRESS VIOLENT EXTREMISM AND PARTICIPATE IN PUBLIC PROBLEM-SOLVING PROCESSES AND PROPOSAL MAKING

As detailed in this book, counterterrorism laws have given states license to limit, control, and censure civil society and the media. An independent civil society and media need civil liberties and freedoms to organize, take part in shaping policies, and play roles in preventing violent extremism. Civil society and media organizations should be able to acquire legal exemptions to have contact with groups on the terror lists in order to understand their interests and grievances, support peaceful change through processes to address political conflicts that may be at the root of terrorism, and provide humanitarian aid to civilians in need. Civil society leaders in diverse corners of the world have come to the conclusion that they must go beyond *protesting* security policies to making *proposals* for alternate ways of supporting human security. Civil society can help to research and identify key factors contributing to violent extremism, provide direct and indirect conciliation between armed groups, and design inclusive peace processes to address political conflict and structural factors linked to violent extremism (Schirch and Mancini-Griffoli 2016).

CONCLUSION

Violent extremism and terrorism are important not only for the costs they bear directly on life, property, and sense of safety. These problems are like toxins spilling out of a barrel, poisoning and polluting other parts of the natural environment and society around it. The spillover effects of violent extremism and terrorism—and current responses to them—affect democracy, human rights, and freedoms for people around the world. This book imagines a different way for our collective response. Instead of causing more problems, a human security response makes the overall global society more healthy by addressing a host of other problems that correlate with violent extremism.

Notes

1. THE LANDSCAPE OF TERROR

1 Other studies determined that over 1 million Iraqis had died from war and its consequences as early as 2006. See Johns Hopkins University, the medical journal the *Lancet*, and British polling institute Opinion Research Business (ORB).

5. RADICAL ISLAMIST AND RADICAL CHRISTIANIST NUCLEAR TERRORISM

1 These remarks are drawn from a longer lecture presented at the conference "Exploring the Religious-Policy/Security Nexus in Responding to Critical Contemporary Regional/Global Challenges," November 1–2, 2016, Austin, TX. I extend my thanks to the Kozmetsky Center, Fletcher School of Law and Diplomacy at Tufts University, and NATO's Public Diplomacy Division.
2 See the prophecy translated by McCants's *The ISIS Apocalypse* in Appendix 2: The Victorious Group.
3 For instance, Erin Miller from the Global Terrorism Database states that a figure of 95 percent of victims being Muslims is "not out of the realm of possibility," although a precise figure is hard to gauge.

7. THE NEUROBIOLOGY OF VIOLENT EXTREMISM

1 The Shankill Butchers was an Ulster loyalist gang active between 1975 and 1982 in Belfast, Northern Ireland, notorious for kidnapping, torturing, and brutally murdering random Catholics.

2 Engineers are overrepresented from everywhere except Saudi Arabia, where engineering skills are prized and engineers are far less likely to be underemployed (Gambetta and Hertog 2016).

8. YOUTH AND THE SECURITY SECTOR: VE AS A FUNCTION OF Y

1 See Goldstone (1991) on youth roles in early modern revolutions, Moller (1968) and Becker (1951) on German youth mobilization from Luther to Hitler, Lewis (2009) on youth roles during the civil rights movement, Zimmerman (2000) on Sandinista youth, and Barber (2001) and Kuzio (2006) on Palestinian youth and Intifada mobilization.

2 See Kuzio (2006), Popovic, Milivojevic, and Djinovic (2006), and Richards (1996) on European "Color Revolutions," Richards (1996) and Shepler (2014) on Sierra Leone "Child Soldiers," and Atran (2015), Hamilton (2012, 2015), and Venhaus (2010), among others, on youth mobilization with militant Islamic groups.

3 This quote draws from a long-term research project (Hamilton 2012) and a more recent conference paper on youth mobilization (Hamilton 2017).

4 This diagram is described elsewhere in the context of an applied system dynamics model (Hamilton 2012, 2017, 10).

5 Helpful conflict analysis resources include Caritas International (2002), Hamilton (2015), and Schirch (2013).

6 UNSCR 2250 linkages and recommendations for youth-security sector engagement were developed for an expert session on "The Role of Young People in Building Peace and Security" at the Woodrow Wilson International Center for Scholars in October 2016.

7 My work at the Inter-American Defense College (IADC), which falls under the umbrella of the Organization of American States, is discussed in Hamilton (2016) and Acemoglu (2003). My comments are not representative of any particular state or intergovernmental organization but come as an interested scholar-practitioner working on these issues.

8 I have found police and military students from the Americas particularly interested in arguments of Acemoglu (2003) and Costa (2012).

9 See discussion of the Ecuadorian case in Johnston (2010) and of Todos Somos Juarez—among other "reverse exclusion" initiatives—in Morse, Isaacson, and Meyer (2011).

10 High-profile nonprofit organizations, business groups, or think tanks may be helpful in such scenarios, or foreign governments with sufficient carrots and sticks to incentive security-sector engagement with civil society.

11 Blackwell (2015) draws on his rich experience as a diplomat and the former secretary of Multidimensional Security for the Organization of American States (OAS) to discuss "Smart Security Approaches" and the importance of evidence-based models.

12 The UPP model is not without critics and has fallen out of favor with local and national politicians. Failures were linked to its limited scope, high cost, and especially the state's failure to deliver on promises of complementary educational and social services. Today once again we see an enhanced militarization of many of the favelas in Rio de Janeiro.
13 Key source material for the master's-level Conflict Analysis and Resolution class at IADC includes Caritas International (2002), Church and Rogers (2006), and Hamilton (2015).

9. ADVANCING A GENDER PERSPECTIVE AND WOMEN'S PARTICIPATION IN PREVENTING AND COUNTERING VIOLENT EXTREMISM

1 The reasons why women join or support terrorist or violent extremist groups remain a topic of debate. For example, see Sutten (2009).
2 Subsequent resolutions include Resolutions 1820, 1888, 1889, 1960, 2106, 2122, and 2422, passed during 2008–2015. For more on these resolutions, see PeaceWomen, "The Resolutions," http://www.peacewomen.org/why-WPS/solutions/resolutions.

11. PRINCIPLES OF EFFECTIVE COUNTERTERRORISM

1 From 2006 onward the Global Center has completed studies on implementing the UN Global Counter-Terrorism Strategy in the Asia-Pacific; South, East, West, and North Africa; Latin America and the Caribbean; South and Southeast Asia; and Oceania—as well as follow-up studies on drivers of violent extremism and linkages to human rights norms, the rule of law, and good governance. All of these studies and reports are available at www.globalcenter.org.

12. OVERCOMING VIOLENT EXTREMISM IN THE MIDDLE EAST: LESSONS FROM THE ARAB SPRING

1 This chapter is based on the findings of Lodgaard (2016). The chapters on US and EU policies toward Egypt, Libya, and Tunisia were written by Jean-Francois Seznec and Rosemary Hollis, respectively. The chapter is based on their contributions and my own "Summary" and "Conclusions" chapter in the book.

13. CIVIL SOCIETY ENGAGEMENT TO PREVENT VIOLENT EXTREMISM

1 With Alistair Millar, Linda Gerber-Stellingwerf, George A. Lopez, Eliot Fackler, and Joshua Weaver. This chapter is drawn from a much longer report with the same title published in 2011. It is based on a series of workshops and consultations sponsored by the Dutch development agency Cordaid, in cooperation with the US-based research team of the Fourth Freedom Forum and the Kroc Institute for International Peace Studies at the University of Notre Dame. It draws from the work of dozens of civil society partner groups in Europe, Asia, Latin America, and Africa and is based on interviews and meetings with hundreds of representatives of civil society organizations (CSOs), donor agencies, research centers, and governments. It benefits especially from the work of CIVICUS, the International Center for Not-for-Profit Law, and the Charity and Security Network.

15. LEGAL RESTRICTIONS AND COUNTERTERRORISM

1 The author has found no public record of exercise of this power in the peacebuilding context.

16. PROSCRIBING PEACE: THE IMPACT OF TERRORIST LISTING ON PEACEBUILDING ORGANIZATIONS

1 This briefing paper and preparatory work was originally published by Conciliation Resources in January 2016 and can be found at http://www.c-r.org/downloads/Conciliation_Resources_Counter-terrorism_brief.pdf. It was prepared with the financial support of the Joseph Rowntree Charitable Trust. The contents are the sole responsibility of Conciliation Resources and do not necessarily reflect the position of the Joseph Rowntree Charitable Trust.
2 Participant, Chatham House discussion, November 11, 2015.
3 Interview with mediation support organization, United Kingdom.

20. ISLAMIZATION, SECURITIZATION, AND PEACEBUILDING APPROACHES TO PREVENTING AND COUNTERING VIOLENT EXTREMISM

1 This is an excerpt from Mohammed Abu-Nimer, "Alternative Approaches to Transforming Violent Extremism: The Case of Islamic Peace and Interreligious Peacebuilding," in Transformative Approaches to Violent Extremism, Berghof Handbook Dialogue No. 13, edited by Beatrix

Austin and Hans J. Giessmann (Berlin: Berghof Foundation, May 2018). http://www.berghof-foundation.org/publications/handbook/handbook-dialogues/13-transforming-violent-extremism/.
2 www.kaiciid.org has a list of over 150 statements by Muslim organizations denouncing violence in the name of religion and especially Islam.
3 Due to the sensitivity of this information, specific attribution of this type of statement cannot be made publicly.
4 In an attempt to capture this process, the Tanenbaum Center for Interreligious Understanding International Peacemakers identified certain trends in "successful/high-impact" techniques. Many included existing techniques and framing, in addition to some new approaches. See the Peacemakers seminar July 2016 report at https://tanenbaum.org/.
5 This was observed by many faith-based organizations (FBO) participants in KAICIID meetings (2015–2017, especially in Nigeria) and by UN Inter-Agency Task Force on Engaging Faith-Based Actors for Sustainable Development and Humanitarian Work (UNIATF).
6 A term used by some peacebuilders, referring to the pressure they experience to incorporate CVE frameworks in framing their proposals to secure funding, as well as to the very high level of international and national spending on P/CVE programs.

21. COUNTERING VIOLENT EXTREMISM; DISARMAMENT, DEMOBILIZATION, AND REINTEGRATION; SOCIAL CAPITAL; AND THE "WOMEN, PEACE AND SECURITY" AGENDA

1 UNSCRs 1325 (2000), OP. 8.a, 13; 1820 (2008), OP. 10; 1888 (2009), PP. 12, OP. 13, 15; 1889 (2009), OP. 13; 1960 (2010), PP. 13; 2106 (2013), OP. 16.a; 2122 (2013) OP. 4.
2 Save for a rhetorical mention in Resolution 2122 (2013) OP. 3: "Threats to international peace and security caused by terrorist acts."

22. ADDRESSING TERRORISM: A THEORY OF CHANGE APPROACH

1 This chapter is reprinted with permission from the Life and Peace Institute. It was originally found in "Somalia: Creating Space for Fresh Approaches to Peacebuilding" (Sweden: Life and Peace Institute, 2011) at https://kroc.nd.edu/assets/227112/somalia_book.pdf.

23. NEGOTIATION AND VIOLENT EXTREMISM: WHY ENGAGE AND WHY NOT?

1 I am grateful to Anthony Wanis St-John for these suggestions.

2 It has been indicated elsewhere that there are two types of stalemate: the Mutually Hurting Stalemate of Ripeness (Zartman 1989, 2000), and the S^5 Situation (soft, stable, self-serving stalemate), also referred to as the Mutually Profitable Stalemate (Zartman 2005; Wennmann 2009). The latter is not discussed here in detail.

27. A PEACEBUILDING APPROACH TO MEDIA AND CONFLICT-SENSITIVE JOURNALISM

1 Parts of this chapter are based on a UN High-Level Panel Discussion, titled "Addressing the Challenges to Safety of Journalists Posed by Terrorist Threat," that was held at the UN Headquarters in New York City on June 27, 2016, organized by the Permanent Mission of Lithuania to the United Nations and the Committee to Protect Journalists (CPJ).

29. PREVENTING VIOLENCE THROUGH A TRAUMA-HEALING APPROACH

1 The opinions stated in this chapter are my own.
2 Detention and mistreatment of torture survivors was a common theme expressed by those (including myself) attending the UN Voluntary Fund for Victims of Torture Expert workshop: "Torture Victims in the Context of Migration: Identification, Redress and Rehabilitation." http://www.ohchr.org/Documents/Issues/Torture/UNVFVT/45thConceptNote.pdf.
3 In addition to our learnings from our direct services programs, many local organizations in Turkey and Iraq have noted with concern that the community consequences of masses of people with untreated severe trauma have led to a "tearing of the social fabric," including social norms. Destruction of traditional taboos that might have previously contained antisocial behavior has led to an increase in sexual violence both in the home and against other community members.
4 The full text of the blog series I wrote during these three months can be found at http://www.cvt.org/JordanCounselingBlogSeries. The quotes represent common sentiments that were expressed repeatedly in the groups.
5 This includes clinical "practice" evidence that the clinical staff hear over and over again as well as outcome studies that show this decrease.

31. PREVENTING AND COUNTERING VIOLENT EXTREMISM THROUGH EMPOWERING WOMEN ECONOMICALLY AND SOCIALLY IN PAKISTAN

1 WASL is an alliance of women and men activists from fifty-nine countries of the South to learn from each other, share, connect, coalesce, and advocate in

international arena around the issue of women peace and security. PAIMAN is one of the founding members of WASL.

2 Anyone siding with the Americans or the West are called infidels. This includes Pakistan security forces as well.

32. THE RADICAL MUSLIM AND THE RADICAL MENNONITE: AN INTERFAITH ENCOUNTER FOR PEACE IN INDONESIA

1 "The Radical Muslim and Mennonite: A Muslim-Christian Encounter for Peace in Indonesia" Edited by Agnes Chen. Semarang, Indonesia, Pustaka Muria City.

33. WHAT WORKS TO PREVENT VIOLENT EXTREMISM: LESSONS FROM EMPLOYMENT AND EDUCATION PROGRAMS

1 These numbers did decrease after the evaluation, due to exogenous factors like a contracting economy.

2 This program was later renamed Somali Youth Learners Initiative.

35. PUTTING HUMAN DIGNITY AT THE CENTER: AN ALTERNATIVE PERSPECTIVE ON "COUNTERING VIOLENT EXTREMISM"

1 Though written to guide NGO operations in disaster relief, the NGO community often transfers the ideals embodied in what is commonly referred to as the "NGO Code of Conduct" to other situations, including complex emergencies and socioeconomic development.

2 The United Nations defines youth as aged fifteen to twenty-four, and this is the primary youth population targeted by CRS youth programming. However, youth programs may include young people between the ages of ten and thirty-five, depending on the country context and/or donor specifications.

3 These five countries are Iraq, Afghanistan, Nigeria, Syria, and Pakistan. It is of note that the United States plays a significant role in all of these conflicts, either as a direct actor or as a major influence.

Bibliography

Abbas, Hassan. 2013. "How Drones Create More Terrorists." *Atlantic*, August 23. https://www.theatlantic.com/international/archive/2013/08/how-drones-create-more-terrorists/278743/.

Abromowitz, Michael J. 2018. *Freedom in the World 2018: Democracy in Crisis*. Washington, DC: Freedom House.

Abu-Nimer, Mohammed, Ilham Nasser, and Seddik Ouboulhcen. 2016. "Introducing Values of Peace Education and Pluralism in Quranic Schools in Western Africa: Advantages and Challenges of the Islamic Peace-Building Model." *Religious Education* 111(5): 537–554.

Acemoglu, Daron. 2003. "Root Causes: A Historical Approach to Assessing the Role of Institutions in Economic Development." *Finance and Development*, June: 27–30.

Ackerman, Spencer. 2010. *NATO-Caused Civilian Casualties Increasing in Afghanistan*. Washington, DC: The Washington Independent.

ACLU. 2015. "More about Suspicious Activity Reporting." Accessed March 20, 2018. https://www.aclu.org/other/more-about-suspicious-activity-reporting.

Action Aid. 2010. *Quick Impact, Quick Collapse: The Dangers of Militarized Aid in Afghanistan*. Washington, DC: Oxfam.

AFT. 2016. "AfT Letter to FBI." August 9. Accessed March 20, 2018. http://www.aft.org/sites/default/files/ltr_dont_be_a_puppet_aug2016.pdf.

Against Violent Extremism. n.d. Accessed January 24, 2017. http://www.againstviolentextremism.org.

Al Arabiya. 2014. "*ISIS leader offers marriage grants to militants*" Al Arabiya News. August 29. Accessed March 20, 2018. http://english.alarabiya.net/en/News/middle-east/2014/08/29/ISIS-chief-declares-marriage-grant-for-.html.

Al Qurtuby, Sumanto. 2013. "Engaging Extremists Key to Peace." *Jakarta Globe*, January 29.

Alexander, Audrey. 2016. "Cruel Intentions: Female Jihadists in America." *The Program on Extremism at George Washington University*. Accessed March 20, 2018. https://cchs.gwu.edu/sites/g/files/zaxdzs2371/f/downloads/Female%20Jihadists%20in%20America.pdf.

Alexander, Ruth, and Hannah Moore. 2015. "Are Most Victims of Terrorism Muslim?" BBC News, January 20.

Ali, Wajahat, Eli Clifton, Matthew Duss, Lee Fang, Scott Keyes, and Faiz Shakir. 2011. *Fear Inc.: The Roots of the Islamophobic Network in America*. Washington, DC: Center for American Progress.

Allam, Rana. 2018. "Unstitching Extremism." *Sisterhood*. March 13. Accessed March 20, 2018. http://sister-hood.com/rana-allam/unstitching-extremism/.

Allard, Eric, and Elizabeth Kensinger. 2014. "Age-Related Differences in Functional Connectivity during Cognitive Emotion Regulation." *Journal of Gerontology* 69 (6): 852–860.

Allison, Simon. 2016. "Kenya: Think Again—Civil Society in Kenya Is Down, but Not Out." *Institute for Security Studies*. January 5. Accessed March 20, 2018. https://issafrica.org/iss-today/think-again-civil-society-in-kenya-is-down-but-not-out.

Al-Obaidi, Muhammad, Nasir Abdullah, and Scott Helfstein. 2009. *Deadly Vanguards: A Study of al-Qa'ida's Violence against Muslims*. Occasional Papers, Combating Terrorism Center at West Point.

Altheide, David. 2016. "Media Logic." In *The International Encyclopedia of Political Communication*, by David Altheide, 1–6. Hoboken, NJ: John Wiley & Sons, Inc.

Amanullah, Shahed. 2015. "Affinis Labs Backs Social Impact Startups that Help Counter Violent Extremism with Startup Incubation, Private Equity Fun." PRWeb. February 19. Accessed March 20, 2018. http://www.prweb.com/releases/2015/02/prweb12523369.htm.

Amnesty International. 2014. "Somalis Are Scapegoats in Kenya's Counter-Terror Crackdown." May. Accessed March 20, 2018. https://www.amnesty.org/en/latest/news/2014/05/kenya-somalis-scapegoated-counter-terror-crackdown/.

———. 2017. "Nigeria: Chibouk Anniversary a Chilling Reminder of Boko Haram's Ongoing Scourge of Abductions." April 12.

Anderson, David. 2014. *The Independent Reviewer on the Operation of the Terrorism Act 2000 and Part 1 of the Terrorism Act 2006*. London: Williams Lea Group.

Annan, Kofi. 2005. *In Larger Freedom: Towards Security, Development and Human Rights for All*. New York: UN Secretary General.

Antiterrorism and Effective Death Penalty Act of 1996. n.d. Pub.L. No. 104–132, 110 Stat. 1214 (See "Providing Material Support to Terrorists" 18 U.S.C. § 2339B).

Aoláin, Fionnuala. 2016. "Masculinity, Jihad and Mobilization." *Just Security*. October 18. Accessed March 20, 2018. https://www.justsecurity.org/33624/masculinity-jihad-mobilization/.

Appleby, R. Scott, and Richard Cizik. 2010. "Engaging Religious Communities Abroad: A New Imperative for US Foreign Policy." *Chicago Council on Global Affairs*. February 23.

as-Suri, Abu Mus'ab. 2004. *The Call for a Global Islamic Resistance*. December. Accessed March 20, 2018. https://archive.org/details/TheCallForAGlobalIslamicResistance-EnglishTranslationOfSomeKeyPartsAbuMusabAsSuri.

Atran, Scott. 2010. *Talking to the Enemy: Faith, Brotherhood, and the (un)Making of Terrorists*. New York: Ecco Press.

———. 2015a. "Role of Youth: Countering Violent Extremism." *Psychology Today*, May 1. https://www.psychologytoday.com/us/blog/in-gods-we-trust/201505/role-youth-countering-violent-extremism-promoting-peace?amp=.

———. 2015b. *Youth, Violent Extremism and Promoting Peace*. April 23. Accessed March 20, 2018. http://blogs.plos.org/neuroanthropology/2015/04/25/scott-atran-on-youth-violent-extremism-and-promoting-peace/.

———. 2016. "The Devoted Actor: Unconditional Commitment and Intractable Conflict across Cultures." *Current Anthropology* (University of Chicago Press) 57 (13): S192–S203. doi:10.1086/685495.

Atran, Scott, and Robert Axelrod. 2008. "Reframing Sacred Values." *Negotiation Journal* 24 (3): 221–246.

Atran, Scott, and Jeremy Ginges. 2012. "Religious and Sacred Imperatives in Human Conflict." *Science*, May 18: 855–857.

Attorney General. 2015. "Pilot Programs Are Key to Countering Violent Extremism Efforts." *Department of Justice Archives*. February 18. Accessed March 20, 2018. https://www.justice.gov/archives/opa/blog/pilot-programs-are-key-our-countering-violent-extremism-efforts.

Babran, Sedigheh. 2008. "Media, Globalization of Culture, and Identity Crisis in Developing Countries." *Intercultural Communication Studies* XVII (2): 212–228.

Bagenal, Flora. 2017. "10 Women Leading the Way in Counter-Extremism." *News Deeply*. March 1. Accessed March 20, 2018. https://www.newsdeeply.com/womenandgirls/articles/2017/03/01/10-women-leading-way-counter-extremism.

Baird, Abigail. 2011. *Think Psychology*. London: Prentice Hall.

Bal, Meike. 2009. *Narratology: Introduction to the Theory of Narrative*. Toronto: University of Toronto Press.

Barber, Briank K. 2001. "Political Violence, Social Integration, and Youth Functioning: Palestinian Youth from the Intifada." *Journal of Community Psychology* 29 (3): 259–280.

Barkun, Michael. 1997. *Religion and the Racist Right*. Chapel Hill: University of North Carolina Press.

Barrett, Richard. 2014. *Foreign Fighters in Syria*. New York: Soufan Group.

Bartlett, Jamie. 2011. "'Wicked' Jihad and the Appeal of Violent Extremism." *Demos*. https://www.demos.co.uk/files/File/wickedjihad.pdf.

Basick, Renee L. 2015. "UChicago Study Explores How ISIS Lights Up the Brains of Recruits." Accessed March 20, 2018. https://socialsciences.uchicago.edu/story/uchicago-study-explores-how-isis-lights-brains-recruits.

Bassuener, Kurt, and Jeremy Kinsman. 2013. *A Diplomat's Handbook for Democracy Development Support*. Waterloo, Canada: Center for International Governance Innovation.

Bateson, Gregory. 1972. *Steps to an Ecology of Mind*. Chicago: University of Chicago Press.

BBC. 2016. "Inside the Home of Indonesia's Most Notorious IS Militant." BBC News, January 18.

Beam, Louise. 1992. "Leaderless Resistance." *Seditionist*, February.

Becker, Howard. 1951. "What the Hitler Youth Inherited: A Methodological Note." *Phlon* 12 (1): 39–54.

Beisar, Elana. 2016. "Turkey's Crackdown Propels Number of Journalists in Jail Worldwide to Record." *Committee for the Protection of Journalists*. December 13. Accessed March 20, 2018. https://cpj.org/reports/2016/12/journalists-jailed-record-high-turkey-crackdown.php.

Belasco, Amy. 2009. *The Cost of Iraq, Afghanistan, and Other Global War on Terror Operations*. Washington, DC: Congressional Research Service.

Bender, Bryan. 2015. "Islamic Leader Says US Officials Unfairly Target Muslims." *Boston Globe*, February 18.

Benjamin, Daniel, and Steven Simon. 2005. *The Next Attack*. New York: Henry Holt and Co.

Bergen, Peter, David Sterman, Alyssa Sims, and Albert Ford. 2016. *ISIS in the West: The Western Militant Flow to Syria and Iraq*. Washington, DC: New America Foundation.

Berger, Jonah. 2016. *Contagious: Why Things Catch On*. New York: Simon & Schuster.

Berman, Eli, Jacob N. Shapiro, Joseph H. Felter, and Michael Callen. 2011. "Do Working Men Rebel? Employment and Insurgency in Afghanistan, Iraq and the Philippines." *Journal of Conflict Resolution* 55 (4): 496–528.

Berry, Damon T. 2017. *Blood and Faith: Christianity in American White Nationalism*. Syracuse, NY: Syracuse University Press.

Bertelsen, Preben. 2015. "Danish Preventive Measures and De-radicalization Strategies: The Aarhus Model." *Panorama* 1: 241–253.

Betz, David. 2008. "The Virtual Dimension of Insurgency and Counterinsurgency." *Small Wars & Insurgencies* 19 (4): 510–540. doi:10.1080/09592310802462273.

Beutel, Alejandro J., Stevan Weine, Aliya Saaed, Aida Mihajlovic, Andrew Stone, John Beahrs, and Stephen Shanfield. 2016. "Field Principles for Countering and Displacing Extremist Narratives." *Journal of Terrorism Research* (The Centre for the Study of Terrorism and Political Violence) 7 (3): 35–49. doi:http://doi.org/10.15664/jtr.1220.

Bharath, Deepa. 2016. "From IRA to Islamists, Former Radicals Unite to Become a Force for Peace." *Christian Science Monitor*, March 6.

Bhui, Kamaldeep S., H. Madelyn Hicks, Myrna Lashley, and Edgar Jones. 2012. "A Public Health Approach to Understanding and Preventing Violent Radicalization." *BMC Medicine*. https://bmcmedicine.biomedcentral.com/track/pdf/10.1186/1741-7015-10-16?site=bmcmedicine.biomedcentral.com.

bin Laden, Osama. 2004. "Full Transcript of bin Ladin's Speech." *Al Jazeera*. November 1. Accessed March 20, 2018. https://www.aljazeera.com/archive/2004/11/200849163336457223.html.

Blackwell, Adam. 2015. *If the War on Drugs Is Over . . . Now What? Security without Easy Answers*. Victoria: Friesen Press.

Blair, Graeme, Christine Fair, Neil Malhotra, and Jacob N. Shapiro. 2013. "Poverty and Support for Militant Politics: Evidence from Pakistan." *American Journal of Political Science* 57 (1): 30–48.

Blattman, Chris, and Laura Ralston. 2015. *Generating Employment in Poor and Fragile States: Evidence from Labor Market and Entrepreneurship Programs*. SSRN.

Bloom, Mia. 2011. *Bombshell: Women and Terrorism*. Philadelphia: University of Pennsylvania Press.

Bolton, Nell, and Myla Leguro. 2016. *Local Solutions to Land Conflict in Mindanao: Policy Lessons from Applying CRS's 3 Bs (Binding, Bonding, Bridging) to Land Conflict*. Baltimore: Catholic Relief Services.

Bond, Michael. 2014. "Why Westerners Are Driven to Join the Jihadist Fight." *New Scientist*, September 10.

Boon-Kuo, Louise, Ben Hayes, Vicki Sentas, and Gavin Sullivan. 2015. *Building Peace in Permanent War: Terrorist Listing and Conflict Transformation*. Transnational Institute, London, Amsterdam: International State Crime Initiative.

Borger, Julian. 2003. "Leaked Memo Exposes Rumsfeld's Doubts about War on Terror." *Guardian*, October 23.

Brakarsh, John. 2009. "Singing to the Lions: A Guide to Overcoming Fear and Violence in Our Lives." *Catholic Relief Services*. Accessed March 20, 2018. https://www.crs.org/our-work-overseas/research-publications/singing-lions.

Breckinridge, James N., and Philip N. Zimbardo. 2007. "The Strategy of Terrorism and the Psychology of Mass-Mediated Fear." In *Psychology of Terrorism*, by Bongar, Bruce, Lisa M. Brown and Larry E. Beutler, 116–133. New York: Oxford University Press.

Briggs, Rachel, and Sebastien Feve. 2013. *Review of Programs to Counter Narratives of Violent Extremism: What Works and What Are the Implications for Government?* London: Institute for Strategic Dialogue.

Brosch, T., E. Bar-David, and E. A. Phelps. 2013. "Implicit Race Bias Decreases the Similarity of Neural Representations of Black and White Faces." *Psychological Science* 24 (2): 160–166.

Brown, Lauretta. 2016. "State Dept.: U.S. Should 'Rehabilitate' and 'Reintegrate' Foreign Fighters Back into Society." September 8. Accessed March 12, 2017. http://www.cnsnews.com/news/article/lauretta-brown/state-dept-director-countering-violent-extremism-us-should-rehabilitate.

Brown, Tricia Gates. 2008. *118 Days: Christian Peacemaker Team Held Hostage in Iraq*. Toronto: Christian Peacemaker Teams.

Brown, Vanda. 2015. "DDR in the Context of Offensive Military Operations, Counterterrorism, CVE and Non-Permissive Environments." In *UN DDR in an Era of Violent Extremism: Is It Fit for Purpose*, by James Cockayne and Siobhan O'Neil, 36–60. Tokyo: UN University.

Brück, Tilman, Neil Ferguson, Valeri Izzi, and Wolfgang Stojet. 2016. *Jobs and Peace*. Berlin: International Security and Development Center.

Buchanan-Clarke, Stephan, and Rorisang Lekalake. 2016. *Violent Extremism in Africa: Public Opinion from the Sahel, Lake Chad and the Horn*. Policy Paper, Afrobarometer.

Burke, Jason. 2015. "Jihad by Family: Why Are Terrorist Cells Made Up of Brothers." *Guardian*, November 17. https://www.theguardian.com/world/2015/nov/17/jihad-by-family-terrorism-relatives-isis-al-qaeda.

CAIR. 2015. "Brief on Countering Violent Extremism (CVE)." *Council on American-Islamic Relations*. July. Accessed March 20, 2018. https://www.cair.com/government-affairs/13063-brief-on-countering-violent-extremism-cve.html.

———. 2016. *Confronting Fear: Islamophobia and Its Impact in the United States*. Washington, DC: CAIR.

Campbell, Charlie. 2017. "ISIS Unveiled: The Story behind Indonesia's First Female Suicide Bomber." *Time Magazine*, March 2.

Campbell, Joseph. 2008. *The Hero with a Thousand Faces (The Collected Works of Joseph Campbell)*. Novato, CA: New World Library.

Cantlie, John. 2016. "The Perfect Storm." *Dabiq*, July 31: 74–77.

Capra, Fritjof. 1996. *The Web of Life: A New Scientific Understanding of Living Systems*. New York: Anchor Books.

Caritas International. 2002. *Peacebuilding: A Caritas Training Manual*. Vatican City: Caritas International.

Carl, Andy, and Sophie Haspeslagh. 2010. *Why Criminalise Dialogue with Terrorists?* n.p.: Open Democracy.

Casey, B. J., Rebecca M. Jones, and Leah H. Somerville. 2011. "Braking and Accelerating of the Adolescent Brain." *Journal of Research on Adolescence* 21 (1): 21–33.

CDC. 2018. *Understanding the Opioid Epidemic*. Atlanta: Center for Disease Control and Prevention.

The Center for Climate and Security. n.d. Accessed March 20, 2018. www.climateandsecurity.org.

Charity Commission. 2013. *Protecting Charities from Harm: Compliance Toolkit*. London: UK Government.

Chatham House. 2012. "Somalia's Transition: What Role for Sub-National Entities." London.

Chatham House in Collaboration with Conciliation Resources. 2010. *The Impact of UK Counterterrorism Legislation on Peace Processes and Mediation with Armed Groups*. London: Chatham House in Collaboration with Conciliation Resources.

Chayes, Sarah. 2016. "Corruption: Violent Extremism, Kleptocracy, and the Dangers of Failing Governance." Testimony to the U.S. Senate Foreign Relations Committee. Washington, DC: Carnegie Endowment for International Peace, June 30.

Chenoweth, Erica, and Maria J. Stephan. 2011. *Why Civil Resistance Works: The Strategic Logic of Nonviolent Conflict*. New York: Columbia University Press.

Cherono, Stella, and David Mwere. 2017. "NGOs: We Were Shut over Plan to Contest Poll Result in Court." *Daily Nation*, August 16.

Choi, Seung-Whan. 2011. *Does U.S. Military Intervention Reduce or Increase Terrorism?* Washington, DC: American Political Science Association.

Church, Cheyenne, and Mark Rogers. 2006. *Designing for Results: Integrating Monitoring and Evaluation in Conflict Transformation Programs*. Washington, DC: Search for Common Ground.

Cialdini, Robert B. 2007. *Influence: The Psychology of Persuasion*. New York: Collins.

Civil Rights Group Letter. 2015. "Grave Concerns regarding 'Countering Violent Extremism' Pilot Programs." February 13. Accessed March 20, 2018. https://www.brennancenter.org/sites/default/files/analysis/Boston%20Organizational%20Letter%20re%20CVE%20Concerns.pdf.

Civil Rights LA Group Letter. 2014. "Groups Serving American Muslim Communities Question Federal Government's CVE Programs as Ill-Conceived, Ineffective, and Stigmatizing." Los Angeles: Asian Americans Advancing Justice, November 13. https://www.advancingjustice-la.org/sites/default/files/20141113%20-%20MR%20-%20CVE%20Statement.pdf.

CNA. 2014. *National Security and the Accelerating Risks of Climate Change*. Alexandria, VA: CNA Military Advisory Board.

Cohen, Andrew. 2017. "The FBI's New Fantasy: 'Black Identity Extremists.'" October 11. https://www.brennancenter.org/blog/fbi-new-fantasy-black-identity-extremists.

Colletta, Nat, and Michelle Cullen. 2000. *Violent Conflict and the Transformation of Social Capital: Lessons from Cambodia, Rwanda, Guatemala and Somalia*. Washington, DC: World Bank.

Conciliation Resources, Centre for Humanitarian Dialogue and Centre on Global Counterterrorism Cooperation. 2012. *Mediation and Engaging with Proscribed Armed Groups*. Summary of expert meeting, London: Conciliation Resources.

Conway, Maura. 2016. "Determining the Role of the Internet in Violent Extremism and Terrorism: Six Suggestions for Progressing Research." *Studies in Conflict & Terrorism* 40 (1): 77–98.

Cooper, Kristi. 2013. "'Amrokraten, Bemodraten and Cemokraten': A Case Study of Denazification and Leadership in World War II, 1944–49." In *Countering Extremism: Building Social Resilience through Community Engagement*, by Jolene Jerard, Salim Mohamed Nasir, and Rohan Gunaratna, 73–90. London: Imperial College Press.

Cordesman, Anthony. 2016. *Comparing Estimates of the Key Trends in the Uncertain Metrics of Terrorism*. Washington, DC: Center for Strategic and International Studies, 12.

———. 2017. "Trends in Terrorism: 1970–2016." *Center for Strategic and International Studies*. Washington, DC, August.

Corman, Steven R., and Kevin J. Dooley. 2008. "Strategic Communication on a Rugged Landscape—Principles for Finding the Right Message." *COMOPS Journal* (Consortium for Strategic Communication—Arizona State University). http://csc.asu.edu/wp-content/uploads/pdf/121.pdf.

Corman, Steven R., Angela Trethewey, and Bud Goodall. 2007. "A 21st Century Model for Communication in the Global War of Ideas—From Simplistic Influence to Pragmatic Complexity." *COMOPS Journal* (Consortium for Strategic Communication—Arizona State University). https://csc.asu.edu/wp-content/uploads/pdf/114.pdf.

Cortright, David, Melanie Greenberg, and Laurel Stone. 2016. *Civil Society, Peace and Power*. Lanham, MD: Rowman & Littlefield.

Cortright, David, and George Lopez. 2007. *Uniting against Terror*. Cambridge, MA: MIT Press.

Cortright, David, Alistair Millar, Linda Gerber, and George Lopez. 2011. *Friend Not Foe*. Goshen, IN: Fourth Freedom Forum.

Coser, Lewis. 1955. *The Functions of Social Conflict*. New York: Free Press.

Costa, Gino. 2012. "Citizen Security and Transnational Organized Crime in the Americas." *Sur: International Journal on Human Rights* 9 (16): 126–146.

Costs of War. 2018. "Brown University Watson Institute for International and Public Affairs." Accessed March 20, 2018. http://watson.brown.edu/costsofwar/.

CPJ. 2017a. "Hamas Detains Palestinian Journalist in Gaza." *Committee for the Protection of Journalists*. June 14. Accessed March 20, 2018. https://cpj.org/2017/06/hamas-detains-palestinian-journalist-in-gaza.php.

———. 2017b. "Journalists Not Terrorists." *Committee for the Protection of Journalists*. September 20. Accessed March 20, 2018. https://cpj.org/reports/2017/09/journalists-not-terrorists-cameroon-anti-terror-imprisoned.php.

CPR. n.d. "Syria/Middle East and North Africa." *Committee to Protect Journalists*. Accessed June 26, 2016. https://cpj.org/mideast/syria/.

Cramer, Christopher. 2010. *Unemployment and Participation in Violence*. Washington, DC: World Development Report Background Paper.

Crawford, Neta C. 2017. *US Budgetary Costs of Post-9/11 Wars through FY2018: $5.6 Trillion*. The Costs of War Project, Brown University.

Crockett, Molly. 2017. "Moral Outrage in a Digital Age." *Nature Human Behavior*, September 18: 769–771.

Cronin, Audrey Kurth. 2008. *How Terrorism Ends: Understanding the Decline and Demise of Terrorist Campaigns*. Princeton, NJ: Princeton University Press.

———. 2009. "How Terrorist Campaigns End." In *Leaving Terrorism Behind*, edited by Tore Bjorgo and John Horgan. New York: Routledge.

CRS. 2008. "Catholic Relief Services Guiding Principles." Baltimore: Catholic Relief Services.

———. 2016. "Healing Personal Trauma to Restore Communities." *Catholic Relief Services*. Accessed March 20, 2018. https://www.crs.org/sites/default/files/tools-research/healing-personal-trauma-to-restore-communities_0.pdf.

———. 2017. *Youth Programming in Latin America and the Caribbean: Unleashing the Power of Youth for Positive Social Change*. Baltimore: Catholic Relief Services.

CSN. 2014. "Permissible Activities for Peacebuilders—Based on Statements by U.S. Officials." *Charity and Security Network*. April 14. Accessed March 14, 2018. https://www.charityandsecurity.org/permissible_peacebuilding_activities.

CTITF. 2009. *Tackling the Financing of Terrorism*. Department of Political Affairs Counter-Terrorism Implementation Task Force, United Nations, United National Counter-Terrorism Implementation Task Force.

Curle, Adam. 1987. *In the Middle: Nonofficial Mediation in Violent Situations*. Bradford, UK: Bradford Peace Studies Papers.

Curt, Gregory A. 2001. "Terrorism and Cancer." *Oncologist* 6: 401.

Dahlberg, Linda. 1998. "Youth Violence in the United States: Major Trends, Risk Factors, and Prevention Approaches." *American Journal of Preventive Medicine* 14 (4): 259–272.

Daily News. 2017. "Hungary Marks Day of National Cohesion." *Daily News Hungary*, June 4.

Dando, Coral. 2016. "What Science Can Reveal about the Psychological Profiles of Terrorists." *Conversation*, May 26. https://theconversation.com/what-science-can-reveal-about-the-psychological-profiles-of-terrorists-78304.

Darby, John, and Roger McGinty. 2008. *Contemporary Peacemaking: Conflict, Peace Processes, and Post-war Reconstruction*. London: Palgrave Macmillan.

Desmond, Molloy. 2017. *Disarmament, Demobilisation and Reintegration: Theory and Practice*. Boulder, CO: Lynne Rienner Publishers.

Dewey, Caitlin. 2013. "Why Nelson Mandela Was on a Terrorism Watch List in 2008." *Washington Post*.

DFID. 2013. *Youth Voices on a Post-2015 World.* CSO Youth Working Group, London: DFID.

Dhamapuri, Sahana. 2013. "Not Just a Numbers Game: Women's Participation in UN Peacekeeping." *International Peace Institute.* July. Accessed March 20, 2018. http://www.ipinst.org/wp-content/uploads/publications/ipi_epub_not_just_a_numbers_game.pdf.

Dharma, Adhi. 2013. "Indonesia: Struggling, Learning, Serving." *Mennonite World Conference*, December 31.

DHS. 2016. "Countering Violent Extremism (CVE) Subcommittee: Interim Report and Recommendation." *Department of Homeland Security.*

Dickey, Christopher. 2009. "Most Suicide Bombers Have Three Things in Common." *Newsweek.*

Dietrich, Simone, and Minhai Mahmud. 2017. "Aiding the Virtuous Circle? International Development Assistance and Citizen Confidence in Government in Bangladesh." *Research and Politics* 4 (4): 1–6.

DoD. 2017. "National Defense Budget Estimates for FY 2018." *Office of the Under Secretary of Defense.* June.

DoJ. 2017. "US Department of Justice—Online Activities to Counter Violent Extremism Online." *Charity and Security Network.* Accessed March 20, 2018. https://www.charityandsecurity.org/node/1499.

Dooley, Brian. 2016. "Kenyan Corruption Undermines Fight against Extremism." *Worldpost.* Accessed March 20, 2018. https://www.huffingtonpost.com/brian-dooley/kenyan-corruption-undermi_b_7737394.html.

Doshi, Vihdi. 2016. "In India, for Example, Entire Villages Are Wiped Out by Mega Dams Developed to Mitigate against the Impacts of Climate Change Droughts And Flooding." *Guardian*, May 18.

Dremann, Sue. 2016. "Kerry: Entrepreneurship Combats Extremism." June 23. Accessed December 16, 2016. http://www.paloaltoonline.com/news/2016/06/23/kerry-entrepreneurship-combats-extremism.

Dudouet, Veronique. 2011. *Anti-Terrorism Legislation: Impediments in Conflict Transformation.* Policy Brief, Berghof Conflict Research.

Dugas, Michelle, and Arie Kruglanski. 2014. "The Quest for Significance Model of Radicalization: Implication for the Management of Terrorist Detainees." *Behavioral Sciences and the Law* May: 423–439.

Duke Law. 2017. "Tightening the Purse Strings: What Countering Terrorism Financing Costs Gender Equality and Security." *Duke Law International Human Rights Clinic and Women Peacemakers Program.* March. Accessed March 20, 2018. https://law.duke.edu/sites/default/files/humanrights/tighteningpursestrings.pdf.

Durkheim, Emile. 1915. *The Elementary Forms of the Religious Life.* New York: Macmillan.

Dyer, Clare. 2007. "There Is No War on Terror." *Guardian*, January 24: 1.

Ehrenreich, Barbara. 1997. *Blood Rites: Origins and History of the Passions of War.* New York: Metropolitan Books.

Eide, Espen Barth. 2015. "How Companies Can Help Defuse Violent Extremism." February 19. Accessed November 23, 2016. https://www.weforum.org/agenda/2015/02/how-companies-can-help-defuse-violent-extremism/.

18 U.S. Code § 2331. 2010. "Definition of International Terrorism."

Elmhirst, Sophie. 2011. "I'd Have Been Ashamed Not to Join the IRA." *New Statesman*.

Eppstein, Susan Epstein, Marian Lawson, and Cory Gill. 2017. *State, Foreign Operations and Related Programs: FY2017 Budget and Appropriations*. Washington, DC: Congressional Research Service.

Erikson, Erik. 1970. "Reflections on the Dissent of Contemporary Youth." *International Journal of Psychoanalysis* 51: 11–22.

Evans, David, Brian Holtemeyer, and Katrina L Kosec. 2018. *Cash Transfers Increase Trust in Local Government*. Policy Research Working Paper WPS 8333. Washington, DC: World Bank Group.

Evans, Peter, Harold Jacobson, and Robert Putnam. 1993. *Double-Edged Diplomacy*. Berkeley: University of California Press.

Ewi, Martin, and Uyo Salifu. 2017. *Money Talks: A Key Reason Youths Join Boko Haram*. Pretoria: Institute for Security Studies. https://issafrica.s3.amazonaws.com/site/uploads/policybrief98.pdf.

Expert Letter. 2013. "Secretary of State John F. Kerry: Remove the Barriers to Peacebuilding." *Charity and Security*. June 20. Accessed March 20, 2018. https://www.charityandsecurity.org/sites/default/files/Peacebuilding%20Petition%202013.pdf.

Ezekilov, J. 2017. "Gender 'Men-Streaming' CVE: Countering Violence Extremism by Addressing Masculinities Issues." *Reconsidering Development* 5 (1).

Fabi, Randy, and Kanupriya Kapoor. 2016. "Indonesia's Most-Wanted Awakens New Generation of Jihadis." *Reuters*, August 26.

Fair, C. Christine, Rebecca Littman, Neil Malhortra, and Jacob N. Shapiro. 2016. *Relative Poverty, Perceived Violence, and Support for Militant Politics: Evidence from Pakistan*. The European Political Science Association, 1–25.

Fair, C. Christine, and Bryan Shepherd. 2006. "Who Supports Terrorism? Evidence from Fourteen Muslim Countries." *Studies in Conflict and Terrorism* 29 (6): 51–74.

Farooq, Sadaf, Saiqa Bukhari, and Manzoor Ahmed. 2017. "Arab Spring and the Theory of Relative Deprivation." *International Journal of Business and Social Science* 8 (1): 126–132.

FATF. 2016. *International Standards on Combatting Money Laundering and Financing of Terrorism and Proliferation*. Paris: Financial Action Task Force.

Faure, Guy Olivier. 2007. "Demonization and Negotiation." *PIN Points* 28: 7–10. Accessed March 20, 2018. http://www.pin-negotiation.org/userfiles/images/pinpoints/PP28.pdf.

Faure, Guy Olivier, and I. William Zartman. 2010. *Negotiating with Terrorists*. New York: Routledge.

FBI. 2016. "Don't Be a Puppet." Accessed March 23, 2018. https://cve.fbi.gov/home.html.

The Federal Council of the Swiss Government. 2015. "Investing in Fragile Environments: The Role of the Private Sector in Countering Violent Extremism." September 29. Accessed January 17, 2017. https://www.admin.ch/gov/en/start/documentation/media-releases.msg-id-58918.html.

Ferguson, Kate. 2016. *Countering Violent Extremism through Media and Communication Strategies : A Review of the Evidence*. Norwich, UK: University of East Anglia, Partnership for Conflict, Crime and Security Research.

Field, Anne. 2016. "Hatching Startups with a Positive Social Impact on Muslims." *Forbes*, April 29. Accessed January 12, 2017. http://www.forbes.com/sites/annefield/2016/04/29/hatching-startups-with-a-positive-social-impact-on-muslims/#2f6dd8d64bb6.

Fink, Naureen C., and Jack Barclay. 2013. *Mastering the Narrative: Counterterrorism Strategic Communication and the United Nations*. Washington, DC: Center on Global Counterterrorism Cooperation.

Fink, Naureen Chowdhurry, Sara Zeiger, and Rafia Bhulai. 2016. *A Man's World: Exploring the Roles of Women in Countering Terrorism and Violent Extremism*. Abu Dhabi and Washington, DC: Hedayah and the Global Center on Cooperative Security.

Fisher, Roger, William Ury, and Bruce Patton. 1991. *Getting to Yes*. New York: Penguin.

Fisher, Ronald. 2005. *Paving the Way: Contributions of Interactive Conflict Resolution to Peacemaking*. New York: Lexington Books.

Flannery, Frances. 2016. *Understanding Apocalyptic Terrorism: Countering the Radical Mindset*. New York: Routledge.

Foa, Roberto, and Yascha Mounk. 2017. "The Signs of Deconsolidation." *Journal of Democracy* 28 (1): 5–16.

Foster, Michelle. 2017. "Media Feast, News Famine: Ten Global Advertising Trends That Threaten Independent Journalism." *Center for International Media Assistance*. January 5. Accessed January 10, 2017. https://www.cima.ned.org/publication/media-feast-news-famine-ten-global-advertising-trends-threaten-independent-journalism/.

Fox, Susannah, and Sydney Jones. 2009. "Depression, Anxiety, Stress or Mental Health Issues." *Pew Research Center*. June 11. Accessed March 20, 2018. http://www.pewinternet.org/2009/06/11/depression-anxiety-stress-or-mental-health-issues/.

Frankel, Viktor. 1956. *Man's Search for Meaning*. Boston, MA: Beacon Press.

Freedom House. 2018. "Freedom in the World 2018: Democracy in Crisis." Washington, DC, 1.

Fromm, Erich. 1941. *Escape from Freedom*. New York: Farrar & Rinehart.

Galtung, Johan. 2000. *Conflict Transformation by Peaceful Means (the Transcend Method)*. Manual, UN Disaster Management Training Programme.

Galula, David. 2006. *Counterinsurgency Warfare: Theory and Practice*. Westport, CT: Praeger Security International.

Gambetta, Diego, and Steffen Hertog. 2016. *Engineers of Jihad: The Curious Connection between Violent Extremism and Education*. New Haven, CT: Princeton University.

Ganor, Boaz. 2010. "If Global Jihad Isn't the Enemy, What Is?" *Jerusalem Post*.

GAO. 2018. *Obligations of Overseas Contingency Operations Funding for Operation and Maintenance Base Requirements*. Washington, DC: U.S. Government Accountability Office.

Garagozov, Rauf. 2012. "Narratives in Conflict: A Perspective." *Dynamics of Asymmetric Conflict: Pathways toward Terrorism and Genocide* 5 (2): 101–106.

Gartenstein-Ross, Daveed. 2011. "Bin Laden's 'War of a Thousand Cuts' Will Live On." *Atlantic*, May 3.

GCCS. 2015. *Strengthening the Case: Good Criminal Justice Practices to Counter Terrorism*. Washington, DC: Global Center for Cooperative Security.

GCCS. 2015. *Strengthening Rule of Law Responses to Counter Violent Extremism: What Role for Civil Society in South Asia*? May. Global Center for Cooperative Security, National University of Singapore, Institute for South Asian Studies, Institute for Inclusive Security.

GCERF. 2015. "Innovative Approaches to Countering Violent Extremism." *Global Community Engagement and Resilience Fund (GCERF)*. June. Accessed December 20, 2016. http://www.gcerf.org/wp-content/uploads/GCERF-at-WEF-Africa-Summit_Innovative-Approaches-to-CVE.pdf.

———. 2016. "Opportunities and Challenges for Mobilizing Resources for Preventing Violent Extremism." *Global Community Engagement and Resilience Fund (GCERF)*. June 21. Accessed December 12, 2016. http://www.organizingagainstve.org/wp-content/uploads/2016/07/Meeting-Summary-Mobilizing-Resources-for-PVE-June-21_Final.pdf.

———. n.d. Accessed December 2, 2016. http://www.gcerf.org.

GCTF. 2015. *Good Practices on Women and Countering Violent Extremism*. Global Counterterrorism Forum (GCTF).

Gelfand, Michele. 2011. "Differences between Tight and Loose Cultures: A 33-Nation Study." *Science* 332 (6033): 1100–1104.

Geneva Call. 2016. "Turkey: The PKK movement signs Geneva Call's Deed of Commitment prohibiting sexual violence and against gender discrimination" March 15. Accessed June 2, 2018. https://genevacall.org/turkey-pkk-movement-signs-geneva-calls-deed-commitment-prohibiting-sexual-violence-gender-discrimination/

Gerecht, Marc Reuel. 2002. *The Gospel According to Osama Bin Laden. Atlantic*.

Ghanem, Hafez. 2015. "Economic Inclusion Can Help Prevent Violent Extremism in the Arab world." Brookings, November 10.

Gill, Paul, John Horgan, and Paige Deckert. 2014. "Bombing Alone: Tracing the Motivations and Antecedent Behaviors of Lone-Actor Terrorists." *Journal of Forensic Science* 59: 425–435.

Gilligan, James. 1996. *Violence*. New York: Putnam.

———. 2001. *Preventing Violence*. London: Thames & Hudson.

Ginsburg, Thomas and Tamir Moustafa. 2008. *Rule by Law: The Politics of Courts in Authoritarian Regimes*. New York: Cambridge University Press.

Gleditsch, Nils Petter, Ragnhild Nordas, and Idean Salehyan. 2007. *Climate Change and Conflict: The Migration Link*. n.p.: International Peace Academy.

Goldin, Nicole. Contributing authors were Veronica Lopez; Susana Puerto Gonzalez; Peter Glick with Nelly Mejia and Francisco Perez-Arce; and Mattias Lundberg, Angela Jhanji, Maria Andersen. 2015. *Toward Solutions for Youth Employment: A Baseline for 2015*. Washington, DC: Solutions for Youth Employment.

Goldstone, Jack. 1991. *Revolution and Rebellion in the Early Modern World*. Berkeley: University of California Press.

GPI. 2017. *Global Peace Index*. Sydney: Institute for Economics and Peace.

Granovetter, Mark. 1978. "Threshold Models of Human Behavior." *American Journal of Sociology* 83 (6): 1420–1443.

Green, Shannon, and Keith Proctor. 2016. "Turning Point: A New Comprehensive Strategy for Countering Violent Extremism." *Center for Strategic and International*

Studies. November 15. Accessed January 15, 2017. https://csis-ilab.github.io/cve/report/Turning_Point.pdf.

Greenberg, Andy. 2016. "Google's Clever Plan to Stop Aspiring ISIS Recruits." *WIRED*, September 7. Accessed December 15, 2016. https://www.wired.com/2016/09/googles-clever-plan-stop-aspiring-isis-recruits/.

Greenwald, Glen, and Murtaza Hussein. 2014. "Meet the Muslim-American Leaders the FBI and NSA Have Been Spying On." *Intercept*, July 9.

Grieg, J. Michael. 2005. "Stepping into the Fray: When Do Mediators Mediate." *American Journal of Political Science* 49 (2): 249–266.

GSX. 2017. "A Global Civil Society Advocacy, Policy Analysis, and Collaboration Platform Dedicated to Preventing Extremism (PVE)." Accessed March 20, 2018. http://www.organizingagainstve.org/wp-content/uploads/2017/02/GSX-Fact-Sheet-FINAL_SA_FP.pdf.

GTD. 2017. *Global Terrorism Database; Codebook: Inclusion Criteria and Variables*. University of Maryland: START National Consortium for the Study of Terrorism and Responses to Terrorism, 9–10.

GTI. 2017. *Global Terrorism Index 2017*. New York: Institute for Economics and Peace.

Gurr, Ted R. 1970. *Why Men Rebel*. Princeton, NJ: Princeton University Press.

Haas, Richard, and Meghan O'Sullivan. 2000. *Honey and Vinegar: Incentives, Sanctions, and Foreign Policy*. Washington, DC: Brookings Institution.

Hafner-Burton, Emilie M., and Jacob N. Shapiro. 2010. "Tortured Relations: Human Rights Abuses and Counterterrorism Cooperation." *Political Science & Politics* (Cambridge Journals) 43 (3): 415–419.

Haider, Syed. 2016. "The Shooting in Orlando, Terrorism or Toxic Masculinity (or Both?)." *Men and Masculinities* 19 (September 16): 555–565.

Haidt, Jonathan. 2003. *The Righteous Mind: Why Good People Are Divided by Politics and Religion*. New York: Penguin.

Halverson, Jeffry R., Steven R. Corman, and H. I. Goodall. 2011. *Master Narratives of Islamist Extremism*. New York: Palgrave Macmillan.

Hamilton, Mark. 2012. "Hamilton Dissertation Data Links." Accessed March 20, 2018. https://sites.google.com/site/hamiltondissertationlinks/.

———. 2015. "A Pedagogy for Peacebuilding: Practicing an Integrative Model for Conflict Analysis and Response." *Revista de Mediación* 8 (2): 1–9.

———. 2016. "Juggling Defense and Security in the Americas: Academic, Diplomatic, and Professional Engagement at the Inter-American Defense College." *Hemisferio: Revista del Colegio Interamericano de Defensa* 2: 114–118.

———. 2017. "Why Rebel? Unpacking the Mechanisms of Mobilization from Sri Lanka to Star Wars." Paper presented at International Studies Association. Baltimore.

Hamilton, Stephen F. 1994. "Social Roles for Youth: Interventions in Unemployment." In *Youth Unemployment and Society*, by Anne C. Peterson and Jeylan T Mortimer, 248–269. New York: Cambridge University Press.

Hancock, Louise. 2013. "Women and Afghan Police." *Oxfam International*. September. Accessed March 20, 2018. https://www.oxfam.org/sites/www.oxfam.org/files/file_attachments/bp-173-afghanistan-women-police-100913-en_3.pdf.

Harris, Gardiner. 2014. "Borrowed Time on Disappearing Land: Facing Rising Seas, Bangladesh Confronts the Consequences of Climate Change." *New York Times*, March 28.

Hasen, Richard L. 2017. "Cheap Speech and What It Has Done (to American Democracy)." *First Amendment Law Review*, Vol. 16, Symposium Issue, 2018.

Haspeslagh, Sophie. 2013. "Listing Terrorist: The Impact of Proscription on Third-Party Efforts to Engage Armed Groups in Peace Processes—A Practitioner's Perspective." *Critical Studies on Terrorism* 6 (1): 189–208.

Hassan, Mehdi. 2014. "This Is What Wannabe Jihadists Order on Amazon before Leaving for Syria." *New Republic*, August 22.

Havlicek, Sasha. 2015. "The Islamic State's War on Women and Girls." Testimony Prepared for the United States House of Representatives Committee on Foreign Affairs. July 28. Accessed March 20, 2018. http://docs.house.gov/meetings/FA/FA00/20150729/103835/HHRG-114-FA00-Wstate-HavlicekS-20150729.pdf.

Hawkes, Keegan, and Alex Amend. 2018. "The Alt Right Is Killing People." *Southern Poverty Law Center*. Montgomery, Alabama, February 5.

Hedayah and International Centre for Counter-terrorism–The Hague. 2014. "Developing Effective Counter-Narrative Frameworks for Countering Violent Extremism." Meeting Note.

Heinrich, Geoff, David Leege, and Carrie Miller. 2008. "A User's Guide to the CRS Integral Human Development (IHD)." *Catholic Relief Services*. Accessed March 2018, 2018. https://www.crs.org/sites/default/files/tools-research/users-guide-to-integral-human-development.pdf.

Hermansson, Patrik. 2017. "My Year Inside the International Alt-Right." Accessed March 20, 2018. https://alternativeright.hopenothate.com/my-year-inside-the-international-alt-right.

Heydemann, Steven. 2014. *Insights: Countering Violent Extremism as a Field of Practice*. Washington, DC: U.S. Institute of Peace.

Hirsch, Michael. 2016. "Inside the FBI's Secret Muslim Network." *Politico*, March 24.

Holder v. Humanitarian Law Project. 2010. 561 (Supreme Court of the United States).

Holmen, Kacey. 2016. "Hundreds March against Islamophobia, Call to End CVE Program." *Minnesota Daily*, September 17.

Home Office. 2015. "Proscribed Terrorist Organisations." London: Home Office.

———. 2016. *For Information Note: Operating within Counter-Terrorism Legislation*. London: Home Office.

Horgan, John. 2014. *The Psychology of Terrorism*. New York: Routledge.

Horowitz, Jonathan. 2013. *Counterterrorism and Human Rights Abuses in Kenya and Uganda: The World Cup Bombing and Beyond*. Washington, DC: Open Society Foundations.

Howard, Ross. 2009. *Conflict Sensitive Journalism*. Handbook, International Media Support and Institute for Media, Policy and Civil Society.

Howell, Jude, Marlies Glasius, Armine Ishkanian, Ebanezer Obadare, and Hakan Seckinelgin. 2008. "The Backlash against Civil Society in the Wake of the Long War on Terror." *Development in Practice*, February 1: 4.

Hoyle, Carolyn, Alexandra Bradford, and Ross Frenett. 2015. "Becoming Mulan? Female Western Migrants to ISIS." *Institute for Strategic Dialogue*. Accessed March 20, 2018. https://www.isdglobal.org/wp-content/uploads/2016/02/ISDJ2969_Becoming_Mulan_01.15_WEB.pdf.

Huckerby, Jayne. 2011. "A Decade Lost: Locating Gender in U.S. Counter-Terrorism." *The Center for Human Rights and Global Justice*. Accessed March 20, 2018. http://chrgj.org/wp-content/uploads/2012/10/Briefing-English-decade-lost.pdf.

———. 2016. "Women, Gender and the U.K. Government's Countering Violent Extremism (CVE) Efforts: Looking Back and Forward." In *A Man's World? Exploring the Roles of Women in Countering Terrorism and Violent Extremism*, by Naureen Chowdhury Fink, Sara Zeiger and Rafia Bhulai, 76–98. Washington, DC: Hedayah and Global Center on Cooperative Security. http://www.globalcenter.org/wp-content/uploads/2016/07/AMansWorld_FULL.pdf.

Hudson, Valerie M. 2009. "The Heart of the Matter: The Security of Women and the Security of States." *International Security* 33 (3): 7–45.

Hug, Erin C. 2013. *The Role of Isolation in Radicalization: How Important Is It?* Monterey, CA: Naval Postgraduate School.

Hughes, Martin. 1990. "Terror and Negotiation." *Terrorism and Political Violence* 2 (1): 72–82.

Human Security Collective. 2013. "10 Human Security Guiding Practices for Countering Violent Extremism." *The Civil Society Network for Human Security*. Accessed March 20, 2018. http://www.hscollective.org/wp-content/uploads/2013/10/10-Human-Security-Guiding-Practices-for-Countering-Violent-Extremism.pdf.

Humanitarian Assistance Facilitation Act of 2013. n.d. H.R. 3526 (U.S. Congress).

Humphreys, Macartan, and Jeremy M. Weinstein. 2008. "Who Fights? The Determinants of Participation in Civil War." *American Journal of Political Science* 52 (2): 436–455.

Hunter, Shireen. 2013. "The Regional and International Politics of Rising Sectarian Tensions in the Middle East & South Asia." *Prince Alwaleed Bin Talal Center for Muslim-Christian Understanding*. Washington, DC: Georgetown University, July 23.

ICG. 2016a. *Exploiting Disorder: Al-Qaeda and the Islamic State*. Brussels: International Crisis Group.

———. 2016b. "Exploiting Disorder: Al-Qaeda and the Islamic State." *International Crisis Group*. March. Accessed March 20, 2018. https://www.crisisgroup.org/global/exploiting-disorder-al-qaeda-and-islamic-state.

———. 2016c. "Nigeria: Women and the Boko Haram Insurgency." *International Crisis Group*. Accessed March 20, 2018. https://d2071andvip0wj.cloudfront.net/242-nigeria-women-and-the-boko-haram%20Insurgency.pdf.

ICRC. 1994. "The Code of Conduct for the International Red Cross and Red Crescent Movement and NGOs in Disaster Relief." Geneva.

Igoe, Michael. 2015. *Will USAID Fund Its Own Mission Statement*. Washington, DC: DEVEX, May 28.

ILO. 2015. *Global Employment Trends for Youth 2015: Scaling Up Investments in Decent Jobs for Youth*. Geneva: International Labour Organization.

Imron, Rasyid. 2006. "Relawan Mujahid Solo Mulai Latihan Fisik." *Tempo*, August 13.

Institute for Economics and Peace. 2017. *Measuring Peacebuilding Cost Effectiveness*. New York: Institute for Economics and Peace.

Institute for Security Studies. 2017. *Armed Conflict Survey 2017*. London: Institute for Security Studies.

Institute for Strategic Dialogue. 2016. "Best Practice Guide Content Creation." *Counter Narratives Toolkit*. www.counternarratives.org.

Intelligence Reform and Terrorism Prevention Act of 2004. n.d. Pub. L. 108–458, 118 Stat. 3638.

International Commission of Jurists. 2009. "Assessing Damage, Urging Action." *Report of the Eminent Jurists Panel on Terrorism, Counterterrorism and Human Rights*. Geneva: International Commission of Jurists.

IPAC. 2017. "Mothers to Bombers: The Evolution of Indonesian Women Extremists." *Institute for Policy Analysis of Conflict*. Accessed March 20, 2018. http://file.understandingconflict.org/file/2017/01/IPAC_Report_35.pdf.

Irwin, Colin. 2005. *The People's Peace Process in Northern Ireland*. Basingstoke, UK: Palgrave Macmillan.

ISS. 2014. *Radicalization in Kenya: Recruitment to al-Shabaab and the Mombasa Republican Council*. Institute for Security Studies, 1–28. Accessed March 2018. https://issafrica.s3.amazonaws.com/site/ uploads/Paper265.pdf.

Izzi, Valeria. 2013. "Just Keeping Them Busy? Youth Employment Projects as a Peacebuilding tool." *International Development Planning Review* 35 (2): 103–117.

Jaeggi, Adrian, Benjamin C. Trumble, Hlilard S. Kaplan, and Michael Gurven. 2015. "Salivary Oxytocin Increases Concurrently with Testosterone and Time Away from Home among Returning Tsimane' Hunters." *Biology Letters*.

Jahangir, Asma, and Fateh Azzam. 2005. *Human Rights*. Vol. 29, in *Towards a Democratic Response: The Club de Madrid Series on Democracy and Terrorism*. Club de Madrid.

Jamal, Nadia. 2014. "Private Sector Has Expertise to Help Counter Violent Extremism." *Point Magazine*, January. Accessed December 10, 2016. http://www.thepointmagazine.com.au/post.php?s=2014-01-21-private-sector-has-expertise-to-help-counter-violent-extremism.

James, Paul, and Jonathon Friedman. 2006. *Globalization and Violence, Vol. 3: Globalizing War and Intervention*. London: Sage Publications.

Jasanoff, Maya. 2016. "The First Global Terrorists Were Anarchists in the 1890s." *New York Times*, April 29.

Jensen, M., P. James, and H. Tinsley. 2016. "Profiles of Individual Radicalization in the United States—Foreign Fighters (PIRUS-FF): Infographics." Office of University Programs, Science and Technology Directorate, U.S. Department of Homeland Security, College Park, MD.

Jervis, Robert. 1999. "Realism in the Study of World Politics." In *Exploration and Contestation in the Study of World Politics*, by Robert O. Keohane, Stephen D. Krasner, and Peter J. Katzenstein, 28–68. Cambridge, MA: MIT Press.

Johnston, Vanessa. 2010. "An Ecuadorian Alternative: Gang Reintegration." In *Small Arms Survey 2010: Gangs, Groups, and Guns*. Geneva: Small Arms Survey.

Jones, Seth G., and Martin C. Libicki. 2008. *How Terrorist Groups End: Lessons for Countering al Qa'ida*. Santa Monica, CA: RAND Corporation.

Judah, Tim. 2008. *Kosovo: War and Revenge*. New Haven, CT: Yale University.

Katzman, Lisa. 2015. "Big Oil Uses Toxic Chemicals to Clean Up Spills." *Mother Jones*, April 24.

Kazungu, Kalume. 2017. "Security Agents Destroy Three Al-Shabaab Camps in Boni Forest." *Daily Nation*, September 12.

Keefer, Philip, and Norman Loayza. 2008. "Terrorism, Economic Development, and Political Openness." *World Bank*. New York: Cambridge University Press.

Kellner, Douglas. 2008. *Guns and Guns Amok: Domestic Terrorism and School Shootings from the Oklahoma City Bombing to the Virginia Tech Massacre*. Boulder, CO: Paradigm Publisher.

Kelly, C. P., S. Mohtadi, R. Seager, M. A. Cane, and Y. Kushnir. 2015. "Climate Change in the Fertile Crescent and Implications of the Recent Syrian Drought." *Proceedings of the National Academy of Sciences* 112 (11): 3241–3246.

Kennedy, David. 2011. *Don't Shoot: One Man, A Street Fellowship, and the End of Violence in Inner-City America*. New York: Bloomsbury.

Kennedy, Robert F. 1964. "Extremism: Left and Right" in The Pursuit of Justice. New York: Harper and Rowe: 3.

Kenya Community Support Centre. n.d. Accessed March 20, 2018. http://www.kecosce.org/index.php/research-and-capacity-building.

"Kenya Human Rights Organizations Are Not Terrorist Organizations." 2015. April 14. https://www.fidh.org/en/region/Africa/kenya/kenya-human-rights-organisations-are-not-terrorist-organizations.

Kenya Today. 2014. "The List of 540 NGOs, Including Church Organisations Deregistered by Uhuru Government." December 16. Accessed March 20, 2018. https://www.kenya-today.com/news/list-ngo-church-organisations-deregistered-uhuru-government.

Kessels, Eelco, and Christina Nemr. 2016. "Countering Violent Extremism and Development Assistance." Global Center on Cooperative Security, February.

Khalid, Hussein. 2015. "Kenya's Wrongheaded Approach to Terrorism." *Washington Post*, May 1.

Khalil, James, and Martine Zeuthen. 2014. "A Case Study of Counter Violent Extremism Programming: Lessons from OTI's Kenya Transition Initiative." *Stability: International Journal of Security and Development* 3 (1): 31.

Khaliq, Bushra. 2010. "Rising Extremism, War on Terrorism and Women's Lives in Pakistan." *International Viewpoint*. February 16. Accessed March 2018. http://www.internationalviewpoint.org/spip.php?article1824.

Khan, Fatima. 2016. "Muslim Advocates Commends Justice Department Decision to Stop Plans for Dangerous CVE Program That Would Trample on Americans' Civil Rights." *Muslim Advocates*. October 4. Accessed March 20, 2018. https://www.muslimadvocates.org/dojendsplansforsrc/.

Khan, Humera. 2015. "Why Countering Extremism Fails." *Foreign Affairs*. February 18. https://www.foreignaffairs.com/articles/united-states/2015-02-18/why-countering-extremism-fails.

Kiai, Maina. 2016. "How Kenya's Executive extrajudicial killings by the police." *Daily Nation*. July 9.

Kimmel, Michael. 2018. *Healing from Hate: How Young Men Get Into and Out of Violent Extremism*. Oakland: University of California Press.

Ki-moon, Ban. 2010. *Secretary General's Message Human Rights Day 2010*. New York: United Nations.

———. 2015. *Plan of Action to Prevent Violent Extremism*. New York: UN Global Counter-Terrorism Strategy.

King, Martin Luther, Jr.. 1963. *Letter from Birmingham Jail*. Boston: Digital Public Library of America.

Klassen, Ben. 1986. *The White Man's Bible*, Reprint Ed. Lighthouse Point, FL: Church of the Creator.

Klein, Gary, Brian Moon, and Robert R Hoffman. 2006a. "Making Sense of Sensemaking 1: Alternative Perspectives." *Intelligent Systems, IEEE* (July/August) 21 (4): 70–73.

———. 2006b. "Making Sense of Sensemaking 2: A Macrocognitive Model." *Intelligent Systems, IEEE* 21 (5): 88–92. doi:10.1109/MIS.2006.100.

Knapton, Sarah. 2014. "Violence Genes May Be Responsible for One in 10 Serious Crimes." *Telegraph*, October 28.

KNCHR. 2015. *The Error of Fighting Terror with Terror*. Nairobi: Kenya National Center for Human Rights.

Knefel, John. 2016. "Trump Should Stop Calling Terrorism a Cancer, and So Should Everybody Else." *Truthout*. October 7. Accessed March 20, 2018. http://www.truth-out.org/opinion/item/37900-trump-should-stop-calling-terrorism-a-cancer-and-so-should-everybody-else.

Koehler, Daniel. 2016. "Right-Wing Extremism and Terrorism in Europe." *Prism* 6 (2): 97.

Kohut, Andrew. 2005. "Arab and Muslim Perceptions of the United States: Testimony to the U.S. House International Relations Committee, Subcommittee on Oversight and Investigations." *Pew Research Center*. November 10. Accessed March 20, 2018. http://www.pewresearch.org/2005/11/10/arab-and-muslim-perceptions-of-the-united-states/.

Koser, Khalid. 2015a. "Five Ways to Engage the Private Sector in Countering Violent Extremism." *Council on Foreign Relations*. February 23. Accessed January 4, 2017. http://blogs.cfr.org/development-channel/2015/02/23/five-ways-to-engage-the-private-sector-in-countering-violent-extremism/.

———. 2015b. "IDPs, Refugees, and Violent Extremism: From Victims to Vectors of Change." *Brookings Institution*. February 20. Accessed March 20, 2018. https://www.brookings.edu/blog/order-from-chaos/2015/02/20/idps-refugees-and-violent-extremism-from-victims-to-vectors-of-change/.

———. 2016. "Preventing Violent Extremism: Turning a Threat into an Opportunity for the Private Sector." *Huffington Post*, July 20. Accessed December 20, 2016. http://www.huffingtonpost.com/dr-khalid-koser/preventing-violent-extrem_b_11009094.html.

Krähenbühl, Pierre. 2011. "The Militarization of Aid Is Perilous." *Stars and Stripes*, January 15.

Kramer, Andrew E. 2016. "Russia Shows What Happens When Terrorists' Families Are Targeted." *New York Times*, March 29.

Kratz, Jackson. 1999. *Tough Guise: Violence, Media and the Crisis in Masculinity*. Northampton, MA: Media Education Foundation.

Kriesberg, Louis. 2006. *Constructive Conflicts: From Escalation to Resolution*. New York: Rowman & Littlefield.

Kriesberg, Louis, and Bruce Dayton. 2009. *Conflict Transformation and Peacebuilding*. New York: Routledge.

Kristof, Nicholas. 2010. "Here's a Woman Fighting Terrorism with Microloans." *New York Times*, November 13.

Krueger, Alan B. 2007. *What Makes a Terrorist: Economics and the Roots of Terrorism*. Princeton, NJ: Princeton University Press.

Krueger, Alan B., and Jitka Maleckova. 2003. "Education, Poverty and Terrorism: Is There a Causal Connection?" *Journal of Economic Perspectives* 17 (4): 119–144.

Kruglanski, Arie, Jocelyn Belanger, Michele Gelfand, Rohan Gunaratna, Malkanthi Hettiarachchi, Fernando Reinares, Edward Orehek, Jo Sasota, and Keren Sharvit. 2013. "Terrorism—A (Self) Love Story: Redirecting the Significance Quest Can End Violence." *American Psychologist* 68 (7): 559–575.

Kruglanski, Arie, Michele Gelfand, Jocelyn Belanger, Anna Sheveland, Malkanthi Hetiarachchi, and Rohan Gunaratna. 2014. "The Psychology of Radicalization and Deradicalization: How Significance Quest Impacts Violent Extremism." *Advances in Political Psychology* 35 (1): 69–93. doi:10.1111/pops.12163.

Kull, Steven. 2007. "Impact of Negative Attitudes towards the U.S. on Efforts against Jihadist Groups." Testimony before the House Committee on Foreign Affairs, Subcommittee on International Organizations, Human Rights, and Oversight. May 17.

Kuperman, Alan, and Timothy Crawford. 2006. *Gambling on Humanitarian Intervention: Moral Hazard, Rebellion and Civil War*. London: Routledge.

Kurtz, John, and Ricardo L Gomez. 2013. "Civic Engagement of Youth in the Middle East and North Africa." In *Islam and Democracy: Perspectives on the Arab Spring*. Newcastle upon Tyne, UK: Cambridge Scholars.

Kurtz, Jon, Beza Tesfaye, and Rebecca Wolfe. 2018. "Can Economic Interventions Reduce Violence." February 2018. Washington, DC: Mercy Corps. Accessed June 20, 2018. https://www.mercycorps.org/sites/default/files/CanEconomicInterventionsReduceViolence_Afghanistan_MercyCorps_Feb2018.pdf

Kuttab, Daoud. 2016. "Palestinian Journalists Facing Dual Restrictions." *Huffpost*, May 9. Accessed March 20, 2018. https://www.huffingtonpost.com/daoud-kuttab/palestinian-journalists-f_b_9861126.html.

Kuzio, Taras. 2006. "Civil Society, Youth and Societal Mobilization in Democratic Revolutions." *Communist and Post-Communist Studies* 39 (3): 365–386.

Labott, Elise. 2015. "General Allen: Failure to Address Root Causes of ISIS Could 'Condemn' U.S. 'to Fight Forever.'" *CNN*. November 12. Accessed March 2018. http://cnnpressroom.blogs.cnn.com/2015/11/12/general-allen-failure-to-address-root-causes-of-isis-could-condemn-u-s-to-fight-forever/.

Ladbury, Sarah. 2009. "Testing Hypotheses on Radicalization in Afghanistan: Why Do Men Join the Taliban and Hizb-i Islami?" Independent Report for the Department of International Development, Department of International Development (DFID), Cooperation for Peace and Unity (CPAU), Kabul, Afghanistan. http://cpau.org.af/manimages/publications/Drivers_of_Radicalisation_in_Afghanistan_Sep09.pdf.

Lakoff, George. 2001. "Metaphors of Terrorism." *University of Chicago Press*. September 16. Accessed March 20, 2018. https://www.cse.buffalo.edu/~rapaport/575/F01/lakoff.on.terrorism.html.

———. 2014. *The ALL NEW Don't Think of an Elephant!: Know Your Values and Frame the Debate*. White River Junction, VT: Chelsea Green Publishing.

Lakoff, George, and Mark Johnson. 2003. *Metaphors We Live By*. Chicago: University of Chicago Press.

LAPD. 2010. "CVE: Los Angeles Police Department Initiative to Develop Training." Accessed March 20, 2018. https://www.brennancenter.org/sites/default/files/CVE%20initiative%20to%20develop%20training.pdf.

Lapowsky, Issie. 2017. "Tech Companies Have the Tools to Confront White supremacy." *Wired*, August 14. https://www.wired.com/story/charlottesville-social-media-hate-speech-online/.

Laub, Zachary. 2014. *The Taliban in Afghanistan*. Washington, DC: Council on Foreign Relations.

Leahy, Patrick. 2011. "Senator Patrick Leahy Letter to Secretary Clinton and Attorney General Holder." *Senator Leahy*. August 3. Accessed March 20, 2018. https://www.leahy.senate.gov/imo/media/doc/080311LeahyToHolderClinton-SomaliaAidRelief.pdf.

Leahy, Robert L. 2008. "Why Is Terrorism Terrifying." *Psychology Today*, March 29. https://www.psychologytoday.com/blog/anxiety-files/200805/why-is-terrorism-so-terrifying.

Lederach, John Paul. 1997. *Building Peace: Sustainable Reconciliation in Divided Societies*. Washington, DC: U.S. Institute of Peace.

Lederach, John Paul, and Scott Appleby. 2010. "Strategic Peacebuilding: An Overview." In *Strategies of Peace*, by Gerald Powers and Dan Philpott. New York: Oxford University Press.

Leutert, Stephanie. 2017. "Climate Change-Induced Migration from Central America." *Lawfare*, June 21.

Lewis, Andrew. 2009. *The Shadows of Youth: The Remarkable Journey of the Civil Rights Generation*. New York: Farrar, Straus and Giroux.

Lewis, Bernard. 2001. "The Revolt of Islam." *New Yorker*, November 19.

Liechtenstein, Stephanie. 2015. "Reflections on Violent Extremism and Radicalization: Can Emotional Literacy be a Game Changer." December 22. https://www.shrmonitor.org/reflections-violent-extremism-radicalization-can-emotional-literacy-game-changer/.

Life after Hate. n.d. Accessed March 20, 2018. https://www.lifeafterhate.org.

Lipka, Michael. 2017. "Muslims and Islam: Key Findings in the US and around the World." *Pew Research Center*. August 9. Accessed March 20, 2018. http://www.pewresearch.org/fact-tank/2017/08/09/muslims-and-islam-key-findings-in-the-u-s-and-around-the-world/.

Little Big Kids. n.d. Accessed January 13, 2017. http://www.littlebigkids.com.

Lodgaard, Sverre. 2004. "Human Security: Concept and Operation." In *From Warfare to Welfare*, by Marie Muller and Bas de Gaay Fortman. Assen, Netherlands: Royal van Gorcum.

———. 2016. *External Powers and the Arab Spring*. Oslo: Scandinavian Press.

Lonsaway, Kim. 2003. “Hiring and Retaining More Women: The Advantages to Law Enforcement Agencies.” *National Center for Women and Policing*. Accessed March 20, 2018. http://womenandpolicing.com/pdf/newadvantagesreport.pdf.

Lopez, George, and David Cortright. 2007. *Uniting against Terror*. Cambridge, MA: MIT Press.

Lopez, Linette. 2017. “Steve Bannon’s Obsession with a Dark Theory of History Should Be Worrisome.” *Business Insider*, February 2.

Luengo-Cabrera, Jose, and Tessa Butler. 2017. “Reaping the Benefits of Cost-Effective Peacebuilding.” *International Peace Institute Global Observatory*. New York, July 31.

Lynch, Jake, Annabel McGoldrick, and Transcend Members. 2003. *Peace Journalism: What Is It? How to Do It?* Publication, Reporting the World, 29.

Lyons-Padilla, Sarah, Michelle J. Gelfand, Hedieh Mirahmadi, Mehreen Farooq, and Marieke van Egmond. 2015. “Belonging Nowhere: Marginalization & Radicalization Risk among Muslim Immigrants.” *Behavioral Science and Policy* (March): 1–12.

Mackintosch, Kate, and Patrick Duplat. 2013. “ ‘Study of the Impact of Donor Counter-Terrorism Measures on Principled Humanitarian Action.” Independent study commissioned by Norwegian Refugee Council and UN Office for the Coordination of Humanitarian Affairs.

Mandaville, Peter, and Melissa Nozell. 2017. “Engaging Religion and Religious Actors in Countering Violent Extremism.” Special Report 413, U.S. Institute of Peace, Washington, DC, 4.

Marcus, Frances Frank. 1983. “Spring Floods Head for Toxic Swamp.” *New York Times*, April 26.

Marshall, D. R., L. Amsel, Y. Neria, M. J. Cook, E. J. Suh, and J. M. Cook. 2007. “The Psychology of Ongoing Threat: Relative Risk Appraisal, the September 11 Attacks, and Terrorism-Related Fears.” *American Psychology* 62 (4):304–316.

Martin, Gus. 2003. *Understanding Terrorism*. London: Sage.

Maslow, Abraham H. 1966. *The Psychology of Science: A Reconnaissance*. New York: Harper and Row.

McCandless, Erin. 2011. *Polarisation and Transformation in Zimbabwe: Social Movements, Strategy Dilemmas and Change*. South Africa: Kwazulu-Natal Press.

McCants, William. 2015. *The ISIS Apocalypse: The History, Strategy, and Doomsday Vision of The Islamic State*. New York: St. Martin’s Press.

McCants, William. 2011. *Testimony, U.S. House of Representatives, Subcommittee on Counterterrorism and Intelligence, Jihadist Use of Social Media: How to Prevent Terrorism and Preserve Innovation*. UNESCO. December 6. Accessed March 20, 2018. https://homeland.house.gov/hearing/subcommittee-hearing-jihadist-use-social-media-how-prevent-terrorism-and-preserve-innovation/.

———. 2015. *The ISIS Apocalypse: The History, Strategy, and Doomsday Vision of The Islamic State*. New York: St. Martin’s Press.

McCauley, Clark, and Sophia Moskalenko. 2011. *Friction: How Radicalization Happens to Them and Us*. New York: Oxford University Press.

———. 2014. "Toward a Profile of Lone Wolf Terrorists: What Moves an Individual from Radical Opinion to Radical Action." *Terrorism and Political Violence* 26 (1): 69–85.

McGill, Michael, and Claire O'Kane. 2015. "Global Partnership for Children and Youth in Peacebuilding." *Evaluation of Child and Youth in Peacebuilding*. July. Accessed March 20, 2018. https://sites.google.com/site/gpcypeace/.

Megged, Moshe. 2015. "Kenya Government Counter-Terrorism Measures against Al Shabaab Islamists." *Intelligence Briefs*. May 27. Accessed March 20, 2018. https://intelligencebriefs.com/kenya-government-counter-terrorism-measures-against-al-shabaab-islamists/.

Mercy Corps. 2011. *Understanding Political Violence among Youth: Evidence from Kenya on the Links between Youth Economic Independence, Social Integration and Stability*. Portland, OR: Mercy Corps.

———. 2015. *Youth & Consequences: Unemployment, Injustice and Violence*. Washington, DC: Mercy Corps.

———. 2016a. *Gifts and Graft: How Boko Haram Uses Financial Services for Recruitment and Support*. Portland, OR: Mercy Corps.

———. 2016b. *Motivations and Empty Promises: Voices of Former Boko Haram Combatants and Nigerian Youth*. Portland, OR: Mercy Corps.

Merriman, Hardy, and Jack DuVall. 2007. "Dissolving Terrorism at Its Roots." In *Nonviolence: An Alternative for Countering Global Terror(ism)*, by Ralph Summy and Senthil Ram. Hauppauge, NY: Nova Science Publishers.

Metcalfe-Hough, Victoria, Tom Keatinge, and Sara Pantuliano. 2015. *U.K. Humanitarian Aid in the Age of Counterterrorism: Perceptions and Reality*. Humanitarian Policy Working Group Paper, London: Overseas Development Institute.

Millar, Alistair, and Eric Rosand. 2016. "Preventing Violent Extremism in 2017 and Beyond: Fading or Renewed UN and US Leadership." *Just Security*. November 16. Accessed March 20, 2018. https://www.justsecurity.org/34545/preventing-violent-extremism-2017-beyond-fading-renewed-u-s-leadership/.

Minkowitz, Donna. 2017. "How the Alt-Right Is Using Sex and Camp to Attract Gay Men to Fascism." *Slate*, June 5. http://www.slate.com/blogs/outward/2017/06/05/how_alt_right_leaders_jack_donovan_and_james_o_meara_attract_gay_men_to.html.

Minnesota Group Letter. 2015. "Minnesota Muslims Concerned about New 'Stigmatizing, Divisive, and Ineffective' CVE Pilot Program." Accessed March 20, 2018. http://files.ctctcdn.com/bd15115b001/d068ad69-9ad8-46a0-bdcd-b9d57454ed20.pdf.

Mo'alla, Noor. 2016. "Countering Violent Extremism in Jordan—Time for a Rethink." *Albany*. June 27. Accessed March 20, 2018. http://www.albanyassociates.com/notebook/2016/06/countering-violent-extremism-in-jordan-time-for-a-rethink/.

Moghaddam, Fathali M. 2005. "The Staircase to Terrorism: A Psychological Exploration." *American Psychologist* (American Psychological Association) 60 (2): 161–169. doi:10.1037/0003–066X.60.2.161.

———. 2010. "De-Radicalization and the Staircase from Terrorism." Chap. 16 in *The Faces of Terrorism: Multidisciplinary Perspectives*, by David Canter. Oxford, UK: Wiley-Blackwell. doi:10.1002/9780470744499.ch16.

Moisi, Dominique. 2007. *The Clash of Emotions*. New York: Foreign Affairs.

Moller, Herbert. 1968. "Youth as a Force in the Modern World." *Comparative Studies in Society and History* 10 (3): 237–260.

Monaco, Lisa. 2014. *Remarks by Assistant to the President for Homeland Security and Counterterrorism*. Washington, DC: The White House.

Moore, John. n.d. "The Evolution of Islamic Terrorism." *Public Broadcasting Service Frontline*.

Morgan, Wesley. 2018. "Pentagon Says Media 'Complicit' by ISIS Ambush Video." *Politico*, March 5.

Morocco on the Move. n.d. http://moroccoonthemove.com/#sthash.wABfXc3o.dpbs.

Morse, Ashley, Adam Isaacson, and Maureen Meyer. 2011. *Tackling Urban Violence in Latin America*. Washington, DC: Washington Office on Latin America.

Muflehun. 2012. www.muflehun.org.

Muggah, Robert. 2014. "Next-Generation Disarmament, Demobilization, and Reintegration." *World Politics Review*, June 17.

Munive, J., and F. Stepputat. 2015. "Rethinking Disarmament, Demobilization and Reintegration Programs." *Stability: International Journal of Security and Development* 4 (1): 48.

Muraya, Joseph. 2016. "Kenya to Launch a National Counter Violent Extremism Policy." *Capital News*, June 28.

Murphy, Shelley. 2014. "Boston to Host Anti-Extremist Pilot Program." *Boston Globe*, September 24.

Nacos, Brigitte. 2016. *Mass Mediated Terrorism: The Central Role of the Media in Terrorism and Counter Terrorism*. Lanham, MD: Rowman & Littlefield.

Naim, Moises. 2009. "What Is a GONGO? How Government-Sponsored Groups Masquerade as Civil Society." *Foreign Policy,* October 13. https://foreignpolicy.com/2009/10/13/what-is-a-gongo/.

Nairn, Tom, and Paul James. 2005. *Global Matrix: Nationalism, Globalism and State-Terrorism*. London: Pluto Press.

Nasser-Eddine, Minerva, Bridget Garnham, Katerina Agostino, and Gilbert Caluya. 2011. *Countering Violent Extremism (CVE) Literature Review*. No. DSTO-TR-2522, Edinburgh, Australia: Defense Science and Technology Organization.

National Security Critical Issues Task Force. 2016. *Countering Violent Extremism-Applying the Public Health Approach*. Center for Security Studies, Georgetown University, Washington, DC: Georgetown Security Studies Review.

Nett, Katharina, and Lukas Rüttinger. 2016. *Insurgency, Terrorism and Organised Crime in a Warming Climate: Analysing the Links between Climate Change and Non-State Armed Groups*. Berlin: Adelphi.

Neumann, Peter. 2007. "Negotiating with Terrorists." *Foreign Affairs* 86 (1): 128–138.

NGO Letter. 2015. "A U.S. Humanitarian, Development and Peacebuilding Statement on the U.S. Global Countering Violent Extremism Agenda." Accessed March 2018. http://www.allianceforpeacebuilding.org/site/wp-content/uploads/2015/07/Statement-FINAL.pdf.

NGO Petition. 2015. "NGO Petition to Kenyan Government on Administrative Harassment." *ESCR-Net*. December. Accessed March 20, 2018. https://www.escr-net.org/petitions/2015/kenya-stop-administrative-harassment-kenya-human-rights-commission-and-other-ngos.

Nguyen, Rosa. 2015. "Civil Rights Groups Protest Federal Program to Combat Extremism, Saying It Targets Muslims." *Boston Globe*, August 7.

Nicole, Flatow, and Esther Yu Hsi Lee. 2014. "New Racial Profiling Guidance Retains Broad Exemptions For Immigration, National Security." *Think Progress*, December 8.

9/11 Commission. 2004. *The 9/11 Commission Final Report*. W. W. Norton and Co., New York: National Commission on Terrorist Attacks upon the United States.

Niyiragira, Yves. 2015. *Current Challenges Facing the Civil Society in Kenya*. Rosa Luxemburg Stiftung.

No H28. n.d. Accessed January 18, 2018. http://www.no2h8.com.

Nordland, Rod. 2010. "Gunmen Kill Medical Aid Workers in Afghanistan." *New York Times*, August 7.

Nowrasteh, Alex. 2016. *Terrorism and Immigration: A Risk Analysis*. Policy Analysis #798, Washington, DC: Cato Institute.

Obama, Barack. 2015. *Remarks by the President at the Summit on Countering Violent Extremism*. Washington, DC: The White House.

O'Brien, Sean P. 1996. "Foreign Policy Crises and the Resort to Terrorism: A Time-Series Analysis of Conflict Linkages." *Journal of Conflict Resolution* 40 (2): 320–335.

Odafen, Onomen E. 2016. *The Northern Nigerian Countering Violent Extremism Project: A Measure of Participation vis-a-vis Outcomes*. SIT Graduate Institute Capstone Collection. 2949.

ODI. 2013. "What Is the Evidence on the Impact of Employment Creation on Stability and Poverty Reduction in Fragile States." London: Overseas Development Institute.

OECD. 2008. *Handbook on Security System Reform: Supporting Security and Justice*. OECD DAC Organisation for Economic Cooperation and Development—Development Assistance Committee.

———. 2016. "States of Fragility Report." Brussels: Organisation for Economic Co-operation and Development.

Office of the President. 2011. "Strategic Implementation Plan for Empowering Local Partners to Prevent Violent Extremism in the United States." Washington, DC: Office of the President of the United States.

———. 2016. "Strategic Implementation Plan for Empowering Local Partners to Prevent Violent Extremism in the United States." Washington, DC: Office of the President of the United States.

Oftedal, Emilie. 2015. *The Financing of Jihadi Terrorist Cells in Europe*. Kjeller: Norwegian Defence Research Establishment.

Oliver, Roy. 2017. "Who Are the New Jihadis." *Guardian*, April 13.

OPIC. 2016. "The Deal Highlights OPIC's Work Bringing Stability to Developing Countries." November 30. Accessed January 5, 2017. https://www.opic.gov/

blog/impact-investing/deal-highlights-opics-work-bringing-stability-developing-countries.

OSCE. 2007. *The Role of Civil Society in Preventing Terrorism*. Barcelona: OSCE Office for Democratic Institutions and Human Rights.

———. 2014. *Preventing Terrorism and Countering Violent Extremism and Radicalization That Lead to Terrorism: A Community Policing Approach*. Vienna: Organization for Security and Cooperation in Europe-OSCE.

Own Your Brain. n.d. Accessed January 25, 2017. http://ownyourbrain.org/about/own-your-brain/.

Patel, Faiza. 2011. *Rethinking Radicalization*. New York: Brennan Center for Justice.

Patel, Faiza, and Meghan Koushik. 2017. *Countering Violent Extremism*. New York: Brennan Center for Justice.

Pauwels, Lieven, Fabienne Brion, Nele Schils, Julianne Laffineur, Antionette Verhage, Brice De Ruyyer, and Marleen Easton. 2014. *Explaining and Understanding the Role of Exposure to New Social Media on Violent Extremism: An Integrative Quantitative and Qualitative Approach*. Science and Society.

"Peacebuilding Exemption Letter." 2011. *Charity and Security Network*. May 12. Accessed March 20, 2018. https://www.charityandsecurity.org/sites/default/files/Ltr%20to%20Clinton%20w%20cover.pdf.

Peracha, Feriha, Raa Raees Khan, and Sara Savage. 2012. "Educational Methods Successfully Countering and Preventing Violent Extremism." In *Terrorist Narratives and Communicative Devices*, by Sara Zeiger, 127–143. Abu Dhabi and Perth: Hedayah and Edith Cowan University.

Perliger, Arie, and Daniel Milton. 2016. *From Cradle to Grave: The Lifecycle of Foreign Fighters in Iraq and Syria*. West Point, NY: Combating Terrorism Center at West Point.

Peters, Allison. 2014. "Countering Terrorism and Violent Extremism in Pakistan: Why Policewomen Must Have a Role." *Institute for Inclusive Security*. March 31. Accessed March 20, 2018. https://www.inclusivesecurity.org/wp-content/uploads/2014/03/IIS-Pakistan-Memo-v5c-web.pdf.

Pew. 2007. *America's Image in the World*. Washington, DC: Pew Research Center.

———. 2012. *The Global Religious Landscape*. Pew Foundation. http://www.pewforum.org/2012/12/18/global-religious-landscape-exec/.

———. 2013. *U.S. Spends over $16 Billion Annually on Counter-Terrorism*. September 13. Accessed March 20, 2018. http://www.pewresearch.org/fact-tank/2013/09/11/u-s-spends-over-16-billion-annually-on-counter-terrorism/.

Phillips, Brian J. 2017. "Do 90 Percent of Terrorist Groups Last Less than a Year? Updating the Conventional Wisdom." *Terrorism and Political Violence* (September): 1–11.

Piedmont, Dean. 2015. "The Role of Disarmament, Demobilization and Reintegration." *Center for Security Governance*, June.

Pierce, William. 2002a. "The Big Lie." July. Accessed March 20, 2018. http://web.archive.org/web/20130510090449/http:/www.natvan.com/free-speech/fs0207a.html.

———. 2002b. *The Turner Diaries*. Hillsboro, WV: National Vanguard Books.

Pillar, Paul R. 2003. *Terrorism and U.S. Foreign Policy*. Washington, DC: Brookings Institution Press.

PIRUS. n.d. "Profiles of Individual Radicalization in the US." Accessed March 20, 2018. http://www.start.umd.edu/data-tools/profiles-individual-radicalization-united-states-pirus.

Poland, Radio. 2017. "Europe Faces 'Clash of Civilizations', Says Polish Minister after Barcelona Attack." August 17.

Pope Francis I. 2017. "Nonviolence: A Style of Politics for Peace." Vatican City: Vatican, January 1.

Popovic, Srdja, Andrej Milivojevic, and Slobodan Djinovic. 2006. *Nonviolent Struggles—50 Crucial Points*. Belgrade: Centre for Applied Non-Violent Action and Strategies.

Solo Pos. 2000. "Corps Hizbullah Independent."

Post Opinions Staff. 2016. "A Transcript of Donald Trump's Meeting with the Washington Post Editorial Board." *Washington Post*, March 21.

Price, Bryan C. 2017. "Terrorism as Cancer: How to Combat an Incurable Disease." *Terrorism and Political Violence* (June 9).

Priest, Dana, and William M. Arkin. 2010. "A Hidden World, Growing beyond Control." July 19. http://projects.washingtonpost.com/top-secret-america/articles/a-hidden-world-growing-beyond-control/print/.

Proctor, Keith, and Shannon N. Green. 2016. *Turning Point: A New Comprehensive Strategy for Countering Violent Extremism*. Washington, DC: Center for Strategic and International Studies.

Proctor, Keith, and B. Tesfaye. 2015. *How Good Governance Can Diminish Support for Violent Extremism*. Portland, OR: Mercy Corps.

PSR. 2015. *Body Bount: Casualty Figures after 10 Years of the "War on Terror" Iraq Afghanistan Pakistan*. Washington, DC: Physicians for Social Responsibility.

Puntland Development Research Centre. 2013. *Puntland Youth*. Garoowe: Ministry of Education.

Purtill, Corrine. 2015. "What Northern Ireland Teaches Us about Today's War on Terror." *PRI*. July 15. https://www.pri.org/stories/2015-07-15/what-northern-ireland-teaches-us-about-todays-war-terror.

Radsch, Courtney. 2016. "CPJ Raises Concerns over UN Agenda on Preventing Violent Extremism." *Committee for the Protection of Journalists*. February 4. Accessed March 20, 2018. https://cpj.org/blog/2016/02/cpj-raises-concerns-over-un-agenda-on-preventing-v.php.

Ranstorp, Magnus, and Xhudo Gus. 1994. "A Threat to Europe? Middle East Ties with the Balkans and Their Impact on Terrorist Activity throughout the Region." *Terrorism and Political Violence* 6 (2): 196–223.

Rapoport, David. 2006. "Four Waves of Modern Terrorism." *UCLA Burkle Center for International Relations*. Accessed March 20, 2018. http://international.ucla.edu/media/files/Rapoport-Four-Waves-of-Modern-Terrorism.pdf.

Reporters without Borders for Freedom of Information. 2016. *2016 World Press Freedom Index: A "Deep and Disturbing" Decline in Media Freedom*. Freedom Index, Reporters without Borders for Freedom of Information.

Resolution, UN General Assembly. 1990. "Convention on the Rights of the Child." *GA 44/25*. New York, September 2.

Richards, Pablo. 1996. *Fighting for the Rain Forest: War, Youth and Resources in Sierra Leone*. Oxford: Currey.

Rieger, Diana, Lena Frischlich, and Gary Bente. 2013. *Propaganda 2.0: Psychological Effects of Right-Wing and Islamic Extremist Internet Videos*. Cologne, Germany: Wolters Kluwer.

Ritzmann, Alexander, interview by Club de Madrid. 2017. *Alexander Ritzmann: "Focus on Hard Measures Might Even Have Fostered Radicalization"* (February 10). http://stoppingviolentextremism.org/qa-with-alex-ritzmann/.

Robbins, James. 2017. "Does U.S. Military Intervention Reduce or Increase Terrorism?" BBC News, May 26.

Robinson, David M. 2016. "Remarks at the Geneva Conference on Preventing Violent Extremism." *Assistant Secretary, Bureau of Conflict and Stabilization Operations*. April 7.

Rogers, Kelly. 2017. "Why More Groups Are Calling on Comedy to Counter Violent Extremism." *Inside Development*, October 3.

Rogers, Mark, Aaron Chassy, and Tom Bamat. 2010. *Integrating Peacebuilding into Humanitarian and Development Programming*. Baltimore: Catholic Relief Services.

Romaniuk, Peter. 2015. *Does CVE Work? Lessons Learned from the Global Effort to Counter Violent Extremism*. Washington, DC: Global Center on Cooperative Security.

Roosevelt, Theodore. 1901a. *First Annual Message*. December 3. Accessed March 2018. http://www.presidency.ucsb.edu/ws/?pid=29542.

———. 1901b. *Office of the President*. December 3. Accessed March 20, 2018. http://www.presidency.ucsb.edu/ws/?pid=29542.

Rosand, Eric. 2016a. "Communities First: A Blueprint for Organizing and Sustaining a Global Movement against Violent Extremism." *The Prevention Project*. Accessed March 20, 2018. http://www.organizingagainstve.org/wp-content/uploads/2016/12/Communities_First_December_2016.pdf.

———. 2016b. "Minding the Gap: A Multi-Layered Approach to Tackling Violent Extremism." *RUSI Newsbrief*, July 5.

Rosand, Eric, and Alistair Miller. 2017. "How the Private Sector Can Be Harnessed to Stop Violent Extremism." *Brookings Institute*. January 31. Accessed February 4, 2017. https://www.brookings.edu/blog/order-from-chaos/2017/01/31/how-the-private-sector-can-be-harnessed-to-stop-violent-extremism/.

Ross, Jeffrey Ian, and Ted Gurr. 1989. "Why Terrorism Subsides." *Comparative Politics* 21 (4): 405–426.

Rosyid, Imron. 2006. "Relawan Mujahid Solo Mulai Latihan Fisik." *Tempo*, August 13.

Roy, Olivier. 2017. "Who Are the New Jihadists?" *Guardian*, April 13. https://www.theguardian.com/news/2017/apr/13/who-are-the-new-jihadis.

Rubenstein, Richard. 1987. *Alchemists of Revolution: Terrorism in the Modern World*. New York: Basic Books.

Rubin, Barry. 1990. *The Politics of Counter-Terrorism*. Baltimore: Johns Hopkins University Foreign Policy Institute.

Russell, Jonathan, and Haras Rafiq. 2016. *Countering Islamist Extremist Narratives: A Strategic Briefing*. London: Quilliam.

RX. 2007. *Aryan Jihad? New Directions for the Aryan Nations*. January 27. Accessed March 20, 2018. http://threewayfight.blogspot.com.es/2007/01/aryan-jihad-new-directions-for-aryan.html.

Sageman, Marc. 2008a. *Leaderless Jihad: Terror Networks in the Twenty-First Century*. Philadelphia: University of Pennsylvania Press.

———. 2008b. "Understanding Terror Networks." University of Philadelphia, Philadelphia, PA, 178.

Saleh, Heba. 2014. "Internet Draws Women to Jihadi Ranks." *Financial Times*, December 17. https://www.ft.com/content/253085e8-80fd-11e4-896c-00144feabdc0.

Saltman, Erin Marie, and Melanie Smith. 2015. *'Till Martyrdom Do Us Part: Gender and the ISIS Phenomenon*. London: Institute for Strategic Dialogue. https://www.isdglobal.org/wp-content/uploads/2016/02/Till_Martyrdom_Do_Us_Part_Gender_and_the_ISIS_Phenomenon.pdf.

Samuel, Thomas Koruth. 2012. *Reaching the Youth: Countering the Terrorist Narrative*. Perpustakaan Negara Malaysia.

Savage, Sara, Anjum Khan, and Jose Liht. 2014. "Preventing Violent Extremism in Kenya through Value Complexity: Assessment of Being Kenyan Being Muslim." *Journal of Strategic Security* 7 (3): 1–26.

Scahill, Jeremy, and Ryan Devereaux. 2014. "Watch Commander: Barack Obama's Secret Terrorist-Tracking System, by the Numbers." *Intercept*, Augsut 5.

Scheuer, Michael. 2008. *Marching toward Hell: America and Islam after Iraq*. New York: Free Press.

Schirch, Lisa. 2005. *Little Book of Strategic Peacebuilding*. Intercourse, PA: Good Books.

———. 2014. *Conflict Assessment and Peacebuilding Planning*. Boulder, CO: Lynne Rienner Press.

———. 2016. *Handbook on Human Security*. The Hague: Alliance for Peacebuilding, GPPAC, Kroc Institute.

Schirch, Lisa, and Deborah Mancini-Griffoli. 2016. *Local Ownership in Security: Case Studies of Peacebuilding Approaches*. The Hague: Alliance for Peacebuilding, GPPAC, Kroc Institute.

Schlaffer, Edit, and Ulrich Kropiunigg. 2016. "A New Security Architecture: Mothers Included!" In *A Man's World: Exploring the Roles of Women in Countering Terrorism and Violent Extremism*, by Naureen Chawdhury Fink, Sara Zeiger, and Rafia Bhulai, 54–75. Washington, DC: Hedayah and Global Center on Cooperative Security.

Schmid, Alex. 2016. *Links between Terrorism and Exclusion*. The Hague: International Center for Counter-terrorism.

Schmid, Alex P. 2011. *Routledge Handbook of Terrorism Research*. London: Routledge, 48.

———. 2012. "Countering Violent Extremism: A Promising Response to Terrorism." *International Centre for Counter-Terrorism*—The Hague. June 12. Accessed May 2017. https://icct.nl/publication/countering-violent-extremism-a-promising-response-to-terrorism/.

Schmitt, E., and Thom Shanker. 2005. "U.S. Officials Retool Slogan for Terror War." *New York Times*, July 26.

Schultz, Julianne. 2005. "The Ideology of Religion." In *The Lure of Fundamentalism*. Nathan Queensland, Australia: ABC Books.

Schumpeter. 2001. "Young, Jobless, and Looking for Trouble." *Economist*, February 3.

Schwartz, Yishai. 2014. "Israel Destroys Homes to Deter Terrorists. A New Study Says It Works—But Is It Moral?" *New Republic*, December 8. https://newrepublic.com/article/120506/study-israels-home-demolitions-policy-works-it-moral.

SCN. 2016. "Briefing Paper 3: Public-Private Community Initiatives." *Strong Cities Network*. Accessed March 29, 2018. http://strongcitiesnetwork.org/wp-content/uploads/2016/05/Briefing-Paper-3.pdf.

———. n.d. Accessed December 20, 2016. http://strongcitiesnetwork.org.

Searcey, Dionne. 2017. "They Fled Boko Haram, Only to Be Raped by Nigeria's Security Forces." *New York Times*, December 8.

Selby, Jan, Omar Dahi, Mike Hulme, and Christiane Fröhlich. 2017. "Climate Change and the Syrian Civil War Revisited." *Political Geography* 60: 253–255.

Sen, Amartya. 2006. *Identity and Violence*. New York: W. W. Norton and Co.

Serwer, Daniel, and Patricia Thomson. 2007. "A Framework for Success: International Intervention in Societies Emerging from Conflict." In *Leashing the Dogs of War*, by Fen Osler Hampson, Pamela Aall, and Chester Crocker, 369–387. Washington, DC: U.S. Institute of Peace.

Sethi, Arjun Singh. 2014. "The US Government Can Brand You a Terrorist Based on a Facebook Post." *Guardian*, August 30.

———. 2016. "The FBI Needs to Stop Spying on Muslim-Americans." *Politico Magazine*, March 29.

Setmariam, Mustafa. 1992. "Leaderless Resistance." *Seditionist*, February.

Sgueo, Gianluca. 2016. *Counter-Terrorism Funding in the EU Budget*. European Parliamentary Research Service.

Shackle, Samira. 2016. "The London Girls Lost to ISIS: What Became of the 'Jihadi Brides.'" *New Statesman*, October 6. https://www.newstatesman.com/culture/observations/2016/10/london-girls-lost-isis-what-became-jihadi-brides.

Shane, Scott. 2015. "Homegrown Extremists Tied to Deadlier Toll Than Jihadists in U.S. since 9/11." *New York Times*, June 24.

Sheikh, Hammad, Ángel Gómez, and Scott Atran. 2016. "Empirical Evidence for the Devoted Actor Model." *Current Anthropology* 57 (S13): S204–S209.

Shepler, Susan. 2014. *Childhood Deployed: Remaking Child Soldiers in Sierra Leone*. New York: NYU Press.

Silber, Mitchell D., and Arvin Bhatt. 2007. *Radicalization in the West: The Homegrown Threat*. New York: NYPD Intelligence Division.

Silke, Andrew, and Tinka Veldhuis. 2017. "Countering Violent Extremism in Prisons: A Review of Key Recent Research and Critical Research Gaps." *Perspectives on Terrorism* 11 (5): 2–11.

Silove, Derrick. 2013. "The ADAPT Model: A Conceptual Framework for Mental Health and Psychosocial Programming in Post Conflict Settings." *Intervention* 11 (3): 237–248.

Silva, Donniell E. 2016. "Innovative, Cross-Sector Approaches in Countering Violent Extremism." *Global Partnerships Week*. March 11. Accessed December 20, 2016.

http://www.p3.co/blog/2016/3/11/innovative-cross-sector-approaches-in-countering-violent-extremism.

Silver, R. C., E. A. Holman, D. N. McIntosh, M. Poulin, and V. Gil-Riva. 2002. “Nationwide Longitudinal Study of Psychological Responses to September 11.” *Journal of the American Medical Association* 288 (10):1235–1244.

Sivaram, Dharmaratnam. 2006. “The Tamil Perspective.” In *Negotiating Peace in Sri Lanka*, by Kumar Rupesinghe. Colombo: FCE.

Smith, Dan, and Janani Vivekananda. 2007. *A Climate of Conflict: The Links between Climate Change, Peace, and War*. London: International Alert.

The Soufan Group and Qatar International Academy for Security Studies. 2013. *Countering Violent Extremism—The Counter Narrative Study*. Doha, Qatar: QIASS. http://www.soufangroup.com/countering-violent-extremism-the-counter-narrative-study/

Spector, Bertram I. 1998. “Deciding to Negotiate with Villains.” *Negotiation Journal*: 43–59.

Stallen, Mirre, Carston De Dreu, and Shaul Shalvi. 2012. “The Herding Hormone: Oxytocin Stimulates In-Group Conformity.” *Psychological Science* (Sage) 23 (11): 1288–1292 .

START. 2017. “Islamist and Far-Right Homicides in the United States Infographic.” *National Consortium for the Study of Terrorism and Responses to Terrorism*. February. Accessed March 23, 2018. https://www.start.umd.edu/pubs/START_ECDB_IslamistFarRightHomicidesUS_Infographic_Feb2017.pdf.

Staub, Ervin. 2010. *Overcoming Evil: Genocide, Ethnic Conflict, and Terrorism*. New York: Oxford University Press.

Steinberg, Laurence. 2013. “The Influence of Neuroscience on US Supreme Court Decisions about Adolescents’ Criminal Culpability.” *Nature Reviews Neuroscience* 14: 513–518.

Stephan, Maria J. 2016. “Defeating ISIS through Civil Resistance? Striking Nonviolently at Sources of Power Could Support Effective Solutions.” *The Olive Branch*, July 11.

Stephan, Maria, and Shaazka Beyerle. 2015. “How to Stop Extremism Before It Starts.” *Foreign Policy*.

Stern, Jason. 2014. “After Journalist Killins, Potential Violations in Gaza Must Be Investigated.” *Committee for the Protection of Journalists*. August 28. Accessed March 20, 2018. https://cpj.org/blog/2014/08/after-journalist-killings-potential-violations-in-.php.

Stern, Jessica. 2003. *Terror in the Name of God*. New York: HarperCollins.

Steuter, Erin, and Deborah Wills. 2009. *At War with Metaphor: Media, Propaganda, and Racism in the War on Terror*. Lanham, MD: Lexington Books.

Stock, Nathan. 2012. “The Wisdom of Reforming Terrorist Designations.” *Foreign Policy*, June.

Stoddard, Abby, Adele Harmer, and Monica Czwarno. 2017. *Aid Worker Security Report 2017*. Washington, DC: Humanitarian Outcomes and USAID, 1–6.

Stohl, Rachel. n.d. “Questionable Reward: Arms Sale and the War on Terrorism.” *Arms Control Association*. Accessed March 20, 2018. https://www.armscontrol.org/act/2008_01-02/stohl.

Strachan, Anna Louise, and Huma Haider. 2015. "GSDRC, University of Birmingham." *Gender and Conflict: Topic Guide*. Accessed March 20, 2018. http://www.gsdrc.org/wp-content/uploads/2015/07/gender_conflict.pdf.

Sukabdi, Zora. 2015. "Terrorism in Indonesia: A Review on Rehabilitation and Deradicalization." *Journal of Terrorism Research* 6 (2): 36–56.

Sutten, Marne L. 2009. "The Rising Importance of Women in Terrorism and the Need to Reform Counterterrorism Strategy." *School of Advanced Military Studies*. May. Accessed March 20, 2018. http://www.dtic.mil/cgi-bin/GetTRDoc?AD=ADA506225.

Tabibnia, Galnaz, and Matthew D. Lieberman. 2007. "Fairness and Cooperation Are Rewarding Evidence from Social Cognitive Neuroscience." *Annals of the New York Academy of Science* 1118 (1): 90–101.

Tarnoff, Curt, and Marian L. Lawson. 2016. *Foreign Aid: An Introduction to US Programs and Policy*. Washington, DC: Congressional Research Service, 6–9.

Tarras-Wahlberg, Louisa. 2016. *Promises of Paradise? A Study on Official ISIS-Propaganda Targeting Women*. Stockholm: Swedish Defence University.

Taylor, Steve. 2015. "The Psychological Roots of Terrorism: How Disorientation Leads to Destruction." *Psychology Today*, December 5.

———. 2016. *Critical Choices*. Washington, DC: Mercy Corps.

Tesfaye, Beza, and Rebecca Wolfe. 2014. *Why Youth Fight: Making Sense of Political Violence in Sub-Saharan Africa*. Portland, OR: Mercy Corps.

Tesfaye, Beza, Topher McDougal, and Beth Maclin. 2018. *"If the Youth Are Given the Chance": Effects of Education and Civic Engagement on Somali Youth Support of Political Violence*. Washington, DC: Mercy Corps.

Third World Forum on Intercultural Dialogue. 2015. *Countering Violent Extremism: The Role of Religious Leaders in Promoting Religious Pluralism and Advancing Shared Well-being*. Baku, Azerbaijan: Third World Forum on Intercultural Dialogue.

Thomas, Alice. 2013. "Sahel Villagers Fleeing Climate Change must Not Be Ignored." *Guardian*, August 2.

Tiwana, Mandeep, and Netsanet Belay. 2010. *Civil Society: The Clampdown Is Real*. Washington, DC: CIVICUS.

Toros, Harmonie. 2008. *"We Don't Negotiate with Terrorist": Legitimacy and Complexity in Terrorist Conflicts*. Oslo: International Peace Research Institute.

Torres, Phil. 2016. "Agential Risks: A Comprehensive Introduction." *Journal of Evolution and Technology* 26 (2): 31–47.

Translation by Federation of American Scientists. 2005. "Letter from Ayman al Zawahiri to Abu Musab al Zarqawi." https://fas.org/irp/news/2005/10/letter_in_english.pdf.

Travis, Alan. 2008. "MI5 Report Challenges Views on Terrorism in Britain." *Guardian*, August 20.

Umar, Musni. 2011. "Dr. Musni Umar: Partisipasi Masyarakat Solo Dan Demokrasi." March 7. https://musniumar.wordpress.com/2011/03/07/dr-musni-umar-partisipasi-masyarakat-solo-dan-demokrasi-bagian-ke-iv/.

UN General Assembly. 2004. *We the Peoples: Civil Society, the United Nations and Global Governance*. New York: Report of the Panel of Eminent Persons on United Nations-Civil Society Relations.

———. 2005. "Resolution Adopted by the General Assembly 60/1." *2005 World Summit Outcome A/Res/60/1*. New York: United Nations, October 24.

UN Human Security Unit. n.d. Accessed March 20, 2018. https://www.un.org/humansecurity/what-is-human-security/.

UN Office of the High Commissioner on Human Rights. 2015. "UN Expert Raises Alarm at Global Trend of Restricting Civil Society Space on Pretext of National Security and Counter-Terrorism." Geneva.

UN SCR 1373. 2001. "United Nations Security Council Resolution 1373." UN Security Council.

UN SCR 2178. 2014. "United Nations Security Council Resolution 2178." UN Security Council.

UN SCR 2354. 2017. "United Nations Security Council Resolution 2354." UN Security Council.

UN SCR 2396. 2017. "United Nations Security Council Resolution 2396." UN Security Council.

UN Security Council. 2011. "Disarmament, Demobilization, and Reintegration." *A/65/741*. March 21.

UN Women. 2015. "Preventing Conflict, Transforming Justice, Securing the Peace: A Global Study on the Implementation of United Nations Security Council resolution 1325." *UN Women*. Accessed March 20, 2018. http://www.peacewomen.org/sites/default/files/UNW-GLOBAL-STUDY-1325-2015%20(1).pdf.

UNDP. 2017a. *Journey to Extremism in Africa*. New York: United Nations Development Programme (UNDP) Regional Bureau for Africa.

———. 2017b. "Journey to Extremism in Africa: Drivers, Incentives and the Tipping Point for Recruitment." New York: UN Development Program. http://journey-to-extremism.undp.org/ content/downloads/UNDP-JourneyToExtremism-report-2017-english.Pdf.

———. 2017c. *Partnering against Violent Extremism*. UN Development Programme.

UNDP Kenya. 2017. *Articulating the Pathways of the Impact of Terrorism and Violent Extremism on the Kenyan Economy*. Nairobi: UN Development Program Strategic Policy Advisory Unit.

UNDPKO. 2010. "2nd Generation Disarmament, Demobilization, and Reintegration Practices in Peace Operations." UN Department of Peacekeeping Operation, January.

UNESCO. 2016. *Time to Break the Cycle of Violence against Journalists*. UN Agency, The International Programme for the Development of Communication, UNESCO, UNESCO.

UNGA. 2015. *Annual Report of the Special Representative of the Secretary-General for Children and Armed Conflict*.

UNHCR. 2014. *Annual Report of the Special Representative of the Secretary General for Children and Armed Conflict*. UN Human Rights Council.

UNSC. 2001. "UN Resolution 1373." *Security Council*.

———. 2014. *Resolution 2178*. UN Security Council.

———. 2015. *Resolution 2250*. UN Security Council.
———. 2016. "Resolution 2325."
———. 2017a. "Report of the Secretary-General on Conflict-Related Sexual Violence." *S/2017/249*. UN Security Council.
———. 2017b. "Resolution 2370." *UN Security Council*.
UNSCR 1325. 2000. *United Nations Security Council Resolution (UNSCR) 1325 on Women, Peace and Security*.
——— 1373. 2001. *UN Security Council Resolution*. Threats to International Peace and Security Caused by Terrorist Acts.
United Nations. 2000a. "The Brahimi Report." *A/55/305—S/2000/809*.
———. 2005. "UN Security Council Resolution 2242." *S/RES/2242*. October 13.
———. 2006a. "United National Global Counter-Terrorism Strategy." *A/RES/60/288*.
———. 2000b. *United Nations Security Council Resolution 1325*.
———. 2008. "United Nations Security Council Resolution 1844." *S/RES/1844*. November 20.
———. 2012. *United Nations Security Council Resolution 2083*.
———. 2015a. "Plan of Action to Prevent Violent Extremism." *A/65/741*. UN Security Council.
———. 2015b. *UN Integrated DDR Standards*.
United Nations Human Rights Council. 2015. "Resolution Adopted by the Human Rights Council on 2 October 2015 30/15. Human Rights and Preventing and Countering Violent Extremism." *United Nations Human Rights Office of the High Commissioner for Human Rights*. October 12. Accessed June 15, 2016. https://documents-dds-ny.un.org/doc/UNDOC/GEN/G15/232/04/PDF/G1523204.pdf?OpenElement.
United Nations Office of the High Commissioner. 1976. "International Covenant on Civil and Political Rights." *United Nations Human Rights Office of the High Commissioner*. March 23. Accessed June 15, 2016. http://www.ohchr.org/en/professionalinterest/pages/ccpr.aspx.
Urdal, Henrik. 2004. *The Devil in the Demographics: The Effect of Youth Bulges on Domestic Armed Conflict 1950–2000*. Washington, DC: World Bank.
———. 2007. "The Demographics of Political Violence: Youth Bugles, Insecurity, and Conflict in Too Poor for Peace." In *Too Poor for Peace? Global Poverty, Conflict and Security in the 21st Century*, by Lael Brainard and Derek Chollet. Washington, DC: Brookings Institution Press.
U.S. Department of State. 2015. *Country Reports on Terrorism 2015—Kenya*. Washington, DC: U.S. Department of State.
U.S. State Department. 2015. "Draft Follow-on Action Agenda." February 19. Accessed March 20, 2018. http://www.globalcenter.org/wp-content/uploads/2015/05/Draft-Follow-On-Action-Agenda-3-April-2015-version.pdf.
USAID. 2009. *Guide to the Drivers of Violent Extremism*. Washington, DC: USAID.
———. 2016. *Joint Strategy on Countering Violent Extremism*. Washington, DC: U.S. Department of State and USAID.
———. 2017. "Countering Violent Extremism: Kenya, Somalia and East Africa." June. Accessed March 20, 2018. https://pdf.usaid.gov/pdf_docs/PBAAH614.pdf.

van Ginkel, Bibi, and Eva Entenmann. 2016. "The Foreign Fighters Phenomenon in the European Union." *International Centre for Counter-Terrorism*. April. Accessed March 20, 2018. https://www.icct.nl/wp-content/uploads/2016/03/ICCT-Report_Foreign-Fighters-Phenomenon-in-the-EU_1-April-2016_including-AnnexesLinks.pdf.

Van Leuven, Dallin, Dyan Mazurana, and Rachel Gordon. 2016. "Analysing Foreign Females and Males in the Islamic State in the Levant (ISIL) through a Gender Perspective." In *Foreign Fighters under International Law and Beyond*, by Andrea de Guttry, Francesca Capone, and Christopher Paulussen, 97–120. The Hague: Asser/Springer.

Venhaus, John M. 2010. *Why Youth Join al-Qaeda*. Washington, DC: U.S. Institute of Peace.

VICE. 2018. "This Indonesian School Is Deradicalizing the Children of Convicted Terrorists." *VICE News*, January 23.

Volkan, Vamik. 2004. *Blind Trust: Large Groups and Their Leaders in Times of Crisis and Terror*. Charlottesville, VA: Pitchstone Publishing.

Wabala, Dominic. 2018. "60 Returnees Recount Pain at the Hands of Al-Shabaab." *Standard Digital*, February 2.

Walsh, Nick Paton, and Salma Abdelaziz. 2018. "US Assault Rifles Are Being Sold on the Telegram Messaging App in Syria." *CNN*, February 20. https://www.cnn.com/2018/02/20/middleeast/us-weapons-telegram-syria-intl/index.html.

Washington Post Editorial. 2010. "The Supreme Court Goes Too Far in the Name of Fighting Terrorism." *Washington Post*, June 22.

———. 2017. "Trump's Homeland Security Department Gives Right-Wing Extremists a Pass." *Washington Post*, August 31.

WASL. 2018. "Uncomfortable Truths, Unconventional Wisdoms: Women's Perspectives on Violent Extremism and Security Interventions." *ICAN*. Accessed March 20, 2018. http://www.icanpeacework.org/wp-content/uploads/2017/03/WASL-Security-Brief-2016.pdf.

Watson, Paul. 2017. "A Melting Arctic Could Spark a New Cold War." *Time*, May 12.

Weine, S. M., B. H. Ellis, R. Haddad, A. B. Miller, R. Lowenhaupt, and C. Polutnik. 2015. "Lessons Learned from Mental Health and Education: Identifying Best Practices for Addressing Violent Extremism." *Final Report to the Office of University Programs, Science and Technology Doctorate*. Compiled by U.S. Department of Homeland Security. College Park, MD: START.

Weinger, Mackenzie. 2016. "The Private Sector Role in Countering Violent Extremism." *The Cipher Brief*. August 2. Accessed December 20, 2016. https://www.thecipherbrief.com/article/exclusive/private-sector-role-countering-violent-extremism-1089.

Wennmann, Achim. 2011. *The Political Economy of Peacemaking*. London: Routledge.

Werrell, Caitlin E., and Francesco Femia. 2013. *The Arab Spring and Climate Change*. Washington, DC: Center for American Progress, Stimson Center, Center for Climate and Security.

West, Sungutu. 2016. "Kenya Unveils New Strategy for Tackling Terror." *Terrorism Monitor* (Jamestown Foundation) 14 (19): 3–5 .

White House. 2011. *Strategic Implementation Plan for Empowering Local Partners to Prevent Violent Extremism in the United States*. Washington, DC: The White House.

———. 2015. *Fact Sheet: The White House Summit on Countering Violent Extremism*. Washington, DC: White House.

White House National Security Council. 2015. *US National Security Strategy*. Washington, DC: White House.

Willebois, Emile van der Does de. 2010. *Nonprofit Organizations and the Combatting of Terrorism Financing : A Proportionate Response*. Washington, DC: World Bank.

Williams, Ray. 2017. "The Rebirth of Macho: Toxic Masculinity and Authoritarianism: How the Convergence of These Three Trends Threaten American Democracy." *Psychology Today*, August 17. https://www.psychologytoday.com/blog/wired-success/201708/the-rebirth-machotoxic-masculinity-and-authoritarianism.

Wilson, Jamie. 2000. "How the Real IRA Recruits Boys into a Life of Terrorism." *Guardian*, November 18.

Wilton Park. 2016. "Statement: Religion, Radicalization and Countering Violent Extremism." April 29. Accessed March 20, 2018. www.wiltonpark.org.uk/wp-content/uploads/Statement-on-religion-radicalisation-and-countering-violent-extremism.pdf.

Wink, Walter. 1986. *Unmasking the Powers: The Invisible Forces That Determine Human Existence*. Philadelphia, PA: Fortress Press.

Winter, Charlie. 2015. *Documenting the Virtual Caliphate*. Quilliam Foundation, 3–4.

Wintour, Patrick. 2017. "Respect for Human Rights Can Prevent 'Vicious Cycle' of Terrorism, Says UN Chief." *Guardian*, November 16.

Witchel, Elisabeth. 2016. "Getting Away with Murder." *Committee for the Protection of Journalists*. October 27. Accessed March 20, 2018. https://cpj.org/reports/2016/10/impunity-index-getting-away-with-murder-killed-justice.php#1.

Wolfe, Rebecca, and Francis Butichi. 2013. *Examining the Links between Youth Economic Opportunity, Civic Engagement and Conflict: Evidence from Mercy Corps' Somali Leaders Initiative*. Portland, OR: Mercy Corps.

Wood, Elisabeth Jean. 2003. *Insurgent Collective Action and Civil War in El Salvador*. Cambridge: Cambridge University Press.

Wood, Graeme. 2015. "What ISIS Really Wants." *Atlantic*, March.

WORDE. 2018. "Building Resilience against Violent Extremism." Accessed March 20, 2018. http://www.worde.org/programs/the-montgomery-county-model/.

World Health Organization. 2017. *Top 10 Causes of Death*. Geneva: World Health Organization.

World Vision. 2008. "Peacebuilding and Conflict Sensitivity." Accessed March 20, 2018. https://www.wvi.org/peacebuilding.

World Vision International. n.d. "Do No Harm." Accessed March 20, 2018. https://www.wvi.org/peacebuilding-and-conflict-sensitivity/do-no-harm.

Yilmaz, Sefer. 2013. "An Analogy between Cancer Cells and Terrorist Organizations." *International Journal of Management Economics and Business* 9 (19): 347–364.

Zartman, I. William. 1983. *The Practical Negotiator*. New Haven, CT: Yale University Press.

———. 1989. *Ripe for Resolution*. New York: Oxford University Press.

———. 1990. "Negotiating Effectively with Terrorists." In *The Politics of Counterterrorism: The Ordeal of Democratic States*, by Barry Rubin, 163–188. Washington, DC: Foreign Policy Institute.

———. 1992. "Internationalization of Communal Strife: Temptations and Opportunities of Triangulation." In *Internationalization of Communal Strife*, by Manus Midlarsky. London: Routledge.

———. 2000. "Beyond the Hurting Stalemate." In *International Conflict Resolution after the Cold War*, by Paul Stern and Daniel Druckman. Washington, DC: National Academy Press.

———. 2003. "Regional Conflict Resolution." In *International Negotiation: Analysis, Approach, Issues*, by Victor Kremenyuk, 348–361. San Francisco, CA: Jossey-Bass.

Zartman, I. William, and Tanya Alfredson. 2010. "Negotiating with Terrorists and the Tactical Question." In *Coping with Terrorism: Origins, Escalation, Counter Strategies and Responses*, by Rafael Reveuny and William Thompson. Albany, NY: SUNY Press.

Zartman, I. William, and Guy Faure. 2011. *Engaging Extremists*. Washington, DC: U.S. Institute of Peace.

Zartman, I. William, and Alvaro deSoto. 2010. "Timing Mediation Initiatives." *U.S. Institute of Peace*. Accessed March 20, 2018. https://www.usip.org/publications/2010/04/timing-mediation-initiatives.

Zenn, Jacob, and Elizabeth E. Pearson. 2014. "Women, Gender and the Evolving Tactics of Boko Haram." *Journal of Terrorism Research* 5 (1): 46–57.

Zimmerman, Matilde. 2000. *Sandinista: Carlos Fonseca and the Nicaraguan Revolution*. Durham, NC: Duke University Press.

Zürcher, Christoph. 2017. "What Do We (Not) Know about Development Aid and Violence? A Systematic Review." *World Development* 89 (C): 506–522.

Index

Note: Page references for figures are italicized.

adventure, 21, 25, 31, 50, 98, 372; and heroism, 31, 35, 95–98, 102, 273, 275, 281, 372
alienation, 21, 39, 40, 71, 129, 137, 297
Al-Qaeda, 24, 31–32, 39, 44, 48, 61, 74, 79, 81–84, 139, 193, 256, 316, 333
Al-Shabaab, 8, 19, 181, 232, 315–20
alt-right. *See* white supremacists
anarchism, 43, 72–73
anti-racism, 34, 76
anxiety, 7, 21, 71, 80, 99, 101, 259
apocalypticism, 22, 43, 81–86
Arab Spring, 36, 116, 120, 139–48, 165, 298, 345
army rule, 47, 52, 63, 71, 129–30, 141
arts and culture, 35, 50, 56, 273, 346, 354
authoritarian rule, 11, 15, 17–18, 42, 44, 52, 71, 83, 136, 151, 367

belonging. *See* social isolation
Black Lives Matter, 19–20, 30, 106
Boko Haram, 33, 91–92, 98, 111–12, 116, 120, 165, 175, 218, 220, 224, 232, 275, 277, 279, 294, 298

charity, 79, 176–79. *See also* humanitarian aid
children. *See* youth
civilian leadership, 130, 191, 194, 196, 227–28
civilians, 5, 9, 11–14, 17, 41, 43, 46, 56, 64, 168–70, 318, 336, 370
civilizations, 31, 71–73, 82–84
civil society, xiv, 11, 19, 41, 54–57, 63, 90, 107, 114, 128, 134, 142, 147, 149–56, 158–59, 166, 245–47, 351–57, 358–69, 373; advocacy, 170–71, 184, 214; counterterrorism impacts on, 154–55, 169–70, 174–84, 321–24; definition, 56; independence of, 57, 174, 182–83, 353, 360, 367; roles of, 150–51, 166, 174, 191, 201–5, 234, 272, 297, 318–21, 324, 334
class, 30, 38, 72, 75, 145, 219, 319, 322. *See also* economy
climate change, 5, 31, 48, 116–21, 373
collective action, 45, 56, 75, 128, 150, 298–99
colonialism, 72, 315, 335
communication, 12, 23, 47, 54, 59, 64, 72; direct *vs*. indirect, 74; horizontal *vs*. vertical, 71–72, 75, 87, 247, 252, 263, 273–75, 288, 294, 336, 362
community engagement, 79, 88, 223

complex environments, ix, xvii, 5, 41, 48, 55–57, 70, 107, 245, 249, 353. *See also* climate change
confusion, 45, 74, 98, 100, 177
countering violent extremism, 54; and civil liberties, 6, 201, 212–17, 319, 370–75; definition, 54; framework, 201–2; prevention and, 54; relevant and specific programs, 201
counternarratives, 45, 52, 284–90, 294, 325
counterterrorism: and civil liberties, 6, 11, 27, 36–37, 152–56; correlation with terrorism, 8; death toll from, *8–9*; defined, 26, 53–54; displacement from, 9; economic impact of, *9–10*; lawfare, 11; spending on, 8
cultural diversity. *See* multiculturalism

DDR (disarmament, demobilization, and reintegration), 28, 41, 187, 226–35
death rates, *6, 9*
democracy, 11, 17, 40, 44, 52, 70–72, 78, 141–42, 147, 195, 319, 322, 365, 370, 372, 376
deradicalization and deprogramming, 28, 46, 205, 208, 319, 329, 351
dialogue, ix, xiii, 35, 46–47, 88, 170, 222, 271–74, 282, 286, 325, 328–29, 345, 356, 362–63; interreligious, xii, 52, 113, 223, 330–31, 333, 336–39; with listed groups, 242, 247–48, 251–53; multistakeholder, 63, 121, 145–46, 157–65, 175, 184, 196, 318; between youth and security sector, 107–9, 319, 375
dignity, 35, 39, 42, 50, 62, 77, 261, 263, 274–75, 280–82, 295, 301–09, 358–69. *See also* social significance

ecology, 5–6, 10, 21
economy: economic grievances, 37–39, 76–77; and greed, 104–5; ideology, 43; income inequality, 71; and open markets, 71, 89; and religion, 44; sustainable economy, 41, 364. *See also* private sector

education, xii—xiii, 10, 28, 30, 35, 38, 40, 46, 56, 74–75, 98, 102, 108, 111, 126, 129, 134, 144–45, 165, 189–90, 199, 201–2, 204, 208, 211, 219–20, 279–80, 318–19, 325, 328, 340–50
elections, 70, 78, 141–46, 261, 315, 321, 359
emotional literacy, 35, 48, 95–100, 190, 198, 243, 270, 285–88, 295, 298–99, 301, 305, 342, 361
employment, 22, 38, 53, 71, 77, 90, 101, 117, 120, 190–92, 226, 281, 315, 340–50
ethnicity, 13, 17, 30, 214, 360; ethnonationalism, 70
evil, 43–44, 60, 74, 81–86, 255–60, 295, 302, 307, 351
extremism, 15–16, 43, 46, 84, 226, 245, 252, 257, 259, 276, 300

family: identification by, 24, 328–30, 354, 365; influence and recruitment by, 25–26, 31, 37, 49, 75, 98, 197, 206–7, 245, 272–73, 286, 289; violence toward, 300–308
fear, 6–7, 12, 14, 32, 35, 41, 50, 52, 62, 99–100, 104, 107, 113, 139, 166, 179, 192, 211, 247, 270, 277, 291, 303–7
freedom, 8, 11, 36, 40–41, 47, 62, 71, 85, 111, 149–56, 202, 224, 292, 294, 299, 319, 321, 371, 373–75

gender, 33–35, 96, 110–15, 130, 137, 219; analysis, 110–12, 228; -based violence, 15, 33, 111, 115, 165, 169, 228–29, 301, 317, 358; and hormones, 96; masculinity, 35; patriarchy and, 17; roles, 33–34, 307, 331–32, 352, 372; -sensitive programs, 229, 232, 234. *See also* women
Global Community Engagement and Resilience Fund (GCERF), 88–90
globalization, 31, 39, 47, 70–72, 77
governance, ix, xii—xiii, 10, 40, 55–57, 59, 64, 71, 120, 130–32, 137, 139–40, 147, 152, 156, 165, 190–96, 202, 219,

227, 230, 251, 255, 269, 297, 315, 319, 322, 343–44, 346, 352, 355, 358, 361, 363, 365–66, 371–73

hormones, 33, 96
humanitarian aid, 34, 58, 120, 125, 144–46, 150, 154–55, 167, 171, 175, 179, 183, 191, 194, 196, 274, 334, 352–56, 360–69, 375
human rights, 11, 19–20, 34, 40–41, 46, 63, 128, 149–56, 158–61, 199, 229, 294, 301, 317, 320, 365; and counterterrorism, 64, 114, 130, 132–34, 146, 151, 176, 179–80, 319–22, 367, 371; Universal Declaration of, 14; violations, 15, 37, 115, 192–93, 219, 228
human security, 3, 7, 10, 12, 41, 62–64, 108, 132, 139, 166, 221, 356, 370–76; contrasted with national security, 62
humiliation, x, 25, 32–33, 35, 44, 50, 193, 301–6, 372

identity, 22, 28, 30–35, 71, 77, 84, 93–94, 97–99, 104–6, 162, 192, 223, 226, 244, 256, 268, 274, 281, 288, 294, 301–5, 358, 361–62, 366, 372; defined, 30; and ideology, 17; in-group and out-group, 30, 32, 39, 42, 77, 84, 104, 205, 249; Islamic identity, 218; national identity, 77; politics of, 71; and religion, 44–45; us and them, 99–100, 303
ideology, 17–18, 25, 28, 30, 42–47, 52, 81–85, 95, 100–101, 153, 198, 200–205, 208, 268, 274, 294, 372–73
interventions, 3, 5–6, 22–23, 26, 30, 35, 42, 45, 47, 53–59, 63, 107–8, 110, 135, 139–46, 153, 199, 205–6, 210, 212, 223–25, 234, 304–9, 315–18, 333–34, 344, 347–50, 370–76; unintended impacts, 58
Irish Revolutionary Army (IRA), 94–95, 97–98
ISIS, 16, 18, 38, 44, 69, 70, 72, 74–75, 78–79, 81–85, 98, 116, 277, 286, 291, 296–99, 334; attack in Barcelona in 2017, 69; attack in Paris in 2015, 69; attack with vehicles in London, Nice, Berlin, and Stockholm, 70

jihad, 27, 29, 33–34, 37, 69–80, 94–101, 141, 194–95, 219, 315, 326, 329, 335
justice, 16, 78, 86, 97–98, 153, 224, 300–309, 315; criminal justice and rule of law, 37, 41–42, 49, 51, 54, 78, 130, 152, 196, 208, 216, 233; economic justice, 52, 149, 155; injustice, 25, 30, 38, 46–48, 52, 104–6, 165, 192–93, 277, 298, 302, 316, 341–49; social, 35, 52, 86, 297, 361–69

Kahanists, 18–19, 43
Ku Klux Klan (KKK), 24, 73–75

law, 229–30, 233–34, 280, 321, 332, 336, 343; to address VE, 42, 156, 157–65, 354, 372–73; and counterterrorism, 11, 41, 130–31, 166–73, 174, 176–77, 179, 181–84, 196, 316–17, 321–23; international law, 12–13, 155, 353; and journalists, 292–94; law enforcement, 54, 79, 113, 132, 152–53, 190–91, 193–94, 197, 200–201, 206–8, 210–17, 279
leaderless resistance, 24, 74
Liberation Tigers of Tamil Eelam (LTTE), xi, 94, 97, 175, 256, 258, 263
local ownership, xiii, 56, 145, 147
lone actors, 21, 23–24, 31, 82
loneliness. *See* social isolation

material support. *See* law: and counterterrorism
meaning and purpose, 21–22, 25, 31, 42, 78–79, 281–82, 301, 368
media, 14, 18, 45–49, 56, 59, 76–79, 161, 273, 284–90, 291–96, 281, 375; coverage, 5, 7, 48–49, 220; images, 7; social media, 26–27, 33, 71, 75, 83, 87, 204, 206, 214, 217

mental health, 33, 35, 50, 136, 201–8, 212–15, 300–309
migration. *See* transition
military intervention, 47, 140, 143, 153–54, 189, 191, 195, 315, 333. *See also* army rule
multiculturalism, 18, 42, 73, 288; cultural tensions, 12, 17, 31–32, 77; purification, 17
multistakeholder coordination, 55–57, 108, 121, 135, 157–64, 198, 212, 220, 230, 242, 270, 296, 325, 355, 373–75

nation-state, 31, 71–72, 220
Nazis, 42, 46, 70, 73, 75, 103
neuroscience, 33, 75, 94–102
nonviolent civil resistance, 16, 19–20, 36, 40, 50, 58, 242, 278, 282, 297–99, 347, 372
nuclear threat, 7, 14–15, 24, 81–86, 140; activism to stop, 78

peacebuilding: definition, 54–55; isolation or engagement in, 241–54; and negotiation, 255–67; principles, 268–76
polarization, 5, 249, 276, 282
politics, 45, 47, 97, 144–45, 222, 262, 267; and grievances, 36–37, 51; and ideology, 42; political terror, 36; and religion, 44
population increases, 71, 120, 277, 340
poverty. *See* economy: economic grievances
private sector, 41, 87–93, 135, 137, 204; and public-private partnerships, 90–93, 128, 269, 319, 363; and virtuous enterprises, 91–92
psychology, 7, 21, 28, 31, 34–35, 42, 49, 71–72, 86, 94–102, 129, 198, 200, 203, 207, 212, 259, 261, 271, 275, 280, 291, 299, 300–309, 320, 325–27, 372
public opinion polls, 7, 15, 21, 43–44, 153

racial integration, 71
racism, 34, 39, 42; and race war, 42, 73–74, 83. *See also* anti-racism
radicalization. *See* recruitment
recruitment, 22–28, 34–35, 37, 49, 55, 58, 90, 92, 105, 111, 115, 127, 129, 135, 272–76, 280, 351, 368; family- and community-based, 25–26, 75, 78–79, 326; forced, 226–35; online, media, and narratives, 26–27, 193, 221, 286–88, 298; prison-based, 28; at religious sites, 27
rehabilitation, 28, 54, 101, 158, 197, 207–8, 275, 280, 300–304. *See also* DDR (disarmament, demobilization, and reintegration)
reintegration. *See* rehabilitation
religion: and fundamentalism, 44, 94, 97, 100–101, 315; and ideology, 43–47; as part of solution, 274–75; as pathway for political and economic grievances, 44; and redemptive violence, 43, 84–86; and religious literacy, 46; as source of identity, 44; and spiritual high, 45; as theological justification, 43
research quality, 21–22
resilience, 35, 37, 42, 55, 59–60, 62, 64, 88, 90–91, 113, 137, 183, 203–4, 212, 226–27, 231–34, 239, 272–73, 281, 300–301, 304, 307–8, 318, 352, 358, 361, 366, 371, 374, 375–76
Revolutionary Armed Forces of Colombia (FARC), 95, 169, 180, 235, 256, 258, 263–64, 289

school shootings, 15, 19–20, 34
securitization, 149, 198, 218–25, 365–66
sex, 30, 33–35, 45–46, 50, 96–97; and sexual orientation, 13–14, 34, 77. *See also* gender
shame. *See* humiliation
social change, 71, 90, 103, 118–19, 253, 256, 361–63

social cohesion, 28, 39–42, 51, 90, 165, 227, 232, 249, 280, 325, 330–31, 355, 358, 361–68
social grievances, 39–40; exclusion, 39, 51, 76, 107, 154, 374; ideology, 42;
social isolation, 22, 31–32, 50, 98, 111, 192, 207, 275; as counterterrorism, 241–54, 256
social significance, 31, 35, 71. *See also* dignity
state-society relations, 40–41, 50, 62, 64, 372–74
systems, xvii, 5, 53, 59, 113, 166, 344

terror: defined, 6; war on, 15
terrorism: correlation with counterterrorism, 8; death toll from, *8–9*; defined, 5, 12–15; displacement from, 9; economic impact of, *9–10*; funding for, 24; legal authority for, 13; spending on, 8; state-sponsored, 14; state *vs*. non-state, 13–15
terrorist listing. *See* law: and counterterrorism
theories of change, xvii, 21–51, 55, 108, 241–53, 350, 374; definition, 22
transition, 31–32, 34, 45, 50, 272, 363–64, 372; anti-immigration policies, 34
trauma, x, 7, 32, 35, 42–49, 61, 113, 226–29, 295, 300–309, 327, 332, 337, 358, 361, 363, 372, 375

urbanization, 71, 117, 119, 232
U.S. policy, 47, 76

violent extremism: defined, 5, 15–20; diagrams, *22, 29*; metaphors and frames for, 59–62
vulnerability, 33, 37, 54–55, 60, 78, 204–5, 233, 281, 302, 318–20, 334, 349

weapons trade, 14, 24, 47–48, 52, 63, 81, 84, 332, 373
white supremacists, 42, 69–80, 91, 195, 218; Aryan Jihad, 76; attack in Charleston, North Carolina, 74; attack in Charlottesville, Virginia, 18, 70; attack in Oklahoma City, 74; Marine Le Pen, 70
whole of government. *See* multistakeholder coordination
wicked problems, ix, 57
women: impact of VE on, 17–18, 20, 26, 30, 33, 110–15, 226–35, 327; roles in addressing VE, 35–36, 106, 110–15, 273, 281, 287, 299, 324–32; support for VE, 33–35, 96, 226–35, 326–27
world order, 72

xenophobia, 70, 77

youth, 35, 38, 40, 53, 70, 75–76, 78–79, 92, 95, 97, 101, 103–9, 127, 129, 135, 136, 142, 160, 163, 190, 199, 204, 210–11, 214–17, 221, 273, 277–83, 298, 319, 325, 328–30, 338, 340–50, 354–55, 358–59, 363–65; and P/CVE, 351–57, 363–64; UN Resolution on Youth, Peace and Security, 103–9, 278; youth bulge, 38, 80

Permissions and Acknowledgements

We wish to acknowledge with thanks the permissions to reproduce the material from the following works, granted by the publisher and authors:

Chapter 4: "Alt-Right and Jihad" by Scott Atran is used with permission and was originally published in Aeon at https://aeon.co on November 6, 2017.

Chapter 13: "Civil Society Engagement to Prevent Violent Extremism" by David Cortright is drawn with permission from a much longer report of the same title published in 2011 sponsored by the Dutch development agency Cordaid, in cooperation with the Fourth Freedom Forum and the Kroc Institute for International Peace Studies at the University of Notre Dame.

Chapters 14, 24, 25, and 26 from Search for Common Ground staff are excerpted with permission from a report by Lena Slachmuijlder in *Transforming Violent Extremism: A Peacebuilder's Guide*, published in Washington, DC, by Search for Common Ground in 2017.

Chapter 16: "Proscribing Peace: The Impact of Terrorist Listing on Peacebuilding Organizations" by Teresa Dumasy and Sophie Haspeslagh is reprinted by permission from Conciliation Resources in January 2016 and can bc found at http://www.c-r.org/downloads/Conciliation_Resources_Counter-terrorism_brief.pdf.

Chapter 20: "Islamization, Securitization, and Peacebuilding Approaches to Preventing and Countering Violent Extremism" by Mohammed Abu-Nimer is excerpted with permission from "Alternative Approaches to Transforming Violent Extremism: The Case of Islamic Peace and

Interreligious Peacebuilding," in *Transformative Approaches to Violent Extremism*, Berghof Handbook Dialogue No. 13, edited by Beatrix Austin and Hans J. Giessmann and published in Berlin by the Berghof Foundation in May 2018. http://www.berghof-foundation.org/publications/handbook/ handbook-dialogues/13-transforming-violent-extremism/.

Chapter 22: "Addressing Terrorism: A Theory of Change Approach" by John Paul Lederach is reprinted with permission from a report titled "Somalia: Creating Space for Fresh Approaches to Peacebuilding" published in Sweden by the Life and Peace Institute in 2011, which can be found at https://kroc.nd.edu/assets/227112/somalia_book.pdf.

Chapter 23: "Negotiation and Violent Extremism: Why Engage and Why Not?" by I. William Zartman and Guy Olivier Faure is reprinted with permission from the book *Engaging Extremists: Trade-offs, Timing, and Diplomacy* copyright 2011 by the Endowment of the United States Institute of Peace, Washington, DC.

Chapter 28: "To Defeat Terrorism, Use 'People Power'" by Maria J. Stephan and Leanne Erdberg is reprinted with permission from the US Institute of Peace's website on March 27, 2018, which can found at https://www.usip.org/publications/2018/03/defeat-terrorism-use-people-power/.

About the Contributors

Mohammed Abu-Nimer is professor of peace and conflict resolution (IPCR) at the School of International Service at American University and senior advisor to KAICIID Dialogue Centre in Vienna, Austria.

Adnan Ansari is cofounder and director of programs at Muflehun, designing and implementing programs in fragile states and postconflict environments.

Scott Atran is director of research in anthropology at the Centre National de la Recherche Scientifique in Paris and cofounder of ARTIS International and of the Centre for the Resolution of Intractable Conflict at Oxford University.

Myriam Aziz is teaching fellow at Eastern Mennonite University's Center for Justice and Peacebuilding in the United States, following years of work with the High Commissioner for Refugees (UNHCR) in the Bekaa, Lebanon.

Gabrielle Belli is program associate at the NGO Working Group on Women, Peace and Security.

Rafia Bhulai is senior programs officer for the Global Center on Cooperative Security, where she conducts research and analysis, manages programs, and helps shape policy related to countering terrorism and violent extremism.

Nell Bolton is senior technical advisor for Justice and Peacebuilding at Catholic Relief Services.

Aaron Chassy is technical director for the Equity, Inclusion and Peacebuilding (EQUIP team) at Catholic Relief Services.

Agnes Chen is regional communications and donor relations officer at Asia Justice and Rights (AJAR) in Indonesia.

Kevin Clements is director of the Toda Peace Institute, based in Tokyo, and director of the National Center for Peace and Conflict Studies (NAPACS) at the University of Otago, New Zealand.

Stone Conroy is the manager for Innovative Finance and the Private Sector at InterAction and senior advisor for Venture Peacebuilding at the International Peace & Security Institute.

David Cortright is the director of Policy Studies at the Kroc Institute for International Peace Studies at the University of Notre Dame and chair of the Board of the Fourth Freedom Forum.

Teresa Dumasy is director of Policy and Learning at Conciliation Resources and senior research fellow within the Conflict Analysis Research Centre (CARC) at the School of Politics and International Relations at the University of Kent in the United Kingdom.

Leanne Erdberg is the director of Countering Violent Extremism (CVE) at the US Institute of Peace and also currently serves as the interim executive director of RESOLVE – Researching Solutions to Violent Extremism.

Guy Olivier Faure is former professor at the Sorbonne University and director emeritus of the French National Centre for Scientific Research.

Mari Fitzduff is founding director of the Masters in Conflict Resolution and Coexistence Program at Brandeis University.

Frances Flannery is director of the Center for the Interdisciplinary Study of Terrorism and Peace (CISTP) and professor of religion in the Department of Philosophy and Religion at James Madison University.

Kay Guinane is director of the Charity & Security Network and a public interest attorney who specializes in the rights of nonprofit organizations, particularly in the areas of free speech, association, and national security.

Mark Hamilton is professor of multidimensional security at the Inter-American Defense College, a multilingual and multinational graduate program for senior military, police, and diplomatic officials from throughout the Americas.

Paulus Hartono is director at Mennonite Diakonia Service and program manager at Lembaga Perdamaian Lintas Agama dan Golongan (the Peace Institute Across Religions and Groups). He is also pastor at Muria Mennonite Christian Church in Surakarta, Indonesia.

Sophie Haspeslagh is a PhD candidate at the London School of Economics and Political Science (LSE), where she is researching the effects of proscription on engaging armed groups in peace processes and a program associate at Conciliation Resources.

Elizabeth Hume is senior director for Programs and Strategy at the Alliance for Peacebuilding.

Humera Khan is the cofounder and executive director of Muflehun and board member of Life after Hate and served as senior advisor on CVE to the UN Security Council Counter-Terrorism Committee Executive Directorate.

Veronica Laveta is international services clinical advisor for Mental Health at the Center for Victims of Torture.

John Paul Lederach is professor emeritus of international peacebuilding with the Kroc Institute at the University of Notre Dame and senior fellow at Humanity United.

Sverre Lodgaard is senior European research fellow at the Toda Peace Institute and senior research fellow at the Norwegian Institute of International Affairs (NUPI).

Alistair Millar is the founder, chairman of the board, and Howard S. Brembeck fellow at the Global Center on Cooperative Security and president of the Fourth Freedom Forum.

Millicent Otieno is the founder and director of Local Capacities for Peace International and also works with Mediators beyond Border for East Africa, the UWIANO Platform for Peace, national and local Mediation Support Units, and CDA Collaborative.

Dean Piedmont is the director for the Peacebuilding, Reintegration and Stabilization Assessment Group to support DDR and CVE work with the US government, the United Nations, and the World Bank.

Lakshitha Saji Prelis is director of children and youth programs at Search for Common Ground and founding cochair of UN Inter-Agency Working Group on Youth and Peacebuilding.

Keith Proctor is a visiting fellow at the Feinstein International Center at Tufts University. Previously, he was a senior advisor for countering violent extremism at the US Department of State and the senior researcher at Mercy Corps.

Mossarat Qadeem is the cofounder and director of the PAIMAN Alumni Trust and national coordinator of Aman-o-Nisa, a coalition of women leaders striving to moderate violent extremism, based in Pakistan.

Lisa Schirch is senior North American research director for the Toda Peace Institute and senior policy advisor for the Alliance for Peacebuilding. She sits on the Independent Review Panel for the Global Community Engagement and Resilience Fund (GCERF) in Geneva.

Matthew J. O. Scott is director of peacebuilding at World Vision International based in Canada.

Arjun S. Sethi is a longtime community activist, civil rights lawyer, writer, and professor based in Washington, DC.

Michael Shipler is Search for Common Ground regional director of Asia Programs, where he oversees program offices in Indonesia, Nepal, Pakistan, Sri Lanka, and Timor Leste.

Lena Slachmuijlder is vice president of programs at Search for Common Ground, where she oversees programming across Africa, Asia, and the Middle East, as well as the institutional learning and children and youth divisions.

Maria J. Stephan is director of the Program on Nonviolent Action at the US Institute of Peace and co-author of *Why Civil Resistance Works: The Logic of Nonviolent Conflict* (2011).

Laura Strawmyer is policy and advocacy associate at the Alliance for Peacebuilding.

Agus Suyanto is pastor at Muria Mennonite Christian Church in Jepara, Indonesia.

Rachel Walsh Taza is children and youth program coordinator for Search for Common Ground.

Rebecca Wolfe is director of evidence and influence on matters related to peace and conflict for Mercy Corps and a fellow at Yale University's Program for Refugees, Forced Migration and Humanitarian Action and the Political Violence Field Lab.

I. William Zartman is professor emeritus in the Paul H. Nitze School of Advanced International Studies (SAIS) at Johns Hopkins University and member of the steering committee of the Processes of International Negotiation (PIN) Program.